Explorer
Britain

Tim Locke

 Publishing

Opposite: Looe Harbour, Cornwall

Written by Tim Locke, Richard Cavendish and Barnaby Rogerson
Additional writing by Nia Williams
Updated by Tim Locke and Colin Follett

Published by AA Publishing, a trading name of Automobile Association Developments Limited, whose registered office is Fanum House, Basing View, Basingstoke, Hampshire RG21 4EA. Registered number 1878835.

ISBN-10: 0 7495 4482 1
ISBN-13: 978-0-7495-4482-9

The contents of this publication are believed correct at the time of printing. Nevertheless, AA Publishing accepts no responsibility for errors, omissions or changes in the details given, or for the consequences of readers' reliance on this information. This does not affect your statutory rights. Assessments of the attractions, hotels and restaurants are based upon the author's own experience, and contain subjective opinions that may not reflect the publisher's opinion or a reader's experience. We have tried to ensure accuracy, but things do change, so please let us know if you have any comments or corrections.

A CIP catalogue record for this book is available from the British Library.

Colour separation by Fotographics Ltd
Printed and bound in Italy by Printer Trento S.r.l.

Find out more about AA Publishing and the wide range of travel publications and services the AA provides by visiting our website at www.theAA.com/bookshop.
Reprinted Feb 2006
Revised sixth edition 2005
First published 1994

Titles in the Explorer series:
Australia • Boston & New England • Britain • Brittany California • Canada • Caribbean • China • Costa Rica • Crete Cuba • Cyprus • Egypt • Florence & Tuscany • Florida France • Germany • Greek Islands • Hawaii • India • Ireland Italy • Japan • London • Mallorca • Mexico • New York New Zealand • Paris • Portugal • Provence • Rome San Francisco • Scotland • South Africa • Spain • Thailand Tunisia • Turkey • Venice • Vietnam

How to use this book

ORGANIZATION

Britain Is, Britain Was
Discusses aspects of life and culture in contemporary Britain and explores significant periods in its history.

A–Z
Breaks down the country into regional chapters, and covers places to visit, including walks and drives. Within this section fall the Focus On articles, which consider a variety of subjects in greater detail.

Travel Facts
Contains the strictly practical information vital for a successful trip.

Hotels and Restaurants
Lists recommended establishments throughout Britain, giving a brief summary of their attractions.

ABOUT THE RATINGS
Most places described in this book have been given a separate rating. These are as follows:

▶▶▶   **Do not miss**

▶▶   **Highly recommended**

▶   **Worth seeing**

MAPS
To make each particular location easier to find, every main entry in this book has a map reference to the right of its name. This comprises a number, followed by a letter, followed by another number, such as 176B3. The first number (176) refers to the page on which the map can be found, the letter (B) and the second number (3) pinpoint the square in which the main entry is located. The maps on the inside front cover and inside back cover are referred to as IFC and IBC respectively.

Contents

5

7

Tim Locke has contributed to more than 30 guides to Britain, having walked, cycled and driven around every county and national park. Richard Cavendish—who wrote most of the Britain Is, Britain Was and Focus On features—has written numerous books on Britain. Travel writer Barnaby Rogerson, the author of _Explorer Britain_'s Scottish chapters, has contributed to other AA books on Scotland.

My Britain

From my house in Sussex I can look upon Lewes Castle, an administrative headquarters set up in Norman times. The town's main thoroughfare slopes down between numerous Georgianized half-timbered buildings, past the White Hart Hotel—where Tom Paine held meetings in the 18th century—to family-run Harvey's brewery, little changed in over a hundred years. A short walk away are the sheep-grazed slopes of the South Downs, dotted with ancient remains. On one slope is the site of the Battle of Lewes, where in 1264 Simon de Montfort defeated Henry III, forcing him to grant rights that paved the way for parliamentary democracy.

I find this sense of continuum an impressive aspect of Britain: its landscapes, both rural and urban, pockmarked with historical incident. I sometimes wonder what else would strike me about Britain if I had never seen it before. I imagine being confronted with a series of cameos: a sheep auction in Mid Wales, with cloth caps and ruddy Celtic faces in abundance; the landscapes of East Anglia, where the quality of light imparts subtle differences each time a view is encountered; a county cricket match at the spa town of Tunbridge Wells; or the hypnotic patter of a dealer at London's Brick Lane market.

Britain, as much as any other corner of the earth, has been much visited and much written about. This book is our selection of the most rewarding places in the kingdom. It doesn't include every city or attraction, but aims to be a balance between the well known and the less obvious.

It constantly surprises me that, in an age ever tending toward standardization, so many aspects of Britain have survived intact: its communities, its lifestyles, its idiosyncracies. The pressure to change is still there, but there has been a realization that we need our heritage as a point of reference to tell us who we are. It would take a great deal to erode that national persona.

Tim Locke

▶▶▶ ABBREVIATIONS USED

NT = *National Trust (see page 102)*

EH = *English Heritage (see page 124)*

Cadw – *Welsh Historic Monuments (see page 187)*

HS = *Historic Scotland (see page 124)*

NTS = *National Trust for Scotland (see page 102)*

Britain is by no means a uniform entity: the more you travel around this compact island, the more there is for you to see and enjoy. Within the boundaries of its 228,000sq km (88,000sq miles) Britain shows an astonishingly rich variety of landscape, architecture, climate, regional accents and cuisine, cultural traditions, social make-up and economic activity.

10

Britain constantly reminds us that it is an island. Once a mighty naval power and the hub of a huge empire, it still has a rich heritage of its past and plenty of unmistakably British hallmarks. The Industrial Revolution began here, as did punk rock, railways and football and it's only in this country that you will find the quintessentially British village *fête* complete with striped tents and bring-and-buy stalls, the seaside pleasure pier, the pub, the English stately home in its landscaped park, Scottish haggis, Welsh cakes and leafy suburbs dotted with Tudor-style semi-detached houses and the odd fish-and-chip shop. British contributions to world culture include an incomparable and all-embracing literary output, from Shakespeare to Winnie-the-Pooh.

THE DIVERSITY Many newcomers to Britain are surprised by how quickly the urban scene gives way to beautiful rural landscapes. Factors include the compactness of many urban areas, restrictive zoning laws and the constant variations in the natural environment: low-level arable fens, rolling hedgerow-lined pastures, craggy dales, blustery moorland, post-glacial mountain scenery, rugged cliffs and shingle shores. This in turn has given rise to numerous types of local architecture: sometimes the bedrock itself supplies the building material, as can be seen in the Cotswolds, Cornwall, rural Wales, the Scottish Highlands and the Pennines, while elsewhere wood and/or bricks predominate. Progress has inevitably eroded some of the finer distinctions in various locales (high-tech agriculture today blankets vast tracts of farmland and chain stores dominate small towns' main shopping streets), but in spite of this, much has either been carefully preserved or has survived. Regional accents, for instance, continue to thrive: a well-trained ear can distinguish from which side of the Pennines, part of Scotland, or even district of London the speaker comes.

Britain's greatest assets for visitors include its sense of history and variety, all of which are packed into one accessible island where the driving distances are never too long between distinctively different landscapes and cultures. The curious explorer will be well served.

Market day (this one is Norwich)— a feast for the senses in every way

The British system of government is that of parliamentary democracy, based on principles of common law. Led by its prime minister (since 1997 Tony Blair, of the Labour party), the country is a 'constitutional monarchy', although there is no written constitution, since it has evolved over the centuries. Queen Elizabeth II gives royal assent to Acts of Parliament, but this is really a mere formality. Universal male suffrage in Britain dates only from 1918 and women did not get the vote until as recently as 1928.

❏ 'Let not England forget her precedence of teaching other nations how to live.'
—John Milton (1644) ❏

The British Isles are the two islands of Britain and Ireland. Britain, or Great Britain, is used to refer to England, Wales and Scotland together. Wales was conquered by England in the 13th century. The King of Scots succeeded the English throne in 1603 and the political union of England and Scotland dates from 1707.

The United Kingdom is England, Wales, Scotland and Northern Ireland, the latter being the six counties of Ulster (predominantly Protestant) that refused to join the rest of Ireland when it broke away from Britain in 1921. Scotland, Wales and Northern Ireland are ruled, like England, from London but in 1999 certain powers were devolved to Scotland and Wales, with the Scottish Parliament in Edinburgh and the Welsh Assembly in Cardiff.

THE SEAT OF POWER The head of state is officially the Queen. Much of the ceremony of British life revolves round **the monarchy**, dating from a time when the monarch ruled the country. Today, power rests with the democratically elected government answerable to **parliament** and to the **House of Commons**, the chief legislative body. The unelected **House of Lords** is the secondary chamber. Britain's relationship with the European Union, however, and the consequences for British sovereignty and parliament are under debate.

❏ 'Great Britain has lost an empire and has not yet found a role.'
—Dean Acheson (1962) ❏

Class distinctions are still important in British life. They involve the most acutely discriminating judgements—concerning people's houses and furnishings, clothes, cars, jobs, education, manners and personal tastes. The simplest clue to someone's class is usually gained by listening to their accent—as George Bernard Shaw once remarked, an Englishman cannot open his mouth without making some other Englishman despise him.

The population of Great Britain numbers more than 58 million. A small and densely populated country, it would fit neatly inside the American state of Oregon, which has a population of only 3 million. Or, keeping the comparison within Europe, the country has about the same number of people as France, in an area less than half the size.

12

EARLY ANCESTRY The British are a nation of mongrels, principally a mixture of Germanic and Celtic strains. The original 'English', or Anglo-Saxons, came across the North Sea in their dragon-prowed

longships from northwest Germany and southern Denmark some 1,500 years ago. They subjugated most of the native Celtic people on the island, whom they dismissively called Welsh, meaning 'foreigners'.

More Germanic invaders came from Denmark and Norway in the Viking Age. Then the famous Norman Conquest of England in 1066 eventually gave all areas of the British Isles a new and initially French-speaking ruling class. From the 16th to the 18th centuries, thousands of French Protestants, known as Huguenots, came to England to escape the religious persecution of Europe. The 19th century brought substantial Irish immigration to Britain and an influx of Jewish families fleeing from persecution in Russia and Eastern Europe. After World War II fresh waves of immigrants came from the West Indies, the Indian subcontinent, Cyprus and many other countries of

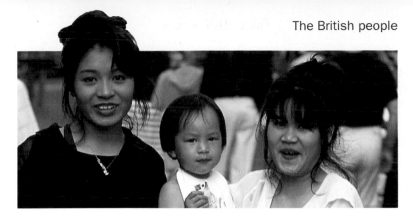

the former British Empire that now form part of the Commonwealth association of nations.

ETHNIC AND RELIGIOUS MIX Despite the presence of many ethnic and religious minorities, statistics show that more than 80 per cent of the UK population is still classified as English, about 10 per cent as Scottish, 2.5 per cent as Irish and 2 per cent as Welsh. Britain is 95 per cent white, with West Indians, Indians and Pakistanis now numbering about 1 per cent each. There are also tiny percentages of Bangladeshis and Chinese. Of the ethnic minority population, close to 50 per cent is British by birth.

The population is overwhelmingly Christian, or thinks of itself that way. More than 85 per cent of the British people regard themselves as Christians, but less than one person in five goes regularly to church or chapel. The Muslim population is about 2 per cent and those of the Jewish faith total 1 per cent.

Male and female members of the population are nearing equality in numbers. In the 20th century the birth rate increased slowly; during the 1970s population fell for a time.

❏ Arthur Koestler, a notable foreign writer who lived in Britain for many years, described the average Englishman as an attractive hybrid between an ostrich and a lion: keeping his head in the sand for as long as possible, but, when forced to confront reality, capable of heroic deeds. ❏

A NATIONAL CHARACTER? Whether there is anything that can be called a British national character is open to question. The Scots, the Welsh and the Irish have retained their separate identities despite (or because of) English domination. Even in England itself, people from London, Yorkshire, Lancashire, the Northeast, the West Country and other areas cherish their regional identities.

Class distinctions are being steadily eroded, but certain national traits live on: reserve, politeness, a sense of fair play, a genius for compromise and a gift for understatement to name but five. Voluntary work plays a major role in the everyday life of many people, with thousands of charity shops, civic societies, women's institutes and fund-raising ventures spread across the country. The affection for gardens, dogs and horses is nationally ingrained. Although they love the countryside, most of them do not actually live in it; walking or hiking in the countryside is by far their most popular activity. They love sport and taught much of the rest of the world organized games, such as soccer and cricket.

Perhaps the most fundamental trait that all the British have in common is a sense of irony which allows them to make fun of themselves with good grace.

If anything causes the British more complaint, anxiety and frustration than the weather, it is the economy. In the Victorian Age, Britain was the most powerful industrial nation on earth, with a mighty economy based on coal, iron and steel, heavy machinery, textiles, ship-building and foreign trade. Queen Victoria ruled the largest empire in history. This commanding position has since been lost and with it the self-confidence of that era.

14

The British economy today is based on private enterprise; in the 1980s many of the nationalized industries were restored to private ownership. Heavy industry has declined while the service sector has grown. Britain used to import raw materials for its factories. Now it is a net importer of manufactured goods from countries that make them better and cheaper. The fishing industry has shrunk after over-fishing led to EU and govern-ment restrictions. Inflation, high in the 1970–1980s, is now under control.

❏ The change that has come over Britain can be observed in the mining valleys of South Wales, where King Coal once ruled over teeming pits and spoil heaps. Today not a nugget of coal is mined in the Rhondda Valley and the valleys are being exten-sively 'greened'. ❏

TRADE AND RESOURCES A strong financial sector brings in more wealth from overseas. Less food is imported today and more grown at home, but only 2 per cent of the population is employed in agriculture. In 1973, Britain joined the European Union (EU), which accounts for more than half of its trade, but did not join the European Economic Community (EEC), later to become the European Monetary Union when the Euro was launched as the European currency in 1999. That year, the trade gap reached a new record with the strength of sterling and a col-lapse in demand from countries hit by the global economic crisis.

The UK was the sixth richest country in the world in 1950, while in 1980 it was only the 22nd richest. All the same, in the 2000s, with two-thirds of British households owning their homes and two-thirds owning cars, Britons have a higher standard of living than ever.

The Bank of England, at the heart of the City of London

Pubs are much more than places in which to drink. They are enclaves of laughter and gossip, arenas for playing games and havens of sympathy in times of trouble. A good pub has its own distinctive atmosphere, complete with its own resident cast of characters.

> ❏ 'When you have lost your inns drown your empty selves, for you will have lost the last of England.'—Hilaire Belloc (1870–1953) ❏

Some pubs are dedicated to thoughtful imbibing and peaceful conversation, others to deafening taped music and clattering slot machines. There are venerable half-timbered Tudor hostelries, leaning at an angle and apparently held up as much by the strength of the ale on tap as they are by their massive black timbers. There are broad-fronted Georgian coaching inns, glittering Victorian 'gin palaces', and dubious little backstreet taverns. There are pubs with romantic tales to tell of smugglers and highwaymen, rose-wreathed pubs idyllically set by rivers and canals, lobster-potted inns gazing over picturesque fishing ports and patronized by sailing enthusiasts, while grim-faced pubs accustomed to wind and weather and perched high on remote moors are frequented by ramblers in thick boots and waterproof jackets.

THEN AND NOW The local pub of today is descended from the local alehouse of Anglo-Saxon and medieval England, an ordinary house whose occupants brewed and sold ale. In the 12th and 13th centuries inns began to open up, providing overnight lodging for wayfarers. In recent years, the traditional pub has found a new identity: serving food—'pub grub'—has become more important and

There are town pubs, village pubs, country pubs ... and boaty pubs

there has been a comeback of 'real ale', meaning old-fashioned beer, once threatened with extinction by the big commercial brewers. Most pubs have become less aggressively masculine and women can feel quite comfortable in them.

WHAT'S IN A NAME? Pubs have picture-signs hanging above their doors, illustrating their names—a custom dating from days when few people could read. Some names are derived from heraldry, like the White Hart and the Red Lion. Others are named for royalty, as in the Crown or the King's Head. Other names reflect country life—the Plough or the Fox and Hounds. There are New Inns that are centuries old and there are strange and enigmatic names: the Pig and Whistle, the Cat and Fiddle. All are part of the richness and variety that keep the British pub a vital institution.

15

Gardens and gardening are often seen as a national passion. Opportunities for self-expression and creativity can be found in the tiniest cottage garden or on the grandest estate. This selected list of gardens that are open to the public gives you an idea of the scope and diversity of the nation's 'backyards'.

The British garden dates from Roman times, when every upwardly mobile villa owner aspired to have an atrium with a small garden. Monastic gardens were merely practical affairs for growing food or cultivating herbs and plants for dyes or for medicinal purposes. With the first great houses of the 16th century came the first true pleasure gardens, with their 'knots' of herbs and flowers. In the next century the aristocratic classes toured France and Italy and saw the formal creations of Le Nôtre; topiary and water parterres were the rage.

The classical 18th century age of English landscaping rejected formality for the naturalistic contrivances of Lancelot 'Capability' Brown and others, who designed green expanses fringed by woodlands, interrupted by lakes and punctuated by classical follies. Victorian times saw formal rockeries, ferneries, roseries and other horticultural extravaganzas back in fashion.

Meanwhile the working classes tended small plots in allotment gardens where they grew their own vegetables, and suburban villas sported lawns and herbaceous borders. In their back gardens, people found a private haven from the outside world.

THE WEST COUNTRY Subtropical species thrive in the gardens of **Tresco Abbey**, on the Isles of Scilly. On the mainland of Cornwall **Glendurgan** (NT), **Penjerrick** and **Trebah** are nearby subtropical havens; **Trelissick** (NT) is noted for rhododendrons and azaleas with blooms all year round; paths wind down to the waterside with glimpses of Pendennis Castle. At **Trewithen** magnolias, rhododendrons

and rare shrubs surround a Georgian mansion, while the **Lost Gardens of Heligan** is Europe's largest garden restoration project, begun in 1991 in a neglected Victorian estate. In Wiltshire, **Stourhead** (NT) is a splendid example of traditional 18th-century landscaping.

SOUTHERN ENGLAND AND LONDON
Kew Gardens (Royal Botanic Gardens) in London is the king of all botanic gardens. The collection of rare specimens from all over the world owes much to the 19th-century botanist Sir Joseph Banks. Don't miss the elegant Palm House and the Princess of Wales Conservatory. **Wisley Garden**, Surrey, was set up in 1904 as experimental gardens for the

Stourhead in Wiltshire, the quintessential landscaped garden

Late spring at Sissinghurst

Royal Horticultural Society: it has many scarce species and an excellent retail outlet. **Winkworth Arboretum** (NT), Surrey, is a great tree collection, splendid for spring and autumn tints. Sussex gardens to head for are **Sheffield Park** (NT), with azaleas and rhododendrons backed by a lake, **Nymans Garden** (NT), full of romantic vistas, **Wakehurst Place** (NT), an outpost of the Royal Botanic Gardens at Kew and of interest year-round and **Great Dixter**, the manor house garden of the gardening writer David Lloyd. In Kent the gardens of **Hever Castle** are strongly Italian in feel and those of **Scotney Castle** (NT) are of the picturesque-romantic style in a lake and island setting. **Sissinghurst Castle Garden** (NT) is the wonderful 1930s creation of Harold Nicholson and Vita Sackville-West.

THE HEART OF ENGLAND Barnsley House, **Hidcote Manor** (NT), **Kiftsgate Court**, **Misarden Park**, **Painswick Rococo Garden** and **Westonbirt Arboretum** are all in the Cotswolds, each offering something different (see panels, pages 118 and 120). **Rousham House**, Oxfordshire, is an example of an 18th-century romantic rural idyll by William Kent.

WALES Powis Castle (NT) in Powys is set amid fine 18th-century terraces.

In Conwy, **Bodnant Garden** (NT) is based on five Italianate terraces with the mountains of Snowdonia as a beautiful backdrop.

NORTHERN ENGLAND Chatsworth in Derbyshire is a masterly marriage of parkland, landscaped by Lancelot 'Capability' Brown and gardens full of surprises that owe much to Joseph Paxton, head gardener from 1827 and later designer of Crystal Palace. **Studley Royal Water Garden** (NT), North Yorkshire, is an ultra-romantic creation around Fountains Abbey.

SCOTLAND Culzean Country Park (NTS), in South Ayrshire, is landscaped park and woodland. At **Edzell Castle** (HS), in Stirling, is a 17th-century 'pleasaunce', while **Branklyn** (NTS), near Perth, is an amazingly stocked suburban garden of modest size. **Crathes Castle**, in Aberdeenshire, is enchanting and innovative. In the wilds of the Highlands, **Inverewe** (NTS) is a spectacular oasis.

❑ The National Gardens Scheme is an umbrella organization for gardens throughout Britain. Included are many private gardens whose owners open them to the public just one or two days a year. See the booklet *Gardens of England and Wales*. ❑

The national calendar of events ranges from the local customs of Mayday dancing and Shrove Tuesday pancake-racing to the royal pageantry of Trooping the Colour and the great sports events held at the Millennium Stadium, Royal Ascot and Lord's Cricket Ground. Local tourist information offices stock details of what's on where and when.

PAGEANTRY AND SPECTACLE

Trooping the Colour, the celebration of the Queen's official birthday, takes place in June in Horse Guards' Parade in central London and shows off the best of royal pageantry. The Lord Mayor's Show in November features the new mayor of the City of London in procession in a golden coach.

Other annual spectacles include the Chelsea Flower Show (May, London), Cruft's Dog Show (March, Birmingham) and the International Airshow (July, even-numbered years, Farnborough, Hampshire).

The Randwick Wap, a Cotswolds mayoral swearing-in

ARTS FESTIVALS

The major arts festival of the year is the Edinburgh Festival in August/September; other sites include Bath, Brighton and Glasgow, plus Gloucester, Herefordshire or Worcestershire for the Three Choirs Festival (see page 117) and Llangollen for the International Musical Eisteddfod in Wales (see page 163). The Promenade Concerts ('Proms') at London's Royal Albert Hall take place from July to September, with classical music, old and new, being performed.

SPORT

Professional soccer matches are held every Saturday between August and May; the FA (Football Association) Cup Final in May is the big match. The cricket season lasts from April to September. Book tickets for Test matches well ahead; there is rarely a problem getting to see a four-day or one-day county game. The Wimbledon Lawn Tennis Championships are held in London late June to early July. As for horse racing, the Grand National is a notoriously tough steeplechase run at Aintree near Liverpool in April and the ultra-fashionable Royal Ascot takes place in June. Regattas are rowed at Henley in late June/early July and a round-the-island yacht race takes place at Cowes on the Isle of Wight in August. In March the Oxford and Cambridge Boat Race is rowed on the Thames in west London.

Numerous traditional sports get an annual revival: variants of medieval football are played in the streets of St. Columb Major in Cornwall and Ashbourne in Derbyshire, while Cumberland wrestling takes place in the Lake District. In Scotland the summer Highland Games at Braemar and elsewhere feature caber-tossing, mountain races and pipe bands.

SHOWS AND FÊTES

County shows have an agricultural emphasis, with livestock and horticultural competitions attracting the nearby farming communities, but also include sport and entertainment.

Village *fêtes* (fairs) are in many ways miniature versions of these, with tombolas (raffles), cake competitions, produce, bric-à-brac stalls and maybe sheep-dog trials—essential for anyone wanting to see the real rural Britain.

FOLK AND RELIGIOUS CUSTOMS

The only nationally celebrated event unique to this country is Guy Fawkes Night, on 5 November, when fireworks are set off and effigies of Guy Fawkes, the conspirator caught attempting to blow up the Houses of Parliament in 1605, are burned on the top of big bonfires.

Locally, an amazing variety of folk customs are celebrated. Some of the oldest owe their origins to Mayday fertility rites, including maypole dancing around the country and, in Cornwall, the Furry Dance in Helston and the 'Obby 'Oss Festival at Padstow. Elsewhere, you can take your pick from such oddities as oyster-blessing at Whitstable (Kent), a pancake (crêpe) race at Olney (Buckinghamshire), or face-pulling through a horse-collar at Egremont (Cumbria). Church customs include rush-bearing (dating from times when churches needed rushes to cover earthen floors) and, in the Peak District, well-dressing, when wells are decorated with pictures made of flowers.

The 'Obby 'Oss Festival, Padstow

The Industrial Revolution began in Britain, in a phenomenal burst of innovation in the late 18th and 19th centuries. In the new millennium, even as Britain's heavy industrial base continues to decline, museums that explore this aspect of the national heritage are a boom industry—and you don't have to be a fan of rusty sprockets and cogwheels to appreciate and learn from them.

Listed here is a selection of the best museums to visit. You can also see evocative reminders of Britain's industrial past—though they haven't been turned into museums as such—in the textile mill towns of West Yorkshire, the valleys of South Wales, the factory villages of Port Sunlight and Saltaire and numerous abandoned mining landscapes such as the tin mines of Cornwall and the lead mines of Swaledale. Many of the sites and museums mentioned below are described more fully in the A–Z section of the book.

THE WEST COUNTRY Coldharbour Mill at Cullompton in Devon is an old wool mill that recalls the heyday of the Devon wool industry; the processes of carding, drafting and spinning are shown and there are some fine old machines. At **Wheal Martyn**, St. Austell, Cornwall's still-surviving china clay industry is explained, with a tour around an abandoned site and a view of the moonscape of working pits nearby.

SOUTHERN ENGLAND At **Amberley Working Museum**, West Sussex, visitors see craftspeople at work in a former chalk pit and lime works. **The Historic Dockyard Chatham** in Chatham, Kent, is the world's largest Georgian dockyard. At Hove in East Sussex, the **British Engineerium** evokes the age of steam power, within a Victorian water pumping station.

THE HEART OF ENGLAND The **Black Country Living Museum**, Dudley (West Midlands), is a skilful reconstruction of an industrial Black Country community of yesteryear, with a colliery, redbrick cottages, a canal where you can try 'legging' along the tunnel in the customary fashion. The **Ironbridge Gorge Museums** (in Shropshire), considered the birthplace of the Industrial Revolution, is the undoubted star of Britain's many distinguished industrial museums.

WALES Visit the **Big Pit National Museum of Wales**, Blaenavon, to get the full experience of going down into a coal mine in the heart of the Welsh valleys. **Sygun Copper Mine** in Beddgelert, Gwynedd and **Llechwedd Slate Caverns** in Blaenau Ffestiniog, Gwynedd, offer imaginatively conceived tours of the old mines and the **Welsh Slate Museum**, Llanberis, is an evocative semi-abandoned slate quarry. The **National Woollen Museum**, at Drefach Felindre in western Wales, has fabric-making demonstrations,

The Museum of Iron at Ironbridge Gorge, a World Heritage Site

The Black Country Living Museum

factory trails and bygone tools and machinery; you can even try your hand at spinning.

NORTHWEST ENGLAND Cromford Mill, in Cromford, Derbyshire, is an exciting monument to Richard Arkwright on the site of his first water-powered cotton mill. In the Potteries area (around Stoke-on-Trent), the **Royal Doulton**, **Wedgwood** and **Spode** factories are open to visitors. The **Gladstone Pottery Museum** is the last surviving 19th-century pottery in the Stoke area, and now has excellent working displays. At Etruria, atmospherically placed between two canals, the **Etruria Industrial Museum** occupies the steam-powered mill where flint was crushed for use in the ceramics industry. The **Paradise Mill and Silk Museum** in Macclesfield, Cheshire, gives the story of the town's heyday when anyone who was anyone wore Macclesfield silk buttons. **Quarry Bank Mill**, Styal, Cheshire, is an excellent restoration of an 18th-century water-powered cotton mill in a fine verdant setting. Authentically clanking old machines can be seen and heard, at the **Helmshore Textile Museums**, in the heartland of the former Lancashire cotton-making country. At **Stott Park Bobbin Mill** in Finsthwaite, Cumbria, former mill workers explain the process of one of the last bobbin mills to be operational in England; it functioned from 1835 until as recently as 1971.

NORTHEAST ENGLAND West Yorkshire has a rich heritage of textile manufacturing. Some of its mills have now become tourist attractions, such as **Armley Mills** in Leeds and the **Bradford Industrial Museum**. **The Beamish North of England Open Air Museum**, Beamish, Co Durham, is a clever evocation of the early 1800s and early 1900s.

SOUTHERN SCOTLAND New Lanark World Heritage Site at New Lanark, South Lanarkshire, is a remarkably well-preserved cotton mill village with working machinery, a period shop and house and craft workshops; the village has a dramatic setting near waterfalls. At Newtongrange, Midlothian, the **Scottish Mining Museum** has a fine working steam engine used for winding. Ambitious displays cover the lives of the miners and some of the colliery buildings can be visited.

Gladstone Pottery Museum

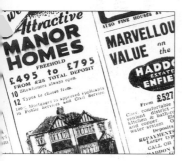

Although it is often taken for granted, the 'semi' is a major component of British cityscapes. Rapidly and cheaply built during the 1930s, semi-detached houses were laid out in neat rows, avenues and crescents. Within two decades a large part of Britain's countryside had given way to suburbanization. The semi may never have been chic, but over the years it has adapted well for modern living and is still going strong today.

Mention the word suburbia in Britain and it is the semi that springs first to mind. The length and breadth of the country, pairs of mirror-image houses under a single roof line the roads that lead into every major town. At first glance, each semi is identical, but closer inspection will reveal certain marks of individuality. For an Englishman's home is his castle and none more so than his semi.

RISE OF THE SEMI Terraced houses, similar to the American row house, had been the dominant feature of 19th-century popular housing in England and Wales (Scottish cities specialized more in tenements); inexpensive and quick to build, the terrace provided housing for the artisan classes. Wealthier folk aspired to semi-detached or detached (separate) properties.

The semi-detached was a feature of the urban scene in Victorian and Edwardian times, but it was in the 1930s Depression years that it really came into its own. The workforce was low-cost and plentiful, cheap materials readily available. Speculative builders were creating new subdivisions in the verdant fringes of major cities and improved rail and road links made commuting more feasible. Advertisements promised a rural idyll.

THE BUILDING BOOM With this boom came the mass-produced semi: a square plan, a common pitched roof, one party wall, a front and back garden, often a garage built onto one side. Since only a modest down payment was needed, the semi was available to virtually anyone with a reasonable income. Rustic and fanciful flourishes were added to the basic design: leaded windows, gables sporting Tudor-style half-timbering, tile-covered walls, stained-glass windows, sunrise motifs. Interior plans varied little: three or four bedrooms and a bathroom, a living room and a small kitchen (in the new age of convenience foods, after all, who needed a big kitchen?). 'Three-piece suites' (a sofa for the children, an armchair for each parent) in the living room exemplified traditional solidity.

The semi has shown itself readily adaptable to modern living, with new porches and extra rooms over the garage being frequent alterations.

A typical semi, in Basingstoke

22

Britain was

England's 'green and pleasant land' is not a natural phenomenon, but the product of 200 generations of hard work. To oversimplify matters, imagine Britain's underlying geology as dividing the country into a highland zone in the north and west, including Scotland, the Pennines, the Lake District and Wales and a lowland zone in the south and east. No matter what the geology, however, hardly any part of the landscape is unaltered by human hand.

24

The first people to make a mark on the landscape were the mesolithic people, nomadic hunters who burned forests and cleared large areas of land in order to gather herds of wild animals together. This lifestyle gradually became more settled over the years as neolithic peoples introduced crops, farming and domesticated animals. In order to make the necessary cropland and pasture for their cattle, sheep and pigs, they made permanent clearings, creating landscapes that were not unlike those we see today, although the actual use of the land was substantially different. Generally, small groups lived in hamlets of a few huts surrounded by an earth bank or a wooden palisade (a tall fence), with fields outside. These were the forerunners of subsequent centuries of village life.

A well-preserved Roman road on Wheeldale in the North York Moors

❑ The stone axes with which neolithic farmers cleared the land were far more effective implements than is generally realized. Experiments indicate that one man working alone could have cleared 0.25ha (0.5 acres) a week. ❑

THE EARLIEST COMMUNITIES Over many centuries, villages grew up where there was fertile soil and an adequate water supply. The 'typical' English village of houses clustered around a village green and duck pond is only one of several types (in Wales and Scotland the green is not a common feature). Other villages are stretched out along a road or have more than one heart or sprawl about in a congenial muddle.

Each village was a service hub for the surrounding countryside, providing a church, a drinking house, artisans, a market for produce. The more successful ones usually had some geographical advantage—they were situated at a ford or an important road intersection, for instance—and they grew into towns. Other towns were founded by landowners looking for profit.

TRACKS AND ROADS The earliest roads were created by farmers and their livestock and many of today's country lanes, lying deep between high banks, may be thousands of years old. Trade also had its part to play and a network of prehistoric 'high roads' can still be traced.

❏ Britain's human history stretches back over a vast period of time to the arrival of manlike beings more than 300,000 years ago. It is conventionally divided into the periods shown here, but the dates should be taken only as extremely rough approximations.

Period	Dates	Outstanding example
Paleolithic (Old Stone Age)	500,000–8,300BC	
Mesolithic (Middle Stone Age)	8,300–4,500BC	
Neolithic (New Stone Age)	4,500–2,300BC	Belas Knap tomb
Bronze Age	2,300–700BC	Stonehenge
Iron Age	700BC–AD43	Maiden Castle hill fort
Roman	AD43–410	Roman Baths, Bath

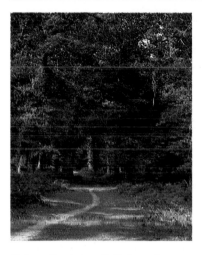

Oak woodlands near Butts Lawn in Hampshire's ancient New Forest

The Romans introduced the first centrally planned road network. The Roman network sufficed until a new era of road-building began in the 1700s. Many of the characteristically long, straight Roman roads survive as modern traffic routes.

❏ 'The great charm...of English scenery is the moral feeling that seems to pervade it. It is associated in the mind with ideas of order, of quiet, of sober well-established principles, hoary usage and reverend custom. Everything seems to be the growth of ages of reverend and peaceful existence.'
—Washington Irving (1820) ❏

FOREST AND WOODLANDS As well as clearing forest for agriculture, neolithic people managed woodlands very successfully. Coppicing is a good example: the tree is cut down to ground level so that several shoots grow up to replace the lost one. Over several years this produces a crop of poles of just the right size for whatever use the woodsman decides upon. And coppiced trees live on almost indefinitely so long as coppicing continues. It is a perfect self-regenerating system. After World War II, men were still using and refining skills such as these, first learned more than 4,000 years ago.

Today, however, most woodlands are managed differently, with concentration on large timber production. Wildlife actually suffers as a result: flowers are shaded out, butterflies lose their habitat.

LANDSCAPE TODAY Despite the changes of the 20th century, the British landscape presents a remarkable historical tableau. Early settlers slashed and burned down the primeval forests, exhausting the soil and leaving moorlands that still cover much of upland Britain. Agricultural and much common land was subject to enclosure from medieval times to the 19th century; the old 'open field' system, where several farmers worked strips within a large single field, was abandoned for smaller enclosures. During that period the hedges (now themselves being removed in many areas) and drystone walls that dominate so much of the lowlands today changed the face of the country.

25

Gaunt and brooding in the British countryside, the shells and ruins of formidable medieval strongholds still defy time and weather. They were sited at strategic points—to control a river crossing, a hill pass, or a port, for example. Many of them saw little or no action, which is testimony to their effectiveness. They were not built to provoke attack, but to deter it.

The Norman Conquest of England made 1066 one of the key dates of British history. The triumphant William the Conqueror—known in his own time, though not to his face, as William the Bastard—divided England between his Norman, French, Breton and Flemish followers. The more important built castles to secure their grip on their new estates and by 1100 there were some 500 of these strongholds in England. The early ones consisted of a mound of earth (the motte), built by conscript workers, with a yard (the bailey) around its base, enclosed by an earth rampart and ditch. Wooden buildings housed the castle's lord, his family and his small private army. The local villagers could take refuge in the bailey in time of danger.

BASTIONS OF STONE Many of these primitive fortresses were soon replaced by daunting strongholds built of stone. A hulking keep was erected on the mound, its walls as

Stark and strong, Corfe Castle in Dorset was built by the Normans

much as 30m (100ft) high and 6m (20ft) thick at the base, pierced by tiny windows through which archers and crossbowmen could fire. The living quarters were in the keep, with the ground floor used for storage and dungeons. Outer walls kept besiegers at a distance and around them might be a water-filled moat crossed by a drawbridge. Castles became ever more elaborate as time went by. The

> ❏ 'The rich man in his castle,
>   The poor man at his gate,
> God made them high and lowly,
>   And ordered their estate.'
> —19th-century hymn ❏

Tower of London, originally built for William the Conqueror himself, is a particularly impressive specimen.

In Wales, both Norman and native warlords built themselves castles. When Edward I of England conquered the country, a chain of powerful fortresses that could be supplied by sea cemented his hold. **Caernarfon**, **Harlech**, **Conwy** and **Beaumaris** castles still testify to the skill of his military engineer, James of St. George. Scotland, where central authority was never as strong, bristles with ferocious and romantic strongholds, led by **Edinburgh** and **Stirling**, high on their lofty crags.

THE MANORIAL ESTATE Castles were extremely costly and only the richest nobles could afford them. In medieval England the basic landholding unit was the manor, ruled by its lord, who lived in the large manor house. Often a manor was a village with its surrounding countryside, but some manors

Harlech Castle, impregnable monument to King Edward I

contained more than one village, while others covered only part of one. The villagers cultivated the land, while the lord's function was to protect them and to keep order. Above the lord, in what is now called the **feudal system**, a chain of greater lords led up to the king himself, each link in the chain owing support to the one above it and protection to the one below.

The lord's manor house was at first just a bigger version of the wood-and-mud hovels of his villagers. By the 13th century, though, manor houses were being built of stone and the fortified manor house appeared— cheaper and more comfortable than a castle, but defensible. They focused on one main room, the hall, where the household ate and slept, while the dogs gnawed bones on the straw- or rush-covered floor and smoke from a central hearth drifted out through a hole in the roof.

Over the centuries the medieval lord of the manor became the less powerful, though still dominant, country squire. Just as the power of kings has ebbed away, so the title of lord of the manor has become a picturesque but empty title.

❑ Perhaps England's best example of a fortified manor house is Stokesay Castle (EH), near Shrewsbury in Shropshire (see page 124), which has preserved its medieval atmosphere to a remarkable degree. ❑

At the same time as being beautiful and satisfying to the senses, churches were originally built as earthly houses for God; symbols of the God-given order of the world and the true purpose of human life. Through the centuries, generations of Christians have prayed in them, joined in the community's spiritual life, been baptized and married and finally, after life's fitful fever, have been laid to rest in eternal peace in the churchyard.

28

From the humblest parish church to the most sumptuous cathedral, in country and town alike, churches are an essential element of the British scene. Almost all of them have been altered, enlarged or rebuilt many times over.

STYLES OF ARCHITECTURE A few **Anglo-Saxon** churches are still standing. Small and plain, they are the oldest British ecclesiastical buildings to survive. The **Normans** built on an altogether more massive and powerful scale, notably with thick round columns supporting the roof and round arches above small doors and windows.

Movingly simple, the Saxon church at Greensted in Essex has walls of split logs

The **Gothic** style, which arrived in Britain in the 12th century, was lighter, airier, more slender, more uplifting to the spirit. Its earliest phases, Early English and the more ornate Decorated, introduced the pointed arch, the flying buttress and the tall spire that directed eyes and thoughts heavenward. These churches were alive with elaborate decoration, carvings in wood and stone, stained-glass windows, statues and wall paintings—the religious textbooks of an age that could not read. (Much of this decoration, unfortunately, was destroyed or painted over by the Puritans when they took over the government in the 17th century.) In the 14th century came the Perpendicular style, named after the strong vertical lines that carry the eye up to the roof. Tall, soaring shafts support a web of fan-vaulting and enormous windows of the most delicate tracery, while graceful towers rise to a riot of pinnacles. The style reached its apogee in the amazing stone cobweb of **King's College Chapel**, Cambridge. In the 19th century the values of medieval architecture were upheld by such architects as Augustus Pugin in the form of the Gothic Revival style.

THE MONASTIC MOVEMENT Among the most haunting legacies that the Middle Ages left to Britain are the now ruined monasteries—**Fountains** (NT and EH), **Rievaulx**, **Glastonbury**, **Tintern** and many more. Medieval abbeys and priories ran a virtual welfare system for the poor, treated the sick, kept scholarship and art alive and gave hospitality to wayfarers, but their primary function was as a focus of prayer and worship. With eight services a day, from matins before dawn to vespers at sunset and compline at bedtime, monks paid humankind's tribute of devotion to God.

The church was always the biggest and finest building in a monastery, usually standing at one side of a quadrangle. Around the other sides were the domestic buildings—the refectory for meals, the kitchen, the dormitory, the infirmary. The monks themselves took vows of poverty, but monasteries accumulated large estates, ran farms and raised sheep.

The soaring ruins of Tintern Abbey

Fountains Abbey in Yorkshire, for example, was the North of England's biggest producer of wool.

The **Reformation** of the 16th century created the Church of England as a separate body, no longer owing allegiance to the Pope and in the 1530s the monasteries were all closed down (the church, however, was often retained by the community as a parish church). Most of the monastic land ended up in the hands of the aristocracy and the country gentry, not only enriching them but making it quite certain that the Dissolution of the Monasteries would never be reversed. Today empty, roofless shells stand quietly where generations of monks once lived and prayed.

❏ Guidebooks often use the following terms for styles of church architecture in Britain. The dates should be considered as rough indications only.

Style	Dates	Outstanding example
Saxon	650–1066	St. Laurence's, Bradford on Avon
Norman (or Romanesque)	1066–1190	Durham Cathedral
Gothic: Early English	1190–1275	Salisbury Cathedral
Decorated	1275–1375	Exeter Cathedral
Perpendicular	1375–1485	King's College Chapel, Cambridge
Classical	17th–18th centuries	St. Paul's Cathedral, London
Gothic Revival	early 19th century	All Saints, Margaret Street, London W1
Victorian	1837–1901	St. Mary's Cathedral, Edinburgh

A long era of relative peace on British soil since the 1500s has left Britain virtually without equal in the number of grand historic houses open for visitors to enjoy. They're packed from floor to ceiling with treasures of art and triumphs of decoration—paintings, sculptures, furniture, porcelain, books, clocks. Surrounded by exquisite gardens and sumptuously landscaped parks, they testify to five centuries of wealth, taste and social prominence.

Britain retains a notable number of timber-framed houses dating from medieval times, though most have been adapted and precise dating is difficult; more important buildings were often constructed in stone. Grander medieval examples include **Haddon Hall** in Derbyshire and **Ightham Mote** in Kent.

Tudor Chenies Manor House, near Amersham in Buckinghamshire

THE VERNACULAR The houses of the ordinary people, and also their agricultural and industrial buildings, were constructed following local traditions and in whatever material was readily at hand, be it stone, flint, or cob, thatch, slate, or pantile.

THE ELIZABETHAN AGE The Tudor era was one of peace and prosperity in which the rich Englishman's home no longer needed to be a fortified castle. The wealthy built ostentatious houses, Cardinal Wolsey and Henry

VIII leading the way with the huge brick palace of **Hampton Court**. Capacious bay windows gazed out upon the countryside, while the fantastically elaborate chimneystacks of grand houses of the 16th and 17th centuries joined the gables, turrets and balustrades that enlivened the roofline to impress passers-by with the owner's wealth.

Much Tudor building was in brick, but in areas where there was plenty of lumber—as in the Southeast and the western Midlands—houses were half-timbered, with rectangular wooden frames enclosing panels of whitewashed plaster or brick. The most lavish examples, like **Little Moreton Hall** (NT) in Cheshire, are a riot of zebra-striped patterns.

THE CLASSICAL IDEAL Outside these houses, a formal symmetrical garden was evidence of the Renaissance enthusiasm for classical Greek and Roman ideals. The first really famous British architects—**Inigo Jones** and **Sir Christopher Wren** in the 17th century—were influenced by classical architecture. Inigo Jones's Queen's House (1616–35) in Greenwich was one of the first houses in Britain to be designed on classical principles. The typical house of Queen Anne's reign was a simple, symmetrical red-brick mansion with large sash windows and a four-sided roof behind a parapet. As the 18th century unfolded, **Sir John Vanbrugh** piled the colossal baroque palaces of **Castle Howard** and **Blenheim** upon the groaning earth, with their splendid domes and porticoes. Most of the English upper class, however, preferred the restrained elegance of the Palladian style of mansion, with its straight lines and pleasing proportions, its classical pillars and pediments. Around the house would stretch a noble park, where smooth lawns escorted the eye to carefully positioned groups of trees, an artificial lake, a bridge and a temple, such as William Kent's **Holkham Hall**, Norfolk. Horace Walpole's **Strawberry Hill** is a playfully picturesque example of the 'Gothick' style.

GEORGIAN ELEGANCE The same style, imposing a calm order upon unruly Nature, created some of Britain's most satisfying townscapes in Bath, London, Edinburgh and other cities. From the 1760s the interiors of Georgian houses were opulently enriched by the genius of **Robert Adam** and his many imitators, who introduced delicate ornamentation into mansions like **Syon House** in Middlesex, in rooms never intended for living in, but for entertaining. In the early 19th-century Regency period John Nash created the flamboyant **Royal Pavilion** in Brighton and the stucco terraces around **Regent's Park.** His contemporary John Soane adopted a highly original style, exemplified by **Sir John Soane's Museum** in London.

VICTORIAN EXUBERANCE Powerful enthusiasm for medieval Gothic Christian architecture gave many Victorian houses an ecclesiastical

Kiftsgate Court, Gloucestershire: a Georgian house in a lovely garden

> ❏ All through the 19th century the Gothic and the classical styles vied for supremacy. In Yorkshire, for instance, the city fathers of Leeds built a magnificent classical temple as their town hall, while rival Bradford erected a Gothic town hall of mammoth proportions. ❏

look, with turrets, pointed windows and stained glass, while Scots magnates built themselves mock baronial palaces. Victorian architects and their patrons took the whole past as their province. They adopted whatever architectural style took their fancy and blended characteristics from different styles to romantic and sometimes wildly excessive effect. In the early 1900s **Richard Norman Shaw** introduced stylised 'vernacular', or countryside, styles (as at Cragside/NT, Northumberland) and **Sir Edwin Lutyens** revived the classical style (as at Great Maytham, Kent).

CHANGING IDEALS A fierce reaction against Victorian and Edwardian 'pastiche' followed in the 20th century as the modern movement in architecture adopted an austere simplicity of straight lines and concrete, often criticized as concrete monstrosities and provoking a more varied approach from the 1980s on, ranging from neoclassical to mock-vernacular. Yet some high-rise blocks are coming back into fashion: Erno Goldfinger's once-hated and much-vandalized 31-floor **Trellick Tower** (1972) in west London is now loved by many residents and acclaimed a masterpiece.

31

In 1066 William the Conqueror, the Duke of Normandy, invaded from France and became the hugely influential William I of England. Richard III was the last medieval king, having wrested power from Edward V whom he declared illegitimate. Richard was killed at the Battle of Bosworth (1485) and Henry Tudor seized the throne to become Henry VII.

Britain's modern history begins in 1485, when the marriage of **Henry VII** of Lancaster to Elizabeth of York ended the 30-year Wars of the Roses— an inheritance dispute between the dukes of Lancaster and York. His son, **Henry VIII**, with a massive frame and small eyes so famously depicted in the Holbein portrait, is best known for his six wives. Two he divorced—breaking from the Catholic Church in Rome in the process—and two he executed, one died in childbirth and the sixth outlived him.

32

Top: Henry V; bottom: Henry VIII with his six wives—Jane Seymour, Anne of Cleves, Catherine Howard, Anne Boleyn, Catherine of Arragon and Catherine Parr

Elizabeth I, 'Virgin Queen'

❏ 'I know I have the body of a weak and feeble woman, but I have the heart and stomach of a king and of a king of England too.'—Queen Elizabeth I, speech to the troops on the approach of the Armada, 1588 ❏

ELIZABETH TUDOR It was typical of Henry's daughter **Elizabeth I** that when a deputation arrived at Hatfield House in Hertfordshire in 1558 to tell her she was queen, the 25-year-old princess was found sitting under an oak tree demurely reading a book. She always had a genius for public relations. A consummate politician, with her father's physical and intellectual prowess combined with feminine grace and charm, she successfully steered her country safely through 44 dangerous years.

THE STUARTS Scotland, meanwhile, had seen a long succession of kings of the Stuart dynasty, who since 1371 had struggled to impose their authority on their rebellious aristocracy. The beautiful **Mary, Queen of Scots** was forced to abdicate in 1567. She escaped to England, where she was politely kept prisoner for 20 years until execution in 1587.

Her son, **James VI of Scotland**, succeeded the childless Elizabeth I in 1603 as **James I of England**. The house of Stuart fared little better in England than in Scotland. **Charles I**, attempting to uphold royal power against Parliament, was defeated by the Puritans under **Oliver Cromwell** in the **Civil War** and executed in London in 1649. **Charles II** was restored to the throne in 1660, after an interregnum of republican rule that proved deeply unpopular. He is remembered for his charm, his cynicism and his prolific sex life. His brother was **James II**, who had a brief anti-Protestant reign before fleeing the throne in 1688; Parliament offered the crown, in the bloodless 'Glorious Revolution', to the Dutch prince **William of Orange**, who reigned jointly with his wife **Mary**, James's daughter. **Queen Anne**, Mary's sister, was the last Stuart ruler.

THE HANOVERIANS On Anne's death in 1714, the Elector of Hanover became king as **George I**. Although he was a German who could not speak a word of English, as a Protestant he was preferred to the Stuart claimants, who made a dashing but unsuccessful last bid for the lost throne in 1745, led by Prince Charles Edward, sentimentally known as **Bonnie Prince Charlie**.

George III, who was much liked for his hearty geniality, was king when the American colonies broke away to become an independent nation. His son, ultimately **George IV**, acted as regent during George III's mental illness and became influential in fashion, architecture and the arts, while his grand-daughter, **Queen Victoria**, enjoyed the longest reign of any British sovereign—64 years from 1837 to 1901. Clad invariably in black after the death of her beloved Prince

A portrait of Charles I

Consort, Albert, in 1861, the widowed queen was ruler of the largest empire in history.

THE HOUSE OF WINDSOR Victoria's grandson, **George V**, sensitive during World War I about the dynasty's German connections, decided to change his family's name (Saxe-Coburg-Gotha) to the House of Windsor. His son **Edward VIII** caused an international scandal by abdicating within months of coming to the throne in 1936, following his marriage to the American divorcée Wallis Simpson, leaving his shy and unprepared brother to rule as **George VI** throughout World War II. Since 1952, **Queen Elizabeth II** has reigned, but the future of the monarchy is constantly under debate.

33

That Britain is an island has formed and influenced its history and character. Britain's greatness was built on seaborne trade and the British Empire rested on the Royal Navy's command of the sea, celebrated in popular patriotic songs from Rule Britannia *to the Gilbert and Sullivan parody* HMS Pinafore. *The sea and seafaring are in Britain's blood.*

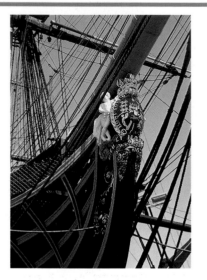

Nelson's flagship, HMS Victory

The sea has played contradictory roles in British history, as both barrier and bridge. Britannia has always needed her 'towers along the steep'—coastal fortifications against attack by sea. They can be seen bristling along England's southern and southeastern shoreline, ranging from Roman forts of the Saxon Shore to medieval and Tudor castles, 19th-century Martello towers and Palmerston forts against the French and World War II fortifications.

OVERSEAS TRADING At the same time, while the sea has served Britain as a defensive moat, it has also been by sea that people, ideas and trade have moved between Britain and the rest of the world. As far back as prehistoric times, ships from the Mediterranean came to Cornwall for tin. In Roman days, Britain exported slaves, oysters and hunting dogs, among other things, to the Continent and imported wine.

The great medieval 'wool churches' of England stand as testimony to the wealth generated by the export trade in wool and cloth. It remained a major factor in the economy into the 16th century, when merchants forged thriving trade links with the world beyond Europe—Asia, Africa and the Americas. The piratical **Sir Francis Drake** sailed away in 1578 in a cockleshell of a ship, which was only the second to circumnavigate the globe. Plundering Spanish possessions on the way, he returned in 1580 with loot estimated at more than £30 million in today's money.

IN COMMAND OF THE SEAS The British navy can trace its history back to **Alfred the Great** in the ninth century; he was the first English king to lead his own squadron in battle, against the Danes. In medieval times, ships and crews were supplied for the royal fleet by the **Cinque Ports** of southeast England—Dover, Sandwich, Hythe, New Romney and Hastings. The Tudor and Stuart kings built up a more effective and powerful force. Along with two other formidable Elizabethan seadogs, Hawkins and Frobisher, Drake

> ❏ 'Britannia needs no bulwarks,
> No towers along the steep;
> Her march is o'er the mountain
>   waves,
> Her home is on the deep.'
> —Thomas Campbell,
> 'Ye Mariners of England'
> (1800–01) ❏

helped defeat the ponderous Spanish Armada in 1588.

Between 1700 and 1780 Britain's foreign trade almost doubled. The port of Bristol took a leading part in the slave trade, which shipped millions of Africans to the American plantations. Meanwhile, Britain became the world's leading colonial power in a struggle against the French in which command of the sea was of paramount importance. The French were driven from India and North America and the British built up the empire on which the sun never set. The 'wooden walls'—the Royal Navy's implacable three-deckers—kept **Napoleon** at arm's length. 'I do not say they cannot come,' said Admiral Lord St. Vincent of the French invasion barges, 'I only say they cannot come by sea.'

ILLUSTRIOUS NAMES The navy was the guardian of British liberty and a succession of naval heroes etched their names on the British conscious-ness—Anson, Rodney, Hood, Howe, St. Vincent, Collingwood, Cochrane. The most admired and loved of them all was **Horatio Nelson**, killed at the Battle of Trafalgar in 1805 as the HMS *Victory* bore down upon the foe. The great ship is lovingly preserved in Portsmouth.

A Martello tower on the south coast, one of many built to counter the threat of Napoleonic invasion

35

❏ 'A willing foe and sea room.' —The Royal Navy's Friday night toast ❏

The British Empire eventually covered a quarter of the land surface of the globe, stretching across the world's heaving waters from Canada to India, Australia, New Zealand, as well as remote islands in the Pacific. It could not be sustained however and World War II demonstrated that command of the sea had eventually passed from Britain to the mightier United States.

Many places in Britain are linked with famous writers and their work. The village of Chawton in Hampshire shelters the modest house where Jane Austen wrote, hiding her papers when any of the household came in. Nearby at Selborne is the home of Gilbert White, the nature writer. Each year, Rochester in Kent commemorates Charles Dickens, who lived nearby. You can explore George Bernard Shaw's home at Ayot St. Lawrence in Hertfordshire, as well as Lord Byron's and D. H. Lawrence's houses near Nottingham, Rudyard Kipling's at Bateman's in East Sussex and Samuel Johnson's in Lichfield and London.

LITERARY SHRINES No writer in English is more admired than **William Shakespeare** and his birth-place town of Stratford-upon-Avon in Warwickshire is the most visited British tourist destination outside London.

In West Yorkshire the once grim little town of Haworth is thronged with pilgrims to the parsonage where **Charlotte**, **Emily** and **Anne Brontë** and their brother **Branwell** lived. Out on the desolate moorland is the ruined farmhouse that may have been the original *Wuthering Heights*.

The Lake District also draws literary pilgrims, to **William Wordsworth**'s homes at Dove Cottage and Rydal Mount and the Lakeland scenes which inspired his poetry. **John Ruskin**, the Victorian art critic and social reformer, owned a house with a magical view over Coniston Water. **Beatrix Potter** also lived at Near Sawrey.

At Laugharne in South Wales the most famous Welsh poet of the 20th century, **Dylan Thomas**, is fondly remembered at his studio, the Boathouse. Scotland's national poet, **Robert Burns**, is cherished at the humble cottage where he was born in the outskirts of Ayr and also in Dumfries, where he spent his last years. **Sir Walter Scott**'s engaging collection of historical curios—Rob Roy's sword, a lock of the Young Pretender's hair and so on—can be admired at Abbotsford, his home in his beloved Borders, while at Kirriemuir is the birthplace of **Sir James Barrie**, author of *Peter Pan*.

The literary trail of **Jane Austen** includes her house from 1809 to 1817 at Chawton (northeast of Winchester), and the city of Bath, where the Jane Austen Centre recalls her work on such novels as *Persuasion* and *Northanger Abbey*. At Coxwold in North Yorkshire is the house where **Laurence Sterne** wrote *Tristram Shandy* and **John Milton** completed *Paradise Lost* in a cottage at Chalfont St. Giles in Buckinghamshire.

❑ Earth has not anything to show
        more fair:
Dull would he be of soul who could
        pass by
A sight so touching in its majesty:
This City now doth like a garment
        wear
The beauty of the morning; silent,
        bare,
Ships, towers, domes, theatres
        and temples lie
Open unto the fields and to the
        sky;
All bright and glittering in the
        smokeless air.
—William Wordsworth
(1770–1850),
Upon Westminster Bridge ❑

RESTING PLACES Interesting literary connections can frequently be found in churchyards. **T. S. Eliot** is buried at East Coker in Somerset, **John Buchan** at Elsfield near Oxford. The country churchyard of **Thomas Gray**'s famous *Elegy* can be found at Stoke Poges in Buckinghamshire. The memory of the evil Count Dracula, **Bram Stoker**'s creation, vampirishly haunts the graveyard at Whitby North Yorkshire. In London, Westminster Abbey's south transept is affectionately known as **Poets' Corner** because Geoffrey Chaucer, Edmund Spenser, Alfred Lord Tennyson, Robert Browning and many other famous poets are buried or have memorials there. Monuments to Shakespeare, Milton, Wordsworth, Burns, Keats and Shelley cluster close to memorials to Lord Byron, T. S. Eliot, W. H. Auden and Dylan Thomas.

> ❏ The curfew tolls the knell of
> parting day,
> The lowing herd winds slowly
> o'er the lea,
> The ploughman homeward plods
> his weary way,
> And leaves the world to
> darkness and to me.
> —Thomas Gray (1716–71),
> *Elegy in a Country Churchyard* ❏

'...MY COUNTRY STILL' Some writers are associated with a whole area of countryside, seen through their eyes and peopled with their own characters. **Thomas Hardy** Country extends over much of Dorset and the museum in Dorchester has an excellent Hardy collection. The 'blue remembered hills' of Shropshire are inseparably linked with the melancholic poetry of **A. E. Housman**.

Alfred, Lord Tennyson is particularly cherished in his native Lincolnshire and there is a noble statue of him outside Lincoln Cathedral. The hub of the **George Eliot** industry is Nuneaton in Warwickshire; the southern part of Tyne and Wear now calls itself **Catherine Cookson** Country in homage to the best-selling romantic novelist.

> ❏ The first fire since the
> summer is lit and is smoking
> into the room;
> The sun-rays spread it through,
> like woof-lines in a loom.
> Sparrows spurt from the hedge,
> whom misgivings appal
> That winter did not leave last
> year for ever, after all.
> —Thomas Hardy (1840–1928),
> *Shortening Days at the
> Homestead* ❏

Sometimes it is the characters more than the author who cast the spell. It is hardly possible to explore Exmoor without recalling *Lorna Doone*, Cornwall without thinking of the heroes and heroines of **Daphne du Maurier** and **Winston Graham** or Dartmoor without memories of Sherlock Holmes, Doctor Watson and the hound of the Baskervilles.

37

Thomas Hardy's statue at the end of the high street in Dorchester, the 'Casterbridge' of his novels

Britain's most characteristic contribution to Western art lies in a long tradition of landscape painting, which inspired such artists as Gainsborough, Constable and Turner. It is this tradition which created the British idea of what the landscape looks like—or at least of what it ought to look like. Visitors enjoying the countryside today still tend to see it through the eyes of the great painters of the past.

The British tradition of landscape painting was founded by **Richard Wilson**, who was born in Wales in 1714 and was deeply impressed by the work of the French painter Claude Lorraine. Unappreciated and poverty-stricken, he struggled to convince the British eye that wild scenery could be beautiful; his paintings of his native Welsh mountains looming above limpid lakes have a classic grandeur and serenity.

THE GREAT NAMES Far more successful financially was **Thomas Gainsborough**, who originally came from Suffolk. He made his money as a fashionable portrait painter in Bath and London, but his true passion was for landscapes—often generalized and idyllic, rather than depicting a particular place. The great Victorian art critic John Ruskin said of him: 'His touch was as light as the sweep of a cloud and swift as the flash of a sunbeam.'

John Constable, arriving on the scene 50 years later, came from the Suffolk-Essex border and his paintings of hayfields, church towers, river scenes, carthorses and wagons have remained hugely popular ever since. Salisbury Cathedral, Hampstead Heath and the South Coast were also popular subjects of his. He believed in the most minute study of Nature, to render, as he said, 'light—dews—breezes—bloom—and freshness' with loving accuracy and he broke free of the formal Claude-inspired landscape.

Constable's contemporary, the prodigious **Joseph Mallord William Turner**, journeyed all over Britain, painting romantic landscapes, castles, cathedrals and great houses. He followed in Richard Wilson's footsteps in Wales, painted extensively at Petworth in West Sussex and in the Thames Valley and rejoiced in the scenery of the Lake District and Wharfedale in Yorkshire. As he grew increasingly fascinated by effects of light, his paintings of Norham Castle in Northumberland depict the ruined fortress and the grazing cattle almost disappearing into abstraction in the glowing sunlit mist.

❏ Britain's country houses and London's National Portrait Gallery house a rich legacy of portraitists. Foreign artists were patronized in earlier times: **Hans Holbein** painted Henry VIII and his court and **Anthony van Dyck** depicted Charles I. In the 18th century the English artists **Sir Joshua Reynolds** and **George Romney** achieved much success. **Sir William Hogarth** created portraits as well as moralizing commentaries such as *The Rake's Progress*. ❏

PLACES OF INSPIRATION Other painters drawn to the Lake District were **Philippe de Loutherburg** and **Joseph Wright**. **L. S. Lowry** painted Lake District scenes, too, though he is better known for his northern industrial townscapes. Over the centuries, the Thames at London has inspired many foreign artists, including **Canaletto**, **Rex Whistler** and **Claude Monet**.

Flatford Mill in Suffolk, still recognizable from Constable's paintings

39

Joshua Reynolds

Some areas have inspired groups of artists, like the **Norwich School** of painters in the early 19th century. **Bristol**'s school of artists was dominated by **Francis Danby** in the 1820s. The **Newlyn School** of artists, based in Cornwall's fishing port, was led by **Stanhope Forbes** from the 1880s, while **St. Ives** in Cornwall was a base for **Barbara Hepworth, Ben Nicholson** and the potter **Bernard Leach**.

Mystical painter **Samuel Palmer** settled at Shoreham, Kent in the 1820s to explore his 'Valley of Vision'. **John Singer Sargent** painted Worcestershire landscapes in the 1880s, **Graham Sutherland** painted in Pembrokeshire pre- and post-World War II. **Cookham**, Berkshire owes its fame to the works of **Sir Stanley Spencer**.

❏ The Pre-Raphaelite Brotherhood of 19th-century English artists painted religious and moralistic scenes, steeped in romantic medievalism and brilliantly hued. Leading figures included **Burne-Jones**, **Rossetti** and **Millais**. London's Tate Britain and the Birmingham Museum and Art Gallery have superb collections. ❏

Crowded, noisy, dirty and packed with life, Manchester was the archetype of the new cities created in Britain by the Industrial Revolution. Instead of a skyline of church spires, hundreds of factory chimneys belched out smoke and fumes. Though horrified by the city's abominable slums and its turbid rivers crawling with filth, many visitors saw Manchester as the symbol of a dawning new age of intense creativity and vitality.

40

The Industrial Revolution was revolutionary in its consequences rather than its speed. The century between 1750 and 1850 ushered in the machine age of factories, mass production and the assembly line, the industrial town and the industrial 'working class'. Why it should all have started in Britain is a disputed question, but the country had certain obvious advantages: ample resources of coal and iron and a growing empire overseas that provided a captive market for British-made products.

THE TEXTILE INDUSTRY The most affected industries in the early stages were textiles, iron and steel, coal mining and pottery. In textiles, a succession of inventions made it possible to increase output while using less human energy. This transformed the making of cloth from a small-scale operation, carried on by skilled workmen and their families at home, to large-scale production in factories where unskilled workers, many of them women and children, toiled as acolytes of the insatiable machines. In 1765 **James Hargreaves** patented the 'Spinning Jenny'—named after his wife—which could spin several threads simultaneously. Four years later a formidable Lancastrian named **Richard Arkwright**, the first great industrial tycoon, patented a spinning frame powered by water. He built a cotton mill and company town at Cromford in the beautiful Derbyshire valley of the Derwent, where people worked in 12-hour shifts as the machines clattered on day and night.

Titus Salt's vast 1853 mill and his model village at Saltaire, Bradford

'And if here man has made of the very daylight an infamy, he can boast that he adds to the darkest night the weird beauty of fire and flame-tinted cloud. From roof and hill you may see on every side furnace calling furnace with fiery tongues and wreathing messages of smoke.'
—Arnold Bennett, *The Potteries* (1898) ❏

THE POWER OF STEAM Arkwright's machinery was powered by water, but in 1779 **Samuel Crompton** invented the so-called mule, a spinning machine that could be powered either by water or steam. Steam was the driving force of the Industrial Revolution and the most important figure in its development, the Scottish inventor **James Watt**, patented the first modern steam engine in 1769. Steam was used to drive all kinds of machinery in factories and mines and was later to propel locomotives and ships, as a transport revolution developed in the 19th century.

'Since the introduction of inanimate mechanism into British manufactories, man, with few exceptions, has been treated as a secondary and inferior machine.'
—Robert Owen, *A New View of Society* (1813) ❏

COAL AND IRON Steam required coal. Britain's coal production doubled between 1750 and 1800 and then grew by 20 times by the end of the 19th century. **Abraham Darby** initiated the mass production of iron ore at **Ironbridge** and new industrial regions grew up close to the principal coalfields in the **Midlands**, the **North of England**, Scotland's **Clydeside** and **South Wales**. The flow of coal from the valleys turned sleepy little fishing villages like Cardiff, Barry and Swansea into busy, blackened ports. At the entrance to the Great Exhibition of 1851 in London's Hyde Park, there stood, appropriately, a towering 24-tonne block of coal.

Towns like Manchester, Birmingham, Glasgow, Leeds, Bradford and Sheffield covered their surrounding countryside with row upon row of workers' housing. Many a lush valley became an inferno of blast furnaces, slag heaps and 'satanic mills'. A new Iron Age introduced iron buildings, iron machines, iron bridges, iron boats, even iron tombstones—as well as the iron regimentation of the assembly line.

Victorian Britain had become 'the workshop of the world', but other countries soon began to overtake it, notably Germany and the United States. In the 1880s Britain enjoyed 37 per cent of the world's trade in manufactured goods, but by 1913 the figure was down to 25 per cent. A new phase of the Industrial Revolution had opened, based on steel, chemicals and electricity and Britain was unable to keep up.

The cotton mill built by Richard Arkwright in Cromford, Derbyshire

LONDON With a population of more than 7 million London is a vast beast, spreading across a great river basin, its haphazard mish-mash of streets revealing exhilarating changes of mood from one moment to the next. Although it is very much a forward-looking thoroughly 21st-century city, there's still a strong sense of the past. To get your bearings, stroll the south bank of the River Thames, hop on a boat, take in the dizzying views from the British Airways London Eye or ride a double-decker bus.

THE WEST END There is more to see here than in any other part of the capital. **Trafalgar Square►►►** is the undisputed centre of London, where a statue of Admiral

43

**TOURIST INFORMATION
(VISIT LONDON)**
Tel: 09068 663344
(60p per minute—
24 hours);
www.visitlondon.com

Nelson stands high on a column guarded by stone lions
fashioned by the artist Edwin Henry Landseer. **St. Martin-
in-the-Fields▶** and the **National Gallery▶▶▶** take up
two sides of the square; Admiralty Arch leads through the
third into the Mall, the grand approach to **Buckingham
Palace▶** (begun 1825), the chief residence of the Queen
with some rooms open in August and September.
Adjacent are the **Queen's Gallery** and the **Royal Mews**
(both open to the public). Flanking the Mall are tree-
shaded **Green Park** and **St. James's Park▶▶**, an alluring
expanse with a lake and bandstand concerts in summer.

The hub of **Westminster** is Parliament Square,
dominated by the clocktower housing the huge Big Ben

Taking a break by the fountains of Trafalgar Square against the backdrop of the National Gallery (left) and St. Martin-in-the-Fields Church (right)

bell, which is part of London's most photographed building, the splendid Gothic Revival **Houses of Parliament**▶ ▶ ▶. The symbol of the seat of government, they were restyled by Charles Barry and Augustus Pugin after fire destroyed an earlier building in 1834. When Parliament is in session you can view from the Strangers' Gallery; Prime Minister's Question Time tends to be the liveliest spectacle (for times and details of guided tours tel: 020-7219 3000; www.parliament.uk). Across the square is **Westminster Abbey**▶ ▶ ▶.

To the west, some of the best addresses in London are in **Mayfair**, chic **Chelsea**, elegant **Knightsbridge** and **Kensington**. Here there is a preponderance of 19th-century stucco in addition to the familiar yellow-toned London stock brick. **South Kensington** is the primary museum quarter. **Hyde Park** and adjacent **Kensington Gardens** constitute a green swathe north of the Royal Albert Hall and the mildly preposterous Albert Memorial.

Covent Garden▶ ▶ ▶, the former fruit and vegetable market hall, has been imaginatively revamped as a lively piazza, with boutiques, street musicians and craft stalls—the scheme was inspired by the renaissance of Faneuil Hall in Boston, Massachusetts. Covent Garden Piazza, laid out by Inigo Jones in 1631, was the first true square in London. The name Covent Garden also denotes the Royal Opera House. **Soho**▶ ▶, farther west, is the heart of the Chinese community (around Gerrard Street the street names are in Chinese) as well as an amalgam of Italian delicatessens, high-class restaurants, nightclubs and sex shops.

Bloomsbury▶ represents the hub of intellectual London: blue plaques (placed on buildings throughout London) indicate the former houses of the famous, including the homes of Charles Dickens (a memorial museum is at 48 Doughty Street) and Virginia Woolf and her 'Bloomsbury Set'. Bloomsbury still has a gracious atmosphere and is a good illustration of how residential

London developed into formal squares and terraces in Georgian and Regency times; Bedford Square continues to be as fashionable as when it was first laid out in 1775. Landmarks include the **British Museum**▶▶▶ and the unusual **British Telecom Tower**, built in 1964.

Regent's Park▶▶ is a gracious tract that was laid out by Regency architect John Nash in conjunction with the supremely elegant stucco terraces on its east side; within the park are **London Zoo**▶▶, an open-air theatre and a boating lake.

Legal London revolves around **Holborn**, with its Gothic Revival High Courts on the Strand and the Central Criminal Courts in the Old Bailey; both have public galleries within the courtrooms. Barristers are attached to chambers within the **Inns of Court** and **Chancery**▶▶ (Gray's Inn, Middle Temple, Inner Temple and Lincoln's Inn), medieval foundations that originally gave lodging to lawyers and legal students; you can wander into the court-yards on weekdays.

THE CITY The 'square mile' of the ancient city of London, the City is where the major financial institutions are concentrated; it retains its medieval street pattern and though the city wall has largely disappeared, its gateways live on in place-names (Ludgate, Aldersgate, Moorgate, etc.); these gates, plus plinths bearing the City griffin, still mark the City boundaries. It is best approached from London Bridge, which has a picture-postcard view of **Tower Bridge**▶▶▶ and the **Tower of London**▶▶▶. **The Monument**▶, designed by Sir Christopher Wren to commemorate the Great Fire of 1666, is a good viewing platform for those fit enough to manage the narrow steps up Richard Rodgers' **Lloyd's Building**▶ in Lime Street and Lord Foster's 30 St. Mary Axe tower (widely nicknamed 'The Gherkin') are two of London's most innovative contributions to high-tech architecture. The **Bank of England** (museum inside), the central bank of the UK, stands opposite the Mansion House, the

45

St. Paul's Cathedral was begun in 1675 and completed 35 years later

Canary Wharf Tower (background), completed in 1991, rises to 240m (790ft)

MORE ON GREENWICH
Greenwich Pier, SE10, is home to the 'tea-clipper' *Cutty Sark*, launched in 1869 and the last of her kind to survive. She is preserved in dry dock as a museum. In Greenwich Park, the **National Maritime Museum**, Romney Road, celebrates Britain's long maritime history, with a fine array of nautical clocks, sea paintings and ship models. The **Royal Observatory**, was designed by Wren, with astronomical and navigational exhibits. Adjacent is the **Greenwich Meridian** (0° longitude), where you can have one foot in each hemisphere.

official residence of the Lord Mayor; Lombard Street, leading east, is London's Wall Street. Close by **St. Paul's Cathedral▶▶▶**, the somewhat bleak-looking Barbican complex comprises 21 high-rise concrete apartment blocks and a confusing maze of walkways; within is the **Barbican Centre**, home of the London Symphony Orchestra and London base of the Royal Shakespeare Company and the **Museum of London▶▶▶**. To the west and outside the City proper, the quiet streets of **Smithfield▶** are a different world, with an endearingly workaday look. The Central London Markets (Smithfield) is an outstanding example of a Victorian market building; adjacent Cloth Fair has a rare wooden house, a survivor of the Great Fire, while the **Church of St. Bartholomew the Great▶▶** represents London's most impressive Norman church architecture.

THE SUBURBS Docklands▶ is Europe's biggest urban development area. Once the East End district around the river docks, now a cityscape of gleaming office blocks and Dutch-looking waterside housing, the area covers the Isle of Dogs, North Woolwich and Rotherhithe on the south bank. The best way to see it is from the elevated Docklands Light Railway (DLR), running from Tower Gateway or Bank to **Canary Wharf Tower**, Britain's tallest building. Canary Wharf and North Greenwich stations are the architectural highlights of the **Jubilee line extension**.

Greenwich▶▶▶ The former hub of the maritime world (see also panel on left), Greenwich Park occupies a hillside above the Thames and within it are the Greenwich meridian line and the **Royal Observatory▶▶** (*Admission free*) of 1676, which houses instruments of navigation and astronomy. Just below, the **National Maritime Museum▶▶** (*Admission free*) and **Queen's House** (*Admission free*), begun in 1616, form a supreme early classical composition by Wren and Inigo Jones. The **Old Royal Naval College** was designed by Wren and the **painted hall▶▶** (*Admission free*) has a superb painted ceiling by James Thornhill.

Hampstead and Highgate▶▶ Hampstead Heath remains pleasantly countrified, with hollows, glades and grassland. Parliament Hill Fields, in the southeast corner of the heath, has a wonderful view over central London. Hampstead village developed as an 18th-century spa and is one of the most fashionable residential districts; psychologist Sigmund Freud and poet John Keats were among its residents—both men's houses can be visited. **Highgate Cemetery▶▶** (*Guided tours*) has a spectacular derelict area where many rich and famous Victorians are buried.

Richmond and Chiswick▶▶ These charming riverside suburbs, are best seen by taking the summer boat service or by walking along the river, for example west from Hammersmith Bridge along Chiswick Mall and on to **Chiswick House▶** (see page 51) or from Kew to Richmond and west past **Ham House▶** (see page 51). Another excellent boat trip is to **Hampton Court Palace▶▶▶** (see page 51). **Richmond Park▶▶** is a former royal hunting park, fenced in by Charles I in 1635 and inhabited by deer; within is the Isabella Plantation, famous for azaleas and heathers. Near the river at Barnes, the **London Wetland Centre▶▶** is a spectacular transformation (created 1995–2000) of reservoirs into a huge nature reserve with birdwatchers' hides. For **Kew Gardens (Royal Botanic Gardens)▶▶▶** see page 16.

Museums and art galleries

Many of London's museums are free, or you might consider purchasing The London Pass, giving entry to more than 50 attractions plus, for an extra charge, travel on public transport and other discounts for one, two, three or six days (tel: 0870 242 9988, www.londonpass.com).

TRAFALGAR SQUARE The **National Gallery▶ ▶ ▶** (*Guided tours* daily at 11.30 and 2.30, plus Wed 6.30pm from the foyer of the Sainsbury Wing. *Admission free*), in Trafalgar Square, WC2, has a superb collection of paintings, many of which will be instantly familiar, from early Renaissance to the French Impressionists. Around the corner, in St. Martin's Place, WC2, is the **National Portrait Gallery▶ ▶** (*Admission free*), as complete a collection of faces of British history as you will find.

COVENT GARDEN AND BLOOMSBURY Somerset House, Strand, WC2 is home to the **Courtauld Institute Gallery▶ ▶**, containing one of Britain's finest collections of French Impressionist and post-Impressionist paintings, the **Gilbert Collection▶ ▶**, home to a bequest of decorative arts, and the

Hermitage Rooms▶ ▶ of treasures from the State Hermitage Museum in St. Petersburg. **London's Transport Museum▶ ▶ ▶**, in the Piazza, Covent Garden, WC2, is a fascinating place which traces the development of London's buses, trams, trains and 'tubes'. Nearby, the **Theatre Museum▶ ▶** (*Admission free*), 1E Tavistock Street, Covent Garden, WC2, is a home for stage memorabilia.

The **British Museum▶ ▶ ▶** (*Admission free; free introductory tours daily*), Great Russell Street, WC1, is one of the greatest collections in the world. The most famous of its artifacts include the Rosetta Stone (which helped historians to decode hieroglyphics), Egyptian mummies, the Elgin Marbles from the Parthenon in Athens and the Mildenhall and Sutton Hoo treasure hoards. The famous Reading Room, where Marx wrote *Das Kapital*, has been transformed into a reference library, surrounded by the Great Court, spanned by a huge glass roof. The **British Library▶ ▶** (*Admission free; charge for tours*) outgrew this space and moved to 96 Euston Road (by St. Pancras railway station); its John Ritblat Gallery has great treasures, including Beatles music manuscripts and the oldest wall map of the world.

London's Transport Museum

EXCURSIONS
The number of possible day trips from the capital is endless. Here we highlight some recommended excursions that can easily be made by train.
Castles: Dover, Windsor.
Historic cities: Cambridge, Canterbury, Oxford, Salisbury, Winchester.
Industrial, railway and naval interest: Amberley Working Museum, Bluebell Railway (near East Grinstead), The Historic Dockyard Chatham, Portsmouth, Watercress Line (Alton to Alresford).
Roman remains: Fishbourne Palace (near Chichester), Lullingstone Villa (near Eynsford), Verulamium (St. Albans).
Coastal resorts: Brighton, Broadstairs, Eastbourne, Hastings.
Small towns: Arundel, Battle, Lewes, Rye, Sandwich,

London

CHANGING EXHIBITIONS OF ART AND DESIGN

The major sites for art exhibitions are the Hayward Gallery in the South Bank Centre, SE1, the Royal Academy of Arts in Piccadilly, W1, the ICA in the Mall, SW1, the Saatchi Gallery in County Hall, on the South Bank, SE1, and the Barbican Art Gallery, Silk Street, EC2. The Serpentine Gallery in Kensington Gardens has exhibitions focusing on younger contemporary artists (*Admission free*).

The Natural History Museum's pattern of terracotta and French Romanesque elements was the creation of Alfred Waterhouse

GREAT SPORTING VENUES

London's major sporting venues double as tourist attractions. The Wimbledon Lawn Tennis Museum (Southfields tube then bus 493) recalls the sport's great moments with the option of a tour of the grounds. For Rugby Union fans, a tour of Twickenham Stadium (Twickenham railway station) includes a visit to its Museum of Rugby (Britain's top sporting museum), while Lord's Cricket Ground (St. John's Wood tube) conducts guided tours on non-match days.

REGENT'S PARK AND BAKER STREET London Zoo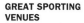 in Regent's Park, NW1, is one of the world's great animal collections and an important research facility. It places emphasis on breeding endangered species and on education. In Marylebone Road, NW1, **Madame Tussaud's**▶ wax museum tops the charts as a paying tourist attraction; be photographed alongside politicians, pop stars and sport celebrities. You may have a long wait for admittance—some may feel the wait and steep admission aren't worth it (for advance booking, allowing immediate entry, tel: 0870 400 3000 or visit www.madame-tussauds.com). Next door at the **London Planetarium**▶ the night sky is projected onto a dome as you are guided around the constellations. The **Sherlock Holmes Museum** at 221b Baker Street, W1, displays memorabilia of the great sleuth at the address used in Arthur Conan Doyle's stories. The **Wallace Collection**▶▶ (*Admission free*), in Manchester Square, W1, has Frans Hals's *The Laughing Cavalier*, plus a superb collection of French paintings and porcelain.

SOUTH KENSINGTON Prince Albert headed the Royal Commission that purchased the museum sites in what was dubbed Albertopolis. The **Victoria and Albert Museum**▶▶▶ (the 'V&A'), Cromwell Road, SW7 (*Admission free*), is a treasure house of decorative art and design, displayed by theme (musical instruments, costume, furniture, etc.) and by civilization (Japan, China, India, etc.). There is something for everyone but too much for one visit. Meanwhile, across the road at the **Natural History Museum**▶▶▶, Cromwell Road, SW7 (*Admission free*), dinosaurs, evolution, blue whales...just about everything is here in this splendid Victorian building. The collection is popular with children. The **Science Museum**▶▶▶, around the corner in Exhibition Road, SW7 (*Admission free*), is also a hit with children, but has plenty for everyone.

CHELSEA AND WESTMINSTER The **National Army Museum▶** (*Admission free*), Royal Hospital Road, SW3, tells a 500-year story of soldiers through the ages. The **Cabinet War Rooms▶** in King Charles Street, SW1, were the subterranean emergency offices for Winston Churchill and his cabinet in World War II; the Map Room and the Transatlantic Telephone Room remain intact.

The **Tate Britain▶▶▶** in Millbank, SW1, is the nation's greatest collection of British art; an excellent headphone tour introduces you to the major works. Entry is free but admission is charged for special exhibitions. A boat service takes you to the Tate Modern. **The Queen's Gallery▶** at Buckingham Palace, SW1, has items from the royal collection, while the **Royal Mews▶** contains the spectacular State Coaches and the Royal Family's sleighs.

SOUTH OF THE RIVER The **Imperial War Museum▶▶▶** (*Admission free*), Lambeth Road, SE1, covers the wars that Britain has been involved in since 1914. There is a Blitz reconstruction and a trench dug out, in addition to weapons, memorabilia, uniforms and a Holocaust exhibition. The latter is particulary harrowing, and is unsuitable for children under 14 years of age. Near Westminster Bridge, County Hall is home to the **London Aquarium▶**. You can hardly miss the slowly rotating 135m (445ft) tall **British Airways London Eye▶▶▶**, the world's tallest observation wheel, erected for the new millennium, whose 32 capusules offer fine views over the city and as far away as 40km (25 miles). Farther east, by Waterloo Bridge, is the National Theatre complex.

In Southwark, on Bankside, the thatched, circular **Shakespeare's Globe▶▶** is a faithful rebuilding of the venue where many of Shakespeare's plays were performed in his own lifetime. There are guided tours, an exhibition and summer performances in this, the only thatched roof structure to be built in London since the Great Fire. The **Tate Modern▶▶▶** (*Admission free*) is a stunning modern art collection housed in a former power station. The **Design Museum▶** at Butler's Wharf, 28 Shad Thames, SE1, is a stylish riverside building housing thematic exhibitions of modern design. At the **London Dungeon** in Tooley Street, SE1, gloomy vaults reveal the dark stories of punishment, torture and witchcraft in times past. Next door, **Winston Churchill's Britain at War Experience** evokes London in the Blitz, with the smells and sounds of an air raid. Moored on the Thames close by (reached from Tower Bridge, via the Thames Path) is **HMS Belfast▶▶**, the last of the Royal Navy's big World War II gunships, launched in 1938.

TOWER HILL AND THE CITY The **Tower of London▶▶▶**, Tower Hill, EC3, is the greatest Norman castle in the kingdom, standing silent sentinel in the shadow of adjacent Tower Bridge; the locale has had a long and gory history from Roman times on. Traditionally dressed Beefeaters still patrol the grounds. The White Tower is the main Norman feature, housing St. John's Chapel while the Crown Jewels are in the Jewel House.

At the **Museum of London▶▶▶** (*Admission free*), London Wall, EC2, is a time-walk display beginning with Roman London, passing a scale model of St. James's Palace in its heyday, and a full-size street of full-size Victorian shops.

THE EAST END
The **Museum of Childhood at Bethnal Green** (*Admission free*), Cambridge Heath Road, Bethnal Green, E2, is an entertaining offshoot of the Victoria and Albert Museum. Toys of all ages and countries are here; among the exhibits are a wonderful collection of dollshouses, a surreal display of dolls' heads and a group of puppet theatres. The **Geffrye Museum** (*Admission free*) occupies a row of early 18th-century almshouses in Kingsland Road, Hackney, E2. Each of a series of rooms is furnished in a different period style, from 1600 to the present day. It is a succinct summary of furniture styles through the ages.

49

SUBURBAN MUSEUMS AND GALLERIES
The **Royal Air Force Museum** (*Admission free*), Grahame Park Way, Hendon (Colindale tube) has more than 200 aircraft, plus a Red Arrow flight simulator and a Battle of Britain Experience. The **Dulwich Picture Gallery**, Dulwich, SE21, is England's oldest public gallery (1814) and housed in a neoclassical building by Sir John Soane. There are works by Gainsborough, Reynolds, Rembrandt and others.

The White Tower, the Tower of London

London

LONDON'S BLUE PLAQUES

A walk around London almost invariably passes at least one building with a blue plaque recalling a famous former occupant. The placing these markers dates back to 1867, when Lord Byron was the first to be thus commemorated. The person must be adjudged to have made 'some important positive contribution to human welfare or happiness'. Responsibility for erecting plaques now falls to English Heritage (see page 124).

50

WHERE THE FAMOUS LIE AT REST

The churchyards of Inner London were so crowded by the early 1800s that they had become revolting and unsanitary. To relieve pressure, massive cemeteries were created farther out, which are the resting places of some of London's most famous dead. Emmeline Pankhurst, the suffragette leader, is buried in Brompton Cemetery; the music-hall queen Marie Lloyd in Hampstead Cemetery; Isambard Kingdom Brunel and Anthony Trollope at Kensal Green; George Eliot and Karl Marx in Highgate Cemetery.

Hampton Court Palace's Pond Gardens started life as fish ponds supplying the royal kitchens

Houses

London has a wide range of houses open to the public, from grand palaces built for monarchs to the more personal homes of the famous or eccentric.

CENTRAL LONDON Sir John Soane's Museum▶▶▶ (*Admission free; charge for guided tours*), 13 Lincoln's Inn Fields, WC2, is wonderfully eccentric; it was designed by the architect Soane (1753–1837), to contain his collection of mostly architectural artifacts. The house is full of inventive lighting effects and quirky details, as well as some great treasures, in particular the paintings of *A Rake's Progress* and *An Election* by Hogarth. At the **Charles Dickens Museum▶**, 48 Doughty Street, WC1, Charles Dickens wrote *Oliver Twist*, the *Pickwick Papers* and *Nicholas Nickleby*. **Dr. Johnson's House**, 17 Gough Square, EC4, hidden away down an alley off Fleet Street, is the house where Samuel Johnson lived between 1749 and 1759 and where he completed his celebrated dictionary. Now it is a museum, with mementoes of Johnson's life and work (see panel, page 122).

Apsley House▶▶, Hyde Park Corner, W1, was the London home of the 1st Duke of Wellington, built in 1778 by Robert Adam with 19th-century alterations by James Wyatt. Its grand interior houses mementoes of the Iron Duke and his campaigns, as well as his impressive collection of paintings. The German composer Georg Friedrich Handel spent many years in London: his house at 25 Brook Street, W1, where he wrote the *Messiah* is now the **Handel House Museum**.

Kensington Palace▶▶ Kensington Gardens, W8, was restyled by Christopher Wren and later William Kent. It was the birthplace of Queen Victoria and was home to

Diana, Princess of Wales. It has the royal collection of pictures and furniture and magnificent court costumes.

Spencer House► (1756–66) was built for the first Earl of Spencer, an ancestor of the Princess of Wales and has sumptuously gilded interiors.

Buckingham Palace►, the official residence of the Queen, is open Aug–late Sep, giving a glimpse of the state rooms and garden; try to book ahead on 020-7766 7300 or visit www.royal.gov.uk, though on-the-day tickets can be purchased from the information office in Green Park.

In Holland Park Road, W14, stands **Leighton House Museum►►** (*Admission free*), created by the Victorian artist Lord Leighton. Paintings by him and members of the Pre-Raphaelite circle adorn the walls, but the astonishing tiled Arab Hall, styled on a Moorish palace, steals the show.

HAMPSTEAD Kenwood House►(EH; *Admission free*), Hampstead Lane, NW8, is handsomely situated on the edge of Hampstead Heath. Robert Adam gave the house its classical proportions; within is a collection of old masters and portraits, including works by Reynolds and Gainsborough. Outdoor summer concerts, often with fireworks, attract big crowds on Saturday evenings. Hampstead's oldest house and one of the grandest, is **Fenton House►**(NT) on Windmill Hill, NW3; it contains antique keyboard instruments, paintings and furniture. You can visit the houses of the poet **John Keats** and the psychoanalyst **Sigmund Freud**. The great Modernist architect Ernö Goldfinger designed **2 Willow Road** (NT) in 1939 for himself.

SOUTH AND WEST Hampton Court Palace►►►, East Molesey, Surrey, is best reached from London by riverboat from Westminster Millennium Pier. The palace was begun in the early 16th century by Cardinal Wolsey and later presented to Henry VIII; it is an enjoyable potpourri of styles and history, with a hammer-beamed hall, Wren's Fountain Court, an Orangerie with Mantegna cartoons and carvings by Grinling Gibbons. The grounds contain a famous maze. **Ham House►►**(NT), Ham Street, Ham, near the Thames towpath close to Richmond Park, is, for London, an outstanding example of Jacobean architecture, built in 1610. **Chiswick House►**(EH), Burlington Lane, Chiswick, W4 (Turnham Green tube then bus or Chiswick railway station) is a Palladian villa (1729) once used for soirées and as a library rather than a house. Styled on Palladio's Villa Capra in Italy, it stands in parkland, naturalistically landscaped in what came to be regarded as the English manner. **Osterley Park►►**(NT), off Great West Road (A4), Osterley (Osterley tube then a 10-minute walk), is a manor house set in parkland, all but engulfed by London's western fringes. Osterley provides an excellent opportunity to see Robert Adam's interiors at their richest. Adam's work dates from 1761 to 1780; the house itself has Tudor origins.

In southeast London, **Eltham Palace►►**(EH), Eltham (Eltham railway station), is a unique architectural mixture: the great hall of a medieval palace and an art-deco mansion. Three stops farther down the same railway line, Bexleyheath is the station for the **Red House►►**(NT), one of Britain's most important Arts and Crafts buildings, designed in 1859 by Philip Webb for the artist, philosopher and furniture designer William Morris and his wife Jancy: it breaks all the conventions of Victorian cluttered interiors.

Kensington Palace became a royal residence when asthmatic William III elected to move away from the unhealthy riverside air of Whitehall Palace

51

ROBERT ADAM

The state rooms at Syon House and Osterley Park (NT)—see left, are among the finest sets of Robert Adam interiors in the country. The brilliant Scottish designer was born at Kirkcaldy in 1728 and was trained, along with his three brothers, by his architect father, William. He set up in London in 1758 and three years later was appointed principal architect to George III. His elegant and graceful classical interiors, lightening the austere accepted Palladian style, were soon all the rage and widely copied. He pioneered several architectural features, notably elliptical rooms. Charlotte Square in Edinburgh (see page 224) is one of his most notable works in his native Scotland. He died in London in 1792.

LONDON WALKS

Walk

Covent Garden, Royal London and Westminster

Start from Covent Garden tube station. Walk down James Street to **Covent Garden►►►**, the former fruit and vegetable market, now transformed into a stylish shopping piazza and popular meeting place. The **Theatre Museum►►** and **London's Transport Museum►►►** are close by. From Henrietta Street, an archway on the right leads into the churchyard of St. Paul's, the innovative design of Inigo Jones. At the heart of London's theatreland, St. Paul's is known as the

actors' church► and its interior walls are covered with plaques in memory of stars of stage and screen. Leave the churchyard via a gate onto Bedford Street; off the next street to the west, Bedfordbury, an arch leads into Goodwin Court, where bow-windowed houses have changed little since the 18th century. As you reach St. Martin's Lane, opposite is Cecil Court, part of the secondhand bookshop quarter. Enter **Trafalgar Square►►►** at the end of St. Martin's Lane, the great pigeon-populated piazza fronted by the church of **St. Martin-in-the-Fields►** and the **National Gallery►►►**. Cross over to Admiralty Arch and enter the Mall. Steps lead up to the right past the Duke of York's column. Walk along Pall Mall, past the long-established concentration of fashionable gentlemen's clubs, distinguished by unobtrusive signs at the entrances.

Big Ben: not the tower, not the clock, but the massive bell inside

Take a detour to look at the east side of St. James's Street with its trio of

old-fashioned shops—Lock's the hat-makers, Berry and Rudd's wine merchants and Lobb's, makers of custom-fitted shoes. Nearby Pickering Place was once used for sword duels.

Cleveland Row skirts **St. James's Palace▶▶**, residence of Prince Charles and others; leave by gates onto Queen's Walk, along the edge of Green Park. Return to the Mall: **Buckingham Palace▶**, the main residence of the Queen, is to the right; the Changing of the Guard takes place (except in very wet weather) daily at 11.30am, Apr–Aug; every other day, rest of year. Cross the Mall and enter St. James's Park, keeping left. Pass through the arch into **Horse Guards Parade▶▶** and on to Whitehall; Downing Street, to the right, has at No. 10 the house of the prime minister. In Parliament Square is Big Ben, part of the **Houses of Parliament▶▶▶**. Across the square is **Westminster Abbey▶▶▶**. Return from Westminster tube station.

53

Walk

Along the South Bank to Tower Hill

Start from Westminster Bridge. The above walk can be extended by following the South Bank (which has a walkway for much of the way) from Westminster Bridge, past the **British Airways London Eye▶▶▶**—a huge observation wheel with the best view in the city—and on to the **Royal Festival Hall▶**. Farther on is **Shakespeare's**

Globe▶▶ (see page 49). The walkway continues east of Waterloo Bridge past an impressive modern office complex, with outstanding views of the City. Pass **HMS *Belfast*▶▶** and carry on to **Tower Bridge▶▶** (the Tower Bridge Exhibition inside the bridge explains its workings and gives access to the high-level walkway, or cross at street level for free); to the right you can see Canary Wharf, Britain's tallest building. On the other side, circle around the moat of the **Tower of London▶▶▶**. Signs to the World Trade Centre lead you to **St. Katharine's Dock▶** yacht haven. Return from Tower Hill tube station.

St. Katharine's Dock

Southwark Cathedral is noted for the many monuments that survived from its days as a monastic church. That of poet John Gower, above, is dated 1408

SIR CHRISTOPHER WREN (1632–1723)

Wren, one of the most celebrated of British architects, was responsible for the rebuilding of St. Paul's Cathedral (in which his monument appears as *lector, si monumentum requiris, circumspice*—'reader, if you seek my monument, look around') and the City churches. He drew up an ambitious plan for the rebuilding of London with Continental-style avenues, but the complexities of land ownership prevented it from being carried out. Member of Parliament for Weymouth in Dorset, he used the local Portland stone regularly in his buildings. The other great architect of the day was Inigo Jones, who designed Covent Garden piazza, the first piazza in London.

The dome of St. Paul's Cathedral

Churches

Although the Great Fire of 1666, the Blitz of 1940 and constant rebuilding have changed London's face repeatedly, there is still an impressive legacy of church architecture, dating from Norman times. There are particularly fine examples of designs of the master architects of the 17th and 18th centuries: Wren, Hawksmoor and Inigo Jones.

THE EARLIEST CHURCHES The only large-scale church of the Norman period in London is **St. Bartholomew the Great▶▶** in West Smithfield, EC1. It is the survivor of a 12th-century Augustinian priory and although the apsidal east end is a 19th-century rebuilding, the atmosphere is of great antiquity. **Southwark Cathedral▶▶**, Montague Close, the cathedral for the South Bank, was founded as the Augustinian priory church of St. Mary Overie in 1106. Although much restored in the 19th century, it is the most substantial medieval artefact in the district of Southwark. The building attained cathedral status in 1905. Previously it was known as St. Mary Overie (meaning 'over' the water from the City).

SIR CHRISTOPHER WREN Wren's domed masterpiece, **St. Paul's Cathedral▶▶▶**, Ludgate Hill, EC4, replaced an earlier Gothic cathedral that perished in the Great Fire of 1666. It no longer dominates the skyline as it did until the mid-20th century, but when seen close up the proportions are overwhelming. Inside the dome, the Whispering Gallery plays acoustic tricks (whispered sounds carry around the great void) and gives splendid interior views. There are tombs of Wren, Nelson, Wellington, Turner and Reynolds in the crypt, views from the Golden Gallery, woodwork by Gibbons and ironwork by Tijou.

After the Great Fire, Sir Christopher Wren graced the City with 51 churches. Among the most celebrated of **Wren's City churches▶▶** are St. Bride's (Fleet Street), St. Margaret's (Lothbury), St. Martin Ludgate (Ludgate Hill), St. Mary Abchurch (Cannon Street), St. Mary-at-Hill (Eastcheap) and St. Stephen Walbrook (Walbrook).

OTHER GREAT CHURCHES St. **Martin-in-the-Fields▶**, Trafalgar Square, WC2, is an 18th-century rebuilding by James Gibbs and a particularly satisfying example of the temple-like architecture of the period, with a characteristic galleried interior.

At **Westminster Abbey▶▶▶**, Parliament Square, SW1, British sovereigns are crowned and many great men and women are buried, among them monarchs, statesmen, poets and scientists. It also has cloisters, a treasury, brass-rubbing and the oldest garden (*Open* Tue–Thu only) in the country. **Westminster Cathedral▶**, in Ashley Place, off Victoria Street, SW1, is Britain's premier Roman Catholic cathedral, a Byzantine brick creation finished in 1903; incense fills the cavernous interior.

Nightlife

THEATRE There are dozens of theatres to choose from, offering everything from Shakespeare to Andrew Lloyd Webber musicals; the capital has an impressive legacy of Victorian theatre architecture. Discount tickets for the day of performance are available from the Society of London Theatre ticket booth in Leicester Square (see panel).

NIGHTSPOTS Soho and Covent Garden constitute the heart of clubland with clubs like the Hippodrome and Empire discotheque by Leicester Square and The Wag in Wardour Street. Ronnie Scott's (47 Frith Street, W1) is a well-established jazz spot and Heaven (under Charing Cross Station) is a leading gay club. Cabaret and alternative comedy are performed at The Comedy Store in Leicester Square. Away from the heart of town is the highly esteemed Fridge, at Town Hall Parade, Brixton Hill, SW2. Watch listings (see panel) for pop/rock concerts at the Carling Apollo (Hammersmith, W6) and Wembley Arena.

CLASSICAL MUSIC London has five resident orchestras. The Royal Festival Hall, the South Bank Centre, on the South Bank (being refurbished 2005–06; plus the smaller Purcell Room and Queen Elizabeth Hall) and the Barbican Hall, Silk Street (Moorgate tube), are major concert halls. Wigmore Hall, Wigmore Street hosts performances by up-and-coming artists. Summer visitors should try to take in a Promenade Concert ('the Proms', see page 18), Europe's biggest music festival, at the Royal Albert Hall. Operas at the Royal Opera House in Covent Garden are performed in the original language with sur-titles, while the English National Opera in the London Coliseum, St. Martin's Lane, gives performances in English. Many churches host lunchtime recitals; most are free, with a collection made at the end.

CINEMA The first-run cinema is the Odeon, Leicester Square, which boasts an organ. The National Film Theatre (NFT) on the South Bank near Waterloo is the leading repertory film theatre; features change daily (tel: 020-7928·3232; www.bfi.org.uk/nft); one-day memberships available.

LISTINGS AND BOOKINGS
The weekly magazine *Time Out* gives listings for all London's entertainments, events and exhibitions and has excellent previews. The *London Theatre Guide*, updated every two weeks, lists theatrical events and is available free of charge from West End theatres, libraries and tourist information points. The *London Evening Standard*'s Thursday supplement is a handy guide to what's on in London.
A useful website is www.officiallondontheatre.co.uk. Buy tickets directly from the box office to avoid paying commissions. Ticket agencies include Keith Prowse (tel: 0870 842 2248; www.keithprowse.com); check for credit card surcharges. Never buy tickets from touts on the street or unofficial agencies. Discounted tickets are available, on the day of performance only, from tkts booth in Leicester Square (*Open* Mon–Sat 10–7, Sun noon–3) and and at Canary Wharf (*Open* Mon–Sat, 11.30–9); note there are separate windows for matinees and evening performances.

55

The lights of Leicester Square

James Smith's redoubtable stick and umbrella shop

LONDON VIEWS
Take the lift up the bell tower of Westminster Cathedral, ride the British Airways London Eye; booking advised (tel: 0870 5000 600; www.ba-londoneye.com), or climb the steps to the top of St. Paul's Cathedral or The Monument (both in the City). There are superb views for free from City Hall, London, Waterloo, Hungerford and Westminster bridges, Primrose Hill (north of Regent's Park) and Parliament Hill Fields (Hampstead Heath).

Shopping

PRINCIPAL SHOPPING AREAS The major West End department stores are clustered along **Oxford Street**, with Selfridges the biggest of them. John Lewis (whose 'never knowingly undersold' policy guarantees a refund if you find the same goods on sale cheaper elsewhere) has a fine stock of furnishings, fashions and decorative items, while the ubiquitous Marks and Spencer is known for good-value clothing and good food halls. Virgin Megastore and HMV have big selections of CDs and cassettes.

Around the corner, **Regent Street** comes into its own in the weeks before Christmas when the illuminations are switched on; during this period, Hamleys, the undisputed king of the toyshops, fills to bursting and has spectacular displays. Nearby is Liberty, renowned for Liberty print fabrics and clothes; the mock-Tudor building itself is worth a look.

Stereos and electrical goods are available at discount prices in the shops along **Tottenham Court Road**. The **British Museum** shop has stylish reproductions of some of its treasures; nearby at 53 New Oxford Street, **James Smith's** umbrella shop has an eye-catching Victorian shopfront boasting 'Life Preservers, Jagger Canes and Swordsticks.'

Charing Cross Road constitutes the heart of London's bookshop territory. Foyles, the largest bookshop, has an impressive stock though the layout can be confusing. There is a particularly fascinating array of specialist secondhand bookshops just off Charing Cross Road on Cecil Court. Round the corner in Trafalgar Square, the **National Gallery shop** has a good selection of art posters, cards and books. **Soho** is densely packed with ethnic food shops, including Chinese supermarkets in Chinatown and numerous Italian delis.

Covent Garden has a wide variety of shops and boutiques, including The Tea House in Neal Street, a cheese shop and bakery in Neal's Yard and a doll's house shop in the piazza itself.

St. James's Street, off Piccadilly, has old-fashioned shops: Berry and Rudd wine merchants, Lock's the hatmakers and Lobb's the shoemakers.

Kings Road in Chelsea is the place for chic fashions, stylish interior design shops and people-watching; a smart antiques market (Mon–Sat) extends along one part.

GREAT FOR WINDOW SHOPPING Harrods, Brompton Road, is the grandest department store of them all; many visitors go just to collect a shopping bag. Harrods prides itself on its range and quality of stock; the food halls conjure up Edwardian grandeur. **Burlington Arcade**, off Piccadilly, is a perfectly preserved Regency shopping arcade, retaining its early 19th-century air with considerable dignity. An immaculately attired beadle patrols the alley and notices forbid 'hurrying or whistling'. **Fortnum and Mason**, on Piccadilly, is the food shop *par excellence*. The famous exterior clock features Mr Fortnum and Mr Mason, who bow to each other on the hour. **New Bond Street** is the home of Sotheby's, the prestigious fine art auctioneers.

Street markets always provide good entertainment. Easily the most atmospheric is **Brick Lane** (Sunday mornings only), off Bethnal Green Road in the heart of Cockney London, now the Bengali community. It is unashamedly shabby and hugely crowded, with wares ranging from cheap stereos to secondhand junk. Note this is not the same as the nearby (and overrated) Petticoat Lane Market. Weekend-long antiques markets are at **Camden Lock** and **Greenwich**. **Portobello Road**, W10/W11, operates Monday to Saturday (junk stalls on Friday, antiques on Saturday); both get absolutely packed. **Grays Antique Market** (Mon–Fri) at 58 Davies Mews, W1, has some 150 dealers within two Victorian warehouses.

Below: some chic window displays verge on the inscrutable

57

SPEAKERS' CORNER
At the corner of Hyde Park, close to Marble Arch at the western end of Oxford Street, Speakers' Corner is a bastion of free speech. It provides memorable free entertainment, at lunchtime Monday to Friday and is at full throttle on Sunday morning. Anyone can set up a soapbox and speak on anything he or she likes as long as there is no blasphemy, defamation, treason, or breach of the peace laws.

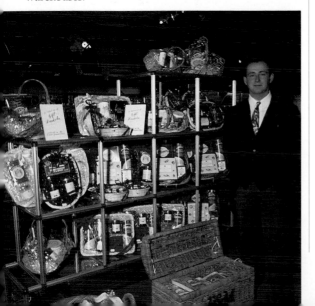

Only the best: a selection of Fortnum and Mason's gift baskets while a frock-coated assistant looks on

RESERVING HOTELS

Visit London publishes a free *Where to Stay in London* guide with 450 entries from luxury hotels to hostels (available from any Tourist Information Centre or tel: 0870 240 4326). It also operates an accommodation booking service, tel: 08456 443020 (8am–11pm) or visit www.visitlondon.com. You can also rent an apartment; Visit London has details of agencies.

In a city of pricey hotels, London's top hotels can be a very expensive experience

Service at its most discreet…

Hotels

HOTELS London is one of the most expensive European capitals for hotel rooms. Those who can afford high prices will appreciate the style and service at such long-established and prestigious establishments as The Ritz, Claridge's, The Savoy, The Dorchester and The Connaught; be prepared for lots of British formality, however, and do not expect air-conditioning as a matter of course. The top modern hotels are generally all in the same price bracket. Among the best areas to stay in the

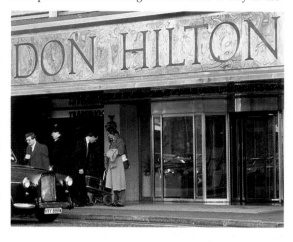

capital are the West End (W1, NW1, SW1, WC2), Bloomsbury (WC1), Kensington (SW7, W2, W8, W11), Knightsbridge (SW1) and Chelsea (SW3).

BED-AND-BREAKFAST Even modest B&Bs costs roughly twice what you would pay outside London. There is a reasonable selection around Victoria (SW1) and Bloomsbury (WC1); the King's Cross area (also WC1) is cheap and drab (Argyle Street WC1, is a reasonable bet if you're really stuck) and there are plenty of places (including some private hostels) in the Earl's Court area (SW5). Out to the west, Hammersmith (W6) is an unprepossessing area but has some large hotels and good Underground connections to central London. Small hotels and B&Bs exist in many suburbs and can cut your hotel costs; aim for a location convenient to the Underground and check the journey time and the timing of the last train back.

HOSTELS AND CAMPSITES The central locations for youth hostelers are on Noel Street, W1, Bolton Gardens, SW5, Queen's Gate, SW7, Holland Walk, W8, Euston Road, NW1 and Carter Lane, EC4; three farther-flung hostels are on Wellgarth Road, Golders Green, NW11, Salter Road, Rotherhithe, SE16, and farther afield on Windmill Lane, Cheshunt, Hertfordshire. Reservations are advised (national YHA tel: 0870 870 8808; www.yha.org.uk). Additionally, numerous colleges offer lodging in the summer. Campsites are obviously farther out; Crystal Palace Caravan Club Site, SE19 (tel: 020-8803 6900), is pleasantly situated, with good public transport links.

Eating out

BREAKFAST For a leisurely start to the day, splurge on **breakfast** at one of the big hotels such as The Savoy (the Strand, WC2; tel: 020-7836 4343). Devotees of Chinese *dim sum* brunch should look no farther than New World (1 Gerrard Place, W1; tel: 020-7434 0396).

LUNCH For quick lunches, sandwich bars and no-frills restaurants are a good bet; there are several of these in the West End. Many pubs and wine bars offer food, though some get crowded and smokey; Gordon's Wine Bar (47 Villiers Street, WC2; tel: 020-7930 1408) is set in a subterranean vault by the Thames. Look around Soho and Covent Garden for Asian restaurants, which offer good-value lunches. You can lunch at some top restaurants for roughly half the price of an evening meal. Big museums and galleries, including the National Gallery, Tate Britain, Tate Modern and Royal Festival Hall, have good self-service cafeterias. A number of inexpensive southern Indian vegetarian restaurants, along Drummond Street, NW1, are handy for Regent's Park. Panton Street, WC2, off Leicester Square, has several budget eateries.

AFTERNOON TEA Tea is served with considerable flair at such prestigious hotels as The Ritz (reservation advisable; Piccadilly, W1; tel: 020-7493 8181), The Savoy (The Strand, WC2; tel: 020-7836 4343) and Claridge's (Brook Street, W1; tel: 020-7629 8860) although prices are high and there is a formal dress code. A less expensive option is Fortnum and Mason (tel: 020-7734 8040)

THE EVENING For a treat, try one of the great Continental-style restaurants such as Bibendum (Michelin House, 81 Fulham Road, SW3; tel: 020-7581 5817) in the eye-catching Michelin Building, or Le Cabanon (35 Great Portland Street, W1; tel: 020-7436 8846). Those who wish to live it up without breaking the bank may like Kettners (29 Romilly Street, W1; tel: 020-7734 6112), in the heart of Soho, part of the Pizza Express chain. London's residential districts Hampstead, Camden Town, Islington, Bayswater, Kensington and Chelsea have a good choice of places to eat. See also hotels and restaurants, pages 276–284.

PUBS IN LONDON
Pubs of special character include the **Cittie of York** (with Britain's longest bar, 22 High Holborn, WC2); the **Lamb and Flag** (in Covent Garden, 33 Rose Street, WC2); the **Museum Tavern** (49 Great Russell Street, WC1, near the British Museum); the **Princess Louise** (spectacular Victorian tiled interior, 208 High Holborn, WC2); the **Lamb** (Bloomsbury, with old fittings, 94 Lamb's Conduit Street, WC1); **Ye Olde Cheshire Cheese** (ancient tavern, former haunt of writers Dickens and Johnson, Wine Office Court, 145 Fleet Street, EC4); the **George Inn** (London's last galleried inn, 77 Borough High Street, SE1); the **Black Friar** (London's finest art-nouveau pub interior, 1/4 Queen Victoria Street, EC4, opposite Blackfriars station); and the **Dove** (riverside pub with terrace, 19 Upper Mall, Hammersmith, W6). Fuller's and Young's are two excellent 'real ale' London brews.

The Ritz was London's very first steel-framed building when erected in 1906

The West Country

★ Walk start point

```
0    10   20   30   40   50 km
0        10        20      30 miles
```

4   5

THE WEST COUNTRY The tapering southwestern peninsula of England culminates in the rugged clifflands of western Cornwall, where Land's End forms the big toe of Great Britain. Called the West Country, the area offers perhaps a fuller range of activities, landscapes and experiences than any other in Britain and, as a result, you'll find many other visitors here, especially during the summer, when the crowds are sometimes overwhelming. People from all over Britain spend their holidays here, in indolent ease or in a whirl of activity. For many of them, the region's diversity is the key to its appeal.

The climate is mild and the sprawling resorts of Torquay and Bournemouth head the sunshine league; this is also a major retirement area. To many, the West Country is synonymous with dairy country; the locals are big cheese-eaters, and you can indulge in a cream tea or even mail home some delicious 'clotted' cream, a cholesterol-watcher's nightmare. Another regional product is lardy cake, a gooey raisin topped cake largely confined to the southern and western counties.

Opposite: Land's End, Cornwall
Bottom: Jamaica Inn on Bodmin Moor

RECOMMENDED COASTAL TOWNS AND VILLAGES
Cornwall: Boscastle, Port Isaac, Padstow, St. Ives, Mousehole, Cadgwith, St. Anthony in Roseland, Portloe, Mevagissey, Charlestown, Fowey, Polperro, Kingsand.
Devon: Lynmouth, Clovelly, Sidmouth, Dartmouth, Salcombe, Newton Ferrers, Plymouth.
Dorset: Lyme Regis, Abbotsbury, Weymouth.
SMALL TOWNS INLAND
Cornwall: Launceston
Somerset: Dulverton, Wells, Dunster, Glastonbury.
Dorset: Beaminster, Sherborne, Shaftesbury.
Wiltshire: Marlborough, Bradford on Avon, Devizes.
HISTORIC CITIES
Bath, Bristol, Exeter, Salisbury.
COASTAL FEATURES
Cornwall: Tintagel Castle, Bedruthan Steps, Gurnards Head (near Zennor), Porthcurno open-air theatre, Logan Rock (near Treen), St. Michael's Mount, Mullion Cove, Fal Estuary, Dodman Point, Rame Head.
Devon: Valley of Rocks, Baggy Point (near Croyde), Hartland Quay, Hobby Drive (near Clovelly), Hooken Cliffs (near Beer), Bolt Head, Bolt Tail (both near Salcombe).
Somerset Porlock Toll Road, Selworthy Beacon, Brean Down
(continued on page 63)

62

CORNWALL In many ways, England's most westerly county almost feels like a separate little world. It was a remote backwater until the opening of the Tamar railway bridge on the Devon border in the 19th century, and despite the summer deluge of tourists, the county still has a distinct sense of place. Most famously Cornwall reveals a quite superlative coastline that twists and turns its way round rocky cliffs, verdant estuaries, idyllic beaches and improbably picturesque fishing villages, and brings to life stories of smugglers and shipwrecks. Defunct tin mines, with their stark ruins of chimneys and engine houses, are as much a feature of the Cornish landscape as the prehistoric sites that proliferate in the windswept granite uplands of Bodmin Moor and Penwith.

There is plenty of scope for pottering around, whether enjoying watersports or sightseeing, although beware that driving on narrow, congested roads can test your patience. On the south coast is a host of lush gardens where exotic species flourish in the mild climate. One of the West Country's top tourist attractions, the Eden Project takes a thought-provoking look at our relationship with the plant world. Architecturally, Cornwall is not richly endowed, but the castles at Tintagel and St. Michael's Mount are wonderfully set. No part of the county is more than 30 minutes away from the coast, where you can usually walk along a coastal path in comparative solitude, surrounded by unsurpassed beauty.

DEVON As with Cornwall, the north and south coasts are strikingly different. North Devon's seaboard is for the most part really rugged, with strange, twisted rock strata around Hartland Quay near the Cornish border, and massive rounded cliffs where moors meet the sea in Exmoor, Devon's longest stretch of unspoiled coast—at its most astonishing around Lynton and Lynmouth, with bare, lonely hills extending far inland. South Devon has the monopoly on beaches, and the climate is noticeably drier and sunnier; as a result it is much more built up, with a string of coastal resorts—Torquay, Teignmouth, Dawlish, Brixham and Exmouth among them. The huge estuaries around Salcombe and the appealing town of Dartmouth are yachting havens. Inland the key attractions are on the high ground. Dartmoor looks almost primeval with its gnarled granite tors and relics of early settlers—a wonderfully liberating place for hiking over boundless moors and through deep, wooded valleys. The two big cities had the misfortune to suffer heavy wartime bombing: Plymouth, a naval town, which nevertheless has some good things to see, including the Barbican area and magnificent National Marine Aquarium; and Exeter, where the medieval cathedral survived miraculously.

SOMERSET While the Somerset coast has little to speak of outside Exmoor (which straddles the Devon border), there is much to explore inland. The little-visited Quantock Hills have a fine heritage of country churches; the Mendip Hills are unspectacular until you encounter Wells, the Cheddar Gorge and Burrington Combe. Southward lie the Levels, a flat, drained marshland once beneath the sea; Glastonbury Tor and the low-rise Polden Hills protrude above the far side. Taunton, the main town in the heart of (hard) cider-making country, has a bland streetscape redeemed by an impressive church and an absorbing museum.

Bath is the obvious first choice among cities to visit in Somerset (although until recently it was in the county of Avon, named after the river that flows through it). It is a delightful city for wandering around, but hellish to drive in. Bristol (now in its own county of Bristol) is a large old port with a great maritime heritage and the elegant suburb of Clifton.

DORSET The home of Dorset Blue Vinny cheese, the county often has the tag 'Hardy's Wessex' applied to it, though the ancient kingdom of Wessex in fact extended into Wiltshire, Somerset and Hampshire. There is scarcely a corner of Dorset that does not appear under a pseudonym in Thomas Hardy's literary output. Although over three-quarters of the county's heathlands have disappeared since 1945, the inland areas still have an ancient, primitive look, with sweeping downs, clumps of beech trees, thatched villages and prehistoric burial sites (tumuli) and hill forts. Villages such as Abbotsbury and Corfe Castle make delightful bases for the best of the remarkably varied and largely undeveloped coast.

RECOMMENDED
(continued from page 62)
Dorset: Lyme Regis under-cliff, Chesil Beach, Portland Bill, Lulworth Cove, St. Aldhlem's Head, Old Harry Rocks, Poole Harbour.
WALKING
The 800km (500 miles) South West Coast Path follows the coast from Minehead (Somerset) to Poole (Dorset); Exmoor, north Cornwall and east Dorset are the most dramatic parts; Dartmoor is best for inland walking; otherwise inland Exmoor, the Dorset Downs, the Mendips, the Quantocks.
OFFSHORE ESCAPISM
Isles of Scilly, Lundy Island.
PREHISTORIC SITES
Wiltshire Downs, west Cornwall.

63

WILTSHIRE An inland county, Wiltshire has a gentle landscape of prairie-like chalk downlands, with its northern reaches of honey-stone villages just in the Cotswolds. Most of its interest is manmade—as in the curious hill 'carvings' of horses and regimental badges on the hillsides. More famous is the legacy of early inhabitants, notably at Stonehenge and perhaps even more memorably at Avebury. Salisbury Cathedral is the pinnacle of the Early English style; a bus service from Salisbury station to Stonehenge helps make it a feasible day-trip from London. Wiltshire's largest town, Swindon, grew up in the railway era (its railway museum is a magnet for train buffs) and witnessed an economic boom in the 1980s; smaller places, including Devizes, Marlborough and Bradford on Avon, are much more attractive.

Thatched roofs and whitewashed walls in Lustleigh: the unspoiled face of Devon

'There is in the Cornish character, smouldering beneath the surface, ever ready to ignite, a fiery independence, a stubborn pride.'
—Daphne du Maurier, *Vanishing Cornwall* (1967)

Walks

Cheddar Gorge, Somerset 61C4

Car park adjacent to Butchers Arms near gorge entrance. Walk along the road at the bottom of the gorge; at the far end (1.5km/1 mile) across from the gate into a nature reserve, take the West Mendip Way on the right, up through woods. Fork right to follow the top edge of the gorge; the views are impressive. Descend by the steps at Prospect Tower. (2 hours)

Lizard, Cornwall 60A1

Start at Lizard village. For the best of this celebrated coast, take the road east to Church Cove and turn right along the coastal path, past Lizard Point, the southernmost point on the mainland and to idyllic Kynance Cove. Follow the toll road inland, branching right by a National Trust sign onto a path back to Lizard village. (2 hours)

Lulworth Cove, Dorset 61B5

Car park at Lulworth Cove. Take the broad path from the car park, joining the coast to reach Durdle Door, a wave-eroded natural arch; on returning, keep along the coast past Stair Hole, for a view of Lulworth Cove. The rugged coast east of the Cove towards Kimmeridge is army training land (open most weekends and public holidays); a path heads down to the cliff where there is a fossil forest. (1 to 2 hours)

Lydford Gorge (NT), Dartmoor 60B3 National Park, Devon

Car parks by gorge; entrance fee. Walk through this densely wooded gorge with the White Lady Waterfall at one end and the Devil's Cauldron, where the River Lyd swirls in a gloomy chasm, at the other. The full trail takes 1.5 hours, or you can take short walks from the car park.

Valley of Rocks, Exmoor 60C3 National Park, Devon

Start at Lynton. Take the small road between the Valley of Rocks Hotel and the church; it becomes the coastal path. The Valley of Rocks and its wild goats soon come into view. Climb Castle Rock, the most prominent feature, for the view and return along the road, branching left after 400m/440yd by a stone shelter to ascend Hollerday Hill and drop into Lynton. (1.5 hours)

Avebury's stones stand silent as daily life goes on around them

64

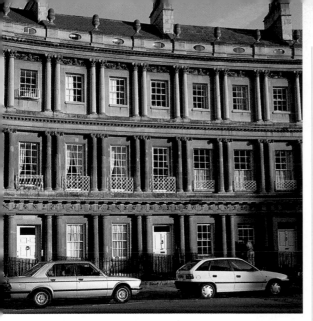

Bath's elegant Circus is built in a perfect circle around a covered reservoir

▶▶▶ Avebury 61C5

(Tourist information tel: 01672 539425; www.visitkennet.co.uk)

Avebury village is surrounded by an astonishingly large 4,000-year-old stone circle and grassy banked henge, classified a World Heritage Site. In the 1930s the marmalade magnate Alexander Keiller bought the entire village, and set about re-erecting the stones—toppled in medieval times by locals who thought the site was the work of the Devil. Near **Avebury Manor** (NT), the **Alexander Keiller Museum** (NT/EH) fleshes out the background of this and the vicinity's other mysterious prehistoric monuments (see panel).

▶▶▶ Bath 61C5

(Tourist information tel. 0906 711 2000 (UK only, 50p per minute), 44 (0)870 444 6442 (overseas callers only); www.visitbath.co.uk)

Britain's finest Georgian townscape is found in this hilly, golden-stone spa town which the Romans knew as Aquae Sulis, a place for taking the waters and paying homage to the goddess Minerva. A new heyday dawned in the early 18th century, when the architects John Wood the Elder and Younger (father and son) laid out parks, squares, the circular piazza known as the Circus and the grand Royal Crescent. The **Roman Baths ▶▶▶** survive as one of the outstanding Roman monuments in the country, and adjoin the chandelier-lit Georgian **Pump Room▶▶**, close to the Perpendicular style **Bath Abbey▶▶**, with its intricate fan-vaulting. The opening of **Thermae Bath Spa** (imminent at time of publication) sees the emergence of a new spa complex.

Browsing the shops and the Saturday flea market is part of Bath's appeal too. Among its excellent museums are The **Museum of Costume▶▶▶** in the Assembly Rooms, with some 150 costumes from the 16th century onwards, the **Bath Museum▶** chronicles the city's transformation and the **Bath Postal Museum▶** replicates the Victorian post office from which the first postage stamped letter was sent in 1840. In a street where she stayed, the **Jane Austen Centre▶** evokes the author's times in Bath, a city that features in her novels *Persuasion* and *Northanger Abbey*.

PREHISTORIC LANDMARKS AT AVEBURY

Avebury's stone circle, which can be walked around in its entirety, connects to the so-called **Stone Avenue**, parallel rows of stones that lead south to the site of another circle, the **Sanctuary**. Across from the car park, a path leading south passes close by **Silbury Hill**, the largest prehistoric earthwork in Europe; it is thought to have played an astronomical or religious role. The path continues south of the A4 to **West Kennet Long Barrow**, an ancient burial chamber, which can be entered.

OUT OF BATH

The surroundings of Bath give scope for several excursions, including boat trips from Pultney Bridge. At Claverton Manor the **American Museum in Britain** has 17th- to 19th-century New World interiors. Set in a valley overlooking the city, **Prior Park Landscape Garden** (NT) is an 18th-century creation by Lancelot 'Capability' Brown; take bus 2 or 4 (there is no car park).

BATH

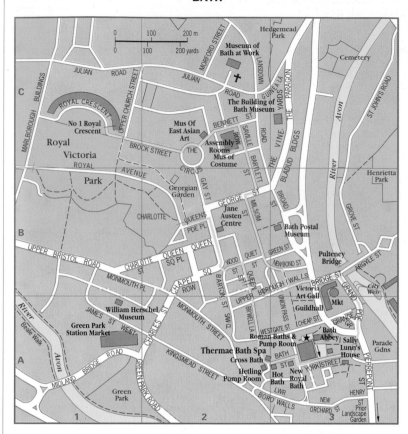

Walk

Central Bath

At the **abbey**▶▶, look at the west front depicting Bishop Oliver's dream of angels that inspired him to rebuild the abbey in 1499. Then walk past the **Roman Baths**▶▶▶, Britain's finest Roman remains: baths, cold plunges, a hypocaust room and part of a Temple to Sulis Minerva, goddess of the springs, can be seen. Next door is the **Pump Room**▶▶, the epitome of Bath's timeless spirit; take afternoon tea to the strains of chamber music by the statue of Beau Nash.

Continue along Old Lilliput Alley. **Sally Lunn's House**, a bakery producing the original Sally Lunn cakes from a secret recipe, is the oldest house in Bath (1482); a kitchen museum tells the story. Follow Grand Parade as far as **Pulteney Bridge**▶▶ (1774, designed by Robert Adam), with shops along both sides.

Walk up Saville Row past the **Assembly Rooms** and **Museum of Costume**▶▶▶. Walk around **The Circus**▶▶▶ (John Wood the Elder, begun 1754) and continue onto **Royal Crescent**▶▶▶ (John Wood the Younger, 1767–74), No. 1 is open to the public. Go through Royal Victoria Park, past the **Georgian Garden**▶ (re-created from its 1770s plan), past the **Jane Austen Centre**▶ and **Queen Square** (1729–36). Return via Bath Street to the abbey.

▶ Bodmin Moor

60B2

(Bodmin tourist information tel: 01208 76616; www.bodminlive.com)

The top of Cornwall comprises bleak open moors dotted with granite tors, ponies and sheep. Brown Willy (419m/1,375ft) is the county's highest point. Tracks onto the moor from the windswept hamlet of **Minions** give excellent views and lead past **The Hurlers** stone circles▶ (Bronze Age).

At nearby Darite, **Trethevy Quoit▶** is a Bronze Age burial chamber with its capstone still in place. Villages ringing the moor are well off the beaten path. **Altarnun▶** is a tranquil haven off the busy A30; its church has magnificent 16th-century bench ends with carvings of a jester, piper and dancers, while the church at **St. Neot** has the finest medieval stained glass in Cornwall.

Launceston▶ occupies a hilltop crowned by a Norman castle keep (EH); one town gateway survives. Near Bodmin are **Lanhydrock▶▶▶** (NT), a house epitomizing aristocratic living at the end of the 19th century, and **Restormel Castle▶** (EH), an impressive Norman fortress.

▶▶ Bradford on Avon

61C5

(Tourist information tel: 01225 865797; www.bradfordonavon.co.uk)

A charming base for the southern Cotswolds, this stone-built town rises steeply, terrace by terrace, with

Bradford on Avon's nine-arched Town Bridge dates from the 14th century; two of its original arches remain

flagged steps connecting its narrow lanes. Former cloth merchants' mansions and humble medieval and 18th-century weavers' cottages set the tone. The oddly named Top Rank Tory is the street with the best views. In Barton Farm Park stands a splendid 14th-century tithe barn.

Lacock Abbey▶ (NT), some 14km (9 miles) northeast, retains 13th-century cloisters, chapter house and sacristy. A barn houses the Fox Talbot Museum, in memory of the pioneering photographer who lived here from 1827 to 1877. The village itself has an 18th-century time-warp feeling and is National Trust property.

THE EDEN PROJECT

Southwest of Bodmin Moor towards St Austell, on the high plateau scarred by the snow-white spoil heaps of the china clay industry, the Eden Project (tel: 01726 811900; www.edenproject.com) has rapidly become one of Britain's foremost tourist attractions since opening in 2001. Gigantic glass structures known as 'biomes' house re-creations of Mediterranean and tropical plant life; the third, called the 'Roofless Biome', represents the temperate zone. The Eden Project aims to promote an awareness of how much we depend on plants and how we should manage them to achieve a sustainable future.

67

A LOST CHURCH

Bradford on Avon's Church of St. Laurence, thought to be seventh to eighth century, is one of Britain's most complete Saxon churches, yet it lay completely forgotten for many years. Looking over the town from a house above the church, a 19th-century vicar noticed the cruciform shape of the building, parts of which had been incorporated into a school, a house and a factory wall. In 1858, restoration was carried out and its interior can once more be seen.

The harsh Atlantic winds buffet a wild, rocky coast, a graveyard for hundreds of wrecked ships. Eerie ruins of tin mines perch on treeless hillsides. The long coast is popular for its beautiful scenery, sights and excellent swimming and surfing beaches. Accordingly, you have to be prepared for crowds at the peak of the season and also for some unsightly resort development, especially between Padstow and Newquay. But it is still easy to get away from it all if you are prepared to walk a few kilometres along the coastal path.

68

TOURIST INFORMATION
For further information contact the Cornwall Tourist Board, Pydar House, Pydar Street, Truro, Cornwall TR1 1EA; tel: 01872 322900; www.cornwalltouristboard.co.uk

PENWITH'S RICH ARCHEOLOGY
Major sites include two Iron Age villages, Carn Euny and Chysauster (EH). Chûn Castle is an Iron Age fort, while Lanyon Quoit is a good Bronze Age burial chamber and Men-an-Tol is a stone hoop of unknown purpose, used in recent times as a folk remedy for rickets; all three sites lie near the Madron–Morvah road. Close by St Buryan, near the road, Merry Maidens stone circle is Bronze Age, the maidens supposedly turned to stone for dancing on the Sabbath.

ARTHUR'S FABLES
The deeds of King Arthur and his castle Camelot mix fact and fiction. He was a real sixth-century chieftain (reputedly born in Tintagel and buried at Glastonbury). But later writers embroidered his exploits— the anonymous *Sir Gawayne and the Greene Knight* (1346), Sir Thomas Malory's *Le Morte d'Arthur* (1485), Tennyson's *Idylls of the King* (1857–85) and works by T. H. White and Mark Twain.

The Devon border to Padstow The village of **Morwenstow▶** bears the indelible stamp of Rev. Robert Hawker, Celtic poet and priest here from 1834 to 1875. He adorned the vicarage with chimneypots in the form of miniature church towers and, on the cliffs nearby, erected a driftwood shack for meditation and opium-smoking (it still stands). His memorial is in the church, which has Norman arches and 16th-century bench ends.

Bude is an unremarkable resort town and a major surfing base, with a large beach; a small museum on the waterfront tells the story of the Bude Canal, which ends here. Inland, **Launcells Church▶**, standing all by itself, escaped the zeal of Victorian restorers and has changed little since the 15th century.

Boscastle▶ occupies a craggy, precipitous creek; the best views are from the clifftop just west of the port. **Tintagel▶** achieved fame for its legendary connections with King Arthur; the ruined medieval castle (EH) postdates Arthur, but the site is nevertheless magnificent, atop an impregnable headland, reached by a steep staircase. The adjacent village is a tourist trap, redeemed somewhat by the Old Post Office (NT), a small-scale manor house preserved as an outstanding example of Cornish domestic architecture. **Port Isaac▶▶** may stake a claim as the most authentic-feeling Cornish fishing village, where there are cottages squeezed around narrow alleyways, and a wholesome whiff of seaweed pervades.

Padstow▶ is a busy resort town of considerable charm. It lacks a beach (try Harlyn Bay, west of town) but has a port area packed with brightly painted craft; fresh fish are on sale at waterfront warehouses and served at a number of good seafood restaurants. Prideaux Place, at the top of the town, looks Elizabethan, but house tours in the summer months reveal whimsical Strawberry Hill Gothick alterations (see Shobdon, page 122) as well as the original Elizabethan plaster ceilings. The adjacent Camel Estuary offers sailing and gentle walks.

Bedruthan Steps to Land's End West from Padstow the summer crowds thicken rapidly. Many of Cornwall's safest and cleanest beaches are found between Padstow and Newquay. The immediate hinterland is spoiled by modern development, but **Bedruthan Steps▶▶** is an impressive coastal feature, comprising massive rock buttresses detached from the cliff itself. **Newquay** has a brash bustle: nightspots, loud-music pubs, theme parks and surfers' shops. It also offers good beaches, a well-stocked zoo and a pretty port. Out of town, **Trerice**▶(NT) is a handsome Elizabethan manor house with a minstrels' gallery and intricate plasterwork ceilings.

St. Ives▶▶, a delightful port turned resort, has attracted artists and beach-loving holiday-makers for a century. Although it has been considerably cleaned up since its heyday as a fishing port, its back streets have unmistakably Cornish character. Sculptress Barbara Hepworth was one of many 20th-century artists who settled here; her studio is now a museum with her sculptures gracing its garden. A branch of the Tate Gallery features the St. Ives School of artists in one of the most striking settings of any gallery.

The westernmost part of Cornwall is known as **Penwith**▶▶▶ and has some of the most dramatic coastal scenery in England, with lonely heather moors inland. At **Zennor** the Wayside Folk Museum has a fascinating selection of Cornish bygones while the church is home to a legendary mermaid, carved on an ancient bench end. **Land's End**, Britain's southwesternmost mainland point, is the place to come if you collect geographical extremities. A signpost gives distances to places throughout the world (add your home town and pose for the photo); the crowds and theme park dwindle to nothing within ten minutes' walk along the cliff southward, where the scenery gets better. The impressive outdoor **Minack Theatre**▶ clings to a breathtaking cliff site at Porthcurno, while eastward the headland of **Treryn Dinas**, near Treen, is one of the most dramatic features of Cornwall's coastline. **Mousehole**▶▶ (pronounced 'Mouzal'), as quaint as its name suggests, was the home of the last solely Cornish speaker, Dolly Pentreath, who died in 1777 aged 102.

A shopkeeper holds some Cornish pasties (hefty meat and vegetable turnovers)

69

MINING IN CORNWALL
Until the 19th century Cornwall was a world leader in copper and tin production (lead was also produced), when Redruth, Camborne and St. Just were busy hubs. The industry has gone, but there is a striking legacy of abandoned mines and engine houses, such as Wheal Coates near St. Agnes Head. At Pool, near Redruth, the National Trust preserves two huge beam engines that pumped water from the mines. In medieval times tin was weighed and stamped at stannary towns, which included Penzance and Truro. Mine accidents were numerous. Cornish innovations which made the job easier included Sir Humphry Davy's miner's safety lamp, Richard Trevithick's steam-powered beam engine and the rock drill.

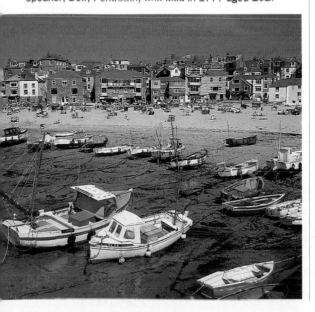

St. Ives' distinctive Mediterranean light qualities attracted artists such as Naum Gabo, Ben Nicholson and Bernard Leach

Eastwards from Penzance, the coast gets more sheltered; the cliffs are less mighty, the seaboard is lusher and more populated than the north coast. Deep-water ports are packed with craft: industrial ships, private yachts and ferries— every village and town seems to have a sign advertising fishing and sharking trips by boat. Visitors in spring and early summer will be on time for Cornwall's famous gardens.

LIZARD TRANSMITTERS
The Lizard peninsula is an important past and present telecommunications hub. A memorial near Poldhu Cove commemorates the birth of transatlantic transmissions—it was from here that in 1901 Marconi sent three dots (a morse 'S') to Newfoundland; his first message which followed was 'What hath God wrought'. Inland, 'the Lizard' is dominated by the space-age form of the Goonhilly Satellite Earth Station, the receiving station for satellite-relayed telephone calls. A tour of the site takes you into an old control tower and you can see the nerve centre of the whole operation.

Penzance to Falmouth The town of **Penzance▶** is pleasantly unprecious, with Georgian streetscapein Chapel Street with its capricious Egyptian House, an early 19th-century precursor to art deco. The National Lighthouse Centre records the essential function of lighthouses on a perilous coast. Surveying the main street is the statue of Sir Humphry Davy, inventor of the miner's safety lamp and the town's foremost son in its tin-mining heyday.

St Michael's Mount▶▶▶(NT) shimmers in the sea, an isle capped by a castle. Those who have seen Mont St-Michel in Brittany can be excused a sense of *déjà vu* and in fact it was the Benedictines from Brittany who founded a church on the site, which became a fortress after the Dissolution in 1539. The owners today are the same family that snatched possession after the Civil War. At low tide you can walk to it along a causeway across the sands; at other times take the little ferry.

The **Lizard peninsula** forms Britain's southernmost acres. **Kynance Cove▶** epitomizes the best of the tumbledown cliffscape of the western Lizard, with a wonderfully sited beach amid the so-called Serpentine Rocks. There are several rock workshops at **Lizard** village, which is itself of little appeal. Eastern Lizard, beyond **Cadgwith▶**, with its thatched cottages stepping down to the sea, has hidden, verdant creeks in the vicinity of the **Helford River**.

These days fishing boats in Mevagissey are still busy, but tourism is the main source of income

Falmouth, Cornwall's largest town, is no great beauty but has a superb **Maritime Museum**►► and is the base for boat trips up Carrick Roads, alternatively known as the **Fal Estuary**►► including excursions upriver to **Truro**, the Cornish capital (not itself of major interest, although it has a 19th-century cathedral). Perfectly preserved Tudor castles, St. Mawes (EH) and Pendennis (EH), guard the great estuary. Subtropical plants abound at the delightful churchyard of **St. Just in Roseland**►, which dips down to the water's edge.

Portloe to the Tamar Charming **Portloe**► is an unspoiled fishing hamlet, hard to get to—and long may it continue to be; it has real character and nothing to attract large-scale commercialization. **Veryan**, inland, is known for its five early 19th-century round houses. **Charlestown**►, a carefully preserved port, is still used by the china clay industry, whose white refuse heaps dominate the area.

Fowey►► rises above the deep-anchorage of Fowey Harbour, terrace by terrace, with Polruan across the water. Blockhouses that used to guard the port stand silent sentinel. An appealing resort town, Fowey comes to life during the late summer regatta.

Mevagissey has become too popular for some people's tastes, with busloads of visitors cramming into its little port, but the place resumes its quiet charm when they have gone; just outside the village the **Lost Gardens of Heligan**►►► are being painstakingly restored to their Victorian glory. Another unmissable plant attraction, in the unlikely moonscape setting of a china clay pit near St. Austell, is the **Eden Project**►►► (see panel, page 67). **Polperro**►►► is even prettier and more groomed than Mevagissey, though no less popular, with a maze of alleys around its photogenic port; park at Talland Bay to the east and walk in along the level coastal path rather than struggle with traffic jams.

The **Tamar Estuary** forms the Devon/Cornwall border; the river can be explored by boat trip from Plymouth. **Antony**► (NT) is the earliest and finest classical-style house in Cornwall, with fine woodland gardens. **Cotehele**►► (NT) is an extraordinary medieval relic, a completely unmodernized house; its estate buildings (saddler, smithy, wheelwright, etc.) are well preserved. By the Tamar is moored *Shamrock*, the last Tamar barge in existence. The **Mount Edgcumbe estate**►, tucked in the far corner of southeastern Cornwall, is a country park looking across to Plymouth; paths through its grounds lead towards quietly characterful Kingsand and Cawsand.

Rising like a dream from Mounts Bay, St. Michael's Mount acquired its monastery after the Archangel Michael appeared in a vision to local fishermen

SUBTROPICAL GARDENS
Penjerrick, Glendurgan (NT) and Trebah gardens, close together west of Falmouth, were all the creation of the Foxes, a Quaker family, who aimed to create Paradise on Earth. For other gardens to visit in south Cornwall, see Gardens, page 16—do not miss the Lost Gardens of Heligan.

Looe, a lively resort in a pleasant setting

CLIFTON

Venture out to the Georgian suburb of Clifton when visiting Bristol. It resembles a mini-Bath with its handsome stone-built squares, crescents and terraces (notably Royal York Crescent). Brunel's majestic Clifton Suspension Bridge (built 1836–64) spans the Avon gorge. Nearby, an 18th-century camera obscura offers views over the city.

Brunel's Clifton Suspension Bridge: when it was completed in 1864, its 214m (702ft) span was the world's greatest

►► Bristol   61C4

(Tourist information tel: 0906 711 2191 (50p per minute); www.visitbristol.co.uk)

There is a new buzz about Bristol nowadays, with much work focusing into improving the look of the city in recent years. As a major port it suffered heavy bombing in World War II, but some gems escaped, among them the **Church of St. Mary Redcliffe►** with its majestic proportions; the **cathedral►** (begun 1142), notable for its Norman chapter house and organ case carved by Grinling Gibbons; and the **Cabot Tower►** a curious architectural folly with far-ranging views. The suburb of **Clifton►►** is the most elegant part of the city (see panel).

Another area to head for is the revamped docklands, where there are boat tours, usually something worthwhile going on at the lively **Arnolfini Arts Centre** *(Admission free)*, plus a stash of other visitor attractions. Particularly Bristol-related are the **Industrial Museum**, and the **SS *Great Britain►►***. Launched in 1843, the latter is now on show in the dry dock where she was built. Entrance also covers the **Maritime Heritage Centre** *(Admission free)*, which charts the city's shipbuilding. The port is also home to **@Bristol** combining Explore (hands-on science), Wildwalk (looking at wildlife) and an IMAX cinema.

Next to the present Temple Meads station, Brunel's original building now houses the **British Empire and Commonwealth Museum►►**, which tells the story of the Empire—and they were by no means all glory days. There is plenty to engage children, who can try on costumes and try out games.

AN L OF AN ACCENT

The hallmark of Bristol speech is the adding of the letter *L* to the ends of words. Thus *area* becomes *areal*, *Australia* becomes *Australial* and *Bristowe*, the old city name, becomes *Bristol*.

► Clovelly   60B2

(Bideford tourist information tel: 01237 477676; www.torridge.gov.uk)

A captivating fishing village, overrun in summer, Clovelly is so steep that cars must park at the Visitor Centre (tel: 01237 431781; www.clovelly.co.uk). Donkeys and sleds make the descent through its cobbled main street. It feels more genuine in the evening, when the crowds have gone.

Hartland Quay►►, to the east, gives access to some of the most formidable cliffs in the West Country, the strata fantastically contorted into bizarre cross-sections.

►►► Dartmoor National Park 60B3

(Dartmoor National Park Authority, High Moorland Visitor Centre (Princetown) tel: 01822 890414; www.dartmoor-npa.gov.uk)

Southern England's largest area of wild country, Dartmoor is a great expanse of blustery moors punctuated by weathered granite outcroppings known as tors. Sheep and Dartmoor ponies graze the open grasslands, wandering between Bronze Age hut circles and burial mounds. The moor can be a bleak place—'nine months winter and three months bad weather'—but there are cob-and-thatch villages to come down to in the lusher valleys (some offering Devon cream teas) and several fine country-house style hotels. Indoor attractions are few: this is a place to be outdoors—picnicking, touring, walking or horse-riding.

On Dartmoor's east side, lush farmland meets the barren moors. **Hay Tor►►** is the most visited viewpoint, easily accessible. **Hound Tor►►**, close by, is well marked by signs and lies next to a well-preserved abandoned medieval village, where you can still make out the fireplaces. West of **Buckland**, whose church clock has the letters MY DEAR MOTHER instead of numerals, **Bel Tor** presides over the Webburn Valley. The **Dart Valley►** is full of choice corners, including Combestone Tor and the medieval 'clapper' bridge, made of great granite slabs, at Dartsmeet, the confluence of the West and East Dart rivers.

Widecombe-in-the-Moor► draws visitors for its valley setting, its fame from the folk song 'Widecombe Fair' and for its church, the 'cathedral of the moor'. **North Bovey►** is much quieter and quite uncommercialized, with a pretty green, thatched cottages, a stone cross and a village pump. **Chagford►** is a large but sleepy village, with enough character and a good location to make it a recommendable base; **Moretonhampstead**, a crossroads town, is a shade busier and has a fine row of 17th-century almshouses.

In northeast Dartmoor the River Teign has carved a course through a deep valley with an enchanting deciduous forest. From **Fingle Bridge►**, an old packhorse bridge, paths lead along the river and up onto moorland viewpoints; the Hunter's Path passes the back entrance to **Castle Drogo►►** (NT), architect Edwin Lutyens' early 20th-century masterpiece, an improbable marriage of granite medievalism and Edwardian Arts and Crafts style. The main entrance is near **Drewsteignton**, which has a charming village square.

Two main roads cross the central moor; the B3212 passes through **Postbridge**, with its notable medieval 'clapper bridge', and grim **Princetown**, dominated by a high-security prison originally built for Napoleonic prisoners of war. For an overview of Dartmoor, go to the **High Moorland Visitor Centre** in Princetown (see above). (Access to the high northern moor is restricted due to military training.)

Two outstanding features justify a visit to the western fringes: **Brent Tor►**, a plain church atop a huge rock and looking far into Cornwall and **Lydford Gorge►►** (see Walks, page 64; NT), a deep and tortuous ravine with a waterfall and whirlpool.

The towns encircling Dartmoor National Park are not of great interest, although **Ashburton** has some attractive streets and **Buckfastleigh** boasts a modern Benedictine abbey, a butterfly park and otter sanctuary and the terminal

Hound Tor: weathering has attacked the joints in the great granite outcrops that dominate the wastes of Dartmoor

73

DARTMOOR'S LETTERBOXES
Many visitors to Dartmoor in the 19th century liked to try to locate Cranmere Pool, scarcely more than a puddle and remotely situated in the moors above Chagford. Someone had the idea of placing a letterbox here, so that a self-addressed postcard would be left here by one walker and picked up and sent on by the next. The fad caught on and now there are some 6,000 official, unofficial and mobile boxes in various places. Today you can record your visit with the rubber stamp provided.

PREHISTORIC PROCESSIONAL ROUTES
Rows of stones erected in the Bronze Age are believed to have marked processional routes. Above the Erme Valley in south Dartmoor, one of these stretches 3km (2 miles) from Stall Moor to Green Hill.

EARLY SETTLERS ON DARTMOOR

The moorland gravels yielded copious quantities of tin, exploited by Bronze Age settlers. Among the most striking of their relics are **Scorhill Stone Circle**, on Shovel Down above Gidleigh (near Chagford), a Bronze Age stone circle of 23 uprights and **Spinsters' Rock**, off the A382 south of its intersection with the A30, a neolithic tomb with its capstone held in place by three uprights.

Grimspound, between Widecombe-in-the-Moor and the B3212, reached by a path up from the road onto Hamel Down, consists of a large walled enclosure with 24 discernible hut circles.

of the steam-powered South Devon Railway (tel: 0845 345 1420; www.southdevonrailway.org) which wends its way 11km (7 miles) to Totnes. The **Museum of Dartmoor Life** at **Okehampton** tells of country life and ways; a fragment of a medieval **castle** (EH) caps a hillock on the edge of town.

Buckland Abbey▶(NT), a former Cistercian monastery, was once home to Sir Francis Drake, born at nearby Tavistock. The house has some relics from his famous ship, *Golden Hind* (including a drum and banners), but it was more Sir Richard Grenville, an earlier occupant, who stamped his character on the house; he added the intricate plasterwork in the Great Hall.

▶▶ Dartmouth   60A3

(Tourist information tel: 01803 834224; www.dartmouth-information.co.uk)

An old naval town, set on steep slopes which drop to the River Dart, Dartmouth has real atmosphere, with small craft on the river and a maze of back streets. The August regatta sees the town at its most exuberant.

Beside Duke Street is the arcaded **Butterwalk**, a former dairy market and now a local museum. In the waterside gardens stands the world's first steam pumping-engine, built in 1725 by Thomas Newcomen, a Dartmouth resident. Two Tudor castles guard either side of the port entrance; **Dartmouth Castle▶** (EH) has a fine view from its roof terrace.

Dartmouth is a base for excursions, including **Totnes▶** with its Norman castle and steep medieval streets and **Salcombe▶**, with a handsome location on an estuary. Ferries cross the Dart to Kingswear, where steam locomotives haul trainloads of day trippers along the **Paignton and Dartmouth Steam Railway** (tel: 01803 555872; www.paignton-steamrailway.co.uk).

The village of Kingswear is just a short ferry-trip across the river from Dartmouth

WALKS NEAR DARTMOUTH

Where you can actually walk along the coast, it is nearly always highly rewarding. But the official coast path in places veers well inland, where the landscape is often unremarkable. The path south from Dartmouth Castle (EH) wriggles round some magnificent coves and rugged cliffs before steering inland at Warren Cove. Other fine uninterrupted coastal stretches are south of Brixham and between Bolt Tail and Start Point either side of Salcombe Harbour; East Prawle is a useful starting point for circular walks.

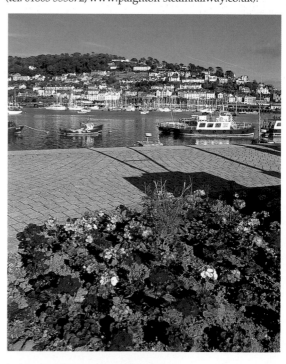

► **Dorchester** 61B4

(Tourist information tel: 01305 267992; www.westdorset.com)
Although not outstandingly attractive, Dorchester is the centre of the countryside of Thomas Hardy's novels, in which the town features as Casterbridge; it is often visited for that reason. The **Dorset County Museum**► celebrates aspects of the county and displaying Hardy's study and a collection of material relating to him. Hardy was also a trained architect and designed **Max Gate** (NT), open to the public; he lived there from 1885 until his death in 1928.

Dorchester, a typical country town, is still recognizable as Thomas Hardy's 'Casterbridge'

75

Maiden Castle►►, on the southwestern edge of Dorchester is Britain's largest Iron Age hillfort; its massive concentric ramparts date from the first century BC.
Hardy's Cottage►(NT), the humble thatched cottage where Thomas Hardy was born in 1840, is furnished as it may have looked in his lifetime. Start from the car park at Higher Bockhampton; either walk along the main track or take the longer Thorncombe Trail, a nature walk through woodland and a fragment of the 'untamed and untameable wild' of Egdon Heath in Hardy's work. Although Hardy is buried at Westminster Abbey, his heart is buried in the family plot at **Stinsford Church**►, Mellstock Church of his novel *Under the Greenwood Tree*.

A prominent tower some 8km (5 miles) southwest of Dorchester, the confusingly named **Hardy Monument**► (NT), commemorates Admiral Thomas Hardy, Nelson's flag-captain at the Battle of Trafalgar. From here there's a view over Chesil Beach and Portland Bill.

THOMAS HARDY COUNTRY

Drive

Thomas Hardy country

This tour (about 110km/68 miles in total) explores the heartland of the countryside immortalized in the writings of Thomas Hardy. Local life has changed beyond recognition, but many elements are still there—thatched villages, rolling downlands, manor houses, ancient monuments.

From **Dorchester** take the A35 east, branching off for **Stinsford▶** and detouring past Hardy's Birthplace at **Higher Bockhampton▶** (see page 75). At **Tolpuddle** the **Tolpuddle Martyrs Museum** (*Admission free*) pays homage to the Tolpuddle Martyrs who formed a trade union and were transported for their pains.

Take minor roads heading north to **Milton Abbas▶▶**, an 18th-century estate village of rustic thatch and whitewash: the owner of Milton Abbey house nearby (which is now a school) had the village rebuilt here to improve the view from his house. The abbey church and finely roofed Abbot's Hall are open.

Take lanes west to **Cerne Abbas▶▶** to look at the famous Giant, best seen from a vista point on the A352 road north. Follow the A352 to **Minterne Magna**, where **Minterne Gardens**, laid out in the 18th century, feature a fine collection of trees and shrubs (open in season).

❑ Looming over the demure village of Cerne Abbas, the prehistoric hill-carving of a naked club-bearing man (the 'Cerne Giant') reveals all for the world to see. Its origins are unclear: it may be a prehistoric fertility symbol or a much later insult to Oliver Cromwell or the local abbot.. ❑

Continue west to **Beaminster▶**, a delightful scene of small-town rural England with an attractive square and past **Parnham House▶** (closed to the public). Drunken lanes meander southeast through **Powerstock**, attractively placed on a hillside and past **Eggardon Hill▶**, an impressively bleak Iron Age hill fort site. Continue on through Littlebredy and up to the **Hardy Monument▶** (see page 75). Drive east via the B3159 and minor roads to pass **Maiden Castle▶▶** (car park on Dorchester side). The A354 leads northwards into Dorchester.

THE FOWLES CONNECTION
At Lyme Regis a sinuous sea wall known as The Cobb gained fame through the film of John Fowles's novel *The French Lieutenant's Woman*, where crazed Sarah Woodruff (played by Meryl Streep) stared out to sea in despair while Charles Smithson (Jeremy Irons) explored natural history in the undercliff just west of town. The Cobb is of medieval origin, and the undercliff, still a wild place and riddled with landslips, is designated a National Nature Reserve.

▶▶▶ Dorset Coast   *61B4–B5*
(Tourist information (Dorchester) tel: 01305 267992; www.westdorset.com for west; (Wareham) tel: 01929 552740; www.purbeck.gov.uk for east)
Beyond Dorset's mighty cliffs lie unspoiled hinterlands that seem to have emerged only recently from the primeval past. The coast is famous for fossils, no place more than **Lyme Regis▶▶**, a charming resort beloved of novelist Jane Austen. The narrow lanes and Regency seafront cottages have changed little since her visits at the turn of the 19th century. Huge ammonite fossils can be seen in garden walls, in **Dinosaurland** (a museum which also gives guided fossil walks along the beach) and in fossil shops. The thatched honey-stone village of **Abbotsbury▶▶** crouches beneath a hillock crowned by a lone chapel; dedicated to St. Catherine, it was once the property of the Benedictine abbey which gave the village its name. A tithe barn and the swannery (very much alive) are other abbey leftovers.

Close by, **Chesil Beach** (or Bank) is one of the most extraordinary features of the British coastline (see panel). **Weymouth▶**, an elegant resort with an early 19th-century ambience, made popular by George III, lies behind a curving bay. Farther east lies **Lulworth Cove▶▶▶**, abutted by amazing cliffs that offer ideal cross-sections for the aspiring geologists who flock here along with fishermen, skindivers, and walkers heading for **Durdle Door** (see Walks, page 64), a fine natural arch. East of Lulworth, army ranges permit only occasional access to rugged cliffs as far as Kimmeridge. **St. Aldhelm's Head** juts into the sea and has a primitive chapel on its summit. Beyond the coastal resort of **Swanage** lie **Old Harry Rocks▶**, chalk stacks detached from the cliff, and the multihued sands of **Studland**, with its fine Norman church; the village lies near the largest remaining heathlands in Dorset. Seaward, views extend to the Isle of Wight. The **Purbeck Ridge** offers a panorama of Poole Harbour and the largest of Dorset's heathlands. The ridge is broken dramatically at **Corfe Castle▶▶▶**, where the pinnacle of a Norman castle rises above the village.

77

THE CHESIL BEACH NATURAL PHENOMENON
The 29km (18-mile) shingle bank was created by the deposit of millions of pebbles through the process of long-shore drift, the lateral shift of material as a result of the waves meeting the shore at an oblique angle. The beach links Portland Bill to the mainland and encloses a lagoon known as the Fleet, a peaceful haven for birds. Because of the steeply shelving seaward side of the beach, it attracts anglers (but swimmers must stay clear: this is one of Britain's most dangerous beaches). The pebbles increase in size from west to east. At the eastern end the Chesil Beach Centre has interactive displays and can arrange glass-bottom boat tours of the Fleet.

Tarr Steps was allegedly built in a single night by the Devil

A LA RONDE
At Exmouth, south of Exeter, A la Ronde (NT) is a delightfully eccentric 16-sided house of 1796, built by Jane and Mary Parminter on returning from a Grand Tour of Europe. It is based on the Byzantine church of San Vitale in Ravenna, Italy and displays many items the sisters collected on their travels.

LUNDY ISLAND
A popular day-trip by ferry from Bideford (in summer also from Ilfracombe) is to Lundy (NT), a little island some 62km (38 miles) north of Hartland Point. Its cliffs are a major site for birdlife; more than 400 species are recorded, including puffins (*lunde* being Norse for puffin). From 1925 to 1954 Lundy's owner Martin Harman tried to make it a separate kingdom; he did not succeed, but the island still issues its own stamps. Lundy's isolation in the Bristol Channel has given it a long history of smuggling. The Marisco Tavern serves beer brewed on the island.

▶ **Exeter**   *60B3*
(Tourist information tel: 01392 265700; www.exeter.gov.uk)
Prior to destruction in a World War II air raid (one of a series targeted on historic sites), Exeter was among southern England's most attractive cities. Amazingly the **cathedral**▶▶ escaped almost unscathed and makes it worth the effort to visit the otherwise largely rebuilt central area. The twin towers are Norman and its nave displays the longest span of Gothic vaulting in the world. Look too for the astronomical clock in the north transept, the bishop's throne and the intricately carved misericords.
    The porticoed **Guildhall** (*Admission free*) in the High Street is England's oldest municipal building. Off High Street, within Romansgate Passage, is the entrance to a 14th-century subterranean water system known as the **Underground Passages**▶ (*Guided tours*).

▶▶ **Exmoor National Park**   *60C3*
(Exmoor National Park Authority (Dulverton) tel: 01398 323841; www.exmoor-nationalpark.gov.uk)
This is a wild, remote part of the coast, with rolling moors stretching inland and merging into high pastures and wooded valleys cut by fast-flowing rivers. Ponies graze the high land, and unusually for England, the moors often reach the clifftops. In the few places where you can reach shore level, the beaches are rocky, and the climate is notoriously wet. Indeed, Exmoor's appeal lies in its scenery, walks, wildlife and sense of escape.

THE COAST ROAD (A39) In the northwest of the national park, **Parracombe's Church of St. Petrock**▶ is a completely unaltered medieval building, preserved thanks to a campaign led by John Ruskin, influential writer, critic and social reformer. **Trentishoe Church** has a tiny musicians' gallery (notice the notch cut out to allow for a double bass's bow); just east, **Heddon's Mouth** is a charming, walkers-only valley which leads from the isolated Hunter's Inn to an abandoned lime kiln on a pebbly beach. At **Lynton**, an amiable resort, strangely shaped crags adorn the **Valley of Rocks**▶▶, where wild goats sniff the sea breezes (see Walks, page 64); **Heddon Valley** is another popular area for walks. A cliff railway connects Lynton with **Lynmouth** below, prettily situated by a small, more animated port. Eastward, the River Lyn lines a magnificent wooded valley; you can walk along the river to an idyllically sited café at **Watersmeet**▶▶, at the joining of the East Lyn River and Farley Water, or head for the hills for the best views; close by, the cliffs near **Countisbury** exceed 300m (985ft) and are some of England's highest. **Oare** and **Malmsmead** are at the heart of Doone Country, the setting of R. D. Blackmore's *Lorna Doone*, based on a real family of outlaws (see panel). **Culbone**, north of the main road, boasts England's smallest church in regular use, alone in the woods. **Allerford**▶ has a pretty packhorse bridge and a fascinating local museum within its old school, while tiny **Selworthy**▶▶ has a group of immaculate thatched cottages and a large church with a fine wagon roof.

INLAND EXMOOR Sheep and ponies roam the breezy hills, red deer the eastern forests. Over the years the moors have dwindled in extent, encroached upon by farmland and pastures, but recent National Park measures have safeguarded what remains. A road tour from Dunkery Hill to Exford, then to Dulverton and west along the Park boundary to Twitchen, gives a good idea of the moor. **Winsford**▶, **Exford** and **Withypool** are three attractive villages in this area; **Dulverton**▶ has lots of small-town charm. South of Withypool, **Tarr Steps**▶ is a 1,000-year-old clapper bridge spanning the River Barle. **Dunkery Beacon**▶▶ is an easily climbed hill, a 10-minute walk from the road, which on a clear day offers a far-ranging view across Devon and Somerset and over the Bristol Channel into South Wales. **Dunster**▶▶▶ rates as one of the most perfect small towns in England, with its ancient yarn market at the hub of its tapering street of medieval buildings and **Dunster Castle**▶▶ (NT) towering above. The fashionable 19th-century architect Anthony Salvin upgraded the castle interior, but it retains earlier features, including a 17th-century staircase and leather wall-hangings that tell the story of Antony and Cleopatra. On the edge of town is a working 18th-century watermill (NT) and there are glorious walks through Dunster Park and along the ridge of Grabbist Hill.

WALKING ON EXMOOR

In addition to the routes into the Valley of Rocks (see page 64) and Hunter's Inn (see page 78), there is outstanding terrain along all of the Exmoor coast. From Lynton head east along the wooded Lyn valley to Watersmeet, and return high above the south side of the valley for coastal views. From Allerford, head to the coast and climb Selworthy Beacon for a huge panorama. Attractive inland walks include Horner Wood beneath Dunkery Beacon, the Grabbist Hill ridge near Dunster, and the moorland valley of Badgeworthy Water in 'Doone Country' south of Malmsmead.

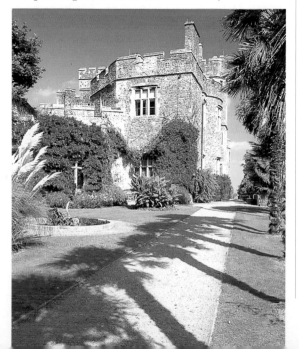

Dunster Castle: there has been a castle on this site since Norman times

LORNA DOONE

Blackmore's Victorian adventure novel takes place in the wilds of Exmoor. The hero, John Ridd, seeks revenge on the Doones for shooting his father and is in love with Lorna Doone, whom the Doones have kidnapped for her large inheritance. Tragedy later strikes at Lorna's wedding at Oare Church. Despite failing to sell for more than a year after publication, *Lorna Doone* has become a minor classic that for many is synonymous with Exmoor.

SIR FRANCIS DRAKE

One of the most immortal examples of cool-headedness was when Sir Francis Drake (c1541–96) insisted on finishing a lawn bowling match on Plymouth Hoe before turning his attention to the Spanish Armada. Devon-born, he was the first Englishman to sail around the world and, as a darling of Elizabeth I, he was knighted for his efforts. In 1588 he achieved the great victory over the Armada; the weather played a major role—a third of the Spanish vessels were shipwrecked. This was Drake's last great naval exploit, although he pioneered a leat (channel) bringing fresh water from Dartmoor to Plymouth.

Gilded ceilings and other adornments at Longleat House were added in the 19th century by the 4th Marquess of Bath

▶ Glastonbury 61C4

(Tourist information tel: 01458 832954; www.glastonburytic.co.uk)

New Age shops dominate the home of the Glastonbury Festival, a huge rock event in summer. A hub for paganism, mysticism and other faiths, the town huddles around the base of Glastonbury Tor, a hill capped by St. Michael's Chapel. The **abbey▶** has long been a place of pilgrimage: the Legend of Glastonbury records Joseph of Arimathaea burying the chalice used at the Last Supper. There are links too with Arthurian legend: Arthur's corpse was supposedly brought here by Sir Lancelot.

▶▶ Longleat 61C5

(tel: 01985 844400; www.longleat.co.uk)

In 1949 Longleat was Britain's first country house to open its doors full-time; side attractions include a Mirror Maze and a safari park. The house, completed in 1580, was ahead of its time: it looks out to its park rather than onto a courtyard. Inside are 16th-century tapestries and 19th-century marquetry and gilded ceilings, added by Italian craftsmen after the 4th Marquess of Bath returned from a Grand Tour. The kitchen dates from this period. Capability Brown landscaped the grounds in 1757 with the world's largest maze.

▶ Plymouth 60A2

(Tourist information tel: 01752 266030 or 304849; www.visitplymouth.co.uk)

A major naval base for centuries, much of Plymouth was rebuilt after World War II bombing, in a monolithic style. Head for the Barbican, west of Sutton Harbour, with the **National Marine Aquarium▶** (Britain's biggest aquarium with Europe's largest tank), the timber-framed **Elizabethan House**, the **Plymouth Gin Distillery** (in operation since 1793) and the **Pilgrim Fathers Memorial**. Carry on past the **Royal Citadel** to **The Hoe▶▶** waterfront area: **Plymouth Dome▶** is a hi-tech evocation of the city's past; entrance covers **Smeaton's Tower**, an 18th-century lighthouse. On Finewell Street is 15th-century **Prysten House** (with a model of 17th-century Plymouth). The **Tamar Bridges** cross into Cornwall: the 1961 suspension bridge and Brunel's 1859 railway bridge.

In Dorset you can walk from Ryme Intrinseca to Beer Hackett; in Kent you can try getting your tongue around Trottiscliffe (pronounced Trozlee); in County Durham you can go to Pity Me; while in Worcestershire, there is a village called Upton Snodsbury. England's place-names have long amused and bemused visitors and locals alike, inspiring both affectionate parody and rhapsodic poetry.

Historical pointers By the time of the Norman invasion in 1066, the settlement pattern in England was already largely established. Place-names give a host of clues as to how and when England developed. Generally the suffix gives the key element, with the prefix acting as a descriptive defining element   Doncaster, for example, tells us of a Roman camp (*castra*) on the River Don.

Settlers from the East As Saxons began to settle in England, they introduced their own place-names rather than using the existing Celtic ones—most of the native place-names that survived adopted natural features such as hills, rivers and valleys. Early Saxon names included heathen names such as those of gods, for instance Woden (Wednesbury) and Thunor (Thunderfield). The suffix -*ing* survives from that period, particularly in Surrey and East Anglia, while later Saxon names included the commonest suffixes, -*ham* (home) and -*ton* (enclosure, farm, or manor).

Scandinavian settlers ensconced themselves in eastern England, where today there are still many names ending with -*by* (Grimsby, Whitby, Wragby, etc.): the vast majority are in the eastern and northwestern counties. Remote areas had names unto themselves: Lympne and Lyminge in east Kent and numerous Cornish names (Trelissick, Marazion, Nanjizal) are unique to those parts. The prefix Chipping (Chipping Campden, Chipping Sodbury, Chippenham, etc.) indicates a marketplace; the word is related to the German *kaufen* (to buy) and appears to be the root of Copenhagen.

Later changes In the 19th century, mining and other industrial settlements created new names—ranging from matter-of-fact New Mills to the intriguing likes of Indian Queens and Booze. The Somerset coastal resort of Weston upgraded itself into Latin and was renamed Weston-super-Mare. The odd euphemism evolved—the Devil's Arse cave was tamed to Peak Cavern and Pigg Hill became Peak Hill. Craven Arms in Shropshire was originally just a pub; a railway town grew around it and the name stuck.

81

THE LYRIC POETS IN SOMERSET

The Quantocks and hills near Culbone inspired *The Lyrical Ballads* (1798) of William Wordsworth and Samuel Taylor Coleridge. Dorothy Wordsworth recorded: 'There is everything here; sea, woods wild as fancy ever painted, brooks clear and pebbly as in Cumberland, villages so romantic.' Coleridge wrote *The Rime of the Ancient Mariner* , Part One of *Christabel* and *Frost at Midnight* at Nether Stowey. His great poem *Kubla Khan* was written at a cottage near Culbone in Exmoor and was inspired by an opium dream, rudely broken off by the alleged arrival of a 'person from Porlock' about some minor matter. The work was never completed.

Salisbury Cathedral

▶ Quantock Hills 61C4
(Taunton tourist information tel: 01823 336344; www.heartofsomerset.com)

A forgotten corner of rural England. The hedges grow high around the sunken, crooked lanes, the churchyards hide behind banks of cow parsley and manor houses lurk behind estate walls. Villages are sleepy, typically of sandstone cottages. Dense woodlands cloak the lower slopes. On the top is a plateau of heather moors crossed by ancient trackways.

Medieval wool-trade prosperity left a legacy of fine churches in the Quantocks: 16th-century carved bench ends are a local craft; the best include those at **Broomfield**, **Spaxton**, **Crowcombe** and **Bicknoller**.

William Wordsworth and his sister Dorothy stayed in 1797 at Alfoxton Park at **Holford**, with fellow poet Samuel Taylor Coleridge (see panel). The latter lived for some years at **Nether Stowey▶**, where his home, **Coleridge Cottage**, has been restored by the National Trust.

The **West Somerset Railway▶** (tel: 01643 704996; www.west-somerset-railway.co.uk), the longest private line in Britain, operates steam and diesel trains along the track from Bishops Lydeard (near Taunton) to Minehead on the coast. Washford station has a small museum devoted to railway memorabilia.

▶▶ Salisbury 61C5
(Tourist information tel: 01722 334956; www.visitsalisbury.com)

Built between 1220 and 1258, entirely in the Early English Gothic style, Salisbury's **cathedral▶▶▶** was the subject of a number of paintings by Constable. Its noble spire, added in 1334–80, soars 123m (404ft), higher than any other in the country. On clear days, it is worth the effort to climb the tower to the base of the spire. Reached through the cloisters, the octagonal chapter house boasts a medieval carved frieze depicting scenes from the books of Genesis and Exodus and the best-preserved of four manuscripts of the Magna Carta, the first bill of rights foisted by barons on King John in 1215. England's largest **cathedral close** surrounds the precincts; houses open to the public are the 13th-century **King's House**, now home to the **Salisbury and South Wiltshire Museum▶** (exhibits include the area's archeological heritage such as

Stonehenge and Old Sarum, as well as costume and lace), **Malmesbury House** (closed for renovation) and **Mompesson House**▶ (NT), a Queen Anne house with a walled garden, period furnishings and a rare collection of English drinking glasses. The rest of the town, laid out on a spacious grid plan in the 13th century, has many attractive corners.

Wilton House▶▶ The 17th-century home of the Earls of Pembroke in nearby Wilton is not on the grandest scale but shows taste; Inigo Jones designed most of it, including the Double Cube Room, hung with Van Dyck portraits. Here too is the room where D-Day invasion planning took place.

From Salisbury there is a bus (No. 3; tel: 01722 336855; www.wdbus.co.uk) to **Old Sarum**▶▶ (see panel) and **Stonehenge**▶▶▶ (see page 84).

▶▶ Scilly, Isles of 60C1

(Tourist information (St Mary's) tel: 01720 422536; www.simplyscilly.co.uk)

An idyllic retreat beyond the southwestern tip of the British mainland, the Scillies comprise five inhabited, strikingly contrasting islands. There is much to interest the naturalist, particularly birdlife. Daffodils, narcissi, irises and tulips are commercially grown.

Hugh Town is the principal township on **St. Mary's**, the largest island (maximum width 5km/3 miles); Star Castle, built in 1593–94 as a fortress, is now a hotel. Paths follow the coastline; there are prehistoric burial chambers to explore, while at Peninnis Head are curiously weathered rocks. **Bryher**, the smallest inhabited island, is windswept, with simple facilities and gorse-clad hillsides. **St. Agnes**, the most southwesterly community in the British Isles, has an old lighthouse of 1680 (now a private house but still providing flashes). Troy Town Maze, a piece of folk art, may have been created by an 18th-century lighthouse-keeper with time on his hands. **St. Martin's** is treeless, with a prominent day-mark cone (1683) at its highest point and has splendid beaches; Higher and Lower Towns between them muster a population of around 100. **Tresco**▶▶, the second-largest isle, is renowned for the subtropical gardens of Tresco Abbey, the major attraction of the Scillies, created by Dorrien Smith. The island is fun to explore (no cars, just tractors), with several forts and many white-sand beaches.

OLD SARUM
Old Sarum (EH), the original site of Salisbury, was finally abandoned in Norman times because of its exposed hilltop position. Old Sarum Church was founded in 1078, but five days afterwards was struck by lightning and largely destroyed. The town moved to New Sarum (present-day Salisbury) soon after, yet up to 1832 the old town was the classic 'rotten borough' represented by two Members of Parliament (including, towards the end, William Pitt) to serve a nonexistent electorate. Old Sarum is on the edge of Salisbury.

83

SCILLY PRACTICALITIES
The archipelago, 45km (28 miles) southwest of Land's End, is reached by a 20-minute helicopter trip from Penzance to St. Mary's and Tresco (tel: 01736 363871; www.islesofscillyhelicopter.com); by plane from Land's End (15 minutes, Newquay (30 minutes), Exeter (1 hour), Bristol (1 hour 10 minutes) and Southampton (1.5 hours) to St. Mary's (tel: 0845 710 5555; www.ios-travel.co.uk); or by a 2.5-hour boat ride from Penzance to St. Mary's (telephone and website as for plane). There is a good boat service between the other islands (tel: 01720 422536). Bicycles can be rented on St. Mary's.

Stonehenge, immense and silent, is thought to have been constructed in three phases

STONEHENGE—THE FACTS

Stonehenge began as a simple ditch and bank (2800BC); sarsen stones from Wiltshire and stones from the Preseli Hills in Wales were added around 2000BC. In the Bronze Age, around 1600–1500BC, the whole site was reworked with uprights and cross-lintels. The central axis aligns with the sun on Midsummer's Day as well as at the midwinter solstice.

STONEHENGE—THE ENIGMA

We may never know the precise mystical, religious, or ceremonial significance of Stonehenge. What seems feasible is that it was erected to mark the position of the winter (rather than the summer) solstice—the crisis time of year when people needed the sun to return. This ties in with other Bronze Age 'Beaker' sites and also explains the 'avenue', (which approaches from the opposite direction): people would process along the avenue to the henge in December, not away from it in June.

▶▶▶ Stonehenge   *61C5*

(tel: 01980 624715; www.english-heritage.org.uk/stonehenge)

Britain's most famous prehistoric stone circle (EH), a World Heritage Site, stands alone on Salisbury Plain, a sparsely populated area of chalk downland studded with mementoes of early inhabitants. Its origins remain a mystery (see panel). Entry includes an audio tour. Visitors flock here in the thousands; a new visitor centre (4km/2.5 miles) and an upgrade in facilities is being planned for completion by 2015.

▶▶ Stourhead   *61C5*

(tel: 01747 841152; www.nationaltrust.org.uk/stourhead)

In 1741, inspired by a Grand Tour of Europe, Henry Hoare II, the son of a wealthy banker, returned home to Stourhead and decided to re-landscape his grounds with classical temples, a triangular lake and rare plants. He created one of the highest achievements of English landscape gardening. The Palladian mansion suffered a fire in 1902 but still has good Chippendale furniture, paintings and a library. This and the village of Stourton are owned by the National Trust.

▶▶▶ Wells   *61C4*

(Tourist information tel: 01749 672552; www.wells.gov.uk)

England's smallest cathedral city is set near the eastern end of the Mendip Hills. The streets of limestone houses are dwarfed by the **cathedral▶▶▶**, significant above all for the richness of its early 13th-century west front (recently restored), adorned with 356 statues. Building started on the choir in about 1180 and finished with the cloisters in 1508, following the designs of Bishop Reginald de Bohun. A problem of subsidence at the crossing was resolved by the innovation of inverted 'scissor' arches, which look timeless in style. Here too is the world's second oldest clock, with its 14th-century face showing phases of the moon and the position of the sun. The stained glass, chapter house and carving deserve time to be appreciated.

Close by is the moated **Bishop's Palace▶▶** with its drawbridge, turrets and medieval hall; a rope dangles for swans to pull when they want to be fed (a trick passed down from one generation to another). Just off the cathedral close, an archway leads into **Vicars' Close▶▶**, a medieval street dating from 1381, claimed to be the most complete medieval street in Europe.

Cheddar Gorge▶▶▶ is the most outstanding feature of the Mendip Hills, themselves a gently rolling whaleback plateau perforated with limestone caverns, some of which have collapsed to form gorges. A road follows the bottom of Cheddar Gorge beneath the massive cliffs; fanciful names have been given to many of the crags. A staircase at the entrance to the gorge, on its south side, leads up to a tin prospect tower; views are even better from above. (See Walks, page 64.) Also by the gorge entrance are the **Cheddar Caves**▶, of which Gough's Cave is recommended for its weird limestone formations. Cheddar itself has a fine medieval market cross.

Axbridge▶ is a pleasing, small town that sees far fewer visitors than Cheddar Gorge or Wells. Its fetching, rather irregular central square is overlooked by the half-timbered King John Hunting Lodge, a 15th-century merchant's house that is home to a local history museum.

Burrington Combe▶ is a lesser version of Cheddar Gorge. During a storm here in 1792, Reverend Augustus Toplady sheltered beneath a rock and composed the hymn 'Rock of Ages'. **Dolebury Warren**▶, a grassy ridge between Burrington Combe and the A38, has good views from its Iron Age hill fort, extending over the Severn Estuary to South Wales and north to Bristol. Jutting out into the Severn Estuary south of Weston-super-Mare, **Brean Down**▶▶ gives phenomenal views of hills and estuary; this too has the site of an ancient hill fort on its summit. **Wookey Hole**▶ is a vividly lit cavern, said to have housed the Witch of Wookey (her alabaster ball and comb and the bones of her goat are in the town museum in Wells). It's a fun place to bring children, with an exhibition re-creating the world of a 9,000-year-old skeleton on display, as well as such contrivances as a mirror maze and an assembly of village penny-in-the-slot machines. Near Wookey Hole, Ebbor Gorge is a secretive limestone ravine with a nature trail through charming woods.

CHEDDAR CHEESE
Cheddar itself is of course best known for Cheddar cheese. The hard cows'-milk cheese was first made here in the early 12th century, perhaps even earlier. The traditional method is to 'cheddar' or cut the firm curd into small pieces and to drain the whey before packing the residual matter into cylinders some 30–38cm (12–15in) in diameter; the cheese is then wrapped in cheese-cloth and coated with wax. It is left to mature (originally this was done in local caves) for anything from three months to two years according to the strength desired. The Cheddar Gorge Cheese Co. Rural Village, Cheddar, makes the authentic product.

85

Witches Kitchen at Wookey Hole

★ Walk start point

| 0 | 10 | 20 | 30 | 40 | 50 km |

| 0 | 10 | 20 | 30 miles |

4

5

SOUTHERN ENGLAND The southeastern counties make up a comparatively affluent corner of Britain. Proximity to the capital and a green-belt policy restricting growth around London have pushed up property prices in this cherished ring of countryside, so that the villages have become affluent commuter caches; beyond the green belt spreads a sizeable stretch of suburbia. Yet for all the urban pressures, the region has surprisingly deep pockets of rural country-side; west Kent, southern Surrey and much of Sussex represent some of the most varied lowlands in Britain.

THE WEALD AND THE DOWNS Many of the region's lushest gardens (see pages 16–17), finest country houses (see pages 102–103) and most appealing villages are found in the Weald, a term given to a somewhat ill-defined area stretch-ing south of London to the coast. Geologically it is identifiable as being between the North and South Downs, two ranges of chalk hills—or 'downs'—that run west to east and end spectacularly in sheer, crumbly cliffs at Dover (the famous White Cliffs) and at Beachy Head near Eastbourne. The Downs rise to no great height, but are much-loved weekend walking grounds, with the long-distance North Downs Way and South Downs Way benefiting from wide views over the Weald itself. The proposed South Downs National Park is intended to cover the chalk uplands of Sussex as well as the sandstone hills of Surrey: it is already an area more visited than any other national park.

Weald comes from a word meaning 'wood', and though many of the trees have been cleared, it has the character of

Opposite: Wye Down, part of the North Downs, in Kent

a wooded area, with clumps of trees and hedge-lined fields. Here the villages tend to be traditional looking, many with timber framed structures, some hung with pantiles and others exposing their beams, plus cottages built with flints, brick or local stone. In Kent you will see oast houses—circular brick kilns built for drying hops for brewing, and now converted to other uses. Regimented poles of hops growing in 'hop gardens', as well as apple and cherry orchards, are also particularly Kentish, though declining in numbers. Between the North and South Downs are the hills (of a sandstone known as greensand) of the High Weald, which include the Ashdown Forest, the wonderfully timeless heathland landscape of the Winnie-the-Pooh stories of A. A. Milne.

KENT, EAST AND WEST SUSSEX AND SURREY Kent is a mixed bag; the north coast is part marshy, part industrial, although the historic dockyard in Chatham and the heart of Rochester are attractive. Inland Kent has numerous pretty villages such as Penshurst, Chiddingstone, Chilham and Shoreham; of its inland towns, Canterbury, Sandwich, Cranbrook and Tenterden stand out the most. On the coast, Dover deserves more than a fleeting visit for its castle, and Broadstairs and Folkestone are pleasant resorts.

The **Sussex** shoreline is almost entirely built up, though the cliffs west of Eastbourne and east of Hastings are notable exceptions. The only decent sandy beach is at Camber, near Rye. Coastal curios include the assembly of houseboats on the tidal mud flats at Shoreham, in West Sussex, and the De La Warre Pavilion, a Bauhaus-inspired design, in the unlikely setting of Bexhill.

The most appealing coastal towns by far are Hastings and Eastbourne, in contrasting styles but both abutting fine cliffs; and Brighton, a pulsating seaside resort, still has tremendous atmosphere, with its Royal Pavilion rating as one of the country's most extravagant follies. Chichester Harbour is the big yacht haven for Sussex. Chichester, West Sussex's cathedral city, lies within easy reach of the county's finest Roman monuments—Fishbourne Palace and Bignor Villa.

88

RECOMMENDED HISTORIC CITIES
Canterbury, Rochester, Winchester.
CASTLES AND ROYALTY
Berkshire: Windsor.
Hampshire: Portchester, Solent forts at Portsmouth, Southsea, etc.
Isle of Wight: Carisbrooke, Osborne House.
Kent: Deal, Dover, Rochester, Walmer.
Sussex: Bodiam, Pevensey.
ROMAN REMAINS
Kent: Lighthouse and Roman Painted House at Dover, Lullingstone Roman Villa (near Eynsford), Richborough Roman Fort (near Sandwich). **Sussex**: Bignor Roman Villa (near Amberley), Fishbourne Roman Palace (near Chichester).
SMALL TOWNS Arundel, Battle, Chichester, Cranbrook, Lewes, Petworth, Rye, Sandwich.
SEASIDE TOWNS
Brighton, Broadstairs, Eastbourne, Hastings.
NAVAL HERITAGE
Chatham, Portsmouth.
COASTAL SCENERY
Sussex: Seven Sisters and Beachy Head (near Eastbourne), Fairlight Cove (Hastings).
Kent: Cliffs between Folkestone and Walmer.

Oast houses are unique to Kent and the Hereford and Worcester areas

Inland Sussex has some prosperous-looking villages and a fair scattering of antiques shops and pleasant country pubs. Highlights include Arundel, with its massive castle towering over its steep main street; Battle, the historic battlefield of 1066 and the abbey founded by William the Conqueror; Rye and Winchelsea, two remarkably unspoiled former ports; Lewes, with its architectural variety and Norman castle; and Alfriston, memorably set beneath the South Downs.

Surrey has been largely developed into an affluent commuter suburb, but it has some delicious countryside, ideal for walking—notably in the greensand country around Haslemere and the vicinities of Shere and Leith Hill, at 294m (965ft) the highest point in the Southeast.

HAMPSHIRE, THE ISLE OF WIGHT AND BERKSHIRE The county of **Hampshire** rolls gently inland, the best of its country in the far east around Selborne and in the far west by the heaths and woodlands of the New Forest. Winchester has a compact but fascinating medieval heart. The coast doesn't offer much aesthetically, but Portsmouth has an important naval heritage. Southampton, a large industrial and commercial hub that was heavily bombed in World War II, has a few corners of historic interest (medieval town walls, Tudor House and the oldest bowling green in the world) as well as archeology, aviation and maritime museums and a fine art gallery. Both these cities and Lymington, have ferry services to the **Isle of Wight**, a pleasant base, with plenty of attractions and scenery to tempt families and walkers, despite the suburbanisation along its eastern coast. The island has an excellent public transport system (some may wish to leave the car on the mainland to avoid the expense of taking it on the ferry) and its south coast is one of Britain's sunniest spots.

Berkshire has a split identity, divided north–south by the M4 motorway, with downlands merging into Wiltshire and Hampshire to the west, while at its flatter eastern edge is Windsor Great Park. At Windsor Castle you can see inside the state apartments of the Queen's residence. Crowds throng the town all year round; you can escape from the bustle by taking a boat trip along the Thames or a walk into Eton or the park. The Thames defines Berkshire's northern border from Windsor to Streatley; the river, which runs down from Buckinghamshire and Oxfordshire, has a placid beauty and a boating scene that can only be found in England.

89

Horsted Keynes Station on the Bluebell Line— so-called because of the bluebell woods through which the railway passes

BRIGHTON'S PAST

In 1754 Dr Richard Russell came to the fishing village of Brighthelmstone and prescribed seawater as a cure for a variety of complaints; many people took his advice and the village acquired spa status. Georgian and Regency houses in terraces followed as the élite arrived in the footsteps of the Prince Regent. Brighton later got a reputation as a rendezvous for lovers' illicit weekends; the railway added a sleazy element. Graham Greene's novel *Brighton Rock* is set in the world of 1930s gang warfare.

▶▶ Bluebell Railway 86B3

(tel: 01825 720800, or for 24-hour recorded information: 01825 722370; www.bluebell-railway.co.uk)

In 1960 the Bluebell was the first standard-gauge steam railway to be reopened as a tourist attraction; in many ways it is the pick of the bunch, with some of its carriages dating from the 1890s and stations furnished with Victorian advertising signs, fire buckets and gas lamps. Its 27km (17-mile) round trip takes an hour (special restaurant trains and other events at weekends) and runs between Sheffield Park and Kingscote via Horsted Keynes (there are bus links to East Grinstead rail station, where the line may eventually extend). Sheffield Park Garden (see page 17) makes a pleasant destination.

▶▶▶ Brighton 86A3

(Tourist information tel: 0906 711255 (50p/minute); www.visitbrighton.com)

Among the oldest, liveliest and most interesting British coastal resorts, Brighton became fashionable when the Prince Regent, later King George IV, came here and virtually initiated the idea of seaside holidays and bathing. He converted a farmhouse bought in 1784 into his capricious **Royal Pavilion▶▶▶**, an oriental extravaganza covered with minarets and onion domes (see panel, page 91). Across the small park, the free **Brighton Museum and Art Gallery▶** *(Admission free)* has an entertaining miscellany, including the story of the town's development, art-nouveau furniture and a fashion section displaying George IV's breeches.

The obvious place to begin is along the **seafront▶▶**. Cream and sky-blue period streetlamps and rows of white stucco houses and hotels proliferate. The best streets lie to the east at **Kemp Town**▶, an example of early 19th-century town planning, with Lewes Crescent at its far end. Towards Hove to the west there are elegant bow-fronted Regency terraces, in Brunswick Square and north of Western Road, while the area just west of the pier is the busiest, with fortune tellers, bookstalls, hair-braiders and bars doing a brisk trade during the warmer months, and games of beach volleyball in progress. There is also a long-established aquarium and a tiny seafront train (**Volk's Electric Railway**). The beach itself is shingle.

Immediately inland from the hub of the seafront, **The Lanes**▶▶ survive from the once humble fishing village of Brighthelmstone; ironically this is now the most chic area of Brighton, with expensive antiques shops, outdoor cafés and galleries in its warren of narrow alleys. The **North Laine**▶ (between the station and North Street) is the vibrant, more atmospheric heart of funky, overtly gay Brighton, with street musicians and alternative shops.

A conspicuously attractive town by the South Downs to the northeast of Brighton, **Lewes**▶▶ is graced with some pleasing streets and paths known as 'twittens', which include steep, cobbled Keere Street. The hilltop castle is Norman and was adapted into a romantic garden feature in the 18th century; it gives a fascinating rooftop view. Many of the half-timbered houses were given a fake brick veneer, fashionable in the 18th century, with the widespread use of 'mathematical tiles', thin fascia tiles resembling bricks. In Southover, the Grange Gardens are a luscious paradise amid walls of stone taken from the nearby, largely vanished medieval priory. The town is famed for the best and heartiest 5 November fireworks night in the country. It also has a notable concentration of antiques shops and auction rooms.

▶▶ Broadstairs

87C5

(Tourist information tel: 01843 583333; www.canterburyandcoastalkent.co.uk)

The prettiest of the coastal resorts in Thanet in East Kent is Broadstairs; all its charm is concentrated on the seafront, with seven sandy coves beneath low cliffs. It is a combination of sedate resort and fishing port; you can still watch fish being unloaded. The town has a pleasantly old-fashioned air. Charles Dickens knew Broadstairs well; he spent several summers at what has since been named 'Bleak House', with the desk at which he wrote *David Copperfield*.

Nearby **Ramsgate**▶ is not in the same league, but worth a stroll for the Regency streets. The coastal walk from Broadstairs to Ramsgate takes about 30 minutes.

91

At this desk at 'Bleak House', Dickens completed David Copperfield

Walks

Tennyson Down, Isle of Wight 86A1

Start from Freshwater Bay. The coastal path leads west along a grassy ridge, with sea views on three sides. Pass the Tennyson monument and continue to the island's western tip; an old fort, Needles Old Battery, gives views of The Needles, a set of rock pinnacles battered by the waves. Return the same way. (2.5 hours)

Ditchling Beacon, West Sussex 86A3

Start from Ditchling Beacon car park, at the site of an Iron Age hill fort on the South Downs. Follow the South Downs Way west along the escarpment edge, enjoying views of the Weald and to the sea. After 3km (2 miles) you reach the famous Jack and Jill windmills. Return the same way. It is excellent terrain for mountain biking. (2.5 hours)

Bewl Water, Kent/East Sussex border 87B4

Start from Visitor Centre car park. An attractive reservoir, Bewl Water is the largest lake in Southeast England and is circled by a well-marked and scenically varied path. It is too long for an entire day's walk, but very pleasant for strolls and mountain biking.

Lullingstone Park, Kent 87B4

Start from car park at Visitor Centre off the A225. Trails take in landscapes of river, woodland and grassland plus Lullingstone Roman Villa and Lullingstone Castle (about 1.5 hours). Longer walks can incorporate the pretty villages of Shoreham, Otford and Eynsford.

Ashdown Forest, East Sussex 87B4

Start at the Poohsticks Bridge car park in Ashdown Forest (take the B2026 south of Hartfield 2km/1 mile, turn west at intersection with minor road; car park is 180m/200yd on north side of road). This is the heartland of A. A. Milne's *Winnie-the-Pooh* stories. A path leads to the bridge where the game of Poohsticks was once played; return to the car park and follow the gravel track east; ignore left forks. Cross the road and take a path rising onto heathland (where Piglet supposedly lived). Walk up to the monument to Milne on Gill's Lap: this is the Enchanted Place of the stories, an ideal picnic spot with a view encapsulating the essence of the 'forest'. Return the same way. (1.5 hours)

Poohsticks Bridge, Ashdown Forest

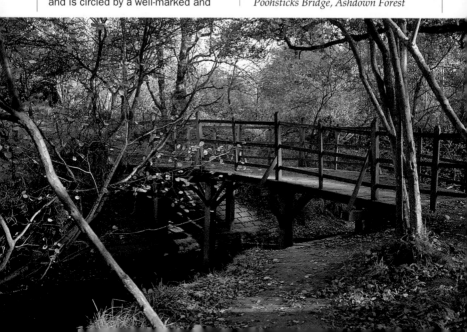

92

▶▶▶ Canterbury   87B5

(Tourist information tel: 01227 378100; www.canterbury.co.uk)

Canterbury has witnessed two very dark hours. One was the murder of Thomas à Becket in the cathedral in 1170, the other a World War II 'Baedeker raid' in 1942 (so called because targets were historic rather than military). The medieval city was destroyed, but the cathedral, seat of the Archbishop of Canterbury and the premier church of England, was miraculously unscathed.

Yet today the city's sense of history is as compelling as ever. You can walk through the **West Gate** (museum inside), as pilgrims have done for eight centuries and pass a number of charitable hospitals founded in medieval times as places to accommodate pilgrims (St. Thomas's Hospital and the **Poor Priests' Hospital** are open to the public, the latter housing the hi-tech **Museum of Canterbury▶**).

The old city is largely contained within the **city wall**, but just outside lie **St. Augustine's Abbey** (EH), founded in 597, its church and cloister foundations still apparent and **St. Martin's Church**, England's oldest church in

CANTERBURY'S STREETSCAPE
The city's surviving older streets show a rich mixture of medieval, Georgian and Victorian styles. Some of the first buildings are: Queen Elizabeth's Guest Chamber, a former inn with a wonderfully over-the-top stucco façade; The Weavers, which is ancient, although its 'half-timbering' is fake and relatively modern; and the Beaney Institute, an elaborate library, a statement of high Victorian exuberance. The major Roman remains are within the Roman Museum in Longmarket.

93

Canterbury's rich architectural heritage is in evidence around the early 16th-century Christ Church Gate

continuous use and once the headquarters of St. Augustine—red Roman bricks can be seen in the walls.

The **cathedral▶▶▶** precincts are entered by Christ Church Gate. The cathedral, built in Caen limestone, boasts several outstanding features, among them Bell Harry, the 72m (236ft) central tower, a collection of 12th- and 13th-century stained glass, a Norman crypt and the Black Prince's tomb. Adjacent is the 15th-century Great Cloister, with a stone marking the spot where Thomas à Becket died.

Behind the cathedral, Green Court is fronted by the Norman Staircase, ruins of the monks' dormitory and the buildings of **King's School**. The **Roman Museum▶** on Longmarket sets the scene of Roman Canterbury, with reconstructions of some dealers' stalls and domestic interiors, before leading past the excavations of a real Roman house with hypocaust system and mosaics. **The Canterbury Tales** brings Chaucer's characters to life in recreations of Canterbury in medieval times.

To the southwest, the village of **Chilham▶** has a fine square, with timber-framed houses on two sides, and the church facing the entrance to the medieval castle.

THE CANTERBURY TALES
In Chaucer's *Canterbury Tales*, the high point of English medieval literature, a party of pilgrims meet at the Tabard Inn, Southwark (now part of London). They agree to travel together and to tell stories to pass the time:
    'And specially, from every shires ende
    Of Engelonde to Caunterbury they wende.'
Chaucer's works are brought to life in theme-park fashion, with tableaux and re-created sounds and smells, in The Canterbury Tales in St. Margaret's Street.

The seaside holiday is one of those great British institutions, which, like other good things, has spread down the class ladder. In the 18th century the only people who could afford a holiday of more than one day were the rich. Later, resorts like Bournemouth and Eastbourne were planned to attract middle-class business. The coming of the railways and the invention of the nationwide 'bank holidays' in Victorian times spurred the development of resorts for the blue-collar class—Blackpool, Margate, Skegness and their like.

BEACH BELLES
When the fashion for 'sea-bathing' began in the 18th century, men and women customarily swam naked, but as it spread, so did modesty. The 'bathing machine' carried people, shielded from view, right out into the waves, but even so, women took to wearing all-enveloping flannel gowns tied with a drawstring at the neck. Elaborate Victorian and Edwardian costumes made of flannel, worsted, or serge looked much like day dresses, with frilly caps, stockings, even shoes. The one-piece swimsuit for ladies came in before World War I; it had sleeves and reached to the knees.

94

Before the 18th century Britons occasionally swam in rivers and lakes, but eyed the sea askance. It was dangerous and it tasted nasty. Even in the Royal Navy, a seaman who could swim was a rarity. When sea bathing began, it was for health rather than pleasure. A drawing of 1735 shows men and women in the sea at Scarborough, a health spa with a mineral spring on the Yorkshire coast. The spring enriched the local doctors and it seems to have occurred to them then that perhaps the rolling brine so plentifully at hand, the salt-laden water and brisk North Sea breezes might be profitably exploited as well.

'Beside the seaside' Certainly this was what happened on the Sussex coast, where the obscure fishing hamlet of Brighthelmstone was transformed into glamorous **Brighton**, queen of the briny. A doctor named Richard Russell, who moved there in 1753, proclaimed the virtues of crabs' eyes, cuttlefish bones and wood lice washed down with a hearty pint of seawater. His successor, an Irishman named Anthony Relham, opportunely discovered the salubrious qualities of fresh sea air, heightened, he said, by Brighton's fortunate lack of noxiously perspiring trees.

The effect of all this nonsense was to draw well-to-do invalids and hypochondriacs to the Sussex shore. When the Prince Regent took to visiting and built for himself the spectacular Royal Pavilion, the new resort's success was assured.

Some fishing villages and minor ports grew gradually into resorts, while others were planned for profit by shrewd local landowners and developers. **Llandudno** on

The splendid onion-domed Brighton Pavilion

the North Wales coast was laid out by the local Mostyn family and remains a charming Victorian resort, lording it over brash **Rhyl** and **Prestatyn**, which were developed later for Lancashire mill-hands. At **Skegness** on the Lincolnshire coast, the Earl of Scarborough built a resort in the 1870s with the intention of attracting the middle classes, but the Great Northern Railway brought hordes of tourists from the Midlands industrial towns and Skegness became a leading blue-collar resort. The first in a chain of Butlin's 'holiday camps' opened there in 1937.

Places with a sandy beach naturally cashed in, as did towns with a mild climate and plenty of summer sunshine. The Thames Estuary resorts of **Margate** and **Southend** enjoy Britain's highest July/August temperatures, followed by those along the south coast from **Torquay** to **Folkestone**. The highest figures for hours of sunshine per day are held by **Sandown** and **Shanklin** on the Isle of Wight.

'So bracing' Health remained a factor—'Skegness Is So Bracing', the posters proclaimed—but sheer fun took precedence as resorts sprouted piers and promenades, amusement parks, cliff railways, zoos, excessively flowery gardens, bandstands, dance halls, freak shows, tattoo parlours, tacky postcards, fortune-tellers' booths, ice-cream and rock kiosks (see panel) to spice up the simpler pleasures of swimming, sunbathing, sand castles and donkey rides. The seaside landlady became a comic cliché, with her iron-bound notions of gentility, strictly regulated mealtimes and green plants in a fussy sitting room. On August Bank Holiday Monday in 1937 more than half a million people swarmed into **Blackpool** in 50,000 motor vehicles and 700 trains, the earliest of which arrived at 3.55am.

Since World War II, with growing affluence, more cars and much longer holidays, patterns have changed. Some people still go faithfully to the same resort every year. Blackpool and Brighton are both going strong, but most British seaside resorts have found themselves unable to compete with the allure of the climate and low prices of package tours abroad. Global warming may, to some extent, help halt the decline as Britain enjoys hotter summers, but the traditional seaside holiday seems increasingly to be a pleasure of the past.

95

Above left: ice-cream and beach huts, Walton on the Naze. Above: just sitting, Brighton Pier

ALL THE WAY THROUGH
A traditional seaside delight is 'rock', a stick of hard mint candy that is usually white in colour with the resort's name in pink letters, mysteriously running through the stick's length. Blackpool and Morecambe both claim to have invented the treat, but there is also a tradition that it originated in the inland industrial town of Dewsbury in the 1860s. As late as the 1970s Blackpool was manufacturing two tonnes of rock a day in the summer.

THE MEDWAY TOWNS

THE MEDWAY TOWNS
The three Medway towns of Rochester, Chatham and Gillingham together form a large industrial sprawl in the north of Kent. The most historic of these is Rochester. Pre-industrial Rochester is compact but impressive, with a medieval cathedral, an absorbing museum within the Guildhall (*Admission free*) and the ruins of a Norman castle (EH) giving mighty panoramas over the River Medway below. The writer Charles Dickens lived in Rochester for a period; the Charles Dickens Centre is in Eastgate House, which features in the *Pickwick Papers* and *The Mystery of Edwin Drood*.

FISHBOURNE'S UNEARTHING
What visitors see at Fishbourne—the mosaics, hypocaust and partition walls—is only one side of a vast palace of AD75, the largest Roman building yet discovered in northern Europe. Part of the rest is under houses and nearby excavations completed in 1999 revealed a military building of similar date to the Roman Conquest in AD43 that some historians believe confirms that the Conquest began at Fishbourne (where local tribes were friendly with the Romans) and not in east Kent as commonly thought.

►► **Chichester**   86A2
(Tourist information tel: 01243 775888; www.visitchichester.org)

The cathedral city for Sussex, Chichester, is based on a simple criss-cross layout focused on a fine 16th-century market cross and, with ancient city walls and handsome Georgian streets, it is an enjoyable place to explore. Its medieval **cathedral►** (early Norman with Early English additions) is unusual—it is not tucked away within its own close and it has a freestanding belfry. The interior has some distinguished modern features: a tapestry by John Piper, a painting by Graham Sutherland and glass by Marc Chagall and unusual older tombs (most famously the medieval Arundel Knight, who breaks with tradition and holds hands with his lady). The **Mechanical Music and Doll Collection** is the most offbeat of the city's museums, while **Pallant House Gallery** specializes in modern British art, displayed within an elegant early 18th-century house.

Fishbourne Roman Palace►►, on the edge of Chichester, is thought to have been built for one Cogidubnus, a Briton who supported the Romans and was made senator. Now much has been re-created, with a dining room, mosaics in full view; remarkably, excavations revealed the exact shape of the bedding trenches in the garden—this has been faithfully replanted and there is a Roman herbarium, with the kinds of plants that would have been familiar to the Romans. (See also panel.)

To the southwest of the town, **Chichester Harbour►** is a big yachting haven. Extending over a huge area, its east side is natural mud flats and complex, marshy inlets. **Bosham** is one of the best places to appreciate the setting: the much-painted village has a picturesque church steeple, waterfront cottages and boating scenes. East Head juts into the south-east corner of the Harbour: here sand dunes and salt marshes make a good setting for an exhilarating stroll. Daily boat tours of the Harbour (in season; also winter bird-watching trips at some weekends) from Itchenor take 1.5 hours (for a recorded timetable tel: 01243 670504; www.chichesterharbourwatertours.co.uk). Due north of Chichester is the **Weald and Downland Open Air Museum►►**, Singleton, a rural museum with more than 45 reconstructed buildings from Kent and Sussex— including a farmhouse, smithy, school and water mill.

A sleepy, unblemished village, much of it thatched, **Amberley►►** is beautifully set beneath the South Downs

Vernacular building styles on show at the Weald and Downland Open Air Museum at Singleton

KINGLEY VALE
Europe's largest yew forest spreads over a shoulder of the South Downs, a wonderful ancient-feeling place, dark and eerie, where trees have collapsed and then continued to grow from their horizontal positions, making a bizarre collection of shapes and forms. A nature trail circles the site (park to the south near West Stoke). The forest's origins are a mystery; could it have been a plantation? Yews were once valued for making bows and arrows.
The view from the Bronze Age bell barrows (burial mounds) on the summit extends over Chichester Harbour.

some 20km (12 miles) northeast of Chichester. Glimpse through the churchyard gate to the 16th-century manor (private) within a massive medieval castle wall, the former residence of bishops of Chichester. It perches on the edge of Amberley Wild Brooks, an area of water meadows known for its rich birdlife and marshland plants. Near the station at the south end of the village, the **Amberley Working Museum▶** has displays of small-scale Sussex industries and crafts, situated in a former chalk pit; here are a blacksmith, potter, woodturner, printer, narrow-gauge railway, vintage buses, wheelwright and even a collection of antique radios. Nearby is the Elizabethan manor house **Parham House▶**, begun in 1577 by Sir Thomas Parham, who later sailed with Sir Francis Drake to Cadiz; its deer park has lakes and a walled garden.

Arundel▶ ▶ is a handsome, compact town. The main street climbs from the canalized River Arun up to the sprawling, much-restored medieval-Victorian **castle▶**— home of the Dukes of Norfolk and their ancestors for more than 700 years—and the nearby superb Roman Catholic **cathedral▶ ▶**. The castle, rich in furnishings and art treasures, is open to the public, as is the adjoining park. At the **Wildfowl and Wetland's Centre▶** (just north of town), you can observe hundreds of geese, swans and ducks at close quarters from specially constructed hides.

To the north, **Bignor Roman Villa▶**, one of Britain's largest Roman houses, has mosaic floors (depicting gladiators, Ganymede and the eagle, etc.). The villa was occupied during the second to fourth centuries. Stane Street, a Roman road now turned into a path, cuts across the downland close by. Its finest section starts from the car park on Bignor Hill (reached by a dead-end lane).

▶ ▶ Dover   87B5

(Tourist information tel: 01304 205108;
www.whitecliffscountry.org.uk)
The major cross-Channel port since Roman times (when it was known as Dubris), Dover has long assumed a military role. It was badly bombed in World War II and redevelopment has been uninspiring—a wasted opportunity, given its cliff and valley setting. But the famous

Chichester: flint walls on St. Richard's Walk

THE CHANNEL TUNNEL
The project to build a link from England to France germinated during Napoleonic times. The final tunnel was completed in 1994 at a cost of £10 billion; **Eurotunnel shuttles** take cars between Folkestone and Calais and the **Eurostar** passenger train runs from London Waterloo to Paris, Lille, Calais and Brussels. The 4.9 million cubic metres (173 million cubic feet) of chalk marl excavated from the tunnel created Samphire Hoe, Britain's newest land—a 30ha (74-acre) coastal grassland beautifully sited beneath the cliff, reached by road tunnel west of Dover.

98

white cliffs (a symbol of homecoming for Britons) still beckon across the Channel. The **castle**▶▶▶(EH), high above the town, stands as one of Britain's finest examples of an intact Norman keep. The views here are superb: Cap Griz Nez on the French coast looks surprisingly near on a clear day. Inside the keep itself are sight- and sound-experiences re-creating the castle under siege in 1216 and during a visit by Henry VIII in 1539. The castle has the longest history of any in the country—wander around with the excellent audio tour and explore the gun emplacements, watch towers and parapets: you will find the Iron Age ramparts, and a Saxon church beside the Pharos, a Roman lighthouse (Britain's tallest Roman building). It is also worth reserving (best on arrival) the tour of the Secret Wartime Tunnels, from where the evacuation of Dunkirk in 1940 was coordinated, and where the wartime telephone exchange, command centre and hospital are preserved. In the middle of town, the major sight is the **Roman Painted House**▶, with its central-heating system and painted walls. For more local history, **Dover Museum** has a comprehensive range, including a Bronze Age boat, the world's oldest seagoing vessel.

Deal and Walmer▶ are both on the coast to the north of Dover and both have castles (EH) built by Henry VIII in the plan of a Tudor rose. Walmer is all neat houses looking over a stony beach; Deal has a pretty ex-fishermen's quarter of narrow streets.

Eastbourne's Victorian pier

▶ **Eastbourne**   *87A4*
(Tourist information tel: 01323 411400; www.eastbourne.org)
A town of genteel hotels and brass bands on the promenade, Eastbourne is a well preserved example of a 19th-century English seaside resort. The South Downs end in style just west of Eastbourne at **Beachy Head** and the **Seven Sisters**▶▶▶. There is a drop of 160m (525ft) at Beachy Head, the chalk cliffs towering above a lighthouse. Farther west, the Seven Sisters are a series of dry valleys chopped off by the sea to form a roller-coaster cliff. There is access to the coastal path at **Birling Gap** and at the **Seven Sisters Country Park** by Cuckmere Haven. Beware of the unfenced edge.

Alfriston▶▶ has a concentration of tile-hung and timber houses, cafés and antiques shops. The 14th-century Clergy House (NT) was the first building acquired by the National

THE FIRST CROSS-CHANNEL FLIGHT
The cliff walk northeast from Dover passes Blériot's monument, commemorating the first powered flight across the Channel. Louis Blériot (1872–1936), whose early flying experiments included towing gliders along the River Seine, made the historic flight from Calais to Dover on 25 July 1909.

Trust and is a half-timbered house with original clay floor. Adjacent, the church, dubbed the Cathedral of the Downs, has 14th-century features. The street also has two fine inns, the Star and the George and the stump of a market cross is a memento of busier days. Nearby and best seen from south of Wilmington village is the **Long Man of Wilmington**▶▶, a chalk carving on the downs of a man bearing a staff in either hand. It could be Anglo-Saxon or earlier, although no written record before the 18th century has been found. East along the coast is **Pevensey Castle**▶ (EH). Its fourth-century Roman walls enclose a medieval castle and Norman keep, damaged in the Civil War. William the Conqueror landed nearby in 1066 to launch his invasion of England (see panel).

▶ Hastings 87A4

(Tourist information tel: 01424 781111; www.hastings.gov.uk)
Dramatically hilly, Hastings is a mixture of a faded seaside resort and an old fishing port. The picturesque, warren-like **old town** lies in a valley to the east; the former fishermen's quarter lies close to tall wooden sheds, called deezes, built for storing fishing nets, and there are caves and a castle to visit. Pleasant walks onto the sandstone cliffs extend east to **Fairlight Cove** along a wild coastline. A **funicular** (Britain's steepest) hauls you up the slope of the old town.

Battle▶▶ (see panels) is a handsome small town, famed for **Battle Abbey and 1066 Battlefield**▶▶(EH); the medieval Almonry houses the **Town Model**, and the **Battle Museum of Local History** and **Buckleys Yesterday's World** (period shop and room displays) justify a full day's visit.

Bodiam Castle▶▶(NT), 19km (12 miles) inland from Hastings, dates from the 14th century—surrounded by a wide moat filled with water lilies and with walls at their original height. A visit can be combined with a steam-hauled ride on the **Kent and East Sussex Railway** to Tenterden.

▶▶ Historic Dockyard Chatham, The 87C4

(tel: 01634 823800, or for 24-hour recorded information: 01634 823807; www.chdt.org.uk)
The historic naval dockyard incorporates Britain's largest concentration of listed buildings. The site includes lifeboats, a shipbuilding exhibition, warehouses, a rope works, shipbuilding sheds, a museum and three warships—a destroyer, a submarine and a Victorian sloop. Combined with Rochester (see panel, page 96), this makes an excellent day out (speedy train services from London).

THE BATTLE OF HASTINGS
The best-known date in British history is 1066, when the Battle of Hastings between William of Normandy and King Harold took place at Battle (as it is now called). Oddly, the great turning point in English history was a surprisingly haphazard affair: the English should have trounced the Normans, who were vastly outnumbered and fighting uphill. However, the English made a strategic blunder in storming downhill when they thought some of the Normans were retreating; the Normans turned round and slaughtered their opponents. The Norman victory is lucidly explained in the battlefield audio tour.

99

BATTLE ABBEY
William I, 'the Conqueror', vowed that if he was victorious he would found an abbey here, on the battlefield where he defeated Harold's English forces; the high altar marks the spot where Harold is said to have fallen, pierced in the eye with a Frenchman's arrow. Today a battlefield trail and an audiovisual display detail the story of the battle. Of the abbey, the gatehouse of 1338 and the oast range are still intact.

Low tide at Birling Gap gives greater access to the beach below the brilliant-white Seven Sisters cliffs, which are slowly being eroded back

Southern England

The Royal Yacht Squadron has its headquarters at Cowes

ISLAND HOUSES
Osborne House (EH) was built as a retreat for Queen Victoria, in 1845 and she died here in 1901. The State Apartments provide a rewarding insight into Victoria's lifestyle.

Dating from the 18th century, **Appuldurcombe House** (EH) stands as a spooky skeleton, with a triumphal gateway to nowhere in its Capability Brown-landscaped grounds.

100

THE TENNYSON CONNECTION
Alfred, Lord Tennyson lived at Farringford Park House (now a hotel) near Freshwater Bay; his Victorian fan club (autograph hunters and all) tracked him down here and he is still remembered by the monument on Tennyson Down.

Cowes High Street

►► Isle of Wight   86A1-A2

(Tourist information tel: 01983 813818; www.islandbreaks.co.uk)

Just 3km (2 miles) over the Solent from the mainland at its nearest point, the diamond-shaped island is reached by ferry' catamaran or hovercraft from Portsmouth (landing in Ryde and Fishbourne), Southsea (landing in Ryde), Southampton (landing in Cowes), or Lymington (landing in Yarmouth). Although developed, the isle has plenty of scenic variety, with chalk downs and splendid coastal cliffs. Public transport is excellent; many visitors leave their cars on the mainland.

On the south coast, grassy whaleback hills provide outstanding views for walkers; at the western end of **Tennyson Down►►** (see Walks, page 92) is a set of chalk pinnacles known as **The Needles**. Close by, the multihued sands of **Alum Bay** are sold in souvenir glass bottles of every shape and size. The island's southernmost point, **St. Catherine's Point►**, has a lighthouse dating from 1840 open to visitors; St. Catherine's Hill is capped by an oratory in the tower of a 14th-century chapel. Farther north, **Yarmouth►** is the most appealing town on the island, a pretty spot with whitewashed cottages and one of the numerous forts (EH) built by Henry VIII to defend the Solent. The coast and rivers have some attractive marshy landscapes, as found along the **River Yar** and **Newtown Estuary**.

The east coast is mostly developed: **Ryde**, **Shanklin**, **Sandown** and **Bembridge** are good spots for low-key holidays. **Dinosaur Isle** in Sandown claims to be one of the biggest exhibitions on the subject. Shanklin has preserved its old village near **Shanklin Chine**, a gorge leading to the sea with a nature trail and other attractions. **Cowes** has a sailing boat atmosphere; in late June the Round the Island Yacht Race features more than a thousand competitors and in August Cowes hosts a regatta. **Ventnor** snuggles beneath an undercliff and has a subtropical **Botanic Garden►►**.

Near Newport, **Carisbrooke Castle►►** (EH) is a well-preserved Norman shell, with rooms dating from 1470; Charles I spent time here pending his execution. The castle has Britain's only surviving donkey wheel, used to haul water from a deep well. **Godshill** is a pretty village of stone and thatch; its church has a rare 15th-century wall painting.

▶ New Forest National Park 86A1

(Lyndhurst tourist information tel: 023-8028 2269;
www.thenewforest.co.uk)

Britain's most recently created national park, the New Forest has survived into the 21st century surprisingly intact. Established in 1079 as a hunting forest for Norman royalty, it still feels incredibly remote. Essentially it is a tract of lowland heath and mixed forest; it is perfect for walking, camping and picnicking. There are no major hills, but there is enough variety to spark interest; it tends to be more open on the west side. Wild ponies and red deer are commonly seen; the former graze on heathlands and are owned by commoners with historic grazing rights. The **New Forest Museum** at Lyndhurst sets the scene.

Lined with conifers, the **Bolderwood** and **Rhinefield ornamental drives▶** are forest drives; species include giant fir, redwood and swamp cypress. Lord Montagu's **National Motor Museum▶▶** at **Beaulieu**, the finest collection of its kind, celebrates the golden age of automobiles; nearby are **Beaulieu Abbey▶** (founded 1204) and **Palace House▶** (the abbey gatehouse), Montagu's stately home (complete with monorail and vintage bus rides). **Buckler's Hard▶** is a nautical hamlet; the story of this former boat-building village is told in its Maritime Museum. **Exbury Gardens** includes outstanding azaleas, rhododendrons, magnolias and camelias, which can be viewed from the narrow-gauge steam railway.

Rhinefield, in the New Forest

101

▶▶ Petworth 86B2

(tel: 01798 342207; www.nationaltrust.org.uk/petworth)

This grand, late 17th-century mansion (NT), built by the Duke of Somerset, has been Percy family property since Norman times. Today the National Trust maintains its interior, which includes virtuoso woodcarving and a collection of paintings unsurpassed by any other National Trust property; there are works by Turner, Blake, Rembrandt, Reynolds and others. The grounds, landscaped by Capability Brown, offer delightful walks. Petworth town (tourist information tel: 01798 343523) lies next to the house; the old streets are most attractive, but suffer appallingly from traffic.

SQUATTERS' RIGHTS
A few scattered thatched hamlets are found in New Forest clearings. Typically such settlements owe their origins to squatters' rights, whereby common land could be occupied by anyone building a house within one day, provided smoke was seen to be rising from the chimney by dusk.

The counties of Kent, West Sussex, East Sussex and Surrey boast a remarkably varied range of houses that are open to the public. Many of those described below make pleasant day-trips from London. Several are included in the Drive on pages 106–107. Some houses may be closed during the winter months, so it is always worth checking on opening times with local tourist authorities.

THE NATIONAL TRUST (NT)

The National Trust is a major landowner; it was formed in 1895 to safeguard Britain's places of historic interest and natural beauty. Property it acquires is held in trust for the nation. Many of the NT's hundreds of country houses, gardens and other places of interest are open to the public. Cards giving free admission to any property are available, on payment of a membership fee, from these and from NT information points, or by post from PO Box 39, Warrington WA5 7WD; or tel: 0870 458 4000. Most properties close in winter. Membership also gives you free entry to properties owned by the National Trust for Scotland (NTS), based at Wemyss House, 28 Charlotte Square, Edinburgh EH2 4ET, tel: 0131-243 9300. In this book, NT and NTS denote staffed properties that charge entrance fees. Websites: www.nationaltrust.org.uk (NT); www.nts.org.uk (NTS).

The Italian Garden at Hever Castle: part of Astor's 20th-century design

102

Towards Tonbridge, **Penshurst Place**▶▶, Penshurst, Kent, lies amid charming lowland countryside, an outstanding example of 14th-century domestic architecture owned by the Sidney family, Earls of Leicester, whose forebears include Sir Philip Sidney, the Elizabethan poet. It has a splendid hall with a chestnut ceiling and a fine, long gallery. Nearby **Hever Castle**▶▶, Hever, Kent, was the birthplace of Anne Boleyn, second wife of Henry VIII. The moated Tudor house owes much of its present appearance to the 20th-century renovation by William Waldorf Astor, a wealthy American. He added mock-medieval features and laid out delightful grounds with great avenues of chestnuts and lindens, a yew maze, yew topiary in the form of chessmen and an Italian garden filled with sculpture. Some 8km (5 miles) north, **Chartwell**▶▶(NT), near Westerham, Kent, was Sir Winston Churchill's home from 1922 until his death in 1965. The house appears as it was when Churchill and his family lived here, a comfortable place filled with mementoes of one of the great men of the 20th century. General Wolfe, general of the British army at the capture of Quebec from the French, was born in 1726 at **Quebec House**▶(NT), Westerham, Kent, close by; an exhibition illustrates the campaign that led to British supremacy in Canada.

Charles Darwin lived the last 40 years of his life at **Down House**▶▶(EH) near Downe, Kent. Here he wrote his seminal work *On the Origin of Species* (1859), the book that changed mainstream thinking on evolution. The rooms are set up as in Darwin's day, and you can imagine the great man ensconced in his study or thinking his theories through on his regular walks in the garden.

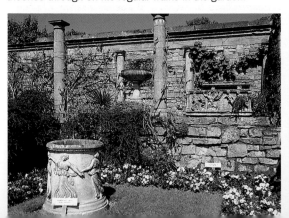

Immediately southeast of Sevenoaks, Kent, **Knole▶▶▶**(NT) is England's largest house, with 365 rooms, 7 courtyards and 52 corridors; little has been altered since the early 17th century. A former archbishop's palace which later fell into the hands of Henry

VIII, Knole has been in the hands of the Sackvilles from the time of Elizabeth I. The huge deer park is always open to the public. **Ightham Mote▶▶▶**(NT), near Shipbourne, Kent, is a 14th-century moated building of great character, with a Tudor chapel with painted ceiling, a splendid Great Hall and a 14th-century chapel and crypt.

Close by the North Downs in northern Kent, **Owletts▶** (NT), near Cobham, is a restrained red-brick 17th-century house, which boasts a plasterwork ceiling and a staircase of the same period. Do not miss the collection of memorial brasses in nearby Cobham Church. Near the village of Shoreham in Kent's Darent Valley, **Lullingstone Castle▶** is a Tudor and Queen Anne family mansion with state rooms and one of the earliest brick gateways (c1497) in the country; a visit can be combined with Lullingstone Roman Villa (see walk on page 92).

Leeds Castle▶▶▶, to the east of Maidstone, Kent, was once a residence of Henry VIII but is not as genuine a stately home as some: the furniture and contents were later brought in with the aim of re-creating a country house; but the grounds and building themselves are real enough and the place has warmth and an idyllic lake setting. About 20km (12 miles) south near Goudhurst, Kent (not far from **Sissinghurst**, see Gardens, page 17), is **Finchcocks▶▶**, an early Georgian house noted for its collection of keyboard instruments. Be sure to catch the demonstration, where the owner gives a witty talk and plays some of the instruments. Some 20km (12 miles) south again at Burwash, East Sussex, is **Bateman's▶**(NT), the 17th-century house where author Rudyard Kipling lived from 1902 to 1936 and completed *Puck of Pook's Hill* and *Rewards and Fairies*. The mill next door houses one of the oldest water-driven turbines, still grinding flour for sale. Kipling's 1928 Rolls-Royce is on display.

Standen▶(NT), near East Grinstead, West Sussex, is a delightful Arts and Crafts house, designed in the 1890s by Philip Webb, a friend of leading artist-craftsman William Morris. It still has its original electric light fittings and has a collection of ceramics by William de Morgan.

The Arcadian beauty of Penshurst Place, famed for its medieval Baron's Hall

THE WEALDEN FORESTS
The Weald has not always been the countryside of fine mansions, charming villages, rich farms and hop-fields that we see today. In centuries gone by, it was deeply forested, its oaks supplying the timber that built the British navy. The trees were also felled by charcoal burners to smelt the Sussex iron. Patches of this ancient forest remain, in the forests of St. Leonards and Ashdown.

Southern England

Nelson's flagship, HMS Victory

PORTSMOUTH'S HISTORIC SHIPS

HMS *Victory* was Lord Nelson's flagship at Trafalgar and is still in commission (thus crewed by serving officers). Henry VIII's splendid battleship, the *Mary Rose*, keeled over on leaving port in 1545, in sight of the king. In 1982 the wreck was brought to the surface and is now kept under special conditions, an intriguing time capsule of Tudor life. HMS *Warrior 1860* was the world's first iron-hulled warship, now restored to its former glory. There is a separate admission charge for each ship (or combined tickets) but visitors are free to walk around the dockyard.

FORTIFICATIONS AT PORTSMOUTH

Among those which can be visited are Southsea Castle, built in 1544, which still has tunnels (exhibits include fish-bone ship models made by Napoleonic prisoners of war); Spitbank Fort, out to sea and reached by a short boat trip, with a labyrinth of passages; and Fort Nelson (*Admission free*) at Fareham. In 1944 Portsmouth was the nerve centre of the Normandy invasion and in 1982 the South Atlantic Task Force was prepared here for battle in the Falklands War.

Church Square, Rye

▶▶▶ Portsmouth 86A2
(Tourist information tel: 023-9282 6722; www.portsmouthand.co.uk)

A sprawling port and industrial city, heavily bombarded in World War II, Portsmouth is unique among British towns in being built on its own island. This has been a naval base since the 12th century and in 1495 was host to the world's first dry dock. For the visitor, Portsmouth rates alongside Greenwich (see page 46) as the place for finding out about Britain's maritime history.

The **Historic Dockyard▶▶▶**, close to Portsmouth Harbour station, is the chief attraction, where a trio of famous warships are berthed (see panel). The **Royal Naval Museum** (*Admission charge* separate, or combined with ticket for historic ships and other attractions in the dockyard) charts naval history from 1485 to the Falklands War and features the Trafalgar campaign and the Siege of Malta. **Port cruises** operate between April and October, weather permitting. For the Millennium, Portsmouth smartened up its waterside, with an ambitious shopping and entertainment complex at **Gunwharf Quays**, public promenades along each waterside and the futuristic 170m (560ft) **Spinnaker Tower**.

To the east lies **Southsea**, an Edwardian coastal resort, where the **D-Day Museum▶** commemorates the Allied invasion of Normandy on 6 June 1944, with the sights and sounds of Britain at war and the 80m (260ft) Overlord Embroidery (a latter-day Bayeux Tapestry). The **Royal Marines Museum** within a grandiose Victorian building that formerly served as the officers' mess, traces the 300-year history of the Marines. Also in Southsea, the **Blue Reef Aquarium** has a ceiling-high 'window onto the ocean'.

Elsewhere in town are **Charles Dickens' Birthplace Museum** (Commercial Road), where the writer was born in 1812; **Portchester Castle▶▶** (EH), originally a Roman stronghold with remains of a Norman church and a palace built by Richard II; and the **City Museum and Records Office** (Museum Road) with old shopfronts and more.

▶▶▶ Rye 87B4
(Tourist information tel: 01797 226696; www.visitrye.co.uk)

This small town of cobblestones and half-timbered houses perches on a rise above Romney Marsh. Mermaid Street is one of the prettiest thoroughfares in southeast England. Once a Cinque Port (see panel, page 105), Rye now lies inland by some 3km (2 miles). In medieval times the town was frequently attacked by the French, who set fire to it in 1377; the **Ypres Tower** is a rare pre-fire survivor and together with the **Rye Castle Museum** (another branch is in East Street) has local history displays. Medieval Landgate guards what was once the only landward entrance. The Gun Garden below looks down the River Rother to Rye Harbour. The novelists Henry James and E. F. Benson lived at Lamb House (NT) at different times; many of Benson's Mapp and Lucia stories are set in Rye.

To the northeast lies **Romney Marsh▶**. The sea has receded leaving the marsh, now drained, and fertile farmland grazed by chunky Romney sheep. Inland the Royal Military Canal, built in Napoleonic times, runs beneath the escarpment marking the old Saxon shore. Romney Marsh is sparsely populated but has some good medieval churches, including the drunkenly askew church at **Brookland**, with its freestanding belfry. **Camber Sands** has the biggest sandy beach in the southeast; a cycle path from Rye avoids the summer traffic.

Winchelsea▶▶ is a quiet hilltop village just southeast of Rye, still ranged around its medieval grid plan, with many handsome old houses and a superb church. The original town was much plundered by the French in the 14th and 15th centuries. Three town gates survive.

Beyond Romney Marsh, the **Romney, Hythe and Dymchurch Railway** (tel: 01797 362353 for schedule), a mere 38cm (15in) gauge, runs along the coast between the picturesque hillside town of **Hythe** (there's a bizarre collection of human skulls in the church crypt) and **Dungeness**, a most surreal place, where fishermen's shacks and converted train carriages crouch on a vast rocky bank beneath the shadow of Dungeness B nuclear power station.

▶▶ Sandwich   87B5

(Tourist information tel: 01304 613565;
www.whitecliffscountry.org.uk)

Though it is of modest size, Sandwich has a remarkably intact medieval centre, all the better for being off the tourist beat. Take a walk beside the river on the earth ramparts, visiting the Barbican, a toll bridge-cum-gateway. **Richborough Roman Fort▶** (EH) was erected after the Roman invasion of AD 43 and a busy town once existed here, dominated by a huge arch that greeted Roman legions at this threshold to Britain. The entrance fee includes an informative audio tour.

THE CINQUE PORTS
During the reign of Edward the Confessor (1042–66) a confederation of Channel ports was formed to defend the coast and for 300 years these Cinque Ports (French for 'five ports') had the monopoly on supplying ships and men for the royal fleet, enjoying privileges in return. The original five ports—Sandwich, Hastings, Hythe, New Romney and Dover—were later joined by Winchelsea and Rye and several other towns were also attached. After the 14th century, as ports silted up and the coastline shifted, the Cinque Ports declined in importance. Today, only Dover is an active port.

105

MARTELLO TOWERS
A feature of the Kent and Sussex coasts is the string of 74 Martello towers (of a type formerly widespread in Europe and named after Cape Mortella in Corsica, where the British Navy captured such a tower in 1794), built 1805–12 to resist a possible French invasion; some are derelict, others are converted to private houses; English Heritage maintains one at Dymchurch, in Romney Marsh (Kent) which opens occasionally (tel: 01304 211067).

Fishing boats on the beach at Dungeness

THE WEALD

The Pantiles, an attractive shopping area in Tunbridge Wells

Drive

The Weald

Starting at Tunbridge Wells, this is a circular tour of approximately 110km (68 miles). You'll see the weather-boarded and pantile-hung cottages, the undulating woodlands and farmland of the Weald and you can visit a host of country houses and attractive gardens. Allow at least a day if you plan to stop at all the places mentioned.

Start at **Tunbridge Wells▶**, a very pleasant old spa town with echoes of its 18th-century heyday (evoked in the exhibition 'A Day at the Wells'), including the delightful Pantiles, a Regency arcade. Leave by the A26, but soon fork right and then left to pass **High Rocks▶**, a popular place for climbers.

At **Groombridge** take the B2188 which rises onto the sandy heathlands of the **Ashdown Forest▶**, the

landscape of A. A. Milne's much-loved *Winnie-the-Pooh* stories (see walk on page 92). Detour south along the B2026—just before the next road intersection, Camp Hill on the right offers a fine viewpoint.

Return north along the B2026 through **Hartfield** and turn off past Cowden railway station to follow back lanes to **Penshurst▶▶**, known for its great house (see page 102) and picturesque cottages.

Continue on the B2176 and then a minor road to **Chiddingstone▶**, where a splendid half-timbered group of buildings owned by the National Trust includes the Castle Inn, named for being close to an eye-catching Gothic castle.

Weave around minor lanes past **Chartwell▶▶** (NT), Churchill's former house (see page 102), through pretty **Ide Hill** village, with its spacious green, around the south side of **Knole Park▶▶▶** (NT) and close to **Ightham Mote▶▶▶** (NT; see page 103).

Return to Tunbridge Wells via **Plaxtol** and **Beltring**, where oast houses mark the site of the **Hop Farm Country Park**, with its displays on the hop industry, shire horses and military vehicles.

King Arthur's 'Round Table'

▶▶▶ Winchester 86B1

(Tourist information tel: 01962 840500; www.visitwinchester.co.uk)

The capital of Saxon England, Winchester became a major religious and commercial hub in medieval times. Its importance has ebbed, but its medieval core is well preserved. Its college is one of Britain's great public schools.

Visitors often spend most of their time in the vicinity of the **cathedral▶▶▶**, the longest medieval cathedral in

WINCHESTER COLLEGE

Students of Winchester College, one of the country's leading 'public' schools (see panel on Eton College, page 109), are known as Wykehamists, harkening to its 14th-century foundation by the Bishop of Winchester, William of Wykeham. Seventy scholars were taught classics and other disciplines here before studying at New College, Oxford (another Wykeham foundation). The school probably was used as a model for Eton College, founded by Henry VI. Both have quadrangles, a chapel and a hall.

108

THE WATERCRESS LINE

Also known as the Mid-Hants Railway, the privately owned 16km (10-mile) railway runs through the Hampshire countryside from Alresford to Alton (where it connects with the main railway line), giving a good idea of train travel in the age of steam. The carriages were formerly used by British Rail, the staff dress in period costume and the stations look and feel right. The watercress beds which gave the line its nickname can still be seen around Alresford and watercress soup is served on the line's weekend dining trains. For details, tel: 01962 733810; www.watercressline.co.uk.

Winchester Cathedral contains the remains of Canute, successor to King Alfred

Europe. It has an outstanding Norman crypt, much Perpendicular work and monuments to Jane Austen and to Isaak Walton, of *Compleat Angler* fame; the chantry of William Wykeham, who funded restoration work, is perhaps the finest monument of all. Walton resided in No. 7 in the **cathedral close**, a charming precinct abutted by the flying buttresses of the cathedral and by the rambling half-timbered Cheyney Court (dating from 1148). Close by is the **City Museum**▶ (*Admission free*), with a strong Roman section.

The **High Street** and **Broadway** have been the main axis of the city since Roman times. At the top end, **West Gate** (*Closed* Nov–Jan. *Admission free*), one of two surviving city gates, occupies a Roman site; a small museum upstairs has a drawing of Wren's scheme for a royal palace (which never got off the ground). Nearby is **The Great Hall** (*Admission free*), where hangs 'King Arthur's Round Table', which lists the names of all his knights but is actually a resplendent medieval fake made about 700 years after his death. Down along Broadway is a 1901 **statue of King Alfred**, King of Wessex, who is buried nearby and the Abbey Gardens, a quiet haven close to the Gothic revival **guildhall** (1871) housing an **art gallery** and the Tourist Information Centre.

The half-timbered **Winchester City Mill** (NT) straddles the River Itchen nearby. On **College Street**, a plaque records the house in which Jane Austen died in 1817, aged 42. **Winchester College**▶ (*Guided tours*) has a 'quad' like those found at the colleges of Oxford and Cambridge universities. **Wolvesey Castle**▶ (EH), a gaunt shell of a bishop's palace built in 1132 and dismantled by Parliamentarians in the Civil War, stands next to elegant **Wolvesey Palace** (1684), which superseded it.

A 15- to 20-minute walk along the riverside meadows to the south brings you to **The Hospital of St. Cross**▶▶, founded in 1136 as a charitable almshouse institution, an extraor-dinary time-warp place with cloistered seclusion, a fine Norman chapel and an antiquated kitchen. By an ancient rule of the charitable trust, Wayfarer's Dole— bread and ale—is still given to anyone who asks for it specifically.

On the banks of the River Test, 16km (10 miles) southwest of Winchester, is the small town of **Romsey**, well worth a visit for its wonderful Norman **abbey church**▶▶, built mainly in the 12th century by Henry de Blois, Bishop of Winchester and with Saxon sculptures among its treasures.

Eton College rowers with Windsor Castle beyond

TOO INNOVATIVE FOR SOME
Windsor's 17th-century guildhall, started by Sir Robert Fitch and completed by Sir Christopher Wren, needed no structural columns beneath its raised floor. The alarmed town burghers insisted that Wren supply some; this he did, but he deliberately built them too short, to prove they were actually unnecessary.

▶▶▶ Windsor and Eton 86C2

(Tourist information tel: 01753 743900; www.windsor.gov.uk)

The two towns are a short walk apart, separated only by the Thames. Although within easy reach of London by train, Windsor and Eton demand a very full day if you want to get around all of the sights. Visitors often tie in a trip to the gardens at **Wisley▶▶** (see page 16).

Windsor is dominated by **Windsor Castle▶▶▶**, Europe's largest, a royal family residence which opens its doors to visitors. The castle dates from the 12th century, but was extended over the next 700 years and was restored following a massive fire in 1992. St. George's Chapel (begun in the 15th century by Edward IV and a superb example of the Perpendicular style, with a fan-vaulted aisle and three-tier stalls), the State Apartments and the extraordinarily detailed Queen Mary's Dolls' House are high points. During the restoration, parts of the building were re-discovered, including an undercroft and medieval well. Guided tours of the castle precincts are included in the admission charge (ticket sales and information tel: 020-7766 7304).

Another royal site is **Frogmore House** (*Open* occasionally; tel: 020-7766 7305), the 17th-century home of Queen Charlotte and Queen Victoria's mother and the burial place of Victoria herself, alongside Prince Albert. **Windsor Park▶▶** is worth exploring on foot (there is public access to most of it), with follies, lakes and a totem pole to discover. **Legoland Windsor** theme park includes a Lego driving school, rides and a miniature re-creation of Amsterdam, London, Brussels and Paris; advance booking advised (tel: 08705 040404; www.legoland.co.uk).

Over the river lies **Eton**, its main street fronted by **Eton College▶▶** (see panel; tours given). Eton was founded in 1440 by Henry VI. The chapel is a fine example of the Perpendicular style. The quad looks like an Oxford University college. Entrance to the college includes admission to the Museum of Eton Life.

From **Windsor**, boat trips run to **Boveney Lock** in the **Thames Valley▶▶**. At **Maidenhead**, villas and gardens back onto the river. **Cookham▶** was immortalized by the artist Stanley Spencer; a gallery has a number of his works. **Henley-on-Thames▶** is famed for its Royal Regatta, first rowed in 1839; the **River and Rowing Museum** gives the full story.

ETON COLLEGE
This is the most famous of Britain's public schools (that is those prestigious private, fee-paying establishments whose headmasters attend the Headmasters' Conference: they are actually quite independent of the state system). The high street has numerous barbers and tailors; one of them, T. Brown, has changed little over the years. Here, boys are fitted out at the start of term in long-tailed jackets and wing collars. 'Old Etonians' include William Gladstone (19th-century prime minster), George Blair (real name Eric Blair; author of *1984*), Ian Fleming (author of the James Bond books) and Thomas Arne (composer of *Rule Britannia*).

THE HEART OF ENGLAND This is a region that reflects, as deeply as any other, that elusively diverse nature of the English landscape: for it includes both the Cotswolds, the epitome of rural England, and the industrial 'Black Country', the economic hub of the Midlands.

THE WEST MIDLANDS AND THE BLACK COUNTRY The Midlands is a nebulous term, often applied to the central industrial manufacturing belt encompassing the cities of Birmingham, Wolverhampton, Coventry, Leicester, Derby, Stoke-on-Trent and Nottingham (some of which fall out-side the scope of this chapter). Most first-time visitors to Britain would give the bulk of the area a miss, but there is plenty of interest in the cityscapes, industrial sights, museums and even areas of unspoiled countryside.

The county of **West Midlands** encompasses the so-called Black Country, dominated by the conurbation of

Eastnor, below the Malvern Hills

Wolverhampton, West Bromwich and others, much of which developed in the 19th century through the exploitation of coal and iron deposits. Some towns developed specialized industries—leather in Walsall, glass in Stourbridge and locks in Willenhall. The industrial heritage is celebrated at the Black Country Living Museum in Dudley (see page 20), and at the Leather Museum in Walsall.

To the east the conurbation merges into **Birmingham** (nicknamed 'Brum'), England's second city, and at first sight an unappealing jungle of motorway overpasses and suburban and industrial sprawl. However, in the last decade or so a remarkable renaissance has come about in its central area, with a new lease of life for its canalside buildings and its Jewellery Quarter as well as its civic and industrial heritage, while the National Exhibition Centre (NEC) and International Convention Centre (ICC) bring in many business visitors. The heaths and woodlands of Cannock Chase and the modest heights of the Clent Hills have pleasant walks just outside the built-up area. East of Birmingham, **Coventry** had its heart knocked out by bombing in 1940, and the ruins of its medieval cathedral stand beside Basil Spence's innovative postwar replacement—endowed with some striking modern art, including glass by John Piper and a huge tapestry by Graham Sutherland. This city too has been imaginatively revived, with the completion of the Phoenix Initiative in 2004 (see page 185), to make a striking balance of old and new.

THE ENGLISH MARCHES Shropshire, **Herefordshire** and **Worcestershire** encompass much in the way of unspoiled countryside, black-and-white and red-brick villages, and the assertive south Shropshire Hills; it is ideal for those who like to make their own discoveries. To the west it adjoins the even lesser-known, and much less populated, Welsh Marches or borderlands. Only the pleasant market town of Ludlow and Ironbridge Gorge, birthplace of the Industrial Revolution, are firmly on the tourist trail; Shrewsbury, Hereford, and numerous smaller towns and villages such as Much Wenlock and Ledbury are well-kept secrets. Walkers may like to head for the hills around Church Stretton and for the Malvern Hills. The russet-earthed territory of rural Herefordshire, its pastures grazed by docile Hereford cattle, is amiably sleepy and has a wealth of half-timbered 'black and white' buildings as well as several outstanding churches, some tucked well away. **Worcestershire** has the cathedral city of Worcester for its showpiece.

THE COTSWOLDS AND THEIR FRINGES East of the fruit and vegetable heartlands of the Vale of Evesham, the buildings change hue dramatically as one climbs up into the **Cotswold Hills** (mostly belonging to **Gloucestershire** and **Oxfordshire**). Its honey-yellow stone villages and towns have enchanted generations of visitors; the area is rich in both places to visit and hotels.

Non Cotswold Gloucestershire includes Gloucester, Cheltenham, and the lowlands abutting the Severn Estuary, the final stages of Britain's longest river. On a waterside site, the naturalist Peter Scott set up the celebrated wildfowl reserve at Slimbridge. In the Forest of Dean, once a coal and charcoal producing area, the villages are not particularly attractive, but there are verdant walks, including the Sculpture Trail (west of Cinderford). The Lower Wye Valley (see under Wales) is close at hand.

The fringes of the Cotswolds have some of the best attractions of central England, including Oxford, Blenheim Palace and Shakespeare's Stratford-upon-Avon. These are close enough to London for day-trips. Notable arrays of stately homes and manor houses open to the public are found in **Warwickshire** (Baddesley Clinton (NT), Charlecote Park (NT), Coughton Court (NT), Farnborough Hall (NT), Kenilworth Castle, Packwood House (NT), Upton House (NT), Warwick Castle) and **Buckinghamshire** (Chenies Manor, Chicheley Hall, Claydon House (NT), Nancy Astor's Cliveden, Dorney Court, Disraeli's Hughenden Manor (NT), West Wycombe Park, and above all the Rothschilds' properties—Ascott (NT), Mentmore Towers and Waddesdon Manor (NT)). Closer to the capital lie the **Chiltern Hills**, whose gently rolling chalk hills and majestic beech woods have been preserved by Green Belt legislation and whose villages look distinctly prosperous.

There are old musical instruments at Snowshill Manor as well as a collection of Japanese Samurai items, toys and bicycles

113

OXFORD ALUMNI
Oxford University's many notable graduates include Sir William Walton (composer) and Lewis Carroll (author), both at Christ Church College; T. S. Eliot (poet), Merton College; Oscar Wilde (playwright) and Sir John Betjeman (poet), both Magdalen College; and T. E. Lawrence ('Lawrence of Arabia'), Jesus College.

Birmingham Museum and Art Gallery

▶▶ Birmingham

110C2

(Tourist information tel: 0121 202 5099; www.beinbirmingham.com)

England's second city, one of the largest manufacturing hubs in the country and a major convention venue, is undergoing a dramatic facelift (trying to rid its image of

SOHO HOUSE

Situated in Soho Avenue off Soho Road, in Handsworth, north of central Birmingham (buses 40X, 74, 78, 79, 440 and 616), Soho House (*Open* Apr–Oct. *Admission free*) was, from 1766 to 1809, the home of Matthew Boulton, one of the industrial pioneers of his day. He set up a huge manufactory (where buckles, buttons, Sheffield plate, silver and ormulu objects were made) and mint and, with James Watt, developed the steam engine. Eminent scientific luminaries from the Lunar Society met here and the house became a hotbed of scientific thought. His house has been preserved; it boasted such comforts as central heating and a water closet.

1960s brutalist architecture and run-down streetscapes). At its heart, Victoria Square speaks of civic pride, with its domed Victorian Council House (city hall), at the back of which is the **Birmingham Museum and Art Gallery▶▶** (*Admission free*), with one of the world's greatest collections of Pre-Raphaelite paintings, plus superb fossils, silverware and wooden marquetry. A walk west from here leads into Centenary Square, flanked by Symphony Hall, which is the home of the City of Birmingham Symphony Orchestra. Off Inge Street the National Trust has restored the city's last remaining courtyard of **Back to Back Houses**; displays tell of life here between 1840 and 1977.

The canals are part of the city's renaissance, with a blend of restored Victorian buildings and gleaming new blocks; along the canals are the fish-shaped **National Sea Life Centre▶**, with aquatic life from the River Severn displayed imaginatively and the **Gas Street Basin**, with narrowboats moored near waterside pubs. To the north, the Jewellery Quarter has some 4,000 workshops and more than 100 shops; the **Museum of the Jewellery Quarter▶▶** (*Open* Apr–Oct. *Admission free*) includes a tour of Smith and Pepper's workshops, little changed since starting business in 1899—(see panel, page 115).

At The University of Birmingham, the **Barber Institute of Fine Arts**▶ ▶ (*Admission free;* train from New Street station to University) is a choice collection with many great artists represented. **Aston Hall**▶ ▶ (*Open* Apr–Oct. *Admission free*), after which Aston Villa Football Club is named, is a splendid Jacobean mansion of 1618–35.

At Bourneville, the Cadbury family set up their chocolate factory in 1879 and near the original village built for workers is **Cadbury World**▶ (booking recommended, tel: 0121 451 4159; www.cadburyworld.co.uk)—not a factory tour, but you see chocolates being made by hand and are allowed to sample the result; there is also a museum.

▶ ▶ ▶ Blenheim Palace   111A3

(tel: 01993 811325 or 0870 602080 (recorded information); www.blenheimpalace.com)

The finest baroque house in Britain, Blenheim is palatial-impersonal in scale but most impressive, with sumptuous state rooms, and door-cases by Grinling Gibbons.

Blenheim was designed by John Vanbrugh for the 1st Duke of Marlborough, one John Churchill. It was a reward from Queen Anne in recognition of his victory over the French at Blenheim in Bavaria in 1704. More recently, in 1874, it was the birthplace of Winston Churchill and the contents include Churchilliana. He is buried in Bladon Church.

The palace stands in a great park laid out by Henry Wise, gardener to Queen Anne, and later modified by Capability Brown. Explore the numerous walks, beech woods and formal features that include the Triumphal Way, Italian Garden, maze, ornamental bridge and Column of Victory. Nearby is the town of **Woodstock**, home to the **Oxfordshire Museum** (*Admission free*).

▶ Bridgnorth   110C2

(Tourist information tel: 01746 763257; www.bridgnorthshropshire.com)

Bridgnorth perches high on a sandstone cliff above the Severn, with a cliff railway connecting the low town. Stroll along Castle Walk past the spectacularly leaning ruin of a Norman castle, blown up in 1646 during the Civil War. From here the **Severn Valley Railway**▶ ▶ (tel: 01299 403816 or www.svr.co.uk for schedule) runs 26km (16 miles) to Kidderminster, recapturing travel of yesteryear, with steam locomotives passing a series of old stations. The journey takes just over an hour and passes through **Bewdley**▶, where the Old Shambles houses the local museum (*Admission free*). To the east, on the A456, is the **West Midland Safari and Leisure Park**, which has themed rides.

BIRMINGHAM'S JEWELLERY QUARTER
This character-laden district just north of the central area narrowly escaped postwar redevelopment. The many workshops mostly employ only one or two people, and are highly specialized, depending on each other as part of the process—one may be a polisher, another a gem-setter or wedding ring maker, while another manufactures bangles or butterfly wings. The Smith and Pepper bangle workshop, now the Museum of the Jewellery Quarter, is the most astonishing time-warp of all. In recent years, numerous retailers have set up locally too.

THE BOTANICAL GARDENS

115

Central Birmingham is strikingly devoid of trees and parks, so the Botanical Gardens (just west of the central area in Westbourne Road, Edgbaston; buses 10, 21, 21E, 22, 23, 29, 103 and 626) makes a welcoming oasis of lush greenery. Ferns, banana trees, cacti and other exotica fill the glass houses, and there are historic and cottage gardens as well as tree collections. Admission is quite expensive, so it is worth making a day of it. From April to September Sunday bandstand concerts enhance the atmosphere further.

A home fit for a world leader: Blenheim Palace was the birthplace of Winston Churchill

WEST WYCOMBE AND THE DASHWOODS

The most notorious member of the Dashwood family was undoubtedly Sir Francis Dashwood (1708–91), who set up the Hellfire Club, a black-magic brotherhood more interested in drinking and whoring than satanic rites. Its meeting places included the West Wycombe Caves (open to the public, just north of the village street) and the hollow gold ball on top of the Church of St. Lawrence. The Dashwood memorials are within the curious roofless, hexagonal mausoleum (1764) next to the church.

Mapledurham Mill, the last working water mill on the Thames

WHIPSNADE WILD ANIMAL PARK

Planned by the Zoological Society of London, Whipsnade is one of Europe's foremost animal collections, situated in a spacious park; close by, Whipsnade Tree Cathedral was created by Edmund Kell Blyth in 1931 as a war memorial, with trees laid out in aisles, transepts and cloisters.

As one who long in populous city pent,
Where houses thick and sewers annoy the air,
Forth issuing on a summer's morn to breathe
Among the pleasant villages and farms
Adjoin'd, from each thing met conceives delight.
—John Milton (1608–74), *Paradise Lost*

▶ Chiltern Hills   111A4

(High Wycombe tourist information tel: 01494 421892; www.wycombe.gov.uk)

Step northwest of London and you are soon into this surprisingly rural area of chalk hills, dotted with fine manor houses and unspoiled country pubs. The beech woods that made the area an important furniture-making hub are still a feature of the landscape. At **Mapledurham▶**, by the Thames, you can visit a working water mill and Elizabethan Mapledurham House. Almost all of **West Wycombe▶** was purchased by the National Trust in 1929; its main street has predominantly

17th- and 18th-century houses. Nearby is **West Wycombe Park▶** (NT), built in 1765 for Sir Francis Dashwood (see panel). Humphry Repton landscaped the park in 1803, adorning it with follies. Benjamin Disraeli, the 19th-century prime minister, lived at **Hughenden Manor▶** (NT) north of High Wycombe; his library and study have been preserved. Near Chalfont St. Giles, traditional Chiltern buildings can be seen at the **Chiltern Open Air Museum▶**; including an Iron Age dwelling, a 19th-century farm and a 1940s prefab.

▶ Coventry   111C3

(Tourist information tel: 024 7622 7264; www.visitcoventry.co.uk)

Devastated by bombing in 1940, Coventry has twice reinvented itself. Postwar rebuilding included the first pedestrian precincts in Britain and, beside the ruins of its blitzed predecessor (preserved as a war memorial), the rather more cherished **cathedral▶▶** of 1962 by Sir Basil Spence. Voted Britain's most popular 20th-century architectural work, it has striking stained glass and a huge tapestry. Around here are the fruits of an inspired revamp completed in 2004, creating two new squares and public art, and joining together the historic core. Past the **Priory Visitor Centre** are **Holy Trinity Church** (with its medieval wall painting) and Millennium Place, framed by the huge Whittle Arches, and flanked by **Coventry Transport Museum▶▶** (*Admission free*), the largest collection of British road transport.

▶ Gloucester

(Tourist information tel: 01452 396572, www.gloucester.gov.uk)

Gloucester's down-to-earth red-brick textures contrast sharply with the golden hues of the nearby Cotswolds, but offers rewards in its small yet absorbing medieval heart and its revived 19th century docks. In summer the Gloucester Civic Trust give guided tours of the historic area.

Just off the historic axis of Westgate Street, with its **Folk Museum** stands the **cathedral▶▶**. It became a place of pilgrimage after the installation of the tomb of Edward II, who was murdered at nearby Berkeley Castle in 1327. From the outside it is a pleasing medieval mish-mash; within, its glory is the glass of its east window, one of England's largest and the 14th-century fan-vaulting in the cloisters, England's earliest. In the Harry Potter movies the cloisters were used for filming Hogwarts School.

Meanwhile, in the **docks**, the warehouses, towers of red bricks, have been partly converted to offices, shops and cafés. Here, in a converted Victorian warehouse, the **National Waterways Museum▶** gives a vivid account of the development of Britain's canals and offers 45-minute cruises along the canal. Close by, the Custom House contains the **Soldiers of Gloucestershire Museum** detailing 300 years of regimental history. Also in the docks is Britain's largest provincial **antiques centre**, with some 140 dealers.

East of Gloucester, **Cheltenham▶** is an elegant Regency spa, with its pump room designed in the best 19th-century Greek Revival tradition. A mineral spring was discovered here in 1715, allegedly by observing the comings and goings of a healthy-looking pigeon population; pigeons feature on the town's crest today. Cheltenham later received the royal approval of George III and acquired its handsome terraces, wrought-iron balconies and leafy thoroughfares. Other attractions are the Art Gallery and Museum (*Admission free*), the **Holst Birthplace Museum** (where the composer of *The Planets* was born in 1874), the annual festivals of music (July) and of literature (October) and the racecourse.

To the northwest, **Tewkesbury▶**, where the Avon and Severn meet, is a handsome town of high-medieval and later façades. The **abbey church▶** is one of England's finest examples of Norman ecclesiastical architecture.

Gloucester cathedral cloisters became part of Hogwarts School for the Harry Potter movies

THREE CHOIRS FESTIVAL
This major music festival takes place in the second or third week of August and rotates in a three-year cycle between Gloucester, Worcester and Hereford cathedrals. Its origins go back to the early 18th century; from the 1890s three organist-conductors (one from each cathedral) were appointed and a distinguished list of works by some of the country's greatest composers were given their first performance, including *Fantasia on a Theme of Thomas Tallis* (1910) by Vaughan Williams, the *Colour Symphony* (1922) by Bliss and the *Choral Fantasia* (1931) of Holst. Elgar directed his own music here until his death in 1934.

Touring country par excellence, the Cotswold Hills are an area of beautiful honey-hued limestone villages, tucked-away manor houses, cottage gardens, russet-earth fields enclosed by drystone walls and lonely, winding country roads leading to nowhere in particular.

Cirencester tourist information tel: 01285 654180. Stow-on-the-Wold tourist information tel: 01451 831082. Website for both: www.cotswold.gov.uk/tourism.

118

SOUTH COTSWOLDS HOUSES
Buscot Park (NT), near Faringdon, is an 18th-century house renowned for its paintings and porcelain. Also near Faringdon is **Great Coxwell Barn** (NT), built by the monks of Beaulieu and considered one of England's finest: in medieval times a tenth of agricultural produce of each parish was handed over as a tax or 'tithe' to the church and was stored in tithe barns. **Owlpen Manor,** a Tudor manor in an old hillside garden of roses and box parterres was restored in the 1920s by Norman Jewson, a follower of the Arts and Crafts movement.

Cotswold architecture: honey-hued walls and stone-mullioned windows

SOUTH COTSWOLDS GARDENS
Among many outstanding gardens are the **Rococo Garden** outside Painswick, **Westonbirt—The National Arboretum** (a Forestry Commission collection of more than 17,000 trees), **Bourton House Gardens** (topiary, herbaceous borders and knot garden), **Batsford Arboretum and Wild Garden** (one of Britain's largest collections of rare trees) and **Misarden Park Gardens** (topiary, shrubs, borders and more).

The Cotswolds present timeless tableaux of rural England. The scenery is pleasant rather than dramatic, with the best views from the western edges. There are plenty of hotels, some very high class indeed and the area is strong on sights (with plenty of interest for children). Wool was the key to the area's medieval prosperity and the wealth it created is commemorated in a striking legacy of grand churches. Almost every town and village seems to have a Sheep Street.

The area is described in two parts, one lying south of the A40, the other north.

The south The undoubted capital of the south Cotswolds is **Cirencester**▶▶, a handsome town with more bustle than most nearby towns and plenty of shops for browsing. In Roman times, only London (*Londinium*) was bigger than Cirencester (*Corinium*) and these and later days are celebrated in the excellent Corinium Museum, which displays original mosaic paving and reconstructions of Roman domestic interiors. Dominating the market square is the cathedral-like parish church, with its fan-vaulted porch and grand interior. One of the finest streets is Cecily Hill, its far end leading into Cirencester Park (pedestrians only), the grounds of Lord Bathurst's stately home.

The drystone wall is the main type of field boundary in the Cotswolds

At **Bibury**▶▶ a triple-arched footbridge over the River Coln leads to Arlington Row, a group of former weavers' cottages. The village is full of pretty cottage gardens and unspoiled corners. The Victorian artist-craftsman William Morris and his Pre-Raphaelite friends 'discovered' the Cotswolds, and in 1871 he came to live at nearby Kelmscott. Morris declared Bibury to be the most beautiful village in England. A 17th-century non-working mill houses the **Arlington Mill Museum**. More low-key charm is found in abundance in the **Colns** (Coln St. Aldwyn, Coln Rogers and Coln St. Dennis) and the **Duntisbournes** (Duntisbourne Abbots, Duntisbourne Leer and Duntisbourne Rouse, the latter having a little Saxon church). **Fairford**▶ prides itself on its splendid 'wool church', famed for its late 15th-century stained glass.

Painswick▶▶ has an appealing, sloping knot of central lanes and stone walls; grand houses jostle cheek by jowl with minute cottages. Best of all is the churchyard, dominated by 99 yews; an explanatory leaflet describes the fine 16th- to 19th-century tombstones. The surrounding area is lush and deep-set, the numerous viewpoints including **Painswick Beacon** and **Haresfield Beacon**. **Slad** was the village of writer Laurie Lee, who captured the pre-automobile age so evocatively in *Cider with Rosie*. Stroud is not particularly attractive, but the atmospherically derelict **Thames and Severn Canal**, near Sapperton, is worth exploring. Farther south are some finely sited towns and villages, including **Wotton-under-Edge** and **Dursley**, snug beneath the escarpment and **Minchinhampton**, on a breezy hilltop site.

Chedworth Roman Villa▶ (NT), excavated 1864–66, has an enchanting atmosphere of Victorian archeological discovery, with a hunting lodge built almost among the ruins, which feature mosaics, bath and heating systems and a water shrine or nymphaeum. **Hetty Pegler's Tump**, named after the wife of its 17th-century owner, is a neolithic burial mound with its stone slabs still in place.

FAMILY ATTRACTIONS (SOUTH)
South of Burford, the **Cotswold Wildlife Park and Gardens** features white rhinos, tigers and more. At **Prinknash Abbey**, a living community of Benedictine monks, there is a bird sanctuary and pottery. At Northleach is **Keith Harding's World of Mechanical Music**, with a beguiling display of antique mechanical instruments. Farther afield, the **Wildfowl and Wetlands Centre** at Slimbridge on the Severn Estuary has a huge collection of wildfowl and **Berkeley Castle** is famous for the dungeon in which Edward II was murdered in 1327.

The Cotswolds

FAMILY ATTRACTIONS (NORTH)
The **Gloucestershire and Warwickshire Railway** operates steam trains between Toddington and Winchcombe, while the **Cotswold Farm Park** (west of Stow-on-the-Wold) is home to rare animal breeds. Just outside Witney, the **Cogges Manor Farm Museum** offers a look at rural Edwardian life in Oxfordshire, with craft and farming demonstrations.

Angular gables, stone roofs and trim lawns: typical of many Cotswold manor houses

NORTH COTSWOLDS HOUSES
Stanway House is a good example of Jacobean architecture, while **Broughton Castle** near Banbury is a moated medieval manor and **Snowshill Manor** (NT) contains a collection of bicycles and Japanese Samurai items. By contrast, **Sezincote** was restyled in the 1800s as an Indian fantasy; the Prince Regent found in it inspiration for his Royal Pavilion in Brighton (see page 90). **Chastleton House** (NT) is a Jacobean manor (must book timed tickets, tel: 01608 674355). **Sudeley Castle**, an imposing part-ruined stately home at Winchcombe, was the burial place of Henry VIII's sixth wife, Catherine Parr.

NORTH COTSWOLDS GARDENS
The magically hidden-away gardens of **Hidcote Manor** (NT), north of Chipping Campden, are pure joy: a 20th-century creation of a series of 'rooms' bounded by hedges and walls. Close by, **Kiftsgate Court Gardens** have rare shrubs and a fine rose collection.

The north In the far north, **Chipping Campden**▶▶▶ should not be missed for its showpiece main street, primitive open-sided market hall and a fine church with Gloucestershire's largest memorial brass. The great manor house of Campden has gone, but its Jacobean lodges and gateway remain. Chipping Campden is just large enough to be a town, but its pace is unhurried and its charms preserved without being commercialized. Beneath the Cotswold escarpment and on the edge of the Vale of Evesham (famed for its fruit and vegetable growing), **Broadway**▶ is a tourist magnet, its elegant main street well lined with gift boutiques and tea rooms. On the top of Broadway Hill and with a huge view to the west, stands a folly known as Broadway Tower; the abrupt transition west from Cotswold stone to Midland red brick is striking.

Other quieter sub-escarpment villages nearby have charm in plenty, including **Buckland**▶ and **Stanton**▶. Within the town of **Winchcombe**▶ you can find a gargoyle-covered church (look for the splendid weathercock) and an

old-fashioned ambience; attractions include The Folk and Police Museum and the Winchcombe Railway Museum (a collection of railway memorabilia). Just out of town by the B4632, **Cleeve Hill**▶ is a blustery highland (only 317m/1,040ft, but it feels higher), a place for strolls, kite-flying and enjoying the view west to the Malvern Hills (see page 125). Beautifully set beneath the Cotswold escarpment, the Cistercian ruin of **Hailes Abbey**▶(EH/NT) was in its day a major pilgrimage site.

Stow-on-the-Wold and **Chipping Norton** are conveniently placed market towns in the area, the latter is the highest town in Oxfordshire. With its series of tiny bridges spanning the Windrush, **Bourton-on-the-Water** is almost too pretty to be believed; it is also the most commercialized village in the Cotswolds, drawing crowds to its miniature model village, Perfumery Exhibition, Model Railway, Birdland aviary, and Cotswold Motor Museum and Toy Collection. By contrast, nearby **Lower Slaughter**▶ is an amazingly unspoiled delight, with cottages and an old mill overlooking a rippling brook. **Burford**▶ has an impressive church and a distinguished main street lined with shops and inns, sloping down to an ancient stone bridge. Close to Witney is **Minster Lovell**▶ with its spooky, ruined 15th-century hall.

THE COTSWOLDS

Drive

The Cotswolds

This tour promises golden stone-built villages, dignified manor houses and fine views (approx 90km/56 miles).

Start from **Burford▶**, descending the main street and continue past **Stow-on-the-Wold** to branch off, past **Sezincote House▶ ▶** and **Blockley**, which still has a few of its old silk-throwing mills. Continue to **Chipping Campden▶ ▶ ▶**; head southwest to the A44 where you turn right (Broadway Tower, a famous scenic viewpoint, is soon off left) to **Broadway▶**. Take the B4632 to skirt peaceful **Buckland▶**; branch off left through **Stanton▶** and **Stanway▶** and rejoin the B4632 close to the turning to **Hailes Abbey▶** (NT). Continue into **Winchcombe▶**, stopping off for **Sudeley Castle▶**. Pass **Belas Knap** prehistoric burial mound and **Guiting Power**. The villages of **Upper Slaughter** and **Lower Slaughter▶** lead up to busy **Bourton-on-the-Water**.

Finish your drive by exploring the quiet countryside around **Great Barrington**.

CIDER IN HEREFORDSHIRE

The alcoholic apple drink has a venerable tradition in the county; in former days, many farms produced hard cider specially for farm workers. True farmhouse 'scrumpy' cider is now a rarity, but the drink has enjoyed a revival in recent years. Bulmer's Cider, one of the largest operations, produces in Hereford. Housed in part of Bulmer's former factory, the Hereford Cider Museum displays cidermaking methods ancient and modern. The museum shop sells numerous varieties of local cider. Near Pembridge, a village on the Black and White Village Trail, Dunkerton's Cider is an engagingly rustic outfit, operating from a barn and Weston's, a much larger company, produces at Much Marcle.

The finely worked 900-year-old carving on the south doorway of Kilpeck Church

DR. JOHNSON (1709–84)

In Lichfield's market square stand statues of this formidably learned and witty man, and his biographer James Boswell. His early years in Lichfield were not dazzling: he dropped out of his studies at Oxford, and had an unsuccessful career as a teacher. But in London he made a living as an essayist and journalist, compiling his famous Dictionary over eight years up to 1755 (see Dr. Johnson's House, page 50), and became one of the capital's greatest literary figures. In 1763 he met Boswell and penned *A Journey to the Western Isles of Scotland* after their travels together.

▶ Hereford *110B1*

(Tourist information tel: 01432 268430; www.visitherefordshire.co.uk)

The capital of Herefordshire, renowned for its eponymous cattle breed and for cider making, stands on the banks of the River Wye. A ring road cuts too close to the heart, but there are some good medieval streets. The highlight is the sandstone **cathedral**▶▶ (begun in 1107) with its library of more than 1,400 chained books and its priceless Mappa Mundi, a 13th-century map of the world.

Southwest is **Abbey Dore**▶. Only a portion of the huge Cistercian abbey remains. Nearby **Kilpeck Church**▶▶ is a perfect Norman building, embellished inside and out with carvings of birds, beasts and angels. Prudish Victorians failed to remove all of the more salacious ones.

The **Black and White Village Trail**▶▶ (available from local tourist offices) is a well-marked car tour west of Hereford through some beautiful, unspoiled half-timbered villages, including **Weobley**, **Pembridge**, **Eardisland** and **Lyonshall**.

At **Shobdon**▶ the stonework of the old church, which may well have been by the same person who sculpted Kilpeck, was turned into a garden ornament in the mid-18th century for a nearby house; the 'new' church built in its place has an interior of wedding-cake 'Strawberry Hill Gothick', a style of architecture named after that used in writer Horace Walpole's 1747 house at Strawberry Hill in Twickenham, near London. Farther north, **Croft Castle**▶ (NT) is a fascinating mixture of medievalism and Georgian Gothic. Walks in the nearby National Trust estate include the ascent of Croft Ambrey, a well-sited Iron Age hill fort with visible ramparts.

▶ Lichfield *111C3*

(Tourist information tel: 01543 308209; www.visitlichfield.com)

The trio of sandstone spires of the mostly 12th- to 15th-century **cathedral**▶ dominates a gracious close of 17th- to 19th-century buildings. There is much Early English and Decorated work. The west front has 113 statues, including 24 English kings. The city's most famous son was man of letters Dr. Johnson (see panel), subject of Boswell's biography; his birthplace is now the Samuel Johnson Birthplace Museum.

The wooded gorge of the River Severn gave birth to the Industrial Revolution in the early 18th century. What happened at Ironbridge heralded the emergence of Britain as the first industrial nation in the world and was the catalyst for a dramatic change in the face of the country, as the Midlands and northern England became a great industrial heartland.

Here in 1709 Abraham Darby first smelted iron ore with coke instead of charcoal, making mass production of iron possible. The gorge soon filled with industrial activity. Today it is a picturesque area, and you have to imagine the din and smoke of the great ironworks and other industries —but the first-rate **Ironbridge Gorge Museums** (tel: 01952 433522) spread over ten sites, skillfully bring it alive. Ironbridge is near Telford (map: *110C2*).

What to see The **Iron Bridge** itself was the world's earliest iron structure of its kind (built in 1779). Staff in period costume enhance the atmosphere of **Blists Hill Victorian Town**▶ ▶ ▶, the largest site, including a toll-house, period shops, a colliery and an inclined railway that linked two canals. **Jackfield Tile Museum**▶ ▶ is housed in a huge Victorian tile factory that had lain abandoned; today it has been reopened and tiles are put on display. The **Coalport China Museum**▶ ▶ marks the original site of the Coalport china factory, based here from the 1790s until the 1920s; today there is a display of china as well as early brick bee-hive kilns. You have to wear a hard hat to enter the gloomy **Tar Tunnel**▶, where bitumen was once extracted. You can also visit the **Darby Houses**, where the ironmasters lived, the **Museum of the Gorge** (history of the Gorge) and the **Broseley Pipeworks**, which manufactured clay smoking pipes ('Broseleys'). At the **Coalbrookdale Museum of Iron**▶ ▶ ▶ you are in historic territory, the very spot where Darby sparked the industrialization of Britain.

History today: the daily round at Blists Hill

DON'T MISS
There is too much to see in a day in the gorge; if you have only a short time, concentrate on Blists Hill, the Iron Bridge, and Coalbrookdale. Children particularly may enjoy Engenuity (though it is aimed at adults too), with fun interactive displays showing how everyday things are made. You can buy separate tickets for each site, or a 'passport' that allows return visits on different occasions. Buses run between the sites. For information: Ironbridge Gorge Museums tel: 01952 433522; for tickets tel: 0800 590258 (free); www.ironbridge.org.uk.

The Iron Bridge gives its name to the town of Ironbridge, which rises steeply from it

Ludlow Castle: the keep

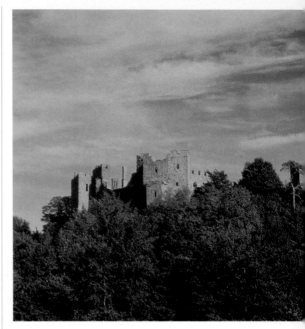

124

The Feathers, one of the finest examples of 17th-century half-timbering in Britain

▶▶▶ **Ludlow**   *110C1*

(Tourist information tel: 01584 875053; www.ludlow.org.uk)
This is often acclaimed as England's most perfect country town—and it is easy to see why. From its hilltop site its streets spread elegantly out from the ancient butter cross and marketplace, on which is found the absorbing **museum** of local history (*Admission free*). Just behind the market cross stands the cathedral-like **Church of St. Laurence▶▶**. Within its soaring interior, the patron saint's life and miracles are celebrated in the east window and there are 15th-century carved misericords. Poet A. E. Housman of *Shropshire Lad* fame (see page 130) is buried in the churchyard.

Broad Street is Ludlow's most celebrated thoroughfare, with its half-timbered Tudor buildings and 17th- to 19th-century brick façades combining happily along the gentle slope to a gateway at the bottom end. The **Feathers Hotel**, a riot of half-timbering, is an outstanding house of its period. **Ludlow Castle▶▶**, founded by Roger Montgomery, Earl of Shrewsbury, in 1085, was built to withstand both Welsh and Norman incursions; its long list of distinguished visitors includes Sir Philip Sidney, Edward IV and Catherine of Aragon. A Norman chapel within the castle has an unusual circular nave. During the Ludlow Festival in June and July, outdoor performances of Shakespeare plays are held in the inner bailey. The town is enjoying a growing reputation for its gastronomy.

Ludlow is splendidly situated for exploring the Welsh Marches and the South Shropshire Hills (see page 130) are within close reach. **Stokesay Castle▶▶** (EH), near Craven Arms, is an outstandingly well-preserved example of a 13th-century fortified manor house; it was designed with windows unusually large for those lawless times. The adjacent church dates mostly from the 17th century but has a Norman doorway.

▶▶ Malvern Hills 110B2

(Great Malvern tourist information tel: 01684 892289;
www.malvernhills.gov.uk)
The jagged Malvern ridge rises between the low plains of
Herefordshire and the Vale of Evesham. From a distance
it looks like a mountain range; close up it reveals itself as
a friendly upland stripe offering superb views from the
easily accessible paths along its spine.

Its advantages as a defensive site were exploited by Iron
Age people: Worcestershire Beacon (the highest point,
425m/1,394ft) and Herefordshire Beacon are both well-
preserved hill forts. To the west there are views of **Eastnor
Castle**▶▶, a 19th-century mock-medieval extravaganza
designed by Robert Smirke and extravagantly decorated
inside by A. W. N. Pugin. In the distance are the hills of the
Welsh Marches; to the east is the Cotswold escarpment.

Malvern Wells and **Great Malvern**▶ lie right under the
Malvern Hills. Malvern water put the area on the map as
a spa after a Dr. Wall wrote in 1756 of the waters' medici-
nal value. Within a modest stone pavilion is St. Ann's
Well, the original source. The priory church, the glory of
Great Malvern, has fine 15th-century stained glass.

Southwest is **Ledbury**▶. The town's broad main street
focuses on John Abel's 16th-century half-timbered market
house. Pretty Church Lane leads to the church, with its
'gold vane surveying half the shire', in the words of
locally born John Masefield, former Poet Laureate.

Worcester▶ is famous as the home of Royal Worcester
Porcelain, which has factory tours (Mon–Fri; tel: 01905
21247, booking advised) and the well displayed **Royal
Worcester Museum**▶. The city was important in the Civil
War, as you can learn from the exhibition in the
Commandery in Sidbury Road, Charles II's headquarters
during the Battle of Worcester. Some post-war development in the city has been uninspired, but spared the
lovely close around the **cathedral**▶▶ (look in for the
monuments, crypt, cloister garden and marble pulpit).

Just west of Worcester, **Lower Broadheath**▶ was the
birthplace on 2 June 1857 of composer Edward Elgar (see
panel). The modest cottage and adjoining Elgar Birthplace
Museum commemorates his life with memorabilia and
his lovingly annotated cycling maps of the area.

125

**SIR EDWARD ELGAR
(1857–1934)**
Elgar's musical education
was derived mainly from
his experience as a violin
player, as a singer at the
church where his father
was organist and from
browsing the scores in his
father's music shop in
Worcester. For a long time
he felt the musical world
was set against him, yet
the fact that he was
mainly self taught proba-
bly gave him a freshness
of vision and made him
perhaps the greatest
English composer since
Henry Purcell.
Elgar's early works were
recognized only locally,
but his international reputation was assured when
Richard Strauss
acclaimed the ever-popu-
lar *Enigma Variations*
(1899). *The Dream of
Gerontius* (1900) enjoyed
success in the Three
Choirs Festival (see panel,
page 117) in 1902. The
First Symphony (1908)
and the *Pomp and
Circumstance Marches*
(1901–30) won
widespread popularity.

*Worcester's spectacular
Guildhall, dated 1722*

CHRIST CHURCH COLLEGE

Tom Quad, the main quadrangle, is so called because of Tom Tower, designed by Sir Christopher Wren and named after the bell, Great Tom, which strikes the hour. Ever since 1682, at 9.05pm it has rung 101 times, commemorating the original number of students; this was the time for students to be back in college. The 16th-century college hall has portraits of some of the college's distinguished former members, including William Gladstone, Lewis Carroll, John Ruskin and W. H. Auden.

126

OXFORD VERSUS CAMBRIDGE

The two universities maintain an ancient rivalry, most obviously displayed in the Oxford and Cambridge Boat Race, rowed on the Thames in west London every spring and in the Varsity rugby match, played at Twickenham in the autumn.

'OXBRIDGE' SUBTLETIES

Oxford and Cambridge universities are referred to jointly as 'Oxbridge'.
● When steering a 'punt', a shallow boat, on the river in Oxford, you stand inside the boat; in Cambridge you stand on its platform.
● Only at Oxford does formal academic dress feature a mortar board as well as a gown.
● In Cambridge, colleges have courtyards; in Oxford they are known as quadrangles (or quads).
● At Cambridge, students' academic work is charted by directors of studies; at Oxford the terminology is tutors.
● There are more colleges at Oxford and they mostly have fewer students than their Cambridge counterparts.

▶▶▶ Oxford   111A3

(Tourist information tel: 01865 726871; www.visitoxford.org)

Home of one of the world's greatest universities (founded about 1200), Oxford has a stunning heritage of historic buildings. Close to the bustling heart of the city lie placid swathes of riverside greenery along Christ Church Meadow. As with Cambridge, there is no single campus in Oxford: the colleges are set in cloistered seclusion behind high walls; most are open to visitors in the afternoon.

Most notable among the university buildings are the **Sheldonian Theatre**, built in 1664 as a ceremonial assembly hall and the **Radcliffe Camera**, a domed building, now a reading room for the **Bodleian Library**, which contains around 7 million volumes. The Bodleian is one of five 'copyright' libraries in the United Kingdom, entitled to receive a copy of every book published in the country. The view from the tower of **St. Mary the Virgin**, the university church on the High Street, extends over the city.

Christ Church▶▶, founded as Cardinal College by Cardinal Wolsey in 1525, is the largest college, has the biggest quadrangle and its chapel (which predates the college) is England's smallest cathedral; the college picture gallery contains works by Dürer and Michelangelo. **Magdalen College**▶▶ (pronounced 'mawdlin') has its own deer park. **All Souls College** has a highly scholarly reputation and admits only post-graduate students, while **St. John's College** is the wealthiest of all and has luscious gardens. **New College**▶ (founded 1379) has a splendid chapel with a statue of Lazarus by Jacob Epstein. Also seek out **Oriel**▶, **Merton**▶▶, **Queen's**▶ and **Keble**▶ **colleges**, the latter a relative newcomer whose ornamental red-brick buildings are Victorian masterpieces.

Of Oxford's museums, the outstanding attraction is the **Ashmolean**▶▶▶ (*Admission free*), a treasure-house of art and antiquities whose exhibits include a ninth-century brooch made for King Alfred, while in its Victorian setting the **Pitt Rivers Museum**▶▶ (*Admission free*) is ranked as one of the world's top six ethnographic collections. The city's history, both town and gown, is illustrated in the **Museum of Oxford**, St. Aldates, while a less traditional approach is provided by the **Oxford Story**, Broad Street, where you sit at moving desks on a voyage through the city's past.

OXFORD

Walk

Start from Magdalen Bridge, pass **Magdalen College**▶▶ and turn right into Queen's Lane, which weaves past

Despite its name, New College was founded in 1379

Magdalen Bridge to the Botanic Garden

St. Edmund Hall▶ (founded 1220) and **New College**▶ (1379). Just before the Bridge of Sighs (which spans the street), take an alley on the right, passing the Turf Tavern, an old pub with an appealing courtyard. Turn left along Holywell Street and continue past the **Sheldonian Theatre**, with its array of sculpted heads of Roman emperors and along **Broad Street** to the **Martyrs' Memorial**, where three bishops were burned for their Protestant beliefs in the 1550s. Diagonally opposite is the **Ashmolean Museum**▶▶. Double back along Broad Street and turn right down Turl Street to the **Radcliffe Camera** and **Bodleian Library**. Cross the High Street, taking Oriel Street on its south side to enter **Christ Church**▶▶ by the gate near the college's picture gallery (if closed, continue along Merton Street to the start of the walk), crossing Tom Quad and leaving by the turnstile at the south side of the college to follow Broad Walk along **Christ Church Meadow**. The **Botanic Garden**▶ is the oldest of its kind in the country.

There are few more pleasant ways to explore Britain's scenery, wildlife and history than an easygoing voyage along the inland waterways. The slow, unhurried pace of a narrowboat gives a chance for once to take a long look at things. Canals run through towns as well as the countryside and supply unexpected perspectives. Spectacular flights of locks, aqueducts, tunnels and bridges, warehouses and workshops, pleasant pubs and inns are the legacy of a time when the canals seemed to hold the future of Britain's transport system.

WATERWAYS HOLIDAYS

Britain's canals are now used primarily for boating trips, fishing and towpath walks. For details about canal holidays, contact: Customer Services, British Waterways, Willow Grange, Church Road, Watford, Hertfordshire WD17 4QA (01923 201400), or visit www.britishwaterways.co.uk for general information) or www.waterscape.com for leisure information.

CANAL ART

During the 19th century a rich tradition of canal art developed. Boat owners covered the boats and their interiors and utensils with a riot of roses and castles, daisies and marigolds in simple patterns and vivid primary hues—a popular art form similar to the one which developed in the same period in touring fairs.

Some 3,200km (1,990 miles) of navigable inland waterways have been described as the British tourist industry's best-kept secret. From prehistoric times down to the 18th century, travel by river was generally faster, safer and more comfortable than travel by road. Rivers like the Severn, the Thames and the Trent bustled with boats carrying goods and people, and the towns along their banks prospered as inland ports.

The Canal Age dawns The trouble with rivers is that they do not always go where you want them to, they silt up, water levels vary and shallows block navigation, as do periodic floods. Attempts to control and improve rivers were made from early times and artificial cuts were made to shorten routes, straighten bends and evade shallows. The Canal Age in the 18th and 19th centuries brought much more radical action. A network of artificial rivers was constructed to mesh with the natural waterways and create an efficient system covering much of the country. The canals were the principal arteries of the first stage of the Industrial Revolution.

The first canal of this period was begun in Lancashire in the 1750s to link St. Helens with the Mersey, but much more excitement arose in the 1760s when the Duke of Bridgewater ordered the construction of a canal to be built to carry coal mined on his estates at Worsley a distance of 12km (7.5 miles) into Manchester. The duke's engineer was an illiterate genius from Derbyshire named James Brindley. The Bridgewater Canal was soon extended to the Mersey, linking Manchester with Liverpool. (The Manchester end is now part of the Castlefield urban heritage area.)

Not only did the duke's canal halve the price of coal in Manchester, but the spectacle of canal boats crossing the River Irwell at Barton on an aqueduct, above the barges on the river, fired the public imagination. A bold plan was swiftly hatched to build a canal joining the Trent and the Mersey—Josiah Wedgwood, the great china-maker, was one of its most eager promoters—from which other canals would run to the Thames and the Severn. This would link Britain's four most important rivers and provide an inland waterway connection between London, Birmingham, Hull, Liverpool and Bristol.

Brindley was the engineer for the Trent and Mersey, which was completed in 1777, five years after his death and the other components of the plan soon followed.

The heyday The success of the early ventures set off 'canal mania', a frenzy that had people flocking to meetings all over the country to invest in new waterways. It reached its peak in 1793, when Parliament passed 24 canal construction acts in that single year. One politician of the time said he hoped his grandchildren would be born with webbed feet, since no dry land would be left in England for them to walk on.

A total of 275km (170 miles) of canal in 1770 grew to 2,575km (1,600 miles) by the end of the century and 6,840km (4,250 miles) in the 1850s as armies of 'navvies' (navigators)—tough, brawling, hard-drinking workers, the terror of peaceful folk—drove the new waterways across country on giant embankments and through cuttings and tunnels. The earliest tunnels had no towpaths and the boats had to be 'legged' through by the crew, lying on their backs or sides, walking along the brickwork.

The canals' brief heyday was ended by the railways from the 1830s on and the development of road transport almost finished them off. Even so, some 4 million tonnes of goods are still carried on the waterways every year, though they are used far more today for recreation. Some have been revived: projects include restoring the Rochdale Canal from Manchester to Halifax and the Huddersfield Narrow Canal through the country's longest canal tunnel.

NARROWBOATS IN THE SKY
Among the most spectacular engineering feats of the canal engineers were flights of locks and aqueducts. The most famous staircase of locks is probably the Bingley Five Rise on the Leeds and Liverpool Canal, which climbs 18m (59ft). The most sensational of aqueducts is the Pontcysyllte near Llangollen in North Wales, designed by the great engineer Thomas Telford in the 1790s. The canal is carried across the aqueduct for 307m (335yd), in an iron trough almost 3.6m (12ft) wide, with an iron towpath set above it. Boats still go across and visitors can also walk across on the towpath.

129

The Rochdale Canal at Hebden Bridge: boats were once pulled by horses plodding along the towpath

Shrewsbury Castle: rebuilt in the 18th century by Thomas Telford, has Norman origins

Decorative quatrefoils in the Square, Shrewsbury

▶ **Shrewsbury** 110C1
(Tourist information tel: 01743 281200; www.shrewsburytourism.co.uk)

The town has a natural defensive site, within a tight loop of the meandering River Severn, with a **castle** to guard the land-linked neck of land. Shrewsbury's collection of Tudor half-timbering and red-brick Georgian buildings, reminders of prosperity brought by the wool trade, is remarkable. Look, for example, at **Owen's Mansion** and **Ireland's Mansion** (both near the arcaded old market hall), and **Council House Court**: the half-timbering includes decorative cable-molding and quatrefoils.

Finds from the Roman city of Wroxeter (*Uriconium*), a short way out of town, are displayed in **Rowley's House Museum** (*Admission free*). **Bear Steps**, a tiny alley, looks medieval, with a hall founded in 1389 as a guild for wool merchants. The Benedictine **abbey** has Norman features and a statue of Edward III on its tower. Street names can bemuse. Butcher Row is self-explanatory (although the butchers are not in evidence) and Grope Lane suggests a variety of possibilities, but Wyle Cop, where Henry VII had a house, may baffle you—it means 'hill top'. The meaning of Dog Pole is uncertain: perhaps a low gate or 'ducken poll' where one had to stoop to get through.

East of Shrewsbury, **Wroxeter Roman City▶** (EH) was, in its day, the fourth largest town in England. The most striking remains are the second-century municipal baths; a museum highlights finds from the site.

The **Shropshire Hills▶▶** are south of Shrewsbury, the heartland of the territory immortalized in A. E. Housman's 1896 collection of poems, *A Shropshire Lad*. **Church Stretton** makes a useful starting point for exploring the **Long Mynd**, a massif of bracken- and bilberry-clad hills deeply cut by valleys such as Ashes Hollow and Carding Mill Valley (parking available in the latter); these and nearby Caer Caradoc, itself best reached by walking from Hope Bowdler, offer magnificent walking, with views into Wales and across the Midlands. To the west, the **Stiperstones** are quartzite rocks strewn along a breezy moorland ridge.

►► Stratford-upon-Avon 111B3
(Tourist information tel: 0870 160 7930;
www.shakespeare-country.co.uk)

Long since celebrated as the birthplace and deathplace of William Shakespeare, Stratford-upon-Avon is swamped with visitors. The Shakespeare connection looms large at every turn; the souvenir shops are stocked with miniature ceramic models of Anne Hathaway's cottage, there is a shopping mall named Bard's Walk. For devotees of the Bard the town is a must; but be warned, some find it a disappointment. The attractions can be divided into three categories: the historic Shakespeare sites, the town itself and the attractions tacked on for visitors who wonder why they have come here. The town has half-timbered buildings and a pleasant boating scene on the Avon; look in Holy Trinity Church for a memorial to Shakespeare, quill pen in hand.

An **open-topped bus** tours the sites every 15–30 minutes (board at any of 14 points on its route). The places in town can be easily reached on foot, but the bus is handy if you want to take in Anne Hathaway's Cottage and Mary Arden's House; a ticket (valid for one day only; tel: 01789 294166) allows its holder cut-price entry to Shakespeare properties. It is possible to get around them all in one very full day.

Foremost among the sites maintained by the Shakespeare Birthplace Trust (tel: 01789 204016; www.shakespeare.org.uk) is obviously **Shakespeare's Birthplace**►► itself. Entrance is through the cottage's garden. Inside, an auction notice describes the property ('a truly heart-stirring relic') when it came up for sale in 1847 and was purchased, for the sum of £3,000, as a national memorial. A miscellanea of Shakespearean bits and pieces make up the exhibits. Shakespeare's daughter Susanna and her husband Dr. Hall lived at **Hall's Croft**, a rather grander house, now furnished with Tudor trappings and home to an exhibition about medicine in Shakespeare's day and the career of Dr. Hall.

Shakespeare died in New Place, a house adjacent to **Nash's House**; New Place is no longer, but an Elizabethan-style knot garden marks the site and Nash's House itself displays Tudor furniture and exhibits relating to Stratford's past. Shakespeare was baptized and buried at **Holy Trinity Church**.

I know a bank whereon
the wild thyme blows,
Where oxlips and the nodding violet grows
Quite over-canopied with
luscious woodbine,
With sweet musk-roses,
and with eglantine:
There sleeps Titania some
time of the night,
Lull'd in these flowers
with dances and delight;
And there the snake
throws her enamell'd
skin,
Weed wide enough to
wrap a fairy in.
—William Shakespeare,
A Midsummer Night's Dream

131

Britain's most hallowed literary shrine: Shakespeare's Birthplace

A NATIONAL TREASURE
Before the auction in 1847, Shakespeare's Birthplace had been in the keeping of two widowed ladies, who had made a good thing out of showing such relics as 'the identical lantern with which Friar Laurence discovered Romeo and Juliet at the tomb'. The house was a ruinous mess but, spurred by the approaching tricentennial in 1864 of Shakespeare's birth and a story that a wealthy American planned to ship the house across the Atlantic, the people of Stratford determined to buy the property. The place was cleaned up, judicious restoration was done and a shilling (5 pence) was charged for admission. The town can never have regretted its investment.

Shall I compare thee to a
summer's day?
Thou art more lovely and
more temperate:
Rough winds do shake the
darling buds of May,
And summer's lease hath
all too short a date...

But thy eternal summer
shall not fade,
Nor lose possession of
that fair thou ow'st
Nor shall death brag thou
wander'st in his shade,
When in eternal lines to
time thou grow'st...
—William Shakespeare,
Sonnet XVIII

Out of town at the village of Shottery, **Anne Hathaway's Cottage▶** was the home of Shakespeare's wife Anne before her marriage; it is a picturesque thatched timber building that gets packed at peak times (you may have to wait to get in). Nevertheless the old-world atmosphere has been kept intact, thanks to the Trust's foresight in purchasing the cottage back in 1892. Less hectic, but an equally good example of domestic Tudor architecture (minus the thatch), is **Mary Arden's House▶**, the farmhouse childhood home of Shakespeare's mother, at the village of Wilmcote. This has been set up as a the Shakespeare Countryside Museum, with falconry flying demonstrations, rare farm breeds and exhibits evoking rural life.

Shakespeare productions are performed at the **Royal Shakespeare Theatre** by the Royal Shakespeare Company (for tickets tel: 0870 609 1110; www.rsc.org.uk); in the Swan Theatre, the **RSC Collection▶▶** exhibits more than 1,000 props and costumes used for past performances. The company has a London base at the Barbican (see page 46). There is a fascinating **backstage tour▶▶** (tel: 01789 403405) of the Royal Shakespeare and Swan theatres. The Dirty Duck is the definitive thespian pub in Stratford.

The **Butterfly Farm** re-creates a jungle environment as a setting for some 1,000 exotic butterfly species and is the largest live butterfly and insect exhibit in Europe. Stratford is also home to the **Teddy Bear Museum**, with teddies ancient and modern.

The Royal Shakespeare Theatre, one of the venues used by the Royal Shakespeare Company

▶▶ Waddesdon Manor   111A4

(tel: 01296 653203; recorded information tel: 01296 653211; www.waddesdon.org.uk)

Ferdinand de Rothschild spared no expense on his French Renaissance-style château in the Buckinghamshire countryside in the 1870s and 1880s. The house and its contents are breathtaking in their opulence. The treasures include clocks, Sèvres porcelain, lace, and paintings by Gainsborough, Rubens and others. Within the grounds are two fountains and an aviary. Waddesdon, in the care of the National Trust, is the grandest of a trio of local Rothschild mansions (*Open* to the public; *admission* to the house by timed ticket): the others are **Mentmore Towers▶** and **Ascott▶** (NT).

▶ ▶ Warwick   111B3

*(Tourist information tel: 01926 492212;
www.shakespeare-country.co.uk)*

Warwick is a pleasant country town with a magnificent castle, one of Britain's most visited stately homes. Indeed, on weekends and at holiday periods your visit may be spoiled by the crowds. The heart of the town was rebuilt after a fire in 1694; a walk around **High Street** and **Northgate Street** takes you past some of the finest buildings, including Court House and Landor House. The **Warwickshire Museum** (*Admission free*) in the market square is a good place for children, with displays including natural history, a model of old Warwick and the historic Sheldon tapestry map of Warwickshire; its **Doll Museum**, on a separate site, displays antique toys and games. Two of Warwick's medieval **gateways** survive, complete with chapels. Westgate Chapel forms part of the **Lord Leycester Hospital**▶, a tottering half-timbered range enclosing a pretty courtyard; since 1571, the building has been used as a hospice for retired soldiers and part of the interior houses the Queen's Own Hussars regimental museum. Pre-fire features of the collegiate **Church of St. Mary**▶ include the fan-vaulted Beauchamp Chapel, with a collection of Warwick tombs and a Norman crypt.

   Warwick Castle▶ ▶ (tel: 0870 442 2000; www.warwick-castle.co.uk) looks its best from Castle Bridge, where the 14th-century walls are reflected in the Avon. There is a walk along the ramparts and, inside, a tour of the mansion takes you from the grim austerity of the original dungeons to the gloomy but sumptuous opulence of rooms later adapted for comfortable living. There are wax figures of a royal weekend party and the Kingmaker Exhibition (with the sounds, sights and smells of the castle getting ready for battle). In the grounds are a re-created Victorian rose garden, the Peacock Garden and parkland, landscaped by Capability Brown.

*Warwick Castle rises
sheer from the River
Avon*

KENILWORTH CASTLE (EH)
On the western edge of Kenilworth, this huge sandstone castle (England's largest castle ruin) is the site for events featuring medieval pageantry, drama and music. The Norman castle was much adapted by the Earl of Leicester, Queen Elizabeth's favourite, whose neglected wife Amy Robsart died nearby in mysterious circumstances (it was never discovered whether her fall down stairs was murder, accident, or suicide). The Virgin Queen was compelled by the resulting controversy to distance herself from Leicester, whom she eventually had executed for treason (admission includes an audio tour).

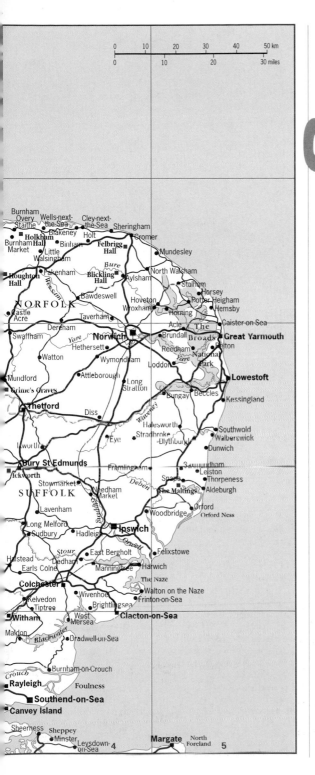

| 0 | 10 | 20 | 30 | 40 | 50 km |
| 0 | | 10 | | 20 | 30 miles |

Burnham Overy Staithe · Wells-next-the-Sea · Cley-next-the-Sea · Sheringham
Holkham · Blakeney · Holt · Cromer
Burnham Market · Holkham Hall · Binham · Felbrigg Hall
Little Walsingham · Mundesley
Houghton Hall · Fakenham · Blickling Hall · Aylsham · North Walsham
Bawdeswell · Stalham · Horsey
NORFOLK · Hoveton · Wroxham · Potter Heigham · Hemsby
Castle Acre · Taverham · Horning · Acle · The Broads · Caister on Sea
Dereham · Norwich · Brundall · Great Yarmouth
Swaffham · Yare · Hethersett · Reedham · Halton
Watton · Wymondham · Loddon · Yare · National Park
Mundford · Attleborough · Lowestoft
Grime's Graves · Long Stratton · Bungay · Beccles · Kessingland
Thetford · Diss
Waveney · Halesworth · Southwold
Ixworth · Eye · Stradbroke · Blythburgh · Walberswick
Dunwich
Bury St Edmunds · Framlingham · Saxmundham · Leiston · Thorpeness
Ickworth · Snape · The Maltings · Aldeburgh
Stowmarket · Needham Market · Deben
SUFFOLK
Lavenham · Orford · Orford Ness
Long Melford · Hadleigh · Woodbridge
Sudbury · Ipswich · Orwell
Stour · East Bergholt · Felixstowe
Halstead · Dedham · Manningtree · Harwich
Earls Colne · The Naze
Colchester · Walton on the Naze · Frinton-on-Sea
Kelvedon · Wivenhoe · Brightlingsea
Tiptree · West Mersea · Clacton-on-Sea
Witham
Maldon · Blackwater · Bradwell-on-Sea
Crouch · Burnham-on-Crouch
Rayleigh · Foulness
Southend-on-Sea
Canvey Island
Sheerness · Sheppey
Minster · Leysdown-on-Sea · Margate · North Foreland

The River Ant near How Hill: typical of the water-scapes of the Norfolk Broads

'On a still day, the light can have the delicate outlines of a Japanese picture. On a stormy day, even in summer, the grey sea batters itself against the shelf [of pebbles], dragging the shingle down with a scrunching, grating, slithering sound. To anyone born on the Suffolk coast, this sound has always meant home.'
—Imogen Holst, *Britten*, in the 'Great Composers' series (1966)

EASTERN ENGLAND This region extends from the northern edge of London to the brink of Humberside. The countryside is agricultural and either flat or gently undulating, with only the Lincolnshire Wolds, Bedfordshire's Dunstable Downs and Leicestershire's Charnwood Forest rising to any appreciable height. Although it is not a region endowed with natural drama, there are imposing country houses set in landscaped parkland, unspoilt villages and country towns, and some beautiful coast.

EAST ANGLIA The most consistently picturesque area of eastern England is East Anglia, the collective term for **Norfolk**, **Suffolk**, northern **Essex** and eastern **Cambridgeshire**: here, above all, the prosperity brought about by the medieval wool trade left a noble legacy of church architecture and villages and towns of handsome half-timbered and plaster-fronted cottages. The countryside was immortalized by the paintings of John Constable on the Essex/Suffolk border with pastel-hued plasterwork ornately decorated with relief patterns known as 'pargeting'. In **Norfolk**, flint walls and Dutch gable ends, reflecting former trading links with the Low Countries, are a common sight. Windmills are ubiquitous, the skies are vast and the light effects subtle.

Scenically, the coast is the most appealing part: south Essex is drably developed around the Thames Estuary, but improves farther north, and east of Ipswich **Suffolk** has lots of interest for the walker and naturalist, although the presence of Sizewell nuclear power station is unfortunate. The **Norfolk Broads** is an excellent place to hire a sail-it-yourself boat. There is a wonderful solitary beauty is abundant along the unspoiled north Norfolk coast.

North of Cambridge lie the **Fens**, a vast expanse of fertile, flat, black-soil farmland, formerly beneath water but drained by cuts and sluices; much of that landscape transformation was begun in the 17th century. Wicken Fen near Ely gives an idea of what the Fens were like before this great agricultural upgrading.

THE INLAND SHIRES There are various pockets of interest inland. **Hertfordshire** has some fine country houses and oases of rural charm such as Ayot St. Lawrence and Benington, but Hertford, Hemel Hempstead and other towns are commuter satellites. **Bedfordshire** has grand houses such as Luton Hoo and Woburn Abbey, but the former hat-making town of Luton and Bedford itself are uninteresting. Northampton is famed for shoemaking and the best of the gentle **Northamptonshire** countryside includes Rockingham Forest and the ironstone villages of Badby and Everdon, while there is an appealing canal scene and canal museum at Stoke Bruerne. Milton Keynes is the newest of Britain's new towns. **Althorp** is the seat of the Spencer family; Diana, Princess of Wales, is buried on a lake island and visitors can pay their respects at a shrine; the house and grounds open from July to September. **Leicestershire** is endowed with some large country estates and rolling countryside on its eastern side, but further west many of its towns belong to the industrial East Midlands; Leicester, the county town, is an industrial hub, though it does have an excavated Roman site within the Jewry Wall Museum and its main attractions and museums are free, making it a good place for day visits. Belvoir Castle, home of the Duke of Rutland, is one of the grandest 19th-century statements of wealth and social prominence. **Nottinghamshire** is the county of Robin Hood, although what is left of Sherwood Forest is inevitably smaller and tamer than in the famous outlaw's day; the great country estates known as the Dukeries include Newstead Abbey and others, while Clumber Park is a popular strolling ground. The writer D. H. Lawrence lived at Eastwood, in the Nottinghamshire coalfield and his house is open as a museum. Nottingham itself is no great beauty but the Lace Market district is attractive and there is an excellent crop of museums.

CAMBRIDGE AND THE CATHEDRAL CITIES Visitors come above all to the university city of **Cambridge**, whose colleges and river combine in perfect composition. Alumni include Oliver Cromwell, John Milton, Isaac Newton, Lord Byron and Charles Darwin. **Ely**, **Norwich**, **Peterborough**, **St. Albans**, **Southwell** and **Lincoln** each have splendid cathedrals, abbeys, or minsters. Of these places, Norwich and Lincoln are less well known, because of their relative isolation, than many of England's other great cathedral cities and deserve a longer look.

BEST PLACES TO GO:
HISTORIC CITIES
Cambridge, Lincoln, Norwich.
SMALL TOWNS
Bury St. Edmunds, Ely, Lavenham, Little Walsingham, Louth, Newark-on-Trent, Saffron Walden, St. Albans, Southwell, Stamford, Thaxted, Woodbridge, Wymondham.
COASTAL TOWNS AND VILLAGES
Aldeburgh, Burnham Overy Staithe, Cley, Dunwich, Southwold, Wells-next-the-Sea.
WALKS
Bedfordshire: Dunstable Downs, Ampthill Park.
Cambridgeshire: Wicken Fen, Cambridge to Grantchester via the river, Grafham Water, Hemingford Grey and St. Ives.
Essex: Sea wall at Tollesbury, Epping Forest, Hatfield Forest.
Hertfordshire: King's Walden and St. Paul's Walden, Ivinghoe Beacon, Tring Reservoirs, Essendon.
Leicestershire: Bradgate Park, Beacon Hill, Burrough Hill, Rutland Water, Grand Union Canal.
Lincolnshire: Lincolnshire Wolds.
Norfolk: Holkham Gap, Cley, Horsey Mere, Yare Estuary, Sandringham country park.
Northamptonshire: Canal towpath at Stoke Bruerne, Knightley Way from Preston Capes to Fawsley Hall.
Nottinghamshire: Clumber Park, Cresswell Crags.
Suffolk: Southwold, Minsmere, Flatford Mill.

137

St. Albans Abbey and the parkland containing remains of the Roman city of Verulamium

THE COLLEGIATE SYSTEM

Colleges are the life and soul of the University of Cambridge, just as they are at Oxford (see page 126). The colleges are where most students live, eat and have their supervisions (in which small groups of students discuss their work with teachers). Lectures, examinations and societies are organized on a university basis, but there are comparatively few 'university' buildings as such.

EXCURSIONS FROM CAMBRIDGE

Wimpole Hall (NT) is Cambridgeshire's grandest house, a formal Georgian composition. It has restored Victorian stables and a large park with lots of walks. Rare breeds of domestic animals and two centuries of farm machinery can be seen at adjacent Home Farm.
Anglesey Abbey (NT), built around 1600, has impressive grounds laid out in the 20th century.
The **Imperial War Museum Duxford** claims to hold Europe's largest collection of historic military aircraft (nearly 200). The museum (tel: 01223 835000; www.iwm.org.uk) runs free hourly buses from Cambridge rail station.

The classical grandeur of the Fitzwilliam Museum

▶ The Broads   135C5

(The Broads Authority (Norwich) tel: 01603 610734; www.broads-authority.gov.uk)

Ever popular with boat enthusiasts and birdwatchers, the Broads is an area of fertile fens, waterways and reedy lakes (called 'broads') formed from peat excavations. Windmills, erected to pump water to drain the farmland and now mostly defunct, proliferate. The Broads (lying within Norfolk and Suffolk) are difficult to see except from a boat; one of the best waterside walks is in the vicinity of Horsey, where the pumping mill is open to the public. The National Trust owns the broad of Horsey Mere; marsh harriers, bitterns and otters make up the population. Other strolls include the banks of the rivers Bure, Thurne and Yare.

▶▶▶ Cambridge   134B3

(Tourist information tel: 0906 586 2526 (60p per minute); www.visitcambridge.org)

Home of one of the world's oldest and greatest universities (founded in 1284), Cambridge is a city ideal for wandering. It is a place of calm, students on bicycles and riverside beauty, as well as a bustling market town. You can go into many colleges, but respect 'Private' notices; some close to visitors from April to June. The Tourist Information Centre, Wheeler Street, offers guided tours.

The university comprises about 30 colleges scattered around the city, of which 16 have medieval origins. **King's College** has the most famous building; its **chapel ▶▶▶**, a symphony of fan-vaulting and magnificent stained glass, is regarded as the finest example of the Perpendicular (15th-century Gothic) style. Nearby **Clare College ▶** is a formal composition, like a Renaissance palace. The grand Palladian **Senate House** is used for formal functions, including graduation ceremonies. **Trinity College ▶▶** has the largest courtyard in Oxford or Cambridge and Christopher Wren's famous library (*Open* to the public) in Nevile Court. **St. John's College ▶▶** has two Tudor courts; beyond them the Bridge of Sighs leads into 19th-century Gothic New Court. More modest in scale is **Queens' College ▶**, with its half-timbered courtyard and painted hall.

CAMBRIDGE

Walk

The colleges, river and streets

With the **Church of Great St. Mary's** (fine view from **tower▶**) on your left, follow King's Parade (which becomes Trumpington Street). On the right is **King's College** with its **chapel▶▶▶**. Pass **Corpus Christi** (its Old Court is hidden at the back) and **Pembroke** (chapel by Wren); farther on are **Peterhouse** (founded 1284, the oldest college) and the **Fitzwilliam Museum▶▶▶**. Enter Little St. Mary's Lane, turn right by the river (you can rent a punt). Pass Mill Inn, cross Silver Street Bridge to pass **Queens' College▶**. Take a path on right across grass for views from **The Backs**. Garret Hostel Lane leads over the river to Trinity Lane. Turn left past **Trinity Hall▶**. Enter **Trinity▶▶** and **St. John's▶▶** colleges from Trinity Street; at river, take walkway on right to a footbridge by the **Lock** and turn right across Jesus Green to Portugal Street. Return past the **Round Church▶** and **Sidney Sussex College** in Sidney Street.

WICKEN FEN

Britain's oldest nature reserve, situated south of Ely and now owned by the National Trust, gives an idea of what the fens were like before they were drained. Villagers left the fen undrained to preserve its supply of reeds for thatching; it is in parts wooded, wetland and meadow, with waterways enclosing the site. A nature trail takes you past a re-erected pumping mill, some bog oaks (logs submerged for thousands of years under the fen and recently unearthed) and the birdwatchers' hide. An information point provides a range of facilities.

For centuries, Ely was dependent on the Ouse as a waterway

The wooden Mathematical Bridge was built without any bolts—until engineers were unable to reassemble it.

Behind Trinity and King's, the River Cam slices through a swathe of greenery, fringed by gardens, known as The Backs. Punts (boats originally designed for gathering reeds for thatching) can be rented near Silver Street Bridge. Walk south through riverside meadows for 3km (2 miles) to Grantchester, or head north from Magdalene Street Bridge to watch college rowing crews training.

The **Fitzwilliam Museum**▶▶▶ (*Admission free*) is a major collection of art, medieval manuscripts and more. The **Cambridge and County Folk Museum**▶ is packed with local memorabilia and **Kettle's Yard**▶ (*Admission free*) is an idiosyncratic private house and modern art gallery.

▶▶ Ely 134C3

(Tourist information tel: 01353 662062; www.eastcambs.gov.uk)
Dwarfed by its great cathedral, Ely occupies a slightly elevated site in the pancake-flat Fenland plain. The region is called the Isle of Ely—a reminder of the days when the town was more or less an island in the undrained marsh.

There is little to see in town, but the **cathedral**▶▶▶ ranks among the greats. Part of the building shows Norman work, including the west front and tower, but restoration was soon needed: in 1250 the east end was rebuilt in Purbeck marble. In 1321 Alan of Walsingham supervised the building of the Lady Chapel; when the central tower collapsed the next year he created the wonderful octagonal lantern, lodged on eight oak pillars, that graces the building today (divine intervention must have prevented a further collapse: the structure has little to support it). Attached to the cathedral are a stained-glass museum and a brass-rubbing facility. Around the precincts are the houses of the King's School, an eminent 'public' school founded by Henry VIII.

▶ King's Lynn 134D3

(Tourist information tel: 01553 763044; www.visitwestnorfolk.com)
Once a member of the Hanseatic League (a powerful commercial association of towns in northern Germany formed in the 14th century), King's Lynn still has a continental look in its darkened red-brick buildings. It traded with northern Europe for many centuries and its docks and

GRIME'S GRAVES (EH)

A major hub of England's neolithic flint industry occupies a site in Thetford Warren, the conifer forest on the low-lying sandy tracts of the Breckland (east of Ely). More than 400 shafts have been discovered; neolithic men climbed down these shafts to work in cramped tunnels, chipping away the flint for use in tools and weapons. One shaft is open to the public.

Lincoln Cathedral: one of the great masterpieces of Gothic architecture

industrial area are still very much functional. St. George's Guildhall (1420) is the oldest guildhall in England and has a beamed roof; this and St. Margaret's Church (Norman, with fine memorial brasses) make a visit to the town worthwhile. Lifestyles of yesteryear are evoked within **True's Yard**, where a pair of fisherman's cottages are a fishing museum.

The villages of **Castle Rising** and **Castle Acre▶**, respectively north and east of King's Lynn, both have Norman castles (EH). West of Castle Acre, the priory church of a Cluniac foundation (EH) survives almost intact.

Fenland churches▶▶ Among the finest of these are **Walpole St. Peter**, with superb benches, font and pulpit and **Walsoken**, a Norman church with a magnificent roof and a 16th-century painting of the *Judgement of Solomon*.

▶▶▶ Lincoln   *134E2*

(Tourist information tel: 01522 873213 or 873256; www.lincoln.gov.uk)

The massive towers of Lincoln's superb cathedral soar high from a hilltop site. The cathedral, castle, museums and historic streets provide plenty of attractions for a full-day visit. However, outside the small historic core much of the city is quite undistinguished.

The **cathedral▶▶**, one of England's finest, was largely rebuilt in the 13th and 14th centuries after an earthquake in 1185 destroyed an earlier structure. Highlights are the elaborate west façade, the carved choir stalls and the stained-glass rose windows known as the Dean's Eye and the Bishop's Eye. High up, is the Lincolnshire Imp carving; the story goes that he got too close to the angels and was turned to stone. Steps lead up the central tower.

Minster Yard, the cathedral close, has Georgian and medieval houses. The **Bishop's Old Palace** dates from the 12th to 15th centuries. **Steep Hill** lives up to its name, climbing from the River Witham, past the Jew's House, inhabited from Norman times and so named because of a Jewish community that once existed there, and continuing beyond the cathedral as **Bailgate**. The street is spanned by Newport Arch, a Roman gateway into the city. Opposite the cathedral's west façade, **Exchequergate** leads to **Lincoln Castle▶** which dates from Norman times and has thick walls, gateways, towers and a 19th-century prisoners' chapel.

141

The perfect tonic for escapists, this remote corner of English coast has a tremendous sense of place and history as well as plenty to interest the naturalist. Dutch gables, flint walls, windmills, huge medieval 'wool' churches and weather-beaten coastal villages supply the human elements—while salt marshes (Europe's largest expanse), vast sandy beaches, prolific birdlife and dramatic skyscapes are among the natural attractions.

NORFOLK HOUSES
Blickling Hall (NT) is a lovely red-brick 17th-century house, famed for the Jacobean plasterwork in its Long Gallery.
Holkham Hall is a neat Palladian mansion built for Thomas Coke, 18th-century agricultural pioneer.
Felbrigg (NT), a tall-chimneyed, 17th-century house in a wooded park, has Georgian furnishings and a fine 18th-century library.
Houghton Hall exudes Palladian elegance and was the seat of Sir Robert Walpole, the first English prime minister.
Sandringham (*Open* only when the Royals are not in residence—Easter Sat to mid-Jul and early Aug–Oct; park and drives always open) was built in the 19th century as a country home for the Prince of Wales, the future Edward VII.

142

A shrimping boat at Wells-next-the-Sea

THE VILLAGES Cromer, famed for its crabs, and **Sheringham** are demure Edwardian resorts atop crumbly cliffs; from the latter a private steam railway heads towards Holt. Inland lies Norfolk's highest land (heathy rises rather than full-fledged hills). **Cley►** has an often-photographed windmill (*Open* periodically). While **Blakeney** is a yachting haven, where mast-stays flap in the wind and a gravelly bank leads to Blakeney Point (still building up westward). Inland, **Binham►** has a superb 13th-century priory church beside the ruins of an 11th-century Benedictine priory.

Wells-next-the-Sea produces 80 per cent of English whelks; the attractive port looks out over wide salt marshes. A walk to the west brings you to **Holkham Gap**, where Corsican pines stabilize the dunes, flanking an immense beach. Another steam railway connects Wells with **Little Walsingham►**, a place of pilgrimage for 900 years with both Roman Catholic and (incense-filled) Anglican shrines to Our Lady of Walsingham. It's fascinating even to non-pilgrims.

The 'Seven Burnhams' are a scattering of hamlets and villages all named with the prefix Burnham. **Burnham Overy Staithe►** broods over salt marshes with a fetching waterside scene—close by are a tower windmill and pretty watermill. **Burnham Thorpe** is famed as Admiral Lord Nelson's birthplace—every other pub hereabouts seems to be called the Nelson or the Hero. The nation's greatest sailor died on board HMS *Victory* (see page 104) after defeating the French and Spanish at Trafalgar in 1805; he was buried in St. Paul's Cathedral in London, but there are memorials in Burnham Thorpe Church. **Burnham Market** is an attractive village set around a spacious green. **Hunstanton** is a quiet resort beside chalk cliffs, with its **Sea Life Centre** tunnel-style aquarium.

THE WILDLIFE Among the best places for observing Norfolk's wildlife are the reserves at **Holme-next-the-Sea**, at **Cley**, a site with reedbeds and shallow lagoons and **Blakeney Point**, reached by boat from Morston or by a long coastal walk over sand and rocky beach from Blakeney. The coast supports a huge population of waders, with wood and curlew sandpipers in summer; great tern colonies exist at Scolt Head island, common and grey seals breed here and there are sizeable numbers of autumnal migrants and wintering birds.

▶▶▶ Norwich 135C4

(Tourist information tel: 01603 727927; www.norwich.gov.uk)
Tucked away in the northeast corner of East Anglia, Norwich is one of the most complete medieval cities in England as well as a bustling university city. For the visitor there is enough to fill a weekend and you can escape to the Norfolk Broads for peace and space (see page 138). The marketplace is one of England's largest, busy six days a week; elsewhere antiques showrooms and shops make for fascinating browsing and there is a fair range of theatres. Wandering through the medieval core reveals an enticing network of gracious old streets—the finest being **Elm Hill**, **Bridewell Alley** and Colegate—a number of ancient buildings (head for the **Guildhall** and **Pull's Ferry**) and a multitude of medieval churches, notably **St. Peter Mancroft** (Perpendicular) and **St. Peter Hungate**, which has a fine hammerbeam roof, a museum of church art and a brass-rubbing facility.

On the northeast side of the central area stands the **cathedral**▶▶▶ (founded 1096), surrounded by a close of houses and boasting remarkable detailing in the roof-bosses, misericords, glass and stone vaulting; its Norman cloister is Britain's largest. More prominent is the Norman **castle**▶, home to a major museum and art gallery (see panel), and which retains impressively grim dungeons.

Pull's Ferry, a 15th-century watergate on the River Wensum at Norwich

▶ Saffron Walden 134B3

(Tourist information tel: 01799 510444; www.uttlesford.gov.uk)
From medieval times until the 18th century this was a hub for the saffron crocus industry. The legacy of its wealth is a knot of historic streets around the largest parish church in Essex, which is in the Perpendicular Gothic style and has notable carvings, roofs and brasses. The Old Sun Inn on Church Street is outstanding among many examples of the East Anglian craft of pargeting (decorative external plasterwork). On the Common is an enigmatic turf maze.

Just west of the town is **Audley End House**▶▶(EH). Although only a fraction of its original size, it represents Jacobean architecture on its grandest scale. Vanbrugh and Robert Adam were responsible for the early 18th-century alterations; Capability Brown landscaped the park.

MUSEUMS IN NORWICH
Castle Museum and Art Gallery, Castle Meadow, displays a celebrated collection of paintings by the Norwich school; ceramics (including the world's largest collection of teapots), archeology and natural history. In the Forum, a stylish modern building, Origins is an interactive journey through local history. **Bridewell Museum**, Bridewell Alley, shows the trades and industries of Norwich over two centuries, in a former prison. On King Street, **Dragon Hall** is a medieval merchant's hall with a fine roof and vaulted undercroft. In Oak Street, **Inspire** is a hands-on science centre in a former church. The **Sainsbury Centre for Visual Arts**, University of East Anglia campus (western edge of the city), has an outstanding art collection, innovatively displayed in a striking building by Lord Foster.

143

AROUND SAFFRON WALDEN
The area's pretty villages make for excellent touring by car or bike, with quiet backroads through gently rolling farmland. To the west are **Clavering**, with its ford and Saxon castle site and **Brent Pelham**, where thatched cottages overlook the old stocks and whipping post. To the south, **Newport's** main street displays many examples of pargeting (ornamental plasterwork).

That national asset, the British countryside, is adored for its infinite variety. Yet the landscapes of Thomas Hardy and John Constable have already been transformed in the name of progress. In recent years public attitudes have become more preservationist, but is it too late?

THE NATIONAL PARKS
Apart from the **Peak** (see opposite), the other National Parks are: the **Lake District**, the **Yorkshire Dales**, **Northumberland** and the **North York Moors** (in northern England); **Snowdonia**, the **Pembrokeshire Coast** and the **Brecon Beacons** (in Wales); **Exmoor, Dartmoor** and the **New Forest** (in southern England); **the Cairngorms** and **Loch Lomond and the Trossachs** (Scotland); proposed is the **South Downs** (southern England).
The Broads has a similar status to a National Park. There are also Areas of Outstanding Natural Beauty such as the Lincolnshire Wolds which have strict planning controls.
For more information tel: 029-2049 9966; www.anpa.gov.uk

Britain's footpaths need a constant watch to ensure that they are in usable condition

SAVING THE LAKES
Early in the 19th century, poet William Wordsworth was anxious about the development of the Lake District and expressed his wish that it should be deemed 'a sort of national property, in which every man has a right and interest who has an eye to perceive and a heart to enjoy.' The children's author Beatrix Potter was another who loved the area and used revenue from her books to acquire local farms and estates, which she donated to the National Trust.

THE SHAPING OF THE LANDSCAPE The countryside is made by a combination of human and natural activity. Patches of the primeval tree cover that once cloaked much of the country exist here and there, but 'slash-and-burn' policies led to a legacy of barren moorland, while farming produced a patchwork of hedge-lined fields and wealthy landowners created great estates and hunting grounds. Yet so embedded in Britain's national culture is the landscape that this unique blend of elements has become 'nature' in the public imagination. No value can be placed on landscape beauty, but the populace tends to expect it to be available for them to enjoy.

THREATENED AND THE SAVED Delicate eco-systems that have thrived for centuries in Britain's varied landscape have suffered greatly since the mid-20th century, with agricultural mass-production, road-building, urban development and other changes in land use. Since 1945, the British countryside has lost 40 per cent of its heathlands, 80 per cent of its chalk downland pastures and 95 per cent of its herb-rich hay meadows. Fortunately the countryside is so prominent in the national conscience that there has been abundant support for saving what remains, from local campaigns to government environmental policies and conservationist bodies like the National Trust.

NATIONAL PARKS AND PUBLIC ACCESS The major catalyst in the formation of National Parks in England and Wales was in 1932, when hikers (or 'ramblers' as they called themselves) mounted a mass trespass against the denial of public access to the hills of the Peak District. Fights broke out with landowners' gamekeepers, who jealously guarded the privately owned moorlands; six ramblers were arrested and five received prison sentences. This event brought the issues of access to the fore and after World War II the Peak became Britain's first such designated area—seen as both valuable and vulnerable for its proximity to industrial cities.

The National Parks that were created in the 1950s (see sidebar) had several aims, including provision of access and facilities for the public, preserving the landscape, protecting wildlife and buildings and maintaining established farming use. However, walkers do not have total freedom of access (although the law may soon allow the 'right to roam' in open country) and the national parks differ from their counterparts in the USA and most other countries in that most of the land is privately owned.

At the same time a unique system of registering public rights of way over private land was set up—giving anyone the right to walk on some 225,000km (140,000 miles) of paths and bridleways in England and Wales—all now shown on Ordnance Survey maps. A new law, being phased in regionally by the end of 2005, gives the 'right to roam' in access areas of open land and common land in England and Wales.

HELPING HANDS The National Trust, a charitable body (see panel, page 102) has since 1895 acquired large areas of coast, downland, upland and forest, which it has the statutory power to declare inalienable (so it can never be sold) for public enjoyment forever. In this way large areas of coastal Devon and Cornwall's magnificent coastal cliffs have been saved for the nation. There is free access on foot to all the Trust's countryside sites.

Some of Britain's most valuable wildlife sites are protected as **National Nature Reserves**. On the South Downs in Sussex, for example, many of the hillsides that attracted a wealth of wildlife have been ploughed up and agriculturally 'improved' since the 1940s; however, a few pockets have been preserved as nature reserves, such as Mount Caburn (near Lewes), with its rare orchids and butterflies and Lullington Heath (near Alfriston), with its unusual mixture of acid and chalky soils. **The Royal Society for the Protection of Birds** (RSPB) is the principal body concerned with wild birds and their environments in the UK and has 120 reserves, many with hides for bird-watchers. For information contact the RSPB at The Lodge, Sandy, Bedfordshire SG19 2DL, tel: 01767 680551 (website: www.rspb.org.uk).

Additionally, numerous specialist bodies play a role in safeguarding wildlife. Based at **Slimbridge** on the Severn Estuary in Gloucestershire, the **Wildfowl and Wetlands Trust** (WWT) is dedicated to the protection of wetland sites—with a huge population of geese, swans and ducks on site—and has wildfowl collections at seven other places in the UK (for information tel: 01453 891900; www.wwt.org.uk). Meanwhile the **Tamar Otter Park** at North Petherwin in Cornwall breeds otters with the aim of reintroducing them to England's rivers.

LONG-DISTANCE PATHS
A web of long-distance paths spans the length and breadth of Britain. It includes the **Pennine Way** along the 'spine' of upland England from Derbyshire to the Scottish Borders; the **West Highland Way** from the edge of Glasgow to the heart of the Scottish Highlands; the **Peddars Way and North Norfolk Coast Path** in the milder scenery of East Anglia. The **South Downs Way** from Eastbourne to Winchester is open to horse riders and mountain bikers as well as walkers. For more information, contact the Ramblers' Association, 2nd Floor, Camelford House, 87–90 Albert Embankment, London SE1 7TW, tel: 020-7339 8500 (website: www.ramblers.org.uk).

145

THE NATIONAL TRUST

HEADON WARREN

THE NATIONAL TRUST
OPEN TO THE PUBLIC
(SUBJECT TO THE BYELAWS
ON THE BACK OF THIS NOTICE)
PLEASE AVOID
LEAVING LITTER
LIGHTING FIRES
DAMAGING TREES
OR PLANTS

VOLUNTARY WORK
The British Trust for Conservation Volunteers (BTCV) runs conservation working holidays and one-day projects (footpath maintenance, drystone walling and so on); participants pay a small amount for food and lodging. For more information, contact the BTCV at the Conservation Centre, 163 Balby Road, Doncaster, South Yorkshire DN4 0RH, tel: 01302 572244 (website: www.btcv.org.uk).

146

Southwold: choose from today's catch at the waterside

▶ **St. Albans**   *134A2*
(Tourist information tel: 01727 864511; www.stalbans.gov.uk)
Less than 30km (19 miles) from London, St. Albans has preserved its provincial character surprisingly well. Its **abbey church**▶ is a medieval foundation built on the site where Alban, the first British martyr, was executed in the fourth century. Its brick-and-flint architecture dates from the 11th century and has been added to in every century since. The Roman city of **Verulamium**▶ lies in a nearby park; excavations include a semicircular amphitheatre, part of the city walls, foundations of houses and a temple. Site finds are well displayed in the Verulamium Museum.

The **Gardens of the Rose**▶ (*Open* Jun–Sep), the Royal National Rose Society's home at Chiswell Green, 3km (2 miles) south of St. Albans, has some 30,000 bushes, at their best in July. East of St. Albans, **Hatfield House**▶▶ has been in the same family since it was built for Robert Cecil in 1611. It has state rooms and knot and scented gardens.

▶ **Southwell**   *134D1*
(Newark-on-Trent tourist information tel: 01636 655765; www.newark-sherwooddc.gov.uk)
The medieval minster (tel: 01636 812649; www.south-wellminster.org.uk; *donation*) in this Nottinghamshire town is not England's best-known, but the chapter house (begun in 1292) boasts some of the country's most breathtakingly intricate carving: a celebration of Sherwood Forest's foliage in stone, featuring oak, maple, vine and ivy leaves. Two of the three Norman towers were rebuilt after a fire in 1711, but the nave, crossing and transept are Norman. Southwell Workhouse (NT) hauntingly evokes the grim yesteryear of the destitute.

▶▶ **Southwold**   *135C5*
(Tourist information tel: 01502 724729; www.visit-sunrisecoast.co.uk)
An enchantingly old-fashioned coastal town, Southwold is an ideal base for exploring the best of Suffolk's coast. It was rebuilt after a fire in 1659 around a charming series of greens edged by flint, brick and pretty cottages. Three cherished landmarks are the huge Perpendicular church, Adnam's Brewery and the lighthouse that gleams behind the Sole Bay Inn, while beach huts and a pier punctuate the sedate seafront. The town museum in the Sailors' Reading Room has displays on maritime life. Around town lie expansive marshes, unspoiled low-lying coast and heathy grassland— the traditional sandlings, or sheepwalks, on which Suffolk's economy depended in the wool-prosperous Middle Ages— making an area of great interest for naturalists.

To the south, **Aldeburgh**▶ is a coastal town, the birthplace of George Crabbe, an 18th-century poet. His poem *The Borough* was adapted by Benjamin Britten for his opera *Peter Grimes*, an evocation of life on this coast, which premièred in 1945. Britten (1913–76) is buried in the churchyard of St. Peter and St. Paul; a memorial window was designed by John Piper. Britten co-founded Aldeburgh's June music festival, which is focused on The Maltings at Snape.

Just north of Aldeburgh is **Thorpeness**▶, a resort village planned in the early 20th century as a weatherboarded and half-timbered 'olde-English' haven. Beside the Meare, the village's artificial lake, is a former grain windmill.

▶▶ Stamford   134C2

(Tourist information tel: 01780 755611; www.southwestlincs.com)

An oasis of mellow, Cotswold-like limestone buildings, Stamford was the first conservation area designated in England. Its clutch of medieval churches includes **St. Martin's**, a complete Perpendicular church with a notable 16th-century alabaster monument to Lord Burghley. Of Stamford's inns **The George** is the most conspicuous, with its 'gallows' inn-sign spanning the street. Look for two good examples of almshouses, 15th-century **Browne's Hospital** and Elizabethan **Lord Burghley's Hospital**.

Capability Brown's landscaped park at **Burghley House▶▶** laps the brink of Stamford. The palatial mansion was built by one William Cecil, chief minister to Elizabeth I, and later Lord Burghley. The Elizabethan exterior belies an interior refurbished 100 years later, full of baroque flourishes, including a dazzling array of Italian plasterwork and painted ceilings by Verrio and Laguerre in the 'Heaven' and 'Hell' rooms, magnificent porcelain, paintings by Veronese and Gainsborough and notable portraits. **Rutland Water▶**, to the west, is a huge reservoir and major recreation area. Farther afield, 22km (14 miles) southeast, **Peterborough** is sprawling and industrial but worth a visit for its Norman **cathedral▶▶** that boasts a superb painted wooden ceiling—Europe's largest. Some 5km (3 miles) from Stamford is **Flag Fen▶** (see panel).

▶▶ Woburn Abbey   134B2

(Abbey tel: 01525 290666; Safari Park tel: 01525 290407; www.woburnabbey.co.uk)

Britain's largest animal safari park forms part of the grounds of this stately home, the seat of the Dukes of Bedford, since 1550. Despite its abbey origins—a Cistercian foundation prior to the Reformation— the house is an 18th century Palladian composition set in a deer park. Within is the finest set of Canaletto paintings to be found anywhere. The house claims to be the birthplace of afternoon tea, and has portraits and possessions spanning many centuries.

FLAG FEN

Discovered in the fens in 1982, the remarkable Flag Fen Bronze Age Monument, 5km (3 miles) east of Peterborough, is the only English site of its era where archaeological excavations are open to the public. The site was once a settlement by a lake, and a wooden causeway consisting of a platform and a line of posts extending about 1km (0.5 miles) once crossed the water. From this remarkable structure deliberately slighted metal objects seem to have been thrown as part of some mysterious ritual. The museum displays some of the best of the many such artefacts unearthed, including the oldest wooden wheel ever found in Britain. Try to take in the guided site tour, and visit the reconstructed Bronze Age and Iron Age houses (tel: 01733 313414; www.flagfen.com).

147

A windmill stands among the tranquil marshes flanking the Blyth Estuary near Southwold

CONSTABLE COUNTRY

Drive

Constable country

The candy tones of local plasterwork, the village greens and the great medieval churches, paid for by the prosperous wool trade, have changed little since Constable's day. The countryside is mild and agreeable if unspectacular: it is the towns and villages, well endowed with tearooms and craft and antiques shops, that have most appeal in this tour (approx 140km/87 miles).

Start at **Sudbury** (Tourist information tel: 01787 881320; www.visit-suffolk.org.uk), where Thomas Gainsborough's birthplace is now a

Gainsborough's House, Sudbury

museum. The route follows the River Stour, along the B1508 to **Bures**, then east through **Stoke-by-Nayland▶**, where the church tower (a familiar feature in Constable's paintings) presides over the Maltings and Guildhall.

Dedham▶▶ has an attractively broad main street and the building of Constable's school survives; the artist Alfred Munnings lived here and his works are displayed in his former house. Near **East Bergholt**, Constable's birthplace, is **Flatford Mill▶▶** (also reached by a pretty 2km/1-mile river path or by boats hired in Dedham); Willy Lott's Cottage by the millpond is still recognizable as the setting for Constable's painting *The Haywain*.

Turn northwest along the B1070 through **Hadleigh▶**, a handsome town by the River Brett with a fine church and half-timbered Guildhall. Detour through **Kersey▶**, a charming village of one street and join the A1141 to **Lavenham▶▶**, with its resplendent half-timbering, a huddle of inns and an outstanding church. To the west, **Long Melford▶** has antique shops, a magnificent church and two fine stately homes nearby.

The A1092 heads past **Cavendish**, a confection of pink rendering and thatch around the green and **Clare**, with its marketplace and flint-built church noted for its woodcarving. Seek out the church, windmill and Recorders' House at **Thaxted▶▶**.

To the east lies **Finchingfield▶** with a delightful green and a windmill. **Castle Hedingham▶▶** has a mighty Norman keep.

The landscape of East Anglia has always held a special fascination for painters. Gainsborough and Constable both came from Suffolk and Gainsborough's birthplace in Sudbury is now a museum. Constable was born at East Bergholt and pictures like The Haywain *and* Flatford Mill *made the winding valley of the Stour 'Constable country' even during the painter's own lifetime.*

While Constable and Gainsborough are the two biggest names (see page 38), many other distinguished artists recorded the East Anglian scene. Philip Wilson Steer painted the Suffolk coast in the 1880s. **Sir Alfred Munnings** painted equestrian scenes and his house at Dedham is now a museum. **John Nash**, a major

Above: from a painting by John Constable

Fishing boats off Yarmouth *by John Sell Cotman*

landscape artist, lived and worked in Essex for years before his death in 1977.

THE NORWICH SCHOOL Norwich's Castle Museum and Art Gallery has a splendid collection of paintings by the Norwich School of painters, which began in 1803. Its chief figures were **John Crome** and **John Sell Cotman**. Crome was much more successful, to the anguished jealousy of Cotman, who is now regarded as the greater painter, admired for his ability to impose simple and satisfying patterns on the natural scene. The work of the Norwich School echoes the Dutch school of landscape painting. They responded to a similar setting—a flat landscape studded by windmills and grazed by cattle beneath a sky of towering cloudscapes.

The wealth and the comparatively isolated position of Norwich in the early 19th century meant that most of its painters were known only locally. The local gentry wanted representations of the scenes they knew—the tranquil Norfolk landscape, picturesquely dilapidated cottages, ruined towers and crumbling abbeys, cattle and sheep, river and coastal views. The Norwich School painted the rural scene as it was in the last days before the Industrial Revolution changed the face of Britain.

EAST ANGLIAN ART ON SHOW
In addition to Gainsborough's house in Sudbury, there are notable collections of works by East Anglian artists at the Castle Museum and Art Gallery and the Sainsbury Centre for Visual Arts, both in Norwich, the Fitzwilliam Museum in Cambridge and at Tate Britain and the National Gallery in London—the latter has Constable's *The Haywain*.

'How much real delight have I had with the study of Landscape this summer. Either I am myself much improved in 'the Art of seeing Nature' (which Sir Joshua Reynolds calls painting) or Nature has unveiled her beauties to me with a less fastidious hand—perhaps there may be something of both so we will divide these fine compliments between us...'
—John Constable, to his future wife (1812)

150

Carmel Head
Holyhead Bay
Amlwch
ISLE OF
ANGLESEY
Holyhead
Holy
Island
Llangefni
Beaumar
Menai Bridg
Llanfair P
Plas Newydd
Llanddona
E
Newborough
Menai
Caernarfo
Caernarfon
Bay
Llanberis
(1085 m
Snowdon)
Penygroes
Beddgelert
Nefyn
Lleyn Peninsula
Porthmadog
D
Aberdaron
Pwllheli
Abersoch
Harlech
Bardsey
Barmout
Tywyn
Aberdyfi
Cardigan   Bay
C
Aberystwyth
Aberaeron
New Quay
CEREDIGION
Templ
Bar
Aberporth
Cardigan
Lampeter
Dinas
Head
Neven
Strumble Head
Pembrokeshire Coast
National
Park
Fishguard
Newcastle
Emlyn
St David's
Head
Mynydd Preseli
PEMBROKESHIRE
CARMARTHENSHIRE
B
St David's
Solva
Carmarthen
Towy
Ramsey
St Non's
Chapel
St Brides Bay
Haverfordwest
Narberth
St Clears
Pontyberem
Skomer
Pembrokeshire Coast
National Park
Kidwelly
Burry
Port
Pontardd
Marloes
Milford
Haven
Llanelli
Dale
Pembroke
Carew
Saundersfoot
Gorseinon
Skokholm
Dock
Castle
SWANSE
Pembroke
Tenby
Carmarthen
Bay
Llanrhidian
Kitte
Bosherston
Manorbier
Caldey
Rhossili
Gower
St Govan's
Chapel
Worms Head
Culver Hole
Oxwich

A

★ Walk start point

0   10   20   30   40   50 km

0   10   20   30 miles

1   2

Chinese human puppets play fighting at the Llangollen International Musical Eisteddfod

THE WELSH LANGUAGE

Visitors to Wales will not need to speak Welsh, but the language—one of Europe's oldest—is in evidence everywhere; on signposts, official notices, on TV and radio and in place names. It is, however, useful to pick up the pronunciation to make it clear which town or village you are talking about. Many places begin with *Llan* (meaning church), the *ll* pronounced as a soft *ch* followed by an *l* sound— put the side of your tongue against your teeth and blow. Other useful rules are: *u* as in wh*ee*l; *y* as in t*i*n or t*u*rn; *f* as in *v*an; *ff* as in *f*un; *th* as in *th*ought; *dd* as in *th*en; *ch* as in lo*ch*; *au* as in m*i*d; and *w* as in l*oo*k. So Fforest Fawr is pronounced *forest vowr*, Llanwrtyd as *chlanuhrtid*; and Caersws as *kairsooce*.

WALES For all its proximity to northwest and central England, Wales feels strikingly different. Cross into South or Mid Wales from the English border and the hills rise immediately. Snaking along the English border from the south to north coast, the exhilarating and hilly 285km (177-mile) **Offa's Dyke Path** roughly follows the line of a ninth-century earthwork built by Offa, King of Mercia and marking the western boundary of his kingdom.

Constitutionally Wales is closer to England than is Scotland; there is no separate legal system, and the two countries have been unified since 1535. Yet the Welsh are proudly independent in culture and outlook; the Welsh language is very much alive (much more so than Gaelic in Scotland) and is taught in schools. Welsh is the first language of many, particularly in North and West Wales; signs ('dim parcio/no parking', 'croeso i Gymru/welcome to Wales') are predominantly bilingual; roughly one in five of its inhabitants is a Welsh speaker. Wales also prides itself on its educational system; it has the highest teacher/pupil ratios in the UK.

Plaid Cymru, a Welsh nationalist party, has sent members to Parliament since 1966, and devolution— restoration of some powers to the local Welsh government—is a current talking point. In September 1997, the Welsh people voted by a narrow margin to establish a Welsh Assembly in Cardiff, which came into existence in 1999. There are strong traditions of choral singing and of Nonconformism (that is, the Protestant denominations such as Methodism that have broken away from the Established Church), virtually every village having at least one chapel. The Welsh love of music, literature, and art manifests itself in the numerous *eisteddfodau* (festivals), in which music, poetry, drama and fine arts feature. Welsh domestic architecture on the other hand is humble—typically sturdy stone-built farmsteads and houses beneath slate roofs; the railway age added red and yellow brick façades. Grand houses are few, but there are plenty of medieval castles to visit.

SOUTH WALES The southern borderland (the border country often being termed as the Marches) is defined precisely by the gorge of the **Lower Wye**, whose scenic reaches are punctuated by features such as Tintern Abbey, Chepstow Castle and Symonds Yat rock. Farther into South Wales lie the former coalfields and the dying industrial heartlands of the **valleys**, which though hardly picturesque have their own fascination. **Cardiff**, the Welsh capital, is the administrative and cultural capital. The coast becomes increasingly seductive as you proceed west; Nash Point near Llantwit Major on the Vale of Glamorgan coast displays extraordinary candy-striped rocks, while **Gower**, on the back doorstep of the industrial city of Swansea, is a peninsula endowed with castles, magnificent bays and cliffs. **Pembrokeshire**, too distant for mere day-trips, is a popular destination for seaside holidays without the host of commercialized trappings found in so many of the English resorts.

MID WALES This nebulous term is applied to a relatively unknown region, sparsely populated except by sheep, which are encountered everywhere (one-quarter of the EU's sheep population is here). The **Brecon Beacons National Park** offers the grandest scenery, with its best-known tracts on its eastern side—the Black Mountains, the Brecon Beacons themselves and the secondhand bookshop town of Hay-on-Wye. Farther west, the **Cambrian Mountains** are scarcely inhabited and largely impenetrable by car, except by a handful of spectacularly lonely mountain roads laid along routes used by drovers taking sheep to market in the pre-automobile era. Aberystwyth is the principal coastal town of Ceredigion (or Cardigan), whose shoreline, though not as scenic as Pembrokeshire, does have a few pleasant places, such as Llangranog, New Quay and Aberaeron.

NORTH WALES Along the north coast stretches a line of resorts, largely undistinguished with the notable exception of Llandudno. But more significantly, North Wales contains the **Snowdonia National Park**; here are the highest mountains in England and Wales and a good range of attractions, including castles, mines and steam trains. Nevertheless, this can be a frustrating area for motorists: roads are often sunk down in the valleys and the scenery slips by quickly; but there are outstanding walks at varying levels of difficulty, from easy forest strolls to tough scrambles up challenging scree-covered mountain slopes.

RECOMMENDED SMALL TOWNS
Carmarthenshire: Llandeilo.
Conwy: Conwy.
Monmouthshire: Chepstow, Monmouth.
Pembrokeshire: St. David's.
Powys: Hay-on-Wye, Llandrindod Wells, Llanidloes, Montgomery, Presteigne.

CASTLES
Caernarfon, Caerphilly, Conwy, Harlech.

COASTAL TOWNS
Llandudno, Tenby.

WALKING AREAS
Brecon Beacons National Park, Gower, Offa's Dyke Path, Pembrokeshire Coast National Park, Snowdonia National Park, Lower Wye Valley. (See Walks, page 158.)

153

INDUSTRIAL INTEREST
Snowdonia National Park, the South Wales mining valleys especially Blaenavon World Heritage Site.

SCENIC DRIVES
Mid Wales: Elan Valley, Beulah to Tregaron, Llanidloes via Dylife to Machynlleth, Rhayader to Aberystwyth.
Brecon Beacons National Park: Gospel Pass (Hay-on-Wye to Llanthony).
Snowdonia National Park: see Drive, page 170.

Rounding up sheep the Welsh way—but sheep dogs normally do the precision work

► Anglesey, Isle of 150E2

(Holyhead tourist information tel: 01407 762622; www.anglesey.gov.uk)

Wales' largest island is flat and fertile and it is its shores that provide most of its attractions to visitors. Good beaches include **Newborough Warren**, which offers distant views of Snowdonia and **Amlwch Bay**.

Pioneering neolithic settlers built an amazing number of chamber tombs on Anglesey, the most notable being **Bryn Celli Ddu** and **Barclodiad y Gawres**. The island's geographical position *en route* to Ireland and its gold and copper inevitably attracted the Celts too; a great hoard of Iron Age chariot fittings and weapons was found at Llyn Cerrig Bach. In medieval times, when the island's farmland provided valuable supplies for granaries in England, Anglesey was held by the English. In the 1290s, Edward I built a stronghold at **Beaumaris►►**; the castle (Cadw) was never attacked and the moated shell survives to this day. The town's former prison houses a museum where you can find ghoulish delights such as the treadmill, the condemned cell and the route to the scaffold.

Between Anglesey and the mainland is the Menai Strait, spanned by Thomas Telford's suspension bridge, the longest such structure in the world when it was built (1826) and one of the engineer's greatest achievements. Overlooking the strait is **Plas Newydd►** (NT), the Pagets' 18th- and 19th-century family home; it has a *trompe l'oeil* mural in the dining room, painted by Rex Whistler in the 1930s. **Holy Island**, attached to Anglesey by a 1km (0.5-mile) causeway, is good for birdwatching and there are good walks on Holyhead Mountain, the island's highest point, which has the remains of a Roman watchtower and traces of third- and fourth-century hut circles. Ferries leave from Holyhead for Dublin in Ireland.

154

THE DRUIDS OF ANGLESEY

The religious leaders of the Celts were the Druids, and Anglesey was famed far and wide as a druidic hub. Tacitus, the Roman historian writing in the first century AD, speaks of Anglesey as the place where youths aspiring to the priesthood were sent to be schooled in philosophy, religion and poetry. In more sinister mode, he also speaks of human blood being smeared on the Druids' altars and human entrails being used for prophecies.

Rugged cliffs embrace Porth Dafarch, on Anglesey's Holy Island peninsula, a popular beach for divers and canoeists

▶▶ Brecon Beacons National Park   151B3

(Brecon Beacons National Park Authority (Brecon) tel: 01874 624437; www.breconbeacons.org)

The park is an east–west upland of four distinct areas, the Black Mountains, Fforest Fawr, the Brecon Beacons themselves and the Black Mountain. It is less rugged than Snowdonia but has some fine views and excellent walks.

The eastern flanks comprise the **Black Mountains**, a series of ridges enclosing deep sheep-grazed valleys. Drive up from **Hay-on-Wye▶**, a small town crowded around its castle and a plethora of secondhand bookshops. Above Hay the **Gospel Pass▶▶** is perhaps the most scenic drive in the park, with easy access to the summit of Hay Bluff. The road dips into a valley, past the ruins of 13th-century **Llanthony Priory▶**. Up a side valley **Patrishow Church▶** boasts a rare musicians' gallery and an eerie mural of a skeleton bearing a shovel, scythe and hourglass. Farther west, the A479 skirts the massif between the attractive towns of **Crickhowell** and **Talgarth** before passing through **Tretower▶**, with its fortified medieval manor (Cadw) by the ruin of an earlier castle.

The **Brecon Beacons** are a sandstone ridge that culminates in Pen y Fan (886m/2,907ft), the highest point in Wales outside Snowdonia. The **Brecon Mountain Railway** (tel: 01685 722988; www.breconmountainrailway.co.uk) is to the south. **Brecon** itself is an amiable market town with a small cathedral and the **Brecknock Museum▶**. South of Brecon, at Libanus, the **Brecon Beacons Mountain Centre** is the main national park information outlet.

Predominantly grassy upland, **Fforest Fawr** includes, near Pont Nedd Fechan, the superlative '**waterfall country**'▶▶ of the wooded Nedd, Hepste and Mellte gorges (see Walks, page 158). **Dan-yr-ogof Caves▶** nearby are part of Britain's largest known cave system; one has a recreation of a Bronze Age dwelling, another presents a history of caving in a sound-and-light show.

To the west, the **Black Mountain** is an expanse of moors and forests dominated by the craggy ridge of **Carmarthen Fan**. Much of it is for the serious walker only, but **Carreg Cennen Castle▶▶** (Cadw), a majestically placed ruin in a valley close to Llandeilo, merits a detour.

The national park includes the highest land in South Wales

LOVE SPOONS

Throughout rural Wales during the 17th, 18th and 19th centuries, young men would spend many long, dark evenings carving ornamental wooden 'love spoons'. These would be presented as tokens to the girls or women they courted; if accepted, it was a sign that courtship would lead to marriage. They are still produced as souvenirs; the Brecknock Museum in Brecon and the Museum of Welsh Life at St. Fagans (see page 157) have fine collections of this genre of folk art.

The industrial valleys of South Wales present a startling transition from the lonely wilds of the Brecon Beacons to the north. Here, stretching from Pontypool in the east (close to the English border) towards Llanelli in the west, is one of the most strongly characterized industrial regions in the whole of Britain.

156

'NYE' AND THE NHS
Aneurin Bevan, or Nye as he was fondly called, was born the son of a miner in 1897. As a boy he was himself a miner and had early trade union experience in the South Wales Miners Federation. In 1929 he was elected Member of Parliament for Ebbw Vale and held the seat until he died in 1960. One of parliament's greatest orators, he has gone down in history as the minister who in 1948 introduced the National Health Service, providing the people of Britain with a comprehensive medical, dental and welfare service funded largely by general taxation.

An old pit head

How green was my valley Between narrow fingers of rising ridges extend the valleys—running deep and roughly north to south, each grooved with long rows of houses built in the heyday of the areas' industrial prosperity.

Near the end of the 18th century, the Industrial Revolution heralded a new dawn; peasants from rural areas migrated *en masse* into the Valleys as ironmasters established works at Aberdare, Dowlais, Hirwaun and Merthyr Tydfil. In 1804 Richard Trevithick gave birth to the age of rail with his steam railway from Merthyr to Abercynon. The Merthyr ironworks supplied cannon for the British forces in the Napoleonic wars and track for railways across the globe.

Coal, choirs and rugby Later, iron production ceased and the Valleys specialized in coal extraction; the coalfield witnessed a great influx of new population. Work was hard and often dangerous, but community life brought its rewards—passions for rugby and choral singing; the Valleys choirs still carry away the prizes at the International Eisteddfod (see panels, pages 160 and 163). Numerous leading socialists were born and bred here, including Aneurin Bevan, a miner's son who was to be the instigator of the National Health Service (see panel) and Neil Kinnock, former leader of the Labour Party.

Facing the future At the height of the Valleys' industrialization, people joked disbelievingly that it would have once been possible for a monkey to have swung from tree to tree along the Rhondda Valley. Now the smoke has gone with closure of the collieries as seams are largely exhausted and greenery is returning: evergreen plantations cloak the upper slopes. Tower Colliery at Hirwaun, once the last of the nationally owned pits, is now owned by its workforce; open-cast mining continues, but only one deep mine and a handful of open-cast mines operate in Wales, providing employment for merely a few hundred people. Unemployment overall is running high and many houses stand empty. Service industries are alive however and the area has awakened to its tourist potential. Former miners take visitors round the inside of abandoned coal mines at the Big Pit National Mining Museum of Wales (*Admission free*) in Blaenavon, and in the Rhondda Heritage Park near Pontypridd, where there are also displays recalling mining through three generations. The 18th-century Blaenavon Ironworks have been preserved under the guardianship of Cadw, and in 2000 the town of Blaenavon gained World Heritage Site status: things may indeed be looking up.

▶▶ Cardiff 151A4

(Tourist information tel: 029 2022 7281; www.visitcardiff.info)
Although it is situated in the industrial heartland of
Wales, Cardiff is a surprisingly clean and livable place.
Despite its status as Welsh capital and as home of Welsh
rugby union and of the (much-acclaimed) Welsh National
Opera, Cardiff is not a particularly Welsh city. Bute Park
cuts a swath by the banks of the Taff, close to the Civic
Centre, a gleaming complex in Portland stone begun in
the 1890s. In St. Mary Street are the city's elegant
Victorian shopping arcades. **Cardiff Castle▶▶** (*Guided
tours*) dates from Norman times but had money poured
into it in the 1860s by the fabulously wealthy 2nd
Marquess of Bute (who built the city's docks and made
Cardiff the world's prime coal port); the result was a
mock-medieval fantasy, designed by William Burges.

Cardiff has an excellent array of **attractions▶▶**. At the
wide-ranging **National Museum and Gallery Cardiff**
(*Admission free*), collections include paintings by French
Impressionists as well as silver, ceramics, fossils, dinosaur
skeletons and shells. Recently Cardiff Bay has undergone
an exciting transformation with the docklands redevel-
oped: you can see a three-dimensional model of the bay in
the **Cardiff Bay Visitor Centre** (tel: 029 2046 3833), enjoy
opera, dance or musicals at the **Wales Millennium Centre**,
look at the **Welsh Assembly building**, and visit
Techniquest, one of the largest hands-on science attractions in the country, for all ages.

The medieval **Llandaff Cathedral▶** is dominated by the figure of *Christ in Majesty* by
Jacob Epstein, an impressive creation in
concrete. The **Museum of Welsh Life▶▶▶**
(*Admission free*) at nearby **St. Fagans** has a
collection of rural dwellings from all over
Wales, including a farmhouse, a terrace from
the mining valleys, a Unitarian chapel and a
Working Men's Institute.

North of Cardiff, double-moated **Caerphilly
Castle▶▶**, dating from the 13th and 14th centuries, is the largest castle in England and Wales after
Windsor. South of Abergavenny, at Blaenavon, the **Big
Pit: National Mining Museum of Wales▶▶** (*Admission
free*), is the best attraction in the industrial Valleys, captur-
ing the atmosphere of a working mine (see opposite page).

*The past is brought to life
at the Museum of Welsh
Life (left); it is a steep
climb to Cardiff Castle's
12-sided Norman keep*

157

CASTELL COCH
Another fairy-tale
concoction of William
Burges was Castell Coch
(Cadw), on the edge of
Cardiff, designed for the
3rd Marquess of Bute. It
was never completed, but
there are hints at what
might have been in the
breathtaking grandeur of
the giltwork, painting,
tiles, statues and
carvings. Murals of
Aesop's fables and the
family's coats of arms
(below) decorate the drawing room, while the ceiling
of Lady Bute's bedroom is
painted with the story of
Sleeping Beauty.

Walks

Dinas Island, Pembrokeshire Coast National Park, Pembrokeshire
150B1

Off the A487 east of Fishguard; car park near Sailors' Safety Inn. The 'island' is in fact a peninsula, ideal for an exhilarating circular walk of 1 to 1.5 hours along the clifftop path, passing Dinas Head, the highest point and Needle Rock, with its large birdlife population. A well-walked public footpath cuts across the narrow neck of land to complete the circuit.

Llyn Idwal, Snowdonia National Park, Gwynedd
151E3

Car park by Idwal Cottage Youth Hostel on the A5. The nature trail around Llyn (lake) Idwal gives straightforward access to supremely dramatic scenery, passing the crags of the Devil's Kitchen beneath Glyder Fawr (1.5 hours). The slopes support rare flora, including alpine species and the area is an officially designated National Nature Reserve. Trail leaflet available on site.

Moel Famau, Denbighshire
151E4

Car park and picnic site on the B5429 between Llanbedr-Dyffryn-Clwyd and Llandyrnog. The walk up from the road to the partly collapsed Jubilee Tower gives views west to Snowdonia and east to the Peak District. Start from the picnic site and walk through the forest (following the blue or red markers); return along the open ridge to drop down to the road, then turn left to the starting point.
(1.5 hours)

The Nedd, Hepste and Mellte Waterfalls, Brecon Beacons National Park, Powys
151B3

Car park at Pontneddfechan, east of Glyn Neath. These mighty waterfalls crash their way along wooded gorges in the southern fringes of the national park. The Hepste and Mellte falls can be reached by a woodland path from Craig y Ddinas car park at the east end of Pontneddfechan or from Porth yr Ogof to the north; the highlight here is Sgwd yr Ira, where you can walk behind the curtain of the fall.
(1–2 hours)

Symonds Yat, Lower Wye Valley, Herefordshire border
151B4

Car park at end of the B4432, north of Coleford. This renowned scenic viewpoint over the Wye gives access to one of the prettiest parts of the gorge. Descend to the west, past a refreshment stand and on a marked path to the riverside Saracen's Head Inn, where a chain ferry takes you across. On the far bank turn left to the wire suspension bridge (it will bounce as you cross); return along the old railway track on the east bank.
(1.5 hours)

▶▶ Elan Valley, Aberystwyth and the Cambrian Mountains
151C3

(Aberystwyth tourist information tel: 01970 612125; www.ceredigion.gov.uk)

One of the best places for spotting the red kite (a huge bird of prey identifiable by its forked tail—see panel), the **Elan Valley** is a chain of reservoirs which graces the great unpopulated wilds of the Cambrian Mountains. The lakes supply water to Birmingham and both the dams and Elan village, built for the reservoir workers, are in characteristically solid Edwardian style. The Elan Valley Visitor Centre (tel: 01597 810898; www.elanvalley.org.uk) in Rhayader has details of walks; the trackbed of an old rail way used in the construction of the reservoirs is a good route for lakeside strolls.

An exciting **mountain road**▶▶ climbs the Cambrian range, leaving Rhayader for the Elan Valley and continuing past abandoned lead and zinc mines to **Devil's Bridge**▶, where three bridges span a gorge. Tiny steam trains run along the scenic narrow-gauge **Vale of Rheidol Railway**▶ (tel: 01970 625819; www.rheidolrailway.co.uk) from here to **Aberystwyth**, the main seaside resort for Cardigan Bay. A crescent of bay-windowed Victorian guest houses on the seafront overlook a rocky beach, which is hemmed in by the bulky bluff of Constitution Hill from where you can see Snowdonia and the Preseli Hills. A cliff railway makes an effortless ascent to the top and a camera obscura enhances the panorama on sunny days.

▶▶ Erddig
151D4

(tel: 01978 355314; www.nationaltrust.org.uk)

Erddig (NT), south of Wrexham, is an excellent introduction to life 'below stairs' in a country mansion. The National Trust rescued the house when mining subsidence threatened the structure; all the service buildings and most of the contents had survived intact and it is now preserved as a fascinating picture of the workings of a country estate in the 18th and 19th centuries.

The Yorkes, who lived here from 1733 to 1973, treated servants kindly and as a visitor you see the house through a servant's eyes, entering through the servants' quarters.

Pennygarreg Reservoir Dam, Elan Valley

THE RED KITE
Less than 20 years ago this majestic bird of prey had become extremely scarce, but has been successfully reintroduced in some areas of Britain and numbers are on the increase. Close to the Elan Valley reservoirs, a good place to see them is just outside Rhayader at Gigrin Farm. The farm has established a Red Kite Feeding Station (tel: 01597 810243; www.gigrin.co.uk) where the birds make an appearance at feeding time (daily at 2pm GMT, 3pm British Summer Time), and where bird hides have been erected. Website: www.welshkitetrust.org.

DOLAUCOTHI GOLD MINES
Remotely sited, just off the A482 southeast of Lampeter, the mines (NT) were periodically worked from Roman times up to the 20th century. Some of the 1930s machinery is still in place and, equipped with helmets and miners' lamps, visitors tour the mine tunnels and pan for gold; stout footwear required. During July and August get there as early as possible or book ahead (tel: 01558 650177).

Far left: the family bicycle collection at Erddig

Look at any holiday brochure or tourist poster for Wales and you are likely to come across the same well-worn images: male voice choirs; young girls playing the harp in Welsh hats; mist-shrouded mountains and lakes; and rugged mining valleys. Like all clichés, they convey only a superficial picture. The reality is far more vital: a combination of reverence for the past and passionate concern for the future. One element links all the strands of politics and culture: a fervent sense of Welsh identity.

THE NATIONAL EISTEDDFOD

Welsh-language culture is seen at its most robust at an *eisteddfod*. All over the country, local *eisteddfodau* (literally 'sittings') are set up in schools and chapels, where singers, dancers, musicians, actors, artists and writers of all ages compete to reach the next level in the categories of Awdl (a complex, ancient form of Welsh poetry) and Pryddest (free verse). The nationwide contest culminates, in the first week of August, in the National Eisteddfod, presided over by the Gorsedd of Bards in druidic robes. For more information tel: 0845 120 9555; www.eisteddfod.org.uk.

DYLAN THOMAS AND LAUGHARNE

One of Wales's cultural giants, Dylan Thomas (1914–53) penned *A Child's Christmas in Wales* as well as the autobiographical short stories of *Portrait of the Artist as a Young Dog* (1940). Born in Swansea, he worked as a newspaper reporter and from 1938 he stayed and eventually settled in Laugharne (northwest of Swansea). The boathouse which he made his haven and the adjacent shed in which he wrote (and drank heavily) now form a museum (Dylan Thomas' Boathouse). He is buried in the churchyard.

Dylan Thomas summed up perfectly the eccentricity and claustrophobia of small-town Welsh life in his play *Under Milk Wood*. The action is set in Llareggub, a mythical fishing community whose name read backwards is the rude phrase 'bugger all'. One of its residents, the Reverend Eli Jenkins, captures the emotional exuberance of Welsh culture with his cry 'Praise the Lord! We are a musical nation!' Music and poetry have an influence which is recognized and nurtured in Wales. The famous male-voice choirs, some of which now perform and record all over the world, are still rooted in the close-knit mining communities of South Wales and the farming and slate-mining areas of the north; and the *Eisteddfod* (presided over by Bards chosen for their contributions to Welsh life), a well-known celebration of Welsh culture, is an important focus for the 500,000 or so Welsh-speakers in Wales (see panel).

The Welsh language The survival of this ancient Celtic language—one of Europe's oldest—does much to explain the defensive pride of the Welsh. Banned from use in official channels by Henry VIII, one of the Welsh Tudor dynasty, the language lived on in the home and in the arts. Fluency in English became essential for anyone wishing to get ahead in life and many parents with ambitions for their children encouraged its use. But Welsh continued to be the language of worship and as Nonconformist chapels (especially Baptist and Methodist denominations) sprang up in the wake of religious revival, it survived as the linchpin of many communities.

Political issues With new generations came new attitudes and the 20th century saw a battle to reestablish Welsh education. Plaid Cymru, a Welsh nationalist party (which now has four MPs in Westminster), began in the 1920s calling for a return to the agrarian, Welsh-speaking way of life—a call not welcomed by the struggling industrial communities of South Wales, where socialism still has a firm hold.

In the 1960s and 1970s, nationalism took a more radical turn, as young members of Cymdeithas yr Iaith Gymraeg (the Welsh Language Society) kept the 'language issue' in the headlines with acts such as painting out anglicized place-names on road signs. In recent

A choir performs at the International Eisteddfod

years the language has enjoyed a revival—It is now included in the statutory school curriculum, a Welsh TV channel has been established and a lively pop culture has developed, willing to absorb the dreaded Anglo-American influence. Today you will hear Welsh spoken by both children and their elders In much of North and West Wales particularly and Welsh is taught at schools.

The current hot political issue in Wales is the influx of English people and the decline of traditional Welsh communities. For example, English 'incomers' living on the northern Lleyn peninsula have been issued with threats and deadlines for leaving the country, but the intermittent arson attacks on such buildings seem to have ceased. Most Welsh people are quick to condemn these acts, which veil the very real fears of communities whose younger generations are leaving in search of work, while cottages are sold at unaffordable prices to absent landlords and stand empty for half the year, turning once vibrant areas into sad and ghostly places.

Conflict in the field For a glimpse of the whole Welsh nation at its sentimental and raucous best, try to get hold of a ticket for one of the international rugby matches at the Millennium Stadium in winter—preferably Wales vs England, when rivalry Is strong and emotions are high. Hearing a stadium full of fans singing the Welsh anthem before watching their national game can bring a lump to the throat—whatever the final score might be.

THE 'WELSH NOT'

In 1847 education commissioners visited schools in Wales. There they heard children using their native Welsh language, which they attacked as immoral and backwards. A campaign to stamp out the use of Welsh was rigorously pursued—often by the Welsh themselves. Pupils overheard slipping into the language were forced to wear wooden boards around their necks bearing the words 'Welsh Not'. The commission's report, bound between blue covers, was never really forgiven and has passed into Welsh history as the Treason of the Blue Books.

CASTLES OF GOWER
Like southern Pembrokeshire, Gower has been a 'little England beyond Wales', with a long history of English-speaking. In the 12th century the Normans held Gower and built a chain of castles, of which remains exist at Oxwich, Oystermouth, Pennard, Penrice and Weobley. Cadw maintain Oxwich, a 16th-century courtyard house, and Weobley, a medieval fortified manor house perched by the marshy north coast.

162

TAKING THE WATERS
Llandrindod Wells, Builth Wells, Llangammarch Wells and Llanwrtyd Wells are the spa towns of Mid Wales. Back in 1732, Rev. Theophilus Evans tried the highly sulphurous waters and thus found a cure for his skin ailment. Chalybeate and saline springs were discovered close by and the area became known as a place for taking the waters. A Mrs Jenkins found a sulphur source in 1736 at Llandrindod and by the 1830s Llangammarch was offering barium chloride as a remedy for heart conditions.

Llandrindod Wells: its hotels recall its heyday as a spa

▶▶ Gower　　　　　　　　　　　　　150A2
(Swansea tourist information tel: 01792 468321; www.swansea.gov.uk or www.explore-gower.co.uk)

The Gower Peninsula stretches out west of Swansea. The residential and industrial outskirts of that city abruptly give way to green countryside, and a coast that, on its southern seaboard, is the rival of Pembrokeshire (see pages 165–166). It has great limestone cliffs and superb sandy beaches, followed for their length by a coastal path, while the north seaboard is low-lying and marshy.

The western tip is the best part of all: here **Rhossili Down▶▶**, a moorland ridge with views of the entire peninsula, dips to a seemingly endless beach; to the west stretches **Worms Head**, a high-tide island accessible on foot by those courageous enough. Nearby, **Mewslade Bay▶▶** shows rock strata tilted and folded. Farther east are good beaches at **Oxwich Bay** and **Brandy Cove**.

▶ Llandrindod Wells　　　　　　　　151C3
(Tourist information tel: 01597 822600; www.visit-llandrindod.co.uk)

The days of taking the waters have gone, but Llandrindod survives as one of Britain's finest 19th-century spas. A few years ago the Victorian pump-room was semi-derelict; today it stands proudly in restored state, and you can sample the rusty-tasting waters spurting from a nearby fountain. Grand red-brick terraces and spa hotels, wrought-iron arcades and balconies, and spacious tree-lined streets suggest something larger than a town of fewer than 5,000 people in the heart of sheep country. In town the main attraction is the **National Cycle Collection▶**, with a range of vintage machines.

Cefnllys▶ is an Iron Age hill fort situated above the River Ithon beside a lone church and the (now robust) Shaky Bridge. There is a nature trail along the river. The **Beulah to Abergwesyn road▶▶**, an old drovers' road to the southwest of the town, takes a spectacular course over the wilderness of the Cambrian Mountains.

The quaintly named waterfall **Water-Break-Its-Neck▶** is to be found north of the A44 in Radnor Forest, a lonely massif of rounded hills and steep-sided valleys. **Old Radnor Church▶** is possibly the finest parish church in Wales, with a medieval screen, Britain's oldest organ case, and a font hewn from a prehistoric monolith. Little has changed for 200 years in the border town of **Presteigne▶**, which has an impressive church. In Broad Street the **Judge's Lodging**▶ ▶ adjoins the former (criminal) assize court, which are the subject of a lively museum, with an audio tour taking you round the house where circuit judges used to stay.

▶ ▶ Llangollen, Vale of 150D4

(Tourist information tel: 01978 860828; www.llangollen.org.uk)
This deep valley, hemmed in by natural terraces of limestone crags, is a landmark on the A5. From it the A542 rises up the hairpin bends of the **Horseshoe Pass**, engineered by Thomas Telford. **Llangollen** itself, site of the international musical *eisteddfod* (see panel), is of little intrinsic interest but is a busy tourist hub, a convenient base for a number of attractions. On the valley floor stand the picturesque ruins of **Valle Crucis Abbey**▶ (Cadw), a Cistercian foundation of 1201; notable features are the Early-English west façade and the vaulted 14th-century chapter house. A wooden roof installed in St Collen's in Llangollen is said to have been taken from here. On the edge of Llangollen, horse-drawn barge trips operate along the **Llangollen Canal**; the canal's proudest moment occurs farther east as it crosses 38m (125ft) above the valley on the Pontcysyllte Aqueduct, built by Telford in 1805. Steam and diesel trains on the **Llangollen Railway** (tel: 01978 860979; www.llangollen-railway.co.uk) run along the valley. Above town is **Panorama Walk**, really a small road. You can get even better views by climbing up to the spectacularly sited 13th-century ruins of **Castell Dinas Brân**▶ ▶.

The view from Castell Dinas Brân, looking at the limestone buttresses that tower above the Vale of Llangollen

THE LLANGOLLEN INTERNATIONAL MUSICAL EISTEDDFOD
Established in 1947, this *eisteddfod* (see panel, page 160) has become a major international musical competition, now attracting competitors from some 40 countries. The hugely popular event takes place in the first week of July. During this time, informal performances by groups of musicians and dancers take place on the Dee Bridge. For more information tel: 01978 862001; www.international eisteddfod.co.uk

Wind turbine at the Centre for Alternative Technology

Right: Pistyll Rhayader, Wales' most spectacular waterfall

THE CENTRE FOR ALTERNATIVE TECHNOLOGY
The centre was established in 1974 as a place for promoting environmentally friendly technologies. A water-powered cliffside train whisks you up to the site entrance and a trail takes you around an informative exhibition that includes an energy-efficient house, ecologically oriented gardens and displays of solar heating and other alternative energy sources. Although obviously an idealized setup, the centre is a great place for talking to people (several workers live on site) and learning how to cut your energy bills, improve your garden and give a greener tinge to your lifestyle. Plenty of appeal for children too (tel: 01654 705950; www.cat.org.uk).

Just south of town, **Plas Newydd▶▶** (NT) is a remarkable mock-Tudor inspiration, home for half a century starting in 1780 to eccentric recluses Lady Eleanor Butler and Miss Sarah Ponsonby, the 'Ladies of Llangollen'. They transformed a cottage into this remarkable half-timbered house, where they entertained a distinguished number of guests, including Sir Walter Scott and the Duke of Wellington. The house is whimsical in the extreme and full of personal touches.

Pistyll Rhayader▶, Wales's tallest waterfall, is at the head of a remote valley south of Llangollen. The fall has been engineered to give the water a twist as it tumbles, but the effect is pleasing. There is easy access by road.

▶**Machynlleth**   151C3
(Tourist information tel: 01654 702401; www.exploremidwales.com)

A market town focused on a clock tower (of a design common to Welsh towns), Machynlleth is comfortably set in the peaceful hills south of the Snowdonia National Park. It is an uneventful place in a pleasant kind of way. The town's hinterland is partly inhabited by a significant hippy population. Topping the bill of local attractions is the excellent **Centre for Alternative Technology▶▶** (see panel).

The scenic **Machynlleth–Dylife road▶** runs over the shoulder of Plynlimon, a boggy upland from which rise the Wye and the Severn, the two great rivers of Wales. At **Dylife** a stream plummets into a gorge via Ffrwd Fawr, a splendid waterfall. A scenic viewpoint at a curve in the road takes in Cader Idris, the major summit in southern Snowdonia. It is worth carrying on past **Llyn Clywedog reservoir** to the unspoiled town of **Llanidloes▶**.

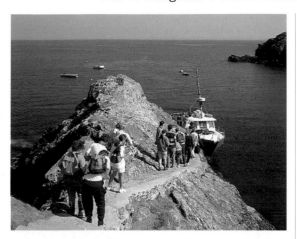

▶ ▶ ▶ Pembrokeshire Coast National Park 150B1

(Pembrokeshire Coast National Park Authority (Pembroke Dock) tel: 0845 345 7275; www.pembrokeshirecoast.org.uk)

As its name implies, the national park is largely confined to a coastal strip. Here are magnificent cliffs, sandy coves (many excellent for swimming if you can bear the chilly water), and a diversity of wildlife which ranks on a par with the best of Cornwall. The south and north parts of the park are strikingly different: a wave cut platform, now raised high above sea level, leaves the southern cliffs mostly level topped, while farther north the scene is more exciting, with assertive bluffs, soaring headlands and dramatic variations in height. Southern Pembrokeshire was for a long time a 'little England beyond Wales', owned by the English, who left a legacy of English place-names and Norman castles for keeping watch over the unruly Welsh Regrettably, the army's foothold on the south coast in the vicinity of Castlemartin means restricted access. Walking is the main draw of the north, which is less populated and consequently less busy in season. Scenic drives are few—the roads generally keep too far inland; a better bet is to take in some of the coastal path, which snakes around the intricate seaboard for some 290km (180 miles). A car will get you into the wilds of the Preseli Hills (see page 166).

TOWNS AND VILLAGES Most famous is undoubtedly **St. David's ▶ ▶ ▶**. Scarcely more than a large village of craft shops, galleries and cafés, it keeps its great Norman cathedral half-hidden in a valley, alongside the considerable ruins of a 14th-century bishop's palace (Cadw). Allegedly, relics of St. David, patron saint of Wales, lie beneath the altar. Of the coastal towns, **Tenby ▶ ▶** is perhaps the most appealing, with its maze of narrow streets, a port surrounded by tiers of Georgian and Tudor merchants' houses, a castle up the hill and a five-arched gate in the town wall. It is very pretty—and it suffers badly for that in summer, with bumper-to-bumper traffic. **Pembroke ▶** is less important than its name suggests, a one-street market town completely dominated by an exceptional Norman castle, which has a 23m (75ft) tower and tunnels to explore. **Fishguard** is split in two by the lie

---

A boat trip leaves Martin's Haven for Skomer Island

ISLAND HOPS

Skokholm and Skomer are major bird sanctuaries, supporting the largest concentration of Manx shearwaters in Britain. Puffins abound on Skomer while Skokholm has a population of storm petrels. Boat trips start from Martin's Haven and for Skokholm also from Dale. Ramsey Island has lots of grey seals (which can also be seen off the mainland) and cliff-nesting birds including choughs; boat trips begin from St. Justinian's. Caldey Island, reached by boat from Tenby, is home to a community of Cistercian monks.

CASTELL HENLLYS

A finely placed Iron Age hill-fort east of Newport, Castell Henllys now is a museum re-creating the lifestyles of its original inhabitants. Iron Age round huts have been reconstructed, and actors demonstrate such crafts as weaving and iron forging.

St. David's Cathedral: 39 steps (or 'Articles') lead down to its door

THE PRESELI HILLS
The national park also encompasses the Preseli Hills (or Mynydd Preseli), a tract of remote upland near Fishguard that is scattered with the burial mounds and hill forts of early settlers. It was from here that the bluestone rocks were transported to Wiltshire for the construction of Stonehenge (see page 84), a feat that has baffled archeologists. The rocks may have been moved by raft (this is technically feasible), but more plausible perhaps is the theory that they were naturally moved closer to Stonehenge by glaciers during the last Ice Age, possibly as far as the Somerset Mendips.

THE WELSHPOOL AND LLANFAIR LIGHT RAILWAY
The privately operated steam train operates along 13km (8 miles) of track between Welshpool and Llanfair Caereinion. Its chief distinguishing features are the narrow 76cm (30in) gauge and the antique wooden cars from the Zillertal in Austria and 1961 carriages from Sierra Leone. For journey times tel: 01938 810441; www.wllr.org.uk

of the land, with the lower town crowded around the port and the upper town grouped around sloping streets. Ferries depart from Pembroke and Fishguard to Rosslare in Ireland. The village of **Solva►** is a boating haven and one-time port prettily set at the end of a narrow, steep-sided bay.

THE BEST OF THE COAST In the south, the indented headlands and bays around **Dale** and **Milford Haven** (itself an industrial port, but worth seeing for its natural anchorage site) have constantly changing views, while **Wooltack Point►►** near Marloes has views across to Skomer and Skokholm islands. At **Bosherston** a series of **lily ponds►** makes a popular walk which can be tacked onto a visit to a fine beach. On the margins of some luscious estuary landscape east of Milford Haven is **Carew Castle**, adjacent to a tide mill and a superb 11th-century Celtic cross. Perched among Pembrokeshire's cliffs are three primitive hermitage chapels, **St. Govan's**, between St. Govan's Head and the towering limestone pinnacles of Elegug Stacks, **St. Justinian's** and **St. Non's** (both near St. David's). **St. David's Head►►** and **Strumble Head►** have rugged grandeur; it is sometimes possible to see the Wicklow Mountains in Ireland from these. Among the most popular swimming beaches are **St. Bride's Bay**, **Tenby**, **Saundersfoot** and **Whitesands Bay**, but smaller beaches offer greater privacy.

►► Powis Castle   151D4
(tel: 01938 551929; www.nationaltrust.org.uk)
A great border stronghold, owned by the Herbert family from 1587 to 1952, Powis (NT) stands just outside Welshpool. It is memorable for its superb gardens (terraced in the 18th century), its architectural diversity through centuries of changes and its lavish state apartments.

　　Montgomery► is more English than Welsh in character: the tiny town focuses on a gracious square with an 18th-century town hall and an assemblage of red-brick Elizabethan façades. The castle mound above town was the stronghold of Roger de Montgomery, who in the 13th century launched assaults on the Welsh.

Tiny St. Govan's Chapel, tucked into the cliffs, can be reached on foot by taking the coastal path from Bosherston Lily Ponds

▶▶▶ Snowdonia National Park *151D3*

(Snowdonia National Park Authority (Penrhyndeudraeth)
tel: 01776 770274; www.snowdonia-npa.gov.uk)
Nowhere else in England and Wales matches Snowdonia
for scenic drama. Long acclaimed for walking and rock-
climbing, it also offers scenic drives, although these tend to
be confined to valley routes and are limited in scope.

The main mountain group is quite compact, focused on
Snowdon, the highest point in England and Wales.
Perhaps the hallmark of Snowdonia is the individuality
of each of the main summits: each has its distinctive
shape. Apart from Great Ormes Head near Llandudno
and the Lleyn peninsula (well to the west of Snowdonia
itself), much of the coast around here is scenically disappointing, however, ribboned by main roads and with no
cliffs to speak of. For sightseeing, on the other hand, you
are spoilt for choice, with a host of nostalgic railways, historic houses, old mines, and castles built by Edward I in
the 13th century to control the Welsh.

THE MAIN SETTLEMENTS In northern Snowdonia **Betws-
y-coed** (pronounced 'Bettus-ee coe-ed') is a touristy
village of Victorian hotels and craft shops. It has grand
scenery on its doorstep and walks along the River Llugwy
and the Swallow Falls and a series of attractive reservoirs
close by to the west; the big mountains keep hidden, however. Also central and with a touch more charm, the
Victorian mountain resort village of **Beddgelert▶** lies
close to Snowdon, and has recently benefited from the
creation of a network of easy paths that can be enjoyed
even when the mists descend over the peaks. A bogus
attraction here is Gelert's Grave, Gelert being the noble
13th-century Prince Llywelyn's dog he supposedly killed
due to an improbable misunderstanding (the grave and
story were actually the invention of a local hotelier keen to
improve trade). Close by, you can tour **Sygun Copper
Mine▶**. Bala, busy in high season, adjoins Wales' largest
lake, but the scenery is not quite so stupendous.

Of the Victorian resorts on the north coast **Llandudno▶** is
by far the most attractive, with its elegant curving sandy
bay, its pier, and a mountain tram up to Great Ormes Head.
Great Orme Copper Mines are a Bronze Age and the oldest
mines in the world open to the public. **Conwy▶▶▶**, also
on the coast, is the only complete medieval walled town in
Wales, with a splendid castle (Cadw), an elegant suspension bridge designed by Thomas Telford (NT) and a house
that claims to be Britain's smallest. **Caernarfon▶▶▶**, too,
boasts a great castle (Cadw). **Harlech▶▶** straddles a slope
above marshland; good beaches lie to the south. The castle
(Cadw) is the key attraction.

Mountains of slate scraps surround **Blaenau Ffestiniog**, at
the heart of the Snowdonia slate industry. Here a visit to the
Llechwedd Slate Caverns▶▶ provides an insight into the
world of the local slate miners, while the **Hydro Centre▶**
gives a tour of the UK's first pumped storage hydroelectric
power station. At **Llanberis** is the **Welsh Slate Museum▶**
and **Dinorwic Discovery▶** which offers trips to the 'Electric
Mountain', underground hydroelectric storage station.

Dolgellau▶, the only town inside the national park, is a
place of stone houses and narrow streets; life revolves
around its marketplace. It makes a good base for

167

**GREAT LITTLE TRAINS
OF SNOWDONIA**
The **Snowdon Mountain
Railway** climbs 1,000m
(3,280ft) from Llanberis to
the summit. Many people
walk back down. **Ffestiniog
Railway**, built for the slate
industry and now one of
the most scenic of all
Britain's private railways,
runs from Porthmadog to
Blaenau Ffestiniog, while
the **Talyllyn Railway** runs
inland from Tywyn to Nant
Gwernol. **Bala Lake** and
Llanberis Lake railways
run alongside the lakes
from which they take their
names. The **Welsh
Highland Railway** will
eventually join together
two existing sections
from Caernarfon and
Porthmadog: currently the
longer section is from
Caernarfon to central
Snowdonia.

CADW MEMBERSHIP
Most of the great castles of
Wales—including Conwy,
Caernarfon, Harlech and
Beaumaris—and other
ancient monuments are in
the care of Cadw, Welsh
Historic Monuments. Cadw
(tel: 029 2050 0200;
www.cadw.wales.gov.uk)
offers 3-day, weekly, and
annual passes for its properties. Cadw, incidentally,
means 'to keep'.

MOUNTAIN SAFETY

Beware! The Snowdonia mountains may not compete in height with the Alps or the Rockies, but they are full of dangers and have claimed many lives. Be sure to be appropriately dressed and equipped; check the weather forecast, take a good map, compass and provisions and tackle only those walks well within your abilities. Leave a note with your hotel of where you are going and when you intend to return.

Classic postglacial scenery: the towering form of Y Garn, seen across Llyn (Lake) Ogwen

touring southern Snowdonia and it has some excellent easier walks on its doorstep, including Cregennan Lakes at the foot of Cadair Idris, the old railway track along the magnificent Mawddach Estuary and the Precipice Walk above the Mawddach Gorge. Farther west, near the coastal resort of Barmouth, the railway bridge across the Mawddach includes a footpath that makes a highly memorable walk in its own right.

THE MAJOR PEAKS The king of them all, **Snowdon** (Yr Wddfa in Welsh) rises high and majestic to 1,085m (3,560ft), five ridges (known collectively as Eryri, 'abode of eagles') radiating from its central pyramid. Not surprisingly, this is the most popular mountain ascent, not just because it is the highest but also because of the views both on the way up and from the top. Paths approach from all directions, or you can cheat and use the Snowdon Mountain Railway (see page 167); the route from Llanberis, parallel to the railway, is the easiest but least interesting path, while the Horseshoe Route (along knife-edge ridges) is the most enthralling and demanding, definitely not for the inexperienced. The first half of the Miners' Track from Pen y Pass (see page 170) takes you into the wilds, rising past lakes and abandoned copper mines to a splendid corrie beneath the summit and main ascent—this initial stage provides an unchallenging way of sampling a great mountain route.

Almost as high as Snowdon and just as spectacular are **Glyder Fawr** (999m/3,278ft) and **Glyder Fach** (994m/3,261ft), two peaks on a great ridge with rock pinnacles and precipitous drops; the **Carneddau group** and (lower but with good views) **Moel Siabod** (872m/2,861ft). The southern giant is **Cadair Idris** (893m/2,930ft), with an exciting path up from the south past a glacial lake, and huge panoramas from the top.

HOUSES, CASTLES AND GARDENS Penrhyn Castle▶▶ (NT) is an imposing mock-Norman structure built by a vastly rich slate magnate in the mid-19th century; architect Thomas Hopper gave it battlements and turrets and a grandiose interior which epitomizes high living of the period. Genuine castles abound in Snowdonia. Most famous of all is **Caernarfon Castle**▶▶▶(Cadw), begun in 1283 after Edward I's conquest of Wales. It was the setting in 1969 for the investiture of the Prince of Wales; his investiture robes are on show here, together with a display of the dynasty of the Welsh princes. **Harlech Castle**▶▶(Cadw), also founded in 1283, has a fine site above the coast; although seemingly impregnable it was taken by Owain Glyndwr in 1404. **Conwy Castle**▶▶▶(Cadw), another of Edward I's foundations, is sited in the town wall; it has 21 semicircular towers and overlooks a castellated suspension bridge, one of some 1,200 bridges designed by Thomas Telford between 1792 and his death in 1834. Less substantial are the castles of **Dolwyddelan**▶(Cadw, near Blaenau Ffestiniog) and **Castell y Bere**▶ (near Abergynolwyn).

Bodnant Garden▶▶(NT), near Llanrwst, rates among Britain's finest horticultural creations. On the coast near Porthmadog, **Portmeirion**▶▶ is an Italianate fantasy village created in the 20th century by Clough Williams-Ellis to show that a scenic site could be developed and retain its beauty. It has often been used as a film set; the cult TV series *The Prisoner* was made here.

Caernarfon Castle, where the monarch invests the eldest royal son with the title of Prince of Wales

The Canal Terrace, Bodnant Garden

SNOWDONIA NATIONAL PARK

Drive

Snowdonia National Park

A circuit of the grandest uplands in Wales (approx 100km/62 miles).

Start at **Betws-y-coed** and take the A5 past the entrance to the spectacular **Swallow Falls▶** to Capel Curig. Continue past Llyn (lake) Ogwen; from the car park at its far end, a short path leads to **Llyn Idwal▶▶**, beneath the

vast crags of the Devil's Kitchen (see Walks, page 158). Beyond the mining town of **Bethesda** take the B4409, then the A4244 and then the A4086 past **Llanberis**, base station for the **Snowdon Mountain Railway▶▶**. At the top of the **Llanberis Pass**, the Miners' Track and Pyg Track leave for an exciting ascent of **Snowdon**. Continue on the A498 past **Beddgelert▶** and along the **Pass of Aberglaslyn**. Take the B4410 and A496 to **Blaenau Ffestiniog**, passing **Ffestiniog Power Station▶** and **Llechwedd Slate Caverns▶▶**. **Dolwyddelan Castle▶**(Cadw), farther up the valley (A470), is supposedly the birthplace of Prince Llewellyn the Great.

SONS OF MONMOUTH
Henry V was born in Monmouth Castle, of which nothing now remains, in 1387. Before the Battle of Agincourt he gained the nickname Harry of Monmouth. The central plaza is named Agincourt Square in his memory.
Charles Rolls was a pioneer of early aviation, engineering and motoring who was a partner in Rolls-Royce. In 1910 he became the first Briton to die in a flying accident. His statue outside the town hall holds aloft a model aeroplane and the town museum has a section devoted to his life.

►► Wye Valley   151B4
(Monmouth tourist information tel: 01600 713899; www.visitwyevalley.com)

The River Wye defines the English/Welsh border for its glorious finale as it enters a sandstone gorge whose slopes are cloaked with woodlands that display breathtaking hues in the autumn. Once the gorge was a hive of industrial activity, the trees supplying charcoal for iron-smelting; brass was invented here in 1568. The valley established a name for itself during the late 18th century Romantic movement, whose poets sought a deeper appreciation of the beauties of nature. **Ross-on-Wye**, though not in the gorge proper, has a mock-Gothic town wall built in the 1830s at the time of this 'picturesque discovery'. Its arcaded market house is two centuries older. **Symonds Yat►**, a rock reached by a stairway, overlooks a bend of the Wye; paths lead down to the river, which is crossed by chain ferry (see Walks on page 158). **Goodrich Castle►** (EH) is an impressive 12th century sandstone bulk, intact until a Parliamentary siege in the Civil War.

The Monnow flows into the Wye at **Monmouth►**, the Monnow spanned by a medieval bridge with a fortified gateway. The **Nelson Museum** (*Admission free*) is a collection devoted to Nelson, including his letters and sword. Above the town, a rustic folly commemorating admirals of the Napoleonic wars caps **Kymin Hill►**, a good place for views. Turner painted and Wordsworth revered the ruins of **Tintern Abbey►►►** (Cadw), an ancient Cistercian foundation set on the valley floor. It is roofless, but standing to its original height and with exquisite tracery in its east window.

Chepstow has a Norman **castle►►** (Cadw) with keep and mighty outer wall. The main street rises to a gateway in the Port Walls, the town wall. Above the east bank, **Wintour's Leap** is a quarried cliff face with a steep drop to the river, while **Wynd Cliff►**, on the west bank, offers a wider view.

One of the world's first iron bridges—the Regency Bridge over the Wye, at Chepstow

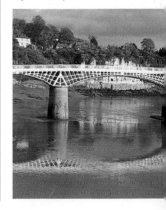

172

Map of Northwest England showing:

NORTHUMBERLAND — Kielder Water, Northumberland National Park, Hadrian's Wall, Morpeth, Newbiggin-by-the-Sea, Cramlington, Blyth, Whitley Bay, Newcastle upon Tyne, Gateshead, Sunderland, Washington, Seaham, Corbridge, Haltwhistle, Hexham, Ponteland

Dumfries, Gretna Green, Glencaple, Caerlaverock Castle, Nith Estuary, Bowness-on-Solway, Silloth, Carlisle, Wetheral, Low Crosby, Stanley, Consett, Castleside, Lanchester, Chester-le-Street, Durham, Peterlee, Hartlepool, Easington

CUMBRIA — Aspatria, Bothel, Caldbeck, Thursby, Wigton, Greystoke, Penrith, Alston, Weardale, Stanhope, Crook, Spennymoor, Sedgefield, Middlesbrough, Stockton-on-Tees, Stokesley

Maryport, Cockermouth, 931m Skiddaw, Workington, Whitehaven, Cleator Moor, Keswick, Buttermere, Pooley Bridge, Shap, Appleby-in-Westmorland, Bishop Auckland, Newton Aycliffe, Darlington, Middleton-in-Teesdale, Barnard Castle, Brough, Bowes

Egremont, Gosforth, Muncaster Mill, Ravenglass, Bootle, Lake District National Park, 978m Scafell Pike, Grasmere, Ambleside, Windermere, Hawkshead, Coniston, Broughton in Furness, Patterdale, Settle Carlisle Railway, 893m Cross Fell, 704m Great Whernside, Kirkby Stephen, Tebay, Reeth, Richmond, Catterick, Northallerton

NORTH YORKSHIRE — Masham, Ripon, Easingwold, Boroughbridge, Knaresborough, Thirsk, Bedale, Leyburn

Millom, Dalton-in-Furness, Ulverston, Grange-over-Sands, Barrow-in-Furness, Isle of Walney, Newby Bridge, Levens Hall, Carnforth, Morecambe, Heysham, Lancaster, Kendal, Sedbergh, Dent, Hawes, Aysgarth, Thwaite, Yorkshire Dales National Park, 693m Pen-y-Ghent, Kirkby Lonsdale, Ingleton, Settle, Malham, Grassington, Buckden

Irish Sea — Fleetwood, Cleveleys, Thornton, Blackpool, Lytham St Anne's, Southport, Formby, Crosby, Bootle, LIVERPOOL, Birkenhead

LANCASHIRE — Bowland Forest, Slaidburn, Gisburn, Hellifield, Bolton Abbey, Blubberhouses, Harrogate, York, Wetherby, Pannal, Otley, Longridge, Clitheroe, Whalley, Colne, Nelson, Burnley, Accrington, Blackburn, Darwen, Todmorden, Preston, Leyland, Chorley, Rochdale

Keighley, Shipley, Bingley, Bradford, LEEDS, Garforth, Halifax, Brighouse, Dewsbury, Wakefield, Pontefract, Huddersfield, Holmfirth, Penistone, Barnsley, Doncaster, Hemsworth

WEST YORKSHIRE, Harewood House

Eccleston, Ormskirk, Skelmersdale, Kirkby, St Helens, Wigan, Bolton, Bury, Middleton, Oldham, Salford, Stretford, MANCHESTER, Chapeltown, Peak District National Park, Rotherham, SHEFFIELD, Worksop, Maltby

Prestatyn, Rhyl, Rhuddlan, St Asaph, Denbigh, Flint, Widnes, Runcorn, Ellesmere Port, Port Sunlight, Warrington, Altrincham, Sale, Stockport, Cheadle, Glossop, Edale, Tideswell, Dronfield, Chesterfield, Warsop, Hardwick Hall

Moel Famau 555m, Chester, Northwich, Tarporley, Tatton Park, Quarry Bank Mill, Macclesfield, Lyme Park, DERBYSHIRE, Buxton, Bakewell, Chatsworth, Haddon Hall, Matlock, Matlock Bath, Sutton in Ashfield

CHESHIRE — Gresford, Wrexham, Nantwich, Crewe, Middlewich, Winsford, Holmes Chapel, Congleton, Biddulph, Arbor Low, Youlgreave, Tissington, Cromford

DENBIGH, Ruthin, Cerrigydrudion, Corwen, Bala, Horseshoe Pass, Ruabon, Llangollen, Plas Newydd, Chirk, Whitchurch, Audlem, Mold, Newcastle-under-Lyme, STOKE-ON-TRENT, Cheadle, Alton Towers, Hucknall, NOTTINGHAM, DERBY, Long Eaton

STAFFORDSHIRE — Market Drayton, Hodnet, Shawbury, Wem, Nesscliffe, Newport, Gnosall, Stafford, Stone, Uttoxeter, Tutbury, Rugeley, Lichfield, Cannock, Burton upon Trent, Ashby-de-la-Zouch, Loughborough, Coalville

ISLE OF MAN — Point of Ayre, Andreas, Ramsey, Ballaugh, Kirk Michael, 620m Snaefell, Laxey, Peel, St John's, Tynwald Hill, Douglas, Port Erin, Castletown, Calf of Man

Shrewsbury, Telford, Ironbridge Gorge, Broseley, Bridgnorth, WOLVERHAMPTON, Dudley, West Bromwich, Walsall, Tamworth, Coleshill, Nuneaton, Hinckley, LEICESTER, BIRMINGHAM, SHROPSHIRE

Severn

★ Walk start point

NORTHWEST ENGLAND This strip covers the region from the industrial northern Midlands to the Scottish border. The most hallowed feature is doubtless the **Lake District**, within the northerly county of Cumbria.

LAKE DISTRICT DELIGHTS Here the lakes, high fells (mountains), pastures and woodlands offer constantly changing vistas of peerless scenic beauty. It is all at a perfect scale for exploration on foot, as equally suited for those wanting a gentle saunter with the mountains as a backdrop as for aspiring rock-climbers. Another option available is to take a boat trip on one of the lakes. Roads and car parks get annoyingly busy in peak periods, but out of season driving is a delight. Public transport is also feasible (Ambleside and Keswick would make good bases), though it restricts what can be visited. The Lake District scores highly for quantity and quality of hotels, for the range of sights suitable for those all-too-frequent rainy days, and for the scope of other outdoor activities, which include sailing, mountain biking, horse-riding and angling (swimming in the lakes is discouraged because of under-currents). As a general rule, the western Lake District has more in the way of spectacle and wildness, while the east is milder, more crowded and has more indoor sights.

THE REST OF CUMBRIA Outside the Lake District, the rest of Cumbria offers a long and not especially beautiful coastline, but an interesting one: along it are the early industrial town of Whitehaven, well worth a visit; St. Bees Head (ideal for birdwatching); and the free visitor information point at Sellafield nuclear reprocessing plant, set up to woo support for the nuclear industry. Northern Cumbria is fairly flat, but it has views across the Solway Firth to southern Scotland and the historic city of Carlisle. Southern Cumbria is fringed by the great expanse of Morecambe Bay, an important site for wading birds and the setting for Britain's fastest incoming tides; tourist offices have details of guided walks over the bay (follow routes precisely to avoid the quicksands).

LANCASHIRE, MERSEYSIDE, AND GREATER MANCHESTER The more built-up parts of Morecambe Bay lie within **Lancashire**—Blackpool, Morecambe and Southport were developed as resorts to serve the cotton-mill towns such as

Below (left): Dove Dale, the best-known limestone valley in the Peak District, deserves time to be appreciated in full
Below: maintaining the dry-stone walls of the region's farmland

Cheshire: Chester.
Derbyshire: Buxton.
Cumbria: Carlisle,
Cockermouth, Kendal,
Kirkby Lonsdale,
Whitehaven.
SCENERY
Lake District, Peak
District, Isle of Man,
Forest of Bowland,
Morecambe Bay
(north side).
TRAIN RIDES
Settle to Carlisle; Arnside
to Ulverston; Barrow-in-
Furness to Whitehaven;
Ravenglass to Boot
(narrow gauge).

174

*View across Morecambe
Bay*

Burnley and Accrington that sprang up in the 19th century. Those towns heralded a major phase in the industrialization of Britain. The mills have closed or changed to other uses, but these urban landscapes, immortalized by the paintings of L. S. Lowry (see panel, page 183), still exist, the straight lines of millworkers' houses being their dominant feature. Manchester and Liverpool were the cities created by this expansion. Liverpool has tremendous atmosphere, while Manchester has experienced a spectacular transformation in recent years. The Forest of Bowland in northern Lancashire is, despite its name, a tract of high, open country, with rugged walks and exhilarating views.

CHESHIRE, DERBYSHIRE AND STAFFORDSHIRE Cheshire extends across a fertile plain from the Welsh border to the brink of the Peak National Park. Black and white half-timbering and red brick are predominant building materials, seen to best advantage in Chester, with its intact city walls. Cheshire, Staffordshire, Derbyshire and South Yorkshire share the **Peak District**; although devoid of true mountain peaks, the Peak has limestone dales, austere gritstone moors, caverns, the contrasting houses of Chatsworth and Haddon Hall, and peaceful stone-built villages. Other outstanding houses in **Derbyshire** include Calke Abbey, a baroque mansion deliberately kept in a state of semi-dilapidation and basically unchanged since 1880, and Hardwick Hall, an outstanding Elizabethan mansion. Although a busy, commercial city, Derby has a surprising amount of open space; the Derby Museum and Art Gallery celebrates the artist Joseph Wright, as well as Derby porcelain, made at Royal Crown Derby, which has factory tours, while an 18th-century silk mill houses the Derby Industrial Museum. Stoke-on-Trent (**Staffordshire**), home of Wedgwood, Spode and others, is Britain's ceramics capital.

Walks

Arnside Knott, Cumbria   172D2
Car park by seafront at Arnside.
The wooded limestone hill is laced with paths to its summit, where a view opens out over the southern Lake District and Morecambe Bay, one of Europe's most important sites for waterbirds of the wader family. The quickest way up is south through the village, on residential roads that give way to paths. (1 hour)

Buttermere, Lake   172F1
District National Park, Cumbria
Car park at Buttermere village.
A well-traversed path leads to Buttermere. The path which runs around the lake is straightforward and level, but is graced with a fine mountain backdrop; the path weaves out of forest, through a section of tunnel and along the water's edge (1.5 hours). Optional add-ons include the ascent of Haystacks, the jagged, dark-topped fell to the south.

Grasmere and   172D1
Rydal Water, Lake District
National Park, Cumbria
Car parks at Grasmere village. Seek out the path along the south side of these two lakes: walk past Grasmere Church on your right, take the left fork of the road to reach the lakeside path, which leaves the road near a boathouse. After a short wooded section, climb up to the level path along Loughrigg Terrace on your right for grandstand views of Wordsworth's valley. Either continue on around Rydal Water or head back by dropping through woods, over a bridge and the A591 to take a minor road to Wordsworth's Dove Cottage at the edge of Grasmere village. (1.5 hours)

Monsal Dale and   172B3
Chee Dale, Peak
National Park, Derbyshire
Car parks at Miller's Dale (old station). Turn left along the railway track (Monsal Trail) to enter Miller's Dale; the trail swings away from the train track as it passes through a tunnel. You pass the Wye's old textile mills, rejoin the train tracks and cross Monsal viaduct (2.5 hours). In the other direction from the car park, the trail soon leaves the railway track for an exciting stepping-stone route along the Wye as it enters a gorge beneath Chee Tor, a popular haunt of rock climbers. (2 hours)

Ullswater, Lake District   172E1
National Park, Cumbria
Car park at Glenridding. Begin this walk by taking the lake steamer from Glenridding across to Howtown and then follow the well-traversed lakeside path back (allow approximately 4 hours); it undulates delightfully and ducks in and out of woods with sudden vistas. An optional add-on is to climb Hallin Fell, close by Howtown, by a path up its southern side.

175

A Lake District scene between Rydal Water and Grasmere

Blackpool: roller-coaster by night

THE ISLE OF MAN
(*Tourist information tel: 01624 686801; www.visitisleofman.com*)
Ruled by Queen Elizabeth II but not part of the UK (it has its own parliament), the Isle of Man has a certain curiosity value. Its residents are called Manx, as is its almost extinct Celtic language. Manx cats are naturally tailless. Located in the Irish Sea, the island does not enjoy the greatest climate and its resorts are somewhat faded. Fish-and-chips is the rule, *haute cuisine* the exception. Yet to some the isle's charms are irresistible: its coastline, particularly in the south around the fishing port of Peel and the seaside resort of Port Erin, is of high, unspoiled cliffs, while inland the hills rise dramatically. A splendid legacy of historic railways has been preserved and the TT Races, an annual motorcycle event since 1907, draws large crowds. Reach the island by ferry or fast ferry from Liverpool, or ferry from Heysham, or by air.

The Citadel, a prominent landmark in Carlisle

▶ Blackpool   *172C1*
(*Tourist information tel: 01253 478222; www.visitblackpool.com*)
In Victorian times this seaside resort was the traditional day out for millworkers from the Lancashire cotton towns, and Blackpool is still going strong in its unique, brash way. The beach suffers from pollution, but the **Blackpool Pleasure Beach** amusement park is Britain's most visited attraction. From the huge **Blackpool Tower** views extend into the Lake District from the top. Trams travel along the seafront to Fleetwood, giving the best view of the famous Illuminations (August to November).

▶ Carlisle   *172E1*
(*Tourist information tel: 01228 625600; www.historic-carlisle.org.uk*)
Cumbria's largest town has recently spruced itself up as a regional shopping hub. It does not rank among the great cathedral cities, but there is enough here for an absorbing half-day in the compact historic heart.

For centuries, Carlisle was plagued by border skirmishes and the **castle▶▶**(EH), dating from 1092, was much attacked and rebuilt (the view from its walls is stomach-churning). The keep is 12th-century; the story of the King's Own Royal Border Regiment is told with uniforms and weapons. Don't miss graffiti carved by prisoners.

Tullie House▶▶, an outstanding city museum, is an evocation of Carlisle's past. Also in the middle of town are some Georgian and earlier streets and the medieval **cathedral▶**, one of Britain's smallest, notable for its east window with its 14th-century glass. Also worth a brief look is the **Guildhall**, a striking timber-framed survivor dating back to 1407.

The scenic **Settle–Carlisle line▶▶**, part of the nation's railway network, was saved by a campaign of volunteers. From Settle, in the Yorkshire Dales, the route crosses the high Pennines in spectacular fashion, over the Ribblehead Viaduct in the shadow of Whernside and along the Eden Valley. Special steam trains sometimes run on the route. By far the most dramatic landscape is between Settle and Appleby-in-Westmoreland, which has a fine castle.

▶▶▶ Chester   172B1
(Tourist information tel: 01244 402111; www.chestertourism.com)

Founded as the Roman city of *Deva*, Chester was a major port until the River Dee silted up in medieval times. Its fortunes slumped until a revival in the 18th century. Today, it has plenty to show for these three periods.

Foremost is Britain's most complete **city wall**▶▶, which provides a fascinating 5km (3-mile) walk, raised above street level for much of the way. A number of its gateways are still in place although much of the wall is medieval some Roman masonry can be seen. A superb set of Roman tombstones are exhibited at the **Grosvenor Museum**▶▶ *(Admission free)*; the museum also includes a Georgian house, and local silver and furniture. By **Newgate**, on the east side, part of the **Roman amphitheatre** can be seen near a park, but more rewarding is the **Dewa Roman Experience**▶▶, an evocation of Roman Chester, with recreated streets, forts and bathhouses, as well as local finds.

Of medieval Chester, the most famous feature is **The Rows**, which feature an upper tier of shops with its own walkway above street level. Nobody quite knows why Chester developed this way, but today it is a thriving shopping area. The central streets house a pleasing mix of half-timbered Tudor, red-brick Georgian and exuberantly elaborate 19th century fake black-and-white buildings. Chester's Victoriana also includes a Gothic style **town hall**, where the Council Chamber and Assembly Rooms are open to the public, on Northgate Street. The red sandstone **cathedral**▶▶ was restored in the 19th century, but its superbly carved 14th-century choir stalls are unaltered. Many of the abbey buildings survived the Reformation in the 16th century, including the chapter house and cloisters.

The famous **Chester Zoo**▶▶ is up the A41 at Upton by Chester. Animal enclosures simulate natural environments.

Chester's streetscape, as seen from The Rows: these Tudor-style buildings are exuberant Victorian pastiche

A WALK ALONG CHESTER'S WALLS: PART 1
From Grosvenor Bridge (the largest single span in the world when erected in 1832), take a counter-clockwise tour of the walls, crossing Bridgegate with its pleasant boating scene a little east (boat rentals available). The walls now turn north, past Newgate and the Roman amphitheatre, over Eastgate with its ornamental clock of 1897.

A WALK ALONG CHESTER'S WALLS: PART 2
Skirt the cathedral precincts (Abbey Square); the northeast tower is known as the King Charles Tower since that king watched from here the defeat of his army by the Parliamentarians on Rowton Heath in 1645. By Northgate the drop on the canal side plummets spectacularly; on the south side is the Bluecoat Hospital (1717) and the sideless Bridge of Sighs, which condemned felons had to cross on their way to prison. From the Water Tower (1322) are views of the Welsh hills. The west side of the walls (where you must follow the road) has less of interest.

The Lake District National Park—Lakeland, the English Lakes, or just the Lakes, call it what you will—is a microcosm of breathtaking variety and scenic perfection. Its character wavers between windswept mountainous upland and dry-stone-walled, lowland pastures. It is outstanding for outdoor pursuits, particularly walking, climbing and sailing, but the climate can be fickle: benign-looking summer days have a habit of clouding over suddenly. Fortunately the area has plenty of indoor attractions, especially for those on a literary pilgrimage.

LITERARY LAKELAND

William Wordsworth was born in Cockermouth in 1770 and a happy childhood there was to influence his poetry in later life. His preferred home was Dove Cottage (*open* to the public and incorporating the Wordsworth Museum), in Grasmere, where he lived from 1799 to 1808. He loved the place and wrote about the area; he is buried in Grasmere churchyard.

The Wordsworths were the focus of a group of friends, among them poet Samuel Taylor Coleridge. Alfred, Lord Tennyson reputedly wrote *Idylls of the King* at Mirehouse, Keswick; later, poet Matthew Arnold and critic John Ruskin both lived here.

Beatrix Potter wrote and illustrated her children's stories at Hill Top (*open* to the public; NT) in Near Sawrey. Arthur Ransome set his *Swallows and Amazons* in the Lakes.

LAKELAND GEOLOGY

The district is formed out of a huge volcanic dome, pushed out from within the earth, subsequently overlain with rocks and sculpted by glaciers into valleys and corries. The Skiddaw Slates, found in northwest Lakeland, make up green slopes, while the volcanic Borrowdale rocks include rugged fells. Limestone predominates in the eastern tracts.

178

Lake District National Park Authority (Kendal) tel: 01539 724555; www.lake-district.gov.uk

THE NORTH AND WEST Keswick▶, the major hub for the northern lakes, is a slate Victorian town, full of walkers, tourists, bed-and-breakfast signs and outdoor sports shops. Here are the traditional **Keswick Museum and Art Gallery** (*Admission free*; with its 'piano' of Cumberland slates), and the unique **Cumberland Pencil Museum**. Just east is the Bronze Age **Castlerigg Stone Circle▶**. The beauties of **Derwent Water▶▶▶** can be appreciated from a public boat or from a shoreside path past Friar's Crag.

Borrowdale appealed to early discoverers of the 'picturesque'; Castle Crag is a good vantage point. The main road over **Honister Pass** skirts **Buttermere▶▶▶**, looking like a miniature Scottish loch. **Cockermouth▶**, outside the park, is a typical Cumbrian market town with attractive houses and with its own brewery.

North of Keswick, the fells flatten and the crowds disappear, but the moors have a beauty of their own. **Hesket Newmarket** is the prettiest village hereabouts. Southeast of Keswick, **Thirlmere▶** is the most popular starting point for walks up Helvellyn (950m/3,117ft). The lake of **Ullswater▶▶▶** twists its way south from Pooley Bridge, the scenery getting better all the time; a steamer plies the length of the lake. By the A592, **Aira Force▶▶** a waterfall, tumbles into a shady chasm at the side of Gowbarrow Park, where Wordsworth saw that host of golden daffodils. East of Ullswater, **Askham▶** is a village of stone cottages.

The Lake District's western tracts are less accessible and a wonderful tonic for escapists. **Wast Water▶▶▶** is one of the great sights, looking to the heights of Great Gable, and Scafell Pike is the highest peak in England at 978m (3,209ft). **Eskdale▶** is mellow and broad; the narrow-gauge **Ravenglass and Eskdale Railway** (tel: 01229 717171; www.ravenglass-railway.co.uk) runs along the valley to the tiny village of Boot with its restored grain mill. Just outside the coastal village of **Ravenglass** stands a Roman bathhouse known as Walls Castle. At the dale's east end, the **Hardknott Pass▶▶▶** is the great scenic drive of Lakeland; the Isle of Man may be visible from the remains of a Roman fort near the top. Drivers can continue along **Wrynose Pass** or into the **Duddon Valley**.

THE SOUTH AND EAST Windermere, England's longest lake, has wooded shores sprinkled with villas built by 19th-century industrialists; steamers serve most parts of the lake and from Lakeside at the southern end a steam train (Lakeside and Haverthwaite Railway; tel: 015394 31594) runs to Haverthwaite. **Bowness-on-Windermere** is a busy lakeside resort; **Windermere town**, away from the lake, is railway-age suburbia. **Ambleside**, at the lake's northern end, is more attractive, particularly up the hill. On Windermere's shores are a number of gardens (**Holehird▶**, **Stagshaw▶** and **Graythwaite Hall▶**), the **Lake District Visitor Centre at Brockhole▶** (tel: 015394 46601; www.lake-district.gov.uk) and the **Windermere Steamboats and Museum▶** (offering cruises on vintage craft).

West of Windermere, the landscape rolls gently, thickly cloaked in trees; in **Grizedale Forest** woodland paths are enhanced by modern sculptures. **Stott Park Bobbin Mill▶** (EH) demonstrates the process of bobbin making. Visit the village of **Hawkshead▶▶** out of season—or wait for the car park and join the crowds in its quaint little streets; its chief sights are the **Beatrix Potter Gallery** (NT), with a changing exhibition of Potter's sketches and paintings, and the **Old Grammar School**, housing the desk on which former pupil William Wordsworth carved his name. Just out of the village, **Tarn Hows▶** is a pretty, if too-visited, pair of tarns artificially merged into one as a landscape feature. Above the village of Coniston, beneath the summit of the Old Man of Coniston, are spectacular relics of its bygone copper mining industry. Glide silently over **Coniston Water** on the National Trust's antique steam yacht, **Gondola▶ ▶**.

North of Ambleside, the A591 enters more mountainous terrain; **Grasmere▶ ▶** and its surroundings are immortalized by the works of Wordsworth (see panel, page 178). To the west loom the craggy **Langdale Pikes**.

Farther south, **Cartmel▶ ▶** is a handsome village, less overrun than Hawkshead, with a fine priory church. Find out about the Lakes at the **Museum of Lakeland Life▶ ▶** at Kendal (just outside the national park).

Far left: the Windermere Steamboats and Museum

> Bliss was it in that dawn to be alive,
> But to be young was very heaven.
> —*The Prelude,* William Wordsworth (1770–1850).

KNOW YOUR LAKELAND TERMS
Small lakes are called *tarns*, mountains are always *fells* (from the Nordic *fjaell*), streams are known as *becks*, spotted black-faced sheep are *Swaledales*, white-faced ones are *Herdwicks*, loose stones created by freeze-thaw weathering are termed *scree. Force* means waterfall. Bassenthwaite Lake is the only lake in Lakeland termed as such: all the others are *meres* or *waters*. 'Lake Windermere' is a useful term to avoid confusion with the town of Windermere, but Lake District purists will shudder if they hear you say it!

179

Grasmere, beloved of William Wordsworth

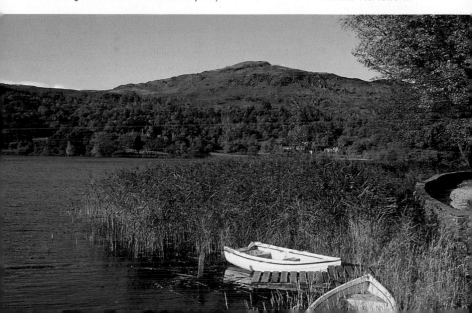

Drive

Lake District

The best of the Lakes (125km/
78 miles), taking in Wordsworth's
Grasmere, spectacular high passes and
the less-visited western areas.

From **Keswick** (tourist information tel:
017687 72645; www.keswick.org) the
route heads south along the A591 past
Thirlmere▶, beneath the shadow of
Helvellyn and past the Wordsworths'
former houses, Dove Cottage at
Grasmere▶▶ and Rydal Mount, **Rydal**.
Turning west at the resort town of
Ambleside, you soon enter **Langdale**,
passing beneath the impressive summits of the Langdale Fells. A minor road
loops around the end of the dale, above
Blea Tarn, to turn right onto the
Wrynose Pass. This leads to the magnificent **Hardknott Pass▶▶▶**, passing
the substantial remains of a Roman fort
on the right after the summit; drop into
Eskdale, with glimpses of its narrow-
gauge railway. Fork right to **Santon
Bridge** (from where you can detour to
majestic **Wast Water▶▶▶**) and continue to **Gosforth**, with its superb
carved **Celtic cross▶** in the
churchyard. Take the A595 to **Calder
Bridge**, then fork right to **Ennerdale
Bridge** via a high-level road with views
of the coast and **Sellafield nuclear
reprocessing plant** (its Visitor Centre is
now a major draw). Beyond **Lamplugh**
bear right and right again on minor
roads to **Loweswater** and the B5289,
where you turn right for a superb finale
past **Buttermere▶▶▶**, up the
Honister Pass, along Borrowdale and
beside **Derwent Water▶▶▶**.

180

❏ Houses open to the public:
Brantwood, east side of Coniston Water: home of critic/artist John Ruskin.
Dalemain, near Penrith: Norman pele tower, Elizabethan rooms, priest's hole.
Dove Cottage, Grasmere: Wordsworth's home during his most productive period.
Hill Top (NT), Near Sawrey: Beatrix Potter's farmhouse.
Holker Hall, near Cartmel: flamboyant Victorian house in Elizabethan style.
Levens Hall, near Levens: Elizabethan manor, gardens. Superb topiary. ❏

THE LAKE DISTRICT

❑ Houses open to the public (continued):
Mirehouse, near Keswick: manuscripts of Tennyson, Wordsworth, etc.
Muncaster Castle, Eskdale: built around pele tower; owl sanctuary, woodland.
Rydal Mount, Rydal: Wordsworth's last house; grander than Dove Cottage.
Sizergh Castle (NT), near Levens: Elizabethan carvings; gardens.
Townend (NT), Troutbeck: traditional Cumbrian farmhouse.
Wordsworth House (NT), Cockermouth: birthplace of William Wordsworth. ❑

In the rejuvenated docklands

MUSEUMS AND GALLERIES IN ALBERT DOCK

The Beatles Story The Fab Four, who immortalized Penny Lane and the Cavern Club, are the focus for this sight-and-sound experience of the music of the 1960s. The two-hour Magical Mystery Tour leaves from here daily; tel 0151 709 3285.

Merseyside Maritime Museum (*Admission free*) An ambitious museum tracing the history of the port: piermaster's house, pilotage building, boat hall, shipbuilding and a display on European emigrants.

Tate Liverpool (*Admission free*) A branch of the great London establishment; modern art.

OTHER MUSEUMS AND GALLERIES IN LIVERPOOL

Liverpool Football Club Museum, Anfield Road: trophies, memorabilia, videos and a look at the pitch on a tour (tel: 0151 260 6677).

Liverpool Museum (*Admission free*), William Brown Street: science and natural history, including a planetarium.

Museum of Liverpool Life (*Admission free*), Pier Head: social history: culture, making a living, voting and much more.

Speke Hall (NT) Fine half-timbered house, dating from 1490. Minibuses from here in the afternoon (or Albert Dock in the morning) for combined tours of **20 Forthlin Road** and **Mendips** (NT; no cars allowed; booking essential; for details tel: 0870 900 0256), the houses where Paul McCartney and John Lennon lived.

The Walker (*Admission free*) William Brown Street: among Britain's finest provincial art galleries.

▶▶ **Liverpool** *172B1*
(*Tourist information tel: 0906 680 6886—25p per minute; www.visitliverpool.com*)

Industrial activity on the River Mersey (Merseyside) has declined and the city's population is less than it was in the early 1900s; run-down streetscapes are testimony to some of the worst urban problem areas in Britain. Yet Liverpool has a strong sense of place, both with it 19th-century heyday as England's second greatest port, and as the birthplace of The Beatles. It now looks forward to becoming European City of Culture in 2008.

The ocean-going liners of the 19th and early 20th centuries have gone—to get a hint of what it was like to arrive by sea, you should take the **Mersey Ferry** to Birkenhead and back. The **Royal Liver Building** (1911) and **Cunard Building** (1917) stand sentinel by the Mersey waterfront. Architecture in the city displays a legacy of wealth and civic pride, at its best around **Dale Street**, **Water Street** and **William Brown Street** and around classical **St. George's Hall** (1854). Restored warehouses around **Albert Dock▶▶** (1846) feature an array of shops, cafés and museums including a branch of the Tate.

At either end of the plum-brick Georgian townhouses of **Hope Street** stand the city's cathedrals. The **Anglican cathedral▶▶**, the largest of its denomination in the world, is a mightily proportioned Gothic edifice, built between 1906 and 1980 to the design of 21-year-old Giles Gilbert Scott. To make the most of its hillside setting, the conventional east–west orientation was not used. An elevator, followed by a flight of more than 100 steps, will take you to the top of the tower for a superb view. By contrast, the **Metropolitan Roman Catholic Cathedral of Christ the King▶** is a squat, tent-like affair set beneath a pinnacled lantern. This design by Frederick Gibberd was adopted after it became apparent that the original plan of Sir Edwin Lutyens was too costly. Of Lutyens' vast building, the foundation stone (1933) and the crypt exist.

▶▶ Manchester 172B2

(Tourist information tel: 0161 234 3157;
www.destinationmanchester.com)

With its Victorian and modern architecture, night scene, gay culture and Chinatown, Manchester stakes a place as one of Britain's most vibrant and rejuvenated cities, around **Salford Quays**▶▶ (see panel) in particular. Near the **cathedral**, the hub of the modest town that was pre-industrial Manchester, a sleek glass building houses **Urbis**▶ (*Admission free*), a celebration of life in cities across the globe. Grandiose Victorian buildings stand as evidence of Manchester's commercial might in the Lancashire cotton industry: these include the Gothic **town hall**▶, with its lavish marble interior by Alfred Waterhouse, and **Barton Arcade**, a Victorian shopping arcade of iron and glass. In Deansgate, the Gothic Revival **John Rylands Library**, (*closed* until 2006) with its richly ornamental façade was founded as a memorial to a Manchester cotton magnate, while just off Deansgate, **St. John Street** is the finest Georgian street in the city.

The revived area of Castlefield includes a reconstruction of a Roman fort that once stood here. The canal basin has an early industrial atmosphere, and you can walk along the Rochdale Canal past Victorian warehouses. Housed in the world's oldest passenger train station, the **Museum of Science and Industry**▶▶ (*Admission free*) has enough to fill a day, with displays such as historic aircraft, a walk-through Victorian sewer, and Xperiment (hands-on science).

Other excellent visits (*All admission free*) are **Manchester Art Gallery**▶▶, with Pre-Raphaelite paintings and modern British art, **Chetham's Library** (Long Millgate; founded 1653 and the Britain's oldest public library, in a building that was originally a college for priests), the **Whitworth Art Gallery**▶ and the **Gallery of Costume**▶ (*Open* last Sat in month) in Platt Hall, covering 400 years of fashion.

Football fans should head for **Old Trafford** to see the Manchester United Museum and tour the huge stadium.

SALFORD QUAYS

Across the Manchester Ship Canal, Salford has been given a new lease of life with two landmark waterside buildings. The Lowry, an arts complex with theatres and galleries is named in memory of L. S. Lowry (see below) and includes a gallery of his paintings. A footbridge connects to the Imperial War Museum North, an inspiring examination of post-1914 warfare and its effects on society, housed in an extraordinary building comprising three shards of steel that represent the world's conflicts on land, sea and air. Both places are open free of charge.

183

Trams have made a comeback on the city's streets

L. S. LOWRY (1887–1976)

Manchester-born Laurence Stephen Lowry studied art in Manchester and Salford and around 1916 developed an interest in painting the bleak landscapes of industrial Lancashire's mill towns. The naïve style of his matchstick figures has been much copied, but at the time his choice of subject was quite apart from the mainstream; many of his works had touches of darkness and satire and an element of the grotesque. A selection of his work is on display at the gallery in The Lowry (see above).

The largest cities in Britain were once its great manufacturing, engineering and trading hubs. They are packed with historical interest and cultural attractions. Yet with the demise of their original industries, many of their inner areas have become run-down, presenting policy challenges for governments since 1945. Many of the problems are now being tackled anew.

'The peculiar character of these streets and the close resemblance each one bears to its neighbour, by no means tends to decrease the bewilderment in which the un-experienced wayfarer through 'the Dials' finds himself involved. He traverses streets of dirty, straggling houses, with now and then an unexpected court composed of buildings as ill-proportioned and deformed as the half-naked children that wallow in the kennels. Brokers' shops, which would seem to have been established by humane individuals as refuges for destitute bugs…are its cheerful accompaniments.'
—Description of Seven Dials, London, from *Sketches by Boz* (1850) by Charles Dickens

Narrow boats in Birmingham's Gas Street Basin

For many centuries, a town was virtually all middle. With its houses and churches, shops and inns huddled tightly together, the typical town was snugly protected from the outside world by its surrounding wall. The Industrial Revolution caused towns to swell out over the surrounding countryside and many became cities, their hearts transformed by grandiose public buildings endowed by proud and philanthropic local entrepreneurs.

Community spirit Despite this vast expansion, the areas around the city's core still enjoyed a strong sense of identity: people lived near their work and often close to their extended families. The tiny back-to-back houses sheltered large families who shared a water tap and latrine at the end of the terrace with other residents, but community spirit was strong even in the most overcrowded streets.

Fall and rise With the decline of Britain's manufacturing base came the inevitable slide in many industrial cities, particularly in northern and central England. But over the past decades, there have been marked improvements, and for the third millennium much money was available from the Millennium Commission (funded by the National Lottery) for a range of projects. One of these was the Phoenix Initiative in Coventry, which was completed in 2004 and has resulted in the transformation of the historic core from a dingy, uninviting area to a pedestrian-friendly zone imaginatively blending old and new. This has been achieved by the creation of exciting new public spaces, outdoor art works, fountains, residential development, restaurants and the opening up of recently discovered historic sites.

184

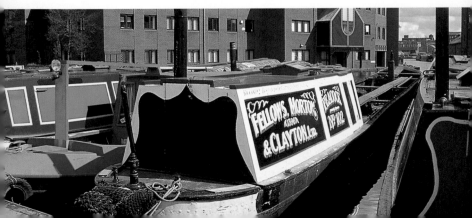

Upwardly mobile Birmingham Long considered England's unglamorous second city, Birmingham has witnessed a remarkable renaissance, has become a major convention destination—boosted by its geographical centrality—and now takes its heritage seriously. The Jewellery Quarter is once again flourishing after the recession-hit 1980s and visitors flock in great numbers to such attractions as Cadbury World at the headquarters of one of the foremost chocolate manufacturers. Neglected canals have been cleaned up, new cobbles laid, towpaths signposted and the waterfront developed with pubs, eateries, smart shops and gleaming offices. Much of the central area is now traffic-free. The early 2000s saw the much-awaited redevelopment of the much-hated Bullring, a massive 1960s brutalist building adjoining New Street Station, into one of Europe's most innovative shopping malls.

Manchester's Millennium Quarter Manchester is another example of revitalization funded by the Millennium Commission. In 1996 a huge terrorist bomb devastated the Arndale Centre, Manchester's vast and drab-looking shopping mall. Fortunately there were no fatalities and this event provided the catalyst for upgrading this area and its surroundings. The medieval town around the cathedral had been a neglected backwater since World War I; the Millennium Quarter scheme linked this area to the central area by means of a city park (Cathedral Gardens)—providing much-needed greenery—and a traffic-free street has been created giving a vista of the cathedral from the main part of the city. Manchester also gained a cathedral visitor centre, encompassing the long-buried medieval bridge that originally served Manchester, and a new cultural attraction called Urbis. The Arndale Centre has been totally refurbished.

Prosperity and pride Environmental pressure on the countryside and congestion on the roads has further led to a revival in the inner cities. In London, the once-neglected warehouse districts around London Bridge, for instance, have become distinctly yuppified, while previously unfashionable Hackney has become the city's major artists' community. The Docklands area virtually died after the end of London as a port, but has been rebuilt with futuristic office blocks and waterside housing, much of it extremely desirable real estate. It is in the inner cities' refurbished buildings, new concert halls, swathes of parkland and new architecture that future visitors should become aware of a reviving sense of civic pride.

Demonstrating a new spirit of enterprise: Manchester's MetroLink trams

THE SECOND BLITZ
Prince Charles once remarked that far more damage had been inflicted on London by developers after World War II than the entire might of Hitler's *Luftwaffe* had achieved during it. The same, unfortunately, is true of many other British cities and towns, devastated by a postwar alliance of urban planners and architects, but the emergence of civic societies and the designation of conservation areas has saved many inner areas in the past 30 years. There is increasing recognition of heritage; even Victorian warehouses that might have been torn down in the 1970s are now being carefully preserved.

London's Docklands: the redevelopment made use of the waterside

185

Monsal Dale: the old viaduct carries the 14km (9-mile) Monsal Trail

WELL DRESSING
A visit to the Peak District between May and September will coincide with the decoration, or 'dressing' of many village wells with mosaics of churches or biblical scenes, formed of petals, mosses, leaves, stones and other natural materials. No one knows how far back the custom of well dressing goes, though it likely originated as a pagan ritual as a thanksgiving for water later taken over by the Church.

On the High Peak Trail

▶▶ Peak District National Park   *172B3*

(Peak District National Park Authority (Bakewell) tel: 01629 816200; www.peakdistrict.org)

Britain's first national park, created in 1951, is encircled by large industrial cities. Though there are no major peaks as such—the district is essentially one of rolling hillscapes—the feeling of escape is exhilarating. The Peak District forms the southern part of the Pennine chain which, in turn, forms the backbone of northern England.

THE WHITE PEAK Most of the southern park comprises the limestone landscapes of the White Peak, where rivers cut deep-grooved gorges, or 'dales', beneath a plateau of stone-walled farmland. Most spectacular of all are **Dove Dale▶▶▶** and its continuation, **Beresford Dale** (despite the crowds), **Monsal Dale▶▶** (with its famous viaduct), the **Manifold Valley▶** just below Wetton and wooded **Lathkill Dale▶** near Youlgreave. Rewarding villages include **Winster, Alstonefield, Tideswell, Ilam, Ashford in the Water** and **Eyam▶**, whose villagers were ravaged by the plague in 1665 when, following their vicar's lead, they confined themselves to their village after an infected box of cloth arrived from London. **Tissington▶▶** has perhaps the loveliest of all Peak village streets, with wide grassy borders and a Jacobean hall. In strong contrast is the industrial village of **Cromford▶**, where Richard Arkwright set up the world's first water-powered cotton mill in 1771 (now a museum). The Peak's finest prehistoric monument is **Arbor Low▶**, south of Monyash, a 4,000-year-old stone circle. **Castleton▶▶** is the hub of the Peak's caving district (see panel): north of the village, a ridge ends at Mam Tor, known as 'Shivering Mountain' because of frequent landslips; Cave Dale looks up to the Norman keep of Peveril Castle (EH), holding its head high above the village.

The national park boundary excludes all the local towns except for **Bakewell▶**, home of Bakewell puddings (made of almond, jam and pastry) which can be sampled at The Old Original Bakewell Pudding Shop. Up the hill around the church is the delightful Old House Museum of relics of the past. Out of town are the Peak's two great houses. **Haddon Hall►►** is a wonderfully preserved medieval house with a gallery, chapel and walled garden; **Chatsworth House►►►**, home of the dukes of Devonshire, has a fine collection of art and furniture. Its grounds were landscaped by Capability Brown and Joseph Paxton (see page 17). Paxton also designed the estate workers' village, **Edensor**.

Buxton►►, an elegant former spa, is the *de facto* Peak capital. Its classically inspired 18th-century Crescent, the Buxton Opera House, pavilion gardens and town hall all contribute to the distinguished air. An excellent town museum and art gallery (*Admission free*) features a Wonders of the Peak exhibition. **Matlock Bath**, another former spa, occupies an extraordinary site in the Derwent Gorge. Cable cars make it easy to explore the **Heights of Abraham**, a park with woodland walks, views and caves. Nearby at Crich is the wonderful **Crich Tramway Village►►**, which offers tram rides and a host of exhibits related to this mode of transport. **Wirksworth►** is a characterful old town amid limestone quarries; the church has a superb eighth-century lead carved coffin lid known as the Wirksworth Stone.

THE DARK PEAK Millstone grit is the underlying rock in the northern Peak. The moors and grassland really are dark; the scenery is bleaker and more rugged. Millstones, for grinding grain, were once a major industry—workings litter abandoned quarries and the stone disks now stand on plinths to mark the national park boundary. The one-street village of **Edale** lies below the peat bog plateau of **Kinder Scout**, the

highest terrain in the Peak (636m/2,087ft). The A57 heads over the **Snake Pass**, displaying the austerity of the northern moors, while the **Derwent Reservoirs►►** near Hope are the most attractive of many manmade lakes. Old cotton-mill towns have a 19th-century workaday character: **New Mills** is one of the most rewarding, with a gorge beneath the Torrs Aerial Walkway. **Lyme Park►** (NT) has a Palladian hall with Grinling Gibbons woodcarving; its park has gentle walks. The gritstone edges such as **Stanage Edge** provide dramatic level tops, with easy paths and challenging rock climbs.

CAVES

Of the five limestone caverns near Castleton that are open to the public, Treak Cliff has some fine stalactites and displays of Blue John (a crystalline fluorspar, worked into jewellery and souvenirs and sold locally), Speedwell Cavern features an underground boat trip along a tunnel that forms part of an old lead mine, while Peak Cavern (the 'Devil's Arse') on the edge of Castleton has a magnificent entrance and is the largest cave in Derbyshire. The Blue John Cavern has Blue John but no stalactites. On the edge of Buxton, Poole's Cavern has the finest formations.

187

The Old Original Bakewell Pudding Shop: 'Bakewell pudding' started life at the White Horse Inn (present-day Rutland Arms), when a cook attempting to make a strawberry tart put the jam in first and poured the egg mixture on top

LEAD MINING

Lead mining was big in the White Peak until the 19th century—the Manifold Valley and Lathkill Dale have traces of past mining activity, Magpie Mine near Sheldon being the most conspicuous relic. Many villages expanded for the purpose; today these stone-built settlements are surprisingly rural and merge into the scenery along with agricultural settlements. At Matlock Bath an excellent mining museum lies close to the reopened Temple Mine, which nonclaustrophobics may like to walk around.

This most famous of factory workers' villages looked forward to a new age of cities: of greenery, clean air and sanitation. It was conceived as a place in which, in the words of its founder, the inhabitants 'will be able to know more about the science of life than they can in a back slum and in which they will learn that there is more in life than the mere going to and returning from work and looking forward to Saturday night to draw their wages'.

VILLAGE TRAIL
The Port Sunlight Heritage Centre (tel: 0151 644 6466; www. portsunlightvillage.com) tells the story of Port Sunlight and a village trail leads visitors around the garden village, taking in the Lady Lever Art Gallery (*Admission free*). Set up by Lever after the death of his wife, the gallery contains a surprising wealth of art, including Pre-Raphaelite paintings and Wedgwood ceramics.

188

Fair deals for the workers Port Sunlight was in fact one of several 19th-century innovations in the Wirral (the peninsula between the River Mersey and Liverpool on one side and the River Dee and Wales on the other). In 1842 Joseph Paxton's Birkenhead Park had been Britain's first public park and in 1853 Prices Patent Candle Company had created Bromborough Pool Village for its workers.

The soap king The industrialist William Hesketh Lever, the first Viscount Leverhulme, was a Liberal Member of Parliament and philanthropist with an interest in the arts and landscape design. He co-owned a soap factory in Warrington; the success of Sunlight Soap was phenomenal and in 1887 he came to the Wirral to set up a new factory. He acquired Thornton Manor and transformed Thornton Hough into a mock-Tudor village for his estate workers.

A vision of the future The factory village of Port Sunlight was to be a haven of peace and cleanliness. Cottages were built to a high standard in half-timbered Tudor and bricky Queen Anne and Elizabethan styles (no two groups of cottages are the same); gardens and parks were liberally provided. The village's visionary design was a predecessor of the garden cities of Ebenezer Howard, which in turn influenced the growth of the garden suburb and of the first 'New Towns'.

▶▶ Quarry Bank Mill   172B2
(tel: 01625 527468; www.quarrybankmill.org.uk)

The showpiece of Styal Country Park—a swathe of green on the fringes of Manchester—is this water-powered cotton mill, built in 1784 and now maintained by the National Trust. It gives an excellent idea of how a weaving mill worked, complete with the deafening clatter of the looms. Exhibits explain cotton processing, the working conditions of the time and the role of the mill owners as factory pioneers. Spinning and weaving demonstrations take place. Visitors can also see living conditions of the 1830s inside the Apprentice House. An 1840 beam engine is in steam in the **Steam Power Galleries**.

▶▶ Stoke-on-Trent (The Potteries)   172B2
(Tourist information tel: 01782 236000; www.visitstoke.co.uk)

Stoke is a conurbation of six towns—Burslem, Fenton, Hanley, Longton, Stoke and Tunstall—but only locals can tell where one ends and the next begins. At first glance the industrial and residential sprawl is unappetizing; but this is the heart of pottery country and anyone interested in the craft should certainly make a visit.

The **Gladstone Pottery Museum**▶▶▶ is a preserved 19th-century pottery with massive bottle-shaped brick kilns (once a common feature of Stoke-on-Trent, now all but vanished). It has pottery demonstrations, informative displays and ceramics ranging from high-class ornaments to Victorian lavatories. The **Etruria Industrial Museum**▶ features the last steam-powered potter's mill in Britain (where bone and flint were crushed to supply the potteries; the engines are usually in steam the first weekend of the month, Apr–Dec). The **Potteries Museum and Art Gallery**▶▶ (*Admission free*) has a fine collection of Staffordshire pottery. Also open to the public and each with museums are the visitor centres for **Spode**▶▶, **Royal Doulton**▶▶ and **Wedgwood**▶▶ (see panel).

Around a courtyard and built in the 15th and 16th centuries, **Little Moreton Hall**▶▶ (NT), north of Stoke, is the best example of half-timbered 'vernacular', with a wainscoted gallery, great hall, chapel and knot garden.

About 24km (15 miles) east of Stoke-on-Trent is **Alton Towers** (tel: 08705 204060; www.altontowers.com). Here the extensive parkland surrounding the ruined home of the Earl of Shrewsbury is today full of the sounds of Britain's most famous amusement park.

VISITING THE POTTERIES
Aim to see the **Gladstone Pottery Museum** (tel: 01782 319232; www.stoke.gov.uk/gladstone) and some of Stoke's many bargain-price factory shops. Then visit one of the potteries (book ahead for factory tours—apart from Wedgwood, available Mon–Fri, except factory holidays).
Wedgwood is famous for its Jasper Ware, (tel: 01782 282986; www.thewedgwoodvisitorcentre.com); **Spode**, specializes in blue and white bone china and still on its original 1770 site (tel: 01782 744011; www.spode.co.uk); and **Royal Doulton** (tel: 01782 292434; www.royal-doulton.com) is famous for its intricate figurines.

189

Stoke-on-Trent is the home of British pottery

NORTHEAST ENGLAND This region includes most of the **Pennines**, the chain of hills that forms the backbone of upland England, from the Peak District in the south to the Scottish borders in the north. It also encompasses **Yorkshire**, the largest county in Britain, divided into North, South, East and West for administrative purposes. It has a reputation for friendliness, with the finest of Britain's medieval cities in York itself and a magnificent heritage of abbey ruins and ecclesiastical architecture.

INDUSTRIAL YORKSHIRE The industrial parts of **West Yorkshire** should not be overlooked. The moorland and the scenically sited, 19th-century stone-built mill towns around Calderdale have a strong and unique personality; you can explore canals and hills and the nearby Brontë country at Haworth. Industrial heritage is the big theme here. Leeds recalls its mill days in the Armley Mills Industrial Museum,

The Swaledale tup, the Yorkshire Dales National Park emblem

RECOMMENDED HISTORIC TOWNS AND CITIES
County Durham: Barnard Castle, Durham.
East Riding of Yorkshire: Beverley.
North Yorkshire: Harrogate, Helmsley, Knaresborough, Middleham, Richmond, Ripon, Scarborough, York.
Northumberland: Alnwick, Hexham.
Tyne and Wear: Newcastle-upon-Tyne.
INDUSTRIAL HERITAGE
Abbeydale Industrial Hamlet, Beamish, Bradford, Halifax, Hebden Bridge, Hull, Saltaire.
SCENERY
North York Moors, Northumberland, South Pennines (Calderdale and Haworth areas), Yorkshire Dales.
COASTAL TOWNS AND VILLAGES
North Yorkshire: Robin Hood's Bay, Runswick Bay, Staithes, Whitby.
Northumberland: Bamburgh, Berwick-upon-Tweed.
HISTORIC SITES AND REMAINS
Fountains Abbey, Hadrian's Wall, Holy Island, Rievaulx Abbey.

and is home to the magnificent Royal Armouries Museum. Bradford is still impressive for its vibrant museums, while on its peripheries Saltaire is an outstanding example of a factory village built by a philanthropic industrialist to improve the lifestyle of his workforce. At Sheffield, in **South Yorkshire**, Abbeydale Industrial Hamlet is a fitting tribute to the city's steel manufacturing days.

THE DALES, THE MOORS, AND THE VALE OF YORK The **Yorkshire Dales** are for lovers of the great outdoors—an excellent area for car touring, walking and caving. East of the Pennines in the **Vale of York** are York itself, the spa town of Harrogate and the enchanting ruins of Fountains Abbey. Southeast Yorkshire is less visited: the flat agricultural scenery may be humdrum, but Selby and Beverley (the latter in the **East Riding of Yorkshire**) each have splendid churches; Hull has a range of sights, including the Hull Maritime Museum (*Admission free*), which celebrates its nautical past; a huge suspension bridge spans the Humber. The **North York Moors** are detached from the Pennine chain and have quite a different character. The coast, with its high cliffs and fishing villages, is a joy. Farther south along the coast are the scalloped chalk cliffs of **Flamborough Head** and the narrow spit of **Spurn Head**.

COUNTY DURHAM, NORTHUMBERLAND, TYNE AND WEAR
The **Pennine** landscape becomes bleaker and more lonely as one proceeds towards Scotland, through Teesdale, in **County Durham** and the Cheviot Hills, in Northumberland. Elsewhere much of County Durham has an industrial face and, like Middlesbrough (in North Yorkshire), is economically depressed. The open-air museum at Beamish is a splendid re-creation of an early 19th-century and an early 20th-century industrial village, while Durham has a great Norman cathedral. **Tyne and Wear** incorporates a conurbation focused on Newcastle-upon-Tyne; locals here are nicknamed Geordies and are known for their quickfire quips and guttural accent. On its back doorstep, **Northumberland**, in total contrast, has wide open spaces, the great Roman structure of Hadrian's Wall and a long and quiet coastline punctuated by imposing castles.

Walks

Hadrian's Wall, Northumberland National Park   190D1

Nearly all the interest is along the wall itself, with its host of Roman features. There is not much reason to go far afield. Simply walking along the wall is a great experience, with views from the ridge of the Great Whin Sill across lonely Northumberland. For a sample, start at Housesteads Fort and walk west, past Crag Lough to Twice Brewed youth hostel and back (2.5 hours). In summer you can use the bus service along the B6318 to take you back.

Holy Island, Northumberland   190E2

Use main car park in village (note tide times). The island's best circular walk is three-quarters coastal, all of it level. Follow Sandham Lane north (turn left and left again out of the car park), turn right beyond the dunes and follow the coast around, past Emanuel Head, where an obelisk looks along the coast into Scotland. Then pass Lindisfarne Castle to finish in the village by Lindisfarne Priory. (1.5 hours)

Ingleton Waterfalls, Yorkshire Dales National Park   190B1

Car park by main entrance to falls. Also known as Ingleton Glen, this

Lindisfarne Castle, Holy Island

splendid gorge is well worth the entrance fee. A circular trail takes in a series of falls of considerable individuality; the most dramatic are the first two, Pecka Fall and Thornton Force. Beyond lies a handily placed refreshment stand, then the path leads into more open country with views of surrounding hills before a finale along the Doe Gorge (2 hours). A booklet available locally explains the geology.

Runswick Bay and Staithes, North York Moors National Park   191C3

Park just above Runswick Bay village. This walk along the clifftops (part of the Cleveland Way) links two captivating coastal villages. From Runswick Bay village, walk up the road; at the top follow the Cleveland Way as it branches off on the right, soon reaching the clifftop for an easy walk past Port Mulgrave and reaching Staithes. Return the same way. (2.5 hours)

Upper Swaledale, Yorkshire Dales National Park   190C1

Roadside parking, Muker village. This walk from Muker enjoys a magnificent steep-sided section of the dale. Walk into the village and find a path out of its north end that leads to a bridge over the Swale; continue north up the dale for 3km (2 miles) to the next bridge (close by Keld). Cross and turn left on the Pennine Way (fork left soon for a short detour to Kisdon Force waterfall). The Way rises slightly, offering fine views. Finally leave it for a farm track that drops to Muker. (2.5 hours)

193

MISERICORDS

The folding seats in the choirstalls of many cathedrals and major churches have a carved under-bracket known as a misericord. When the seats were turned up, the misericords made ledges for the monks to rest on during the long periods of standing in their services. Frequently carved in fanciful designs, the misericords were deliberately made so narrow that there was no chance of dozing off.

Sun-dial (below) and open-top omnibus (right), Beamish

SALTAIRE

This famous example of a 'factory village' dates from the 1850s, when Titus Salt, an enlightened industrialist of liberal views and temperance ideals, decided to house his workforce in this garden village of parks and spacious streets, free from Bradford's smog. The place, a World Heritage Site, has scarcely changed, though the houses are now mostly privately owned. The mill itself is used for a variety of purposes. Paintings by native son artist David Hockney are on display in the 1853 Gallery. Other sections are released for commercial use. Website: www.visitsaltaire.com.

▶▶ Beamish, The: North of England Open Air Museum *190D2*

(tel: 0191 370 4000; www.beamish.org.uk; reduced operation in winter)

Life in northern England in the early 1800s and 1900s is re-created in meticulous detail here, divided into five sections: the colliery village, the town, the manor house, the railway and the farm. Costumed actors play roles in the museum.

▶▶ Beverley *191B3*

(Tourist information tel: 01482 867430; www.visiteastyorkshire.com)

Beverley has pleasing Georgian brickwork, the North Bar (the only survivor of five town gates), a Saturday market and, above all, two gems of church architecture. Begun in Norman times, the **Minster▶▶** is famed for its Gothic stone-carving, its 68 misericords (see panel) made by the Ripon school of woodcarvers and its fine-towered west front. **St. Mary's Church▶** has a 15th-century west façade and a chancel ceiling depicting early kings, all cloaked and crowned against a gold background.

▶ Bradford *190A2*

(Tourist information tel: 01274 433678; www.visitbradford.com)

A patchily impressive Victorian city (knocked about by post-war planning), Bradford is the fruit of the textile-mill age; the Gothic Revival **town hall** and the spectacular tombs of **Undercliffe Cemetery▶** are monuments of past achievement. The entertaining **National Museum of Photography, Film and Television▶▶▶** *(Admission free)* has put Bradford on the map: encounter the animator's world, the story of British TV, the Kodak Gallery of still photography, and the power of advertising. The museum *(closed* Mon except public and school holidays) is attached to an IMAX cinema *(Admission charge;* reservations tel: 0870 701 0200; www.nmpft.org.uk).

The **Colour Museum**▶ explores the use of colour chemistry and the **Bradford Industrial Museum**▶, with rebuilt back-to-back houses, has a tour through the world of textile production. The **Cartwright Hall Art Gallery** (*Admission free*) has a good display of 19th- and early 20th-century paintings. Recommended visits (easy by rail) are **Saltaire**▶▶ (see panel) and **Leeds**▶▶ (see page 197).

▶▶ Calderdale   190A1
(*Halifax tourist information tel: 01422 368725;
www.calderdale.gov.uk*)

A former textile valley in the heart of the Pennines, Calderdale is rich with local life. Sturdy rows of stone cottages and the geometry of stone-walled fields stripe the sides of the valley. Some of the best views are to be had by taking the train from Bradford to Huddersfield. The largest settlement, **Halifax**▶, is unjustifiably ignored by many visitors; in fact it is the best-preserved of West Yorkshire's industrial towns, with the galleried **Piece Hall**▶▶, the former cloth market built around a courtyard. **Eureka!**, Discovery Road, is a lively hands-on museum for children.

Hebden Bridge▶ is magnificently set at the meeting of two valleys, its houses rising row by row up the hillside. From the original Hebden Bridge itself, a cobbled path rises steeply to the hilltop village of **Heptonstall**▶▶, a fascinating place with cobbled streets, a ruined church and the world's oldest Methodist chapel in continuous use (since 1764). There is folded landscape in the deep valleys of Luddenden Dean and Cragg Vale close by.

▶▶▶ Castle Howard   191B3
(*tel: 01653 648333; www.castlehoward.co.uk*)

In the gentle Howardian Hills, this early 18th-century house stands surrounded by a park adorned with ornamental lakes, a colonnaded mausoleum and a 'temple' designed by Vanbrugh. He is commonly attributed with the design of the house, yet he was then a man of no architectural experience; it seems extremely likely that his clerk of works, architect Nicholas Hawksmoor, lent a helping hand. The house has portraits by Holbein, statues, tapestries, porcelain, furniture, a costume collection and an exhibition on women in the Yorkshire country house from 1660 to 1960.

WALKS IN CALDERDALE
Calderdale is an excellent walking area, with a dense network of footpaths, including the Pennine Way and Calderdale Way. From Hebden Bridge, walk along the Rochdale Canal towpath in either direction for glimpses of typical Pennine features, such as back-to-back cottages and old mills. Combine this with a walk up to Heptonstall, which abuts the top of a dramatic gorge known as Colden Clough. The area just north of Hebden Bridge offers riverside strolls through a densely wooded valley, or up to Hardcastle Crags.

195

The handsome mill at Saltaire, pre-eminent in its day

CATHEDRAL FIRSTS

Durham Cathedral represents the highest achievement of the Norman style. In addition to the characteristic use of rounded arches, the building has what are thought to be the earliest transverse Gothic-style pointed arches in English architecture: since the cathedral was largely built during a single period, this really shows a transition between the two building techniques. The sense of scale is created by the hitherto unprecedented use of rib-vaulting, which creates greater space between load-bearing columns.

Durham Cathedral stands high above the Wear

ST. CUTHBERT

The Chapel of the Nine Altars in the cathedral contains the relics of St. Cuthbert, brought here by Lindisfarne monks who escaped from Holy Island (see page 199) when Danish raiders arrived in 875. Cuthbert was a shepherd boy from the Lammermuir Hills who decided to dedicate his life to God, living on Holy Island and later the Farne Islands. He remained a lover of all animals.

►►► Durham 190C2

(Tourist information tel: 0191 384 3720; www.durhamtourism.co.uk)

Few places in Britain can rival the drama of Durham's setting, its majestic cathedral soaring high over sandstone cliffs and woodlands ribboning the tight curve of the River Wear. The historic heart is compact and largely traffic-free. **Durham Heritage Centre and Museum** in St. Mary le Bow Church chronicles the city's history.

The nave, chancel and transepts of the **cathedral►►►** were built over a single period (1070–1140). The sense of balanced might and soaring space is enthralling—it is Britain's finest Norman church architecture. In the cathedral precincts is College Green, the most complete example of a Benedictine monastery in England. Durham was until 1836 a 'palatinate', enjoying royal rights and ruled by prince bishops, who were secular and religious leaders.

The main entrance to the cathedral is via **Palace Green**, where other buildings belong to the **university**, England's third oldest. The **castle►►** (*Guided tours*) dates from the 1070s. The university rebuilt the octagonal keep in 1840 but several early features survive, including the Great Hall (1284) and the Black Staircase (1662). For the best views, follow the **riverside path►►**, cross over **Prebends Bridge**, beside weirs and old mills (one houses the **Durham Museum of Archaeology**), up to **South Street**. To the north, **Crook Hall and Gardens►** is a 14th-century manor house with gardens. In the university the **Oriental Museum►**, Elvet Hill, is a treasure house of exotica, including Egyptian mummies and jade.

▶▶▶ Fountains Abbey and   190B2
Studley Royal Water Garden

(tel: 01765 608888; www.fountainsabbey.org.uk)

In medieval times, **Fountains Abbey** (NT) had grange farms and lands across much of northern England and was a major wool producer. Its former prosperity is evident in what are regarded as Britain's greatest abbey ruins and a World Heritage Site. Founded for 12 Benedictine monks who later changed to Cistercian rule, the abbey still has a 12th-century nave and transepts, a tower completed shortly before the Dissolution and buildings where the monks lived and worked. The **Studley Royal** estate has an 18th-century park with one of the best surviving examples of a Georgian water garden and a medieval deer park with dramatic vistas of the abbey.

▶ Haworth   190B1

(Tourist information tel: 01535 642329;
www.visitbrontecountry.com)

The **Brontë Parsonage Museum** (see page 198) and a walk to the Brontë Waterfalls and Top Withins justify a literary pilgrimage to this popular Pennine village. The village is a stop on the **Keighley and Worth Valley Railway▶**, which steams along between Keighley and Oxenhope.

▶ Leeds

(Tourist information tel: 0113 242 5242; www.leeds.gov.uk)

Victorian municipal swagger does not come much stronger than Leeds Town Hall and the covered shopping arcades. Industry and commerce is writ large—the glass-roofed market is Yorkshire's biggest, and the former Corn Exchange has become a cheerful hall of shops and eateries. The **Royal Armouries Museum▶▶▶** (*Admission free*) is an illuminating survey of arms through the ages, and has daily events. The heady days of textile making are evoked in the **Armley Mills Museum▶**, a former woollen mill crammed with machinery and memories. The excellently presented **Thackray Museum▶** delves into all things medical.

Trips out of the city north include **Harewood House▶▶** (see panel) and the spa town of **Harrogate▶**.

Fountains Abbey

197

RIPON AND ITS CATHEDRAL
From the park road in the Studley Royal estate, there is a contrived vista of nearby Ripon Cathedral. This mostly medieval building is notable for its west front, misericords and Saxon crypt. The daily blowing of the nightwatch horn at 9pm in the spacious market square of this appealing town is a tradition dating back to 886.

HAREWOOD HOUSE
Completed in 1771, the seat of the Earls of Harewood boasts an impressive list of credits: interiors and furniture by Robert Adam, exterior by John Carr, murals by Angelica Kauffman, gardens by Charles Barry and parkland by Capability Brown. Painted ceilings, porcelain and intricate plasterwork further grace the building, and there is an aviary of exotic birds.

Charlotte (1816–55), Emily (1818–48) and Anne (1820–49) Brontë were the daughters of an Irish clergyman. The Brontës' lives were constantly beset by ill health and unfortunate circumstance. Charlotte had an unhappy love affair in Brussels, Emily had no close friends and Anne had a tendency to religious melancholy. Meanwhile, their brother Branwell, disillusioned with his attempts to be a writer and artist, took to drink and opium.

'My sister Emily loved the moors. Flowers brighter than the rose bloomed in the blackest heath for her; out of a sullen hollow in a livid hillside her mind would make an Eden. She found in the bleak solitude many and dear delights; and not the least and best loved was—liberty.'
—Charlotte Brontë (1816–55)

Haworth's cobbled main street is today lined with gift shops .

THE BRONTË NAME
The family name was originally Brunty or Prunty but the form Brontë was adopted after Lord Nelson was given the title Duke of Brontë by the King of Naples after the Battle of the Nile in 1798.

The Brontës lived in the bleak parsonage (now a museum) in Haworth (see page 197), overlooking a graveyard that polluted the water supply, severely reducing villagers' life expectancy. The girls consequently escaped into fantasy worlds. It was Charlotte's determination that got the Brontës into print, after she had chanced upon some secret poetry of Emily's and had been convinced of its worth; the three contributed works to a volume published in 1846 under the pen names of Acton (Anne), Currer (Charlotte) and Ellis (Emily) Bell; the sales were dismal (two books in the first month), but with Charlotte's drive, the sisters each submitted novels. Emily's *Wuthering Heights*, probably set in the now-ruined farmhouse of Top Withins and Anne's *Agnes Grey* were published in 1847. Charlotte failed to get *The Professor* published, but the constructive comments of one publisher gave her encouragement: she completed *Jane Eyre* soon after and it won immediate acclaim—Thackeray read it in a single sitting.

Hard times But the sisters had to spend much time nursing their brother Branwell and the money from the books went to paying off his debts; after his death in September 1848, Emily contracted tuberculosis ('consumption') and died three months later. Anne too fell ill and died the next year at Scarborough, after writing *The Tenant of Wildfell Hall*.

Charlotte was brought to London as a literary celebrity; here she made friends with the successful novelist Mrs Gaskell, who later wrote a biography of Charlotte. Meanwhile, Charlotte worked on *Villette*, based on her time in Brussels and married Arthur Bell Nicholls, their curate, after two years of strong opposition from her father. She died nine months later in pregnancy.

IN MEMORY OF
EMILY JANE BRONTË
WHO DIED DEC.19TH 1848.
AGED 30 YEARS.
AND OF
[...]TE BRONTË
[...] APRIL 21[...]
[...] MARCH 31ST 1855

▶▶ Northumberland Coast   190E2

*(Alnwick tourist information tel: 01665 510665;
www.alnwick.gov.uk or www.visitnorthumberland.com)*

England's northeasternmost seaboard is low-lying and virtually unspoiled, characterized by expansive beaches, profuse birdlife, quiet resorts with golf courses and sands and wind-haunted castle ruins.

Berwick-upon-Tweed▶▶ changed hands 13 times between England and Scotland between 1100 and 1510. The Tweed, a salmon river which runs just south beneath a trio of bridges (including 17th-century Berwick Bridge with its 15 arches), would seem a natural border, but the town has been English since 1482. An excellent walk follows the 16th-century **walls**, the best-preserved fortification of its date in Britain, which encircle the town; you'll pass the restored waterfront, **Berwick Barracks▶** of 1717 (EH; Britain's oldest purpose-built barracks; with an exhibition re creating the life of infantrymen; plus a regimental museum, part of the Burrell art collection) and a church built in 1652.

BERWICK TRIVIA
● Although the town of Berwick is English, the old county of Berwickshire was in Scotland and Berwick Rangers play as a Scottish football team.
● With the coming of the railway, Berwick's castle was pulled down to make way for the station and much of its stone was used in Stephenson's railway bridge.
● Berwick cockles are not molluscs but an old-fashioned peppermint.

199

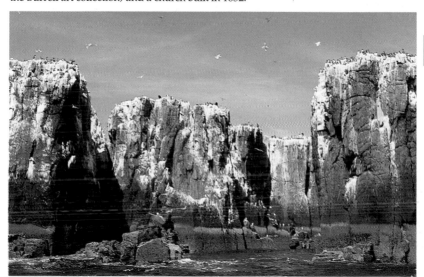

The Farne Islands

Holy Island▶▶ is accessible by car at low tide (times are given on noticeboards both on the island and mainland) via a causeway. It is excellent for walks (see page 193) and is regarded as the cradle of Christianity in England (see panel). **Lindisfarne Castle** (NT), lone by the shore, was converted in the 1900s by architect Sir Edwin Lutyens and is open to the public. **Bamburgh▶** close by has a Norman castle, revamped in the 18th and 19th centuries. The **Grace Darling Museum** (*Admission free*) pays tribute to the woman who helped rescue nine shipwrecked marines in a gale in 1838. **Dunstanburgh Castle▶** (EH/NT) is an eerie ruin, the largest of the Northumbrian coastal strongholds, begun in 1313. It is an easy walk along the coast from the port of **Craster**, which has a workaday port and kipper smokeries. Inland lies **Alnwick▶**, a dignified stone-built market town and a pleasant base for exploring the area. **Alnwick Castle▶** dates from Norman times, but has a Renaissance-style interior, fine Meissen china and paintings by Reynolds and

HOLY ISLAND
In 635, at the request of the king of Northumbria, a missionary landed here from the Scottish island of Iona. St. Aidan founded the Lindisfarne Priory (EH) on what is today known as Holy Island and from this spot Christianity spread across northeastern England. Lindisfarne became a Benedictine monastery in 1082. A museum tells the story. *The Lindisfarne Gospels*, an illuminated manuscript of c700, is now in the British Library.

LINDISFARNE NATIONAL NATURE RESERVE

Home to wildfowl and waders, a major site for wigeon and the only British wintering ground for pale-bellied Brent geese, the nature reserve includes mud flats and dunes around Holy Island and the farther-flung Farne Islands. The latter are an important habitat for seals and seabirds; April and August to September (May to July is the breeding season) cruises depart from Seahouses (NT information tel: 01665 721099)—it is an exciting boat ride that offers really close encounters with the surprisingly tame wild birds.

Man-made beauty: the huge Kielder Water amid the conifers of Kielder Forest

Titian; Anthony Salvin, the Victorian architect, was responsible for much of the building and a century earlier the parkland was landscaped by Capability Brown. The extensive Hulne Park, next door, is ideal for woodland walks; there is a Carmelite priory and an 18th-century folly tower. At the mouth of the River Coquet, **Warkworth▶** has a medieval castle and 14th-century hermitage chapel (both EH) cut out of the cliffs, with the hermit's living quarters still intact (walk along the river and take a ferry across).

In complete contrast, **Newcastle-upon-Tyne▶** is a sprawling industrial conurbation, definitely not pretty at first sight, but with plenty of atmosphere. For the new millennium, an innovative footbridge and cycleway has been built across the Tyne, bringing the total number of bridges up to seven. A cluster of medieval waterside buildings, the 17th-century guildhall and the castle are pre-industrial survivals, while Grey Street and Eldon Square are fine examples of early 19th-century townscaping. Newcastle's big three museums (www.twmuseums.org.uk) are the **Laing Art Gallery** (*Admission free*), the region's premier art collection; **Discovery Museum** (*Admission free*), with interactive science, plus costumes, displays on Tyneside inventors, the 30m (100ft) vessel *Turbinia* and a hands-on social history of the city; and the **Hancock Museum**, with natural history, a Living Planet environmental gallery and Egyptian artefacts.

▶▶ Northumberland National Park   190D1

(Northumberland National Park Authority (Hexham) tel: 01434 605555; www.northumberland-national-park.org.uk)
Stretching up to the Scottish border this is a beautifully remote corner of the northeast, with rustic villages and farming hamlets scattered around the strikingly empty grassy hills and peaceful valleys. Even at the height of summer you often have only Cheviot sheep and the occasional hill walker for company. Vast Kielder Forest spreads its seemingly endless evergreen plantations, home to red squirrels and deer, over western Northumberland. Kielder

The Roman ruins of Housesteads Fort, on Hadrian's Wall

Water and the forest trails offer a retreat and there is an 19km (12-mile) forest drive. You can also hire boats and canoes.

The **Cheviot Hills** reach to the Scottish border. The best of the walks involve treks along solitary sheep-drovers' roads, now quiet grassy tracks, to the ridge which forms the border, taking in the summits of Windy Gyle (619m/3,031ft) and The Cheviot (816m/2,677ft). The scenic drives tend to be of the there-and-back variety as no roads lead right across the massif apart from the A68; notable among these is the road along **Coquetdale** from Rothbury, past the craggy Simonside Hills, to Alwinton and beyond. **Rothbury** itself is an attractive sandstone town with a sloping green and a spacious main street; **Cragside**▶ (NT) on the edge of the town was built by the 19th-century architect Norman Shaw and was the first house in the world to be lit by hydroelectric power. The wooded grounds here are laced with trails and have lakes, a formal garden and a fine show of rhododendrons. **Chillingham Castle** has for more than 700 years been home to Wild White cattle, a breed that was kept by ancient Britons. **Ford** is a model estate village for Ford Castle and has craft workshops.

The southern part of the national park holds the finest surviving stretch of **Hadrian's Wall**▶▶▶ (EH), the largest Roman monument in Britain and a World Heritage Site (see panel). Of its 118km (73-mile) length, remains can be seen along 16km (10 miles), the best sections being between points north of Haltwhistle and Hexham. Walkers may like to make use of a summer bus service which runs along the main road parallel to the wall.

Housesteads Fort (NT), which still has a hospital and latrines, and Chesters, a cavalry fort, are particularly well preserved. At Vindolanda Fort a section of wall is reconstructed as it would have been at the time of the Roman occupation, while at Corbridge are the remains of the garrison town of *Corstopitum* and a museum of finds. Also try to take in Birdoswald Fort, situated over the border in Cumbria, and the Visitor Centre at Once Brewed.

Hexham▶ (tel: 01434 652220; www.hexhamnet.co.uk) makes an attractive base. It has an abbey church; the crypt and bishop's throne are Anglo-Saxon—before destruction in 875 it was the largest church in northern Europe. Local history features at Border History Museum (in an old prison).

HADRIAN'S WALL
This great fortification at the northernmost point of the Roman empire was planned in AD122 by Emperor Hadrian from Newcastle to the Solway Firth on the Cumbrian coast. The natural feature of the Great Whin Sill, a ridge of hard rock, made an ideal base to the construction for much of its length. To the north lay wilderness and the Picts and it still feels primevally wild on the wall today. Structures known as milecastles were placed at intervals of Roman miles; the Vallum, or southern rampart, was below the wall and is visible in places. Seventeen forts, housing 13,000 infantrymen and 5,500 cavalrymen, were connected by a military road. The best preserved is Housesteads (NT). At Wallsend (just east of Newcastle-upon-Tyne) a museum and reconstructed bath house stand beside the remains of Segedunum Fort. Website: www. hadrianswallcountry.org.

MORE NORTH YORKSHIRE PRIORIES AND ABBEYS

Byland Abbey (EH), near Coxwold, had the largest priory church in England—the shattered rose window gives a scant idea of its glory. Mount Grace Priory (EH), near the attractive village of Osmotherley, was a Carthusian house; the lifestyle was austere, with vows of silence and prison-like confinement; one cell has been reconstructed. Guisborough Priory, an Augustinian foundation at the edge of Guisborough in Cleveland, is now largely razed but retains a huge east window. The substantial ruins of Whitby Abbey (EH) overlook the sea; an inscription on a stone cross commemorates the Creation Hymn, one of the first poems in the English language, penned by Caedmon, an Anglo-Saxon herdsman.

The ruins of Rievaulx (pronounced 'reevo') Abbey, desolate and still in sheltered Ryedale

RIEVAULX ABBEY

Before Henry VIII started his Dissolution of the monasteries in 1536, there were more monasteries in Yorkshire than in any other county in England. In North Yorkshire Rievaulx Abbey (EH) is the undoubted star. Founded in 1131, it became very prosperous, rich in sheep and by the 1160s there were 140 monks and 500 lay brothers. By the Dissolution numbers had dropped to 22. The ruins occupy a site of remote beauty in Ryedale.

▶▶ North York Moors National Park   191C3

(North York Moors National Park Authority (Helmsley) tel: 01439 770657; www.northyorkmoors-npa.gov.uk)

The North York Moors, one of England's most distinctive landscapes, has a variety of moods. The moors themselves are a great plateau of England's largest tract of heather, dotted with ancient stone crosses. The plateau is cut by a series of lush green dales (valleys) scattered with red-roofed, yellow-stone farms and hamlets. Then the moors dip steeply on three sides to the plain, while to the east runs a sublime stretch of coast, with weather-beaten fishing villages and sandstone cliffs—the highest on the east coast.

THE MOORS AND DALES Farndale, celebrated for its wild daffodils and **Rosedale**, once an ironstone-mining hub, typify the contrasts of moorland plateau and lush vales. **Helmsley▶** is a small market town with craftshops, bookshops and a handsome market square; close by are the east tower of the Norman castle (EH) and Duncombe Park, a revamped Palladian mansion memorable for its fine classical entrance hall and saloon and for its grass terrace complete with temples.

The village street of **Coxwold▶** is without blemish, all trim grass-edged lanes and stone cottages; Laurence Sterne lived and wrote *The Life and Times of Tristram Shandy* at what is now known as Shandy Hall (house open). Lonely St. Gregory's Minster in **Kirkdale** has a remarkably preserved Anglo-Saxon sundial from 1060. **Hutton-le-Hole▶▶**, with its sloping, sheep-nibbled green, is home to the Ryedale Folk Museum, where rural buildings have been rebuilt to give an insight into the life of yesteryear. **Lastingham Church▶** is built over a Norman crypt and the touristy village of **Thornton-le-Dale▶** has some pretty corners by its brook. The major attraction, the **North Yorkshire Moors Railway▶▶** (tel: 01751 472508; www.northyorkshiremoorsrailway.com) runs from Pickering to Grosmont along unspoilt dale scenery in about an hour.

Enthusiasts reopened this line as the North Yorkshire Moors Railway in 1973; it had closed eight years earlier

CAPTAIN JAMES COOK
The great explorer was born in 1728 at Marton (now part of Middlesbrough, Cleveland), where a museum charts his life and travels. The site of the Cooks' house at Great Ayton is marked by an obelisk and the school James attended is a modest museum. After being a shop apprentice in Staithes, he was apprenticed to a Quaker ship-owner in Whitby (the house where he lived with his master is a museum of Cook's life— Captain Cook Memorial Museum). From 1768 he undertook his voyages of discovery to New Zealand, the east coast of Australia and the Pacific Isles. He was killed by natives in Hawaii in 1799. Website: www.captaincook.org.uk

Pickering▶ itself is a bustling market town with a lively local museum and the remains of a Norman castle (EH); look around the church for the set of 15th-century murals, one of the most complete in all of England. **Goathland** has a long green and sheep are everywhere; from the Mallyan Spout Hotel a path drops down to **Mallyan Spout**, a waterfall, while south of the village you can walk along a section of Roman road, **Wade's Causeway**▶. At **Grosmont** you can peer into the locomotive shed or take a train into **Eskdale**.

Much of the eastern moors is dominated by commercial forestry, including **Dalby Forest**, laid out with trails, picnic sites and a drive; it abuts **Bridestones Nature Reserve**, where mushroom-shaped rocks are clustered on the moor. The western and northern escarpments, followed by the long-distance **Cleveland Way** footpath, offer grandstand views towards the Pennines and over industrial Teesside respectively; **Sutton Bank**▶▶, by the A170, is an inland cliff with a dizzying view across the Vale of York to the Pennines; at its southern end is the Kilburn White Horse, a 96m (315ft) hill carving created by local schoolchildren and their teacher in 1857.

ALONG THE COAST A footpath (the end of the Cleveland Way) follows the coast continuously; roads reach the coast in only a few places. **Staithes**▶▶ is an authentic-looking fishing village, with fishing craft squeezed into a tiny harbour; **Runswick Bay**▶ is a tight jumble of cottages beneath the cliff. **Whitby**▶▶ was once a famous whaling port, hence the whalebone arch above town from where you can look across to the ruined abbey (EH) and St. Mary's Church. The town has expanded as a resort but has kept its character in its old streets around the port; a few shops still specialize in Whitby jet ornaments. The densely stocked Whitby Museum displays some impressive local fossils. A sandy beach extends north to Sandsend.

Red-roofed **Robin Hood's Bay**▶▶▶, a tightly huddled fishing village, clings to steep slopes that drop to the shore, where low tide reveals tide pools and fossils; tales of smuggling haunt the quaint hotchpotch of lanes. **Scarborough**▶, just outside the Park, is both a Regency spa and a Victorian resort with a castle on a headland between two sandy bays. Wood End Museum displays natural history and has a section on the literary Sitwell family, who used to live in this house. The Rotunda, a purpose-built museum of 1828, features a Bronze Age tree trunk burial and displays on Victorian Scarborough.

The Laurel Inn, Robin Hood's Bay

York Minster, one of the wonders of Gothic architecture, as seen from the north corner of the city wall

THREATS FROM BELOW AND ABOVE

In the 1960s York Minster's lantern tower was threatened with imminent collapse. Only a major project, with supports erected between 1967 and 1972, saved the day; the undercroft exhibition gives a view of this repair operation. In 1984 the Minster was struck by lightning and was badly damaged by the fire that ensued. Some people interpreted this as an act of God after the Bishop of Durham, one of the Church of England's less traditional bishops, had made outspoken remarks that revealed his doubts about the literal truth of the Virgin Birth.

▶▶▶ York   *190B2*

(Tourist information tel: 01904 621756; www.visityork.org)

York is England's unsurpassed showpiece cathedral city: nowhere else has such a concentration of medieval and other historic treasures. There are far more museums than can be visited in a single day (see page 206): the Castle Museum, the National Railway Museum and Jorvik are the top three. Around every corner are examples of buildings of every period, including medieval churches and time-warp streets like the Shambles, with its overhanging upper floors. Shoppers, sightseers and street performers throng the central area; much of it is pedestrianized and a pleasure to explore on foot. York prospered as a hub of the wool trade in medieval times, when it was second only to London in importance.

THE CITY WALL▶▶▶ The Romans built the original defensive wall around the settlement of *Eboracum*, at the confluence of the rivers Ouse and Foss; in Viking times the city was known as Jorvik, later corrupted to 'York'. Today's wall is largely medieval. It can be followed along its top for much of its 4.5km (3-mile) length and provides a splendid city overview (see Walk, page 205); west of the river, the wall skirts a railway-age residential area. The wall's gateways are known as bars; on Micklegate Bar during the Wars of the Roses, the heads of enemies would be exhibited on spikes.

THE MINSTER▶▶▶ Built 1220–1475, this is the largest medieval cathedral in Britain and the city's crowning glory. Its magnificent glass dates from 1150—look for the depictions of Genesis and Revelations in the east window, as well as the 'Five Sisters' windows within a quintet of lancets. Look too for the rich interior of the chapter house, the painted roof of the nave, the carved rood screen, the undercroft display and the Treasury. Climb the tower for superb views of the city.

YORK

Walk

City highlights

Outside **Castle Museum**▶▶▶, face **Clifford's Tower**▶▶, turn left to take a path to the near side of the tower; beyond Ouse Bridge view the city from the north riverbank; recross by Lendal Bridge. Enter the **Museum Gardens**, pass fragments of medieval **St. Leonard's Hospital**; **Multangular Tower**, a Roman relic beside a section of Roman wall; and the ruins of **St. Mary's Abbey**. The **Yorkshire Museum**▶▶ is also in this park.

Find a gate into Marygate and go to **Bootham Bar**; join the walkway along the top of the wall, with superb views of the Minster. Leave the wall at Monk Bar; the **Treasurer's House**▶(NT) is filled with 17th- and 18th-century décor, while **St. William's College** has an exhibition on the **Minster**. Skirt the **Minster**▶▶▶ to its main entrance. Pass **St. Michael-le-Belfrey Church** (fine 15th- and 16th-century glass), detour to Stonegate for its shopfronts; go on along Low Petergate, detour left to Goodramgate for **Holy Trinity Church**▶. Find the **Shambles**▶▶ York's most famous street. From Fossgate visit the **Merchant Adventurers' Hall**▶▶; beyond Coppergate are **Jorvik**▶▶ and the elegantly Georgian **Fairfax House**▶.

205

The Shambles, originally a street of butcher shops

York's museums

The **York Pass** (available from the tourist office or www.yorkpass.com)—for one, two or three days—gives free entry to more than 30 attractions plus other discounts. If you are visiting the city from November to March, check with the tourist office for half-price entry to many attractions.

ARC▶ St. Saviourgate: hands-on archeology for all; learn how to sort and label real Roman finds and weave on a reproduction Viking warp-weighted loom.

Bar Convent Blossom Street: still a convent, but housing a museum on early Christianity in northern England.

Castle Museum▶▶▶ Eye of York: this alone justifies a visit to York. Collections include a full-scale cobbled street of shops, re-creations of domestic interiors over the centuries and a working water mill by the river.

Clifford's Tower▶▶ (EH) Tower Street: this medieval keep was the site of a horrifying event in English Jewry's history. In 1190, York's small Jewish community gathered inside the tower for protection from a violent mob. Many people took their own lives; others died when the tower was set alight.

Fairfax House▶ Castlegate: a Georgian town house with late 17th-century furniture, clocks and paintings, mostly from Joseph Terry, a Quaker confectionery magnate.

Guildhall St. Helen's Square (*Admission free*): a re-creation of the original 15th-century building, destroyed in an air raid.

Jorvik▶▶ Coppergate: entertaining and realistic time-travel journey into 10th-century Viking York. Go early or late when it is likely to be less busy.

Merchant Adventurers' Hall▶▶ Fossgate: the most impressive half-timbered building in the city; the 14th-century hall of a city merchants' guild, still in use.

National Railway Museum▶▶▶ Leeman Road (*Admission free*): Britain's finest historic locomotives. With working demonstrations and hands-on exhibits.

Richard III Museum Monk Bar: the medieval monarch on trial—guilty or not guilty?

York Art Gallery (*Admission free*) Exhibition Square: includes nudes by local artist William Etty.

York Dungeon Clifford Street: a chilling glimpse into a world of punishment and death.

Yorkshire Museum▶▶ Museum Gardens: Roman, Saxon, Viking and medieval treasures, including a Viking ship and the Middleham Jewel.

The Castle Museum's re-created cobbled street, Kirkgate, takes its name from Dr. John Kirk, who started the museum with his collection of everyday miscellanea

Drive

This tour (approx 90km/56 miles) takes in waterfalls, Castle Bolton, unspoiled dales and lonely moors.

From the busy little town of **Hawes** at the heart of Wensleydale, take the

The Yorkshire Dales (see also pages 208–209)

A684 Sedbergh road, turning off very soon for an unclassified road leading to Kettlewell. Here you'll enter the northern end of **Wharfedale** at **Hubberholme** (with its charming church). The B6160 leads over into Bishopdale and **West Burton▶**, with its long village green. Proceed past **Aysgarth Falls**, taking the road rising up to the formidable fortress of **Castle Bolton▶▶**.

Beyond this, the road rises onto Redmire Moor; pause to admire the views at the top and drop down into **Swaledale** at **Grinton**. The odd castellated structure on the right as you descend is a former shooting lodge and now a youth hostel.

Grinton Church, grandiosely dubbed 'Cathedral of the Dales', is worth a short pause, while **Reeth▶**, with its inns ranged around a sloping green, makes a good halfway stopping point.

The route goes along bleak **Arkengarthdale**, rising to the incredibly remote **Tan Hill Inn**, England's highest pub, near the meeting of Cumbria, North Yorkshire and County Durham.

Re-enter **Swaledale** at **Keld**; beyond **Thwaite** the road to Hawes is known as the **Buttertubs Pass**, so-called because of the natural limestone 'sinks' into which farmers used to place their butter to keep it cool on long journeys

Grassington, in Wharfedale

208

NIDDERDALE AND TEESDALE

Although outside the national park, Nidderdale's scenery matches the best of the Dales; but access is limited by grouse shooting (season: 12 Aug–10 Dec) and reservoirs. How Stean Gorge has small cliffs; near Pateley Bridge (fine folk museum) are Brimham Rocks, a weird, naturally sculpted landscape of tors. Stump Cross Caverns are a tour-it-yourself show cave. North of the park, within County Durham, lies Teesdale in the midst of the wildest and emptiest tracts of the Pennines. High Force is the mightiest waterfall in England. With its harsh climate and unusual soils, the official nature reserve protects Arctic and alpine species, including the rare Teesdale violet.

A traditional landscape: Swaledale has 750 stone barns and numerous drystone walls

► ► ► **Yorkshire Dales National Park** *190B1*
(Yorkshire Dales National Park Authority (Leyburn) tel: 01969 650456; www.yorkshiredales.org.uk)

The great Pennine mass that forms the backbone of England has its proudest moments here, in the limestone dales and gritstone moors of the Yorkshire Dales National Park, where villages and field walls are almost universally stone. Spend a few days in the area and you will see the subtle differences between one dale and another.

WHARFEDALE This is a long dale, with several moods. Around **Bolton Abbey►**, all is pastel-shaded and gentle, graced by the ruined Augustinian priory and the functioning priory church; upriver the Wharfe swirls through a chasm in Strid Wood. **Burnsall**, with its old bridge and green and **Arncliffe** are two idyllic villages; **Grassington** is larger and busier, with a range of shops and places to eat around its central square. Looming over the dale is **Kilnsey Crag**, England's largest overhang, a challenge for rock climbers. Like many Dales places, **Buckden** and **Kettlewell** grew up around the lead-mining industry; relics litter the moors. **Hubberholme** has a gem of a church, with a rare musicians' gallery of 1558.

AIREDALE England's most famous limestone scenery is concentrated in the area around **Malham► ► ►**, where the subterranean River Aire reappears at the base of Malham Cove, a great inland cliff. A short walk away, formidable Gordale Scar waterfall impressed the early Romantics. Other local walks include to Janet's Foss waterfall and Malham Tarn, with its rich plant and bird life. Downstream lies **Skipton**, a market town with a rewarding castle restored by Lady Anne Clifford after Civil War damage; the Embsay and Bolton Abbey Steam Railway heads into Wharfedale.

SWALEDALE Stone barns, abandoned lead mines (notably in Gunnerside Gill) and Swaledale sheep are features of the landscape along with the Swale itself. **Reeth►**, ranged around a spacious green, is a charming large village and well placed for walks into nearby Arkengarthdale.

The enchanting market town of **Richmond► ► ►** crowns a hilltop site, its mighty Norman **castle► ►** (EH) staring down to the Swale and over the marketplace. There are

One of the deep limestone shafts on Buttertubs Pass, a high route between Swaledale and Wensleydale

two museums (the Richmondshire Museum and the Green Howards Regimental Museum), and some choice streetscapes such as Frenchgate and Newbiggin Broad. Beyond one of two surviving town gateways, Cornforth Hill leads to a view of Culloden Tower, a fetching Georgian folly. Richmond's **Georgian Theatre Royal ▶▶** (1788), the oldest in its original form in England, is concealed by a barnlike exterior (*Open* for tours). There are tempting strolls beside the Swale, through Hudswell Woods or to the ruins of **Easby Abbey**.

WENSLEYDALE Cheese-making heritage is illustrated by rural relics in the Dales Countryside Museum in **Hawes** and shops sell the crumbly Wensleydale cheese. Villages such as **Askrigg, Bainbridge** and **West Burton▶** have more appeal, while **Middleham▶▶** has a pretty square (around which horses from the nearby racing stables are paraded) and a 12th-century castle (EH), former home of Richard III. Of the dale's many waterfalls, **Aysgarth Falls** are the most well-known, with the best view a short walk downstream from the bridge. Look into Aysgarth Church, with its superb screen brought from **Jervaulx Abbey▶**, whose ruins can be seen farther east. **Hardraw Force ▶**, the tallest single-drop waterfall in England, is reached through the pub at Hardraw. **Castle Bolton▶▶** is an impregnable-looking bulk, little altered since the 14th century; Mary, Queen of Scots was imprisoned here (1568–69). **Masham▶** is attractively set around its large cobbled marketplace.

RIBBLESDALE AND DENTDALE Settle is a likeable market town, if noisy with quarry traffic; the train ride to Carlisle gives great views (see page 176). The 'Three Peaks'— **Whernside** (737m/2,418ft), **Ingleborough** (723m/2,372ft) and **Pen-y-ghent** (693m/2,274ft)—are nearby, a popular challenge walk, often started from Horton-in-Ribblesdale, takes in all three. Ingleborough is dotted with potholes and caves, including **Ingleborough▶** and **White Scar▶** caverns (both *Open* to the public) and Gaping Gill, big enough to hold London's St Paul's. Ingleton is the base for walks into **Ingleton Glen▶▶** (see page 193). Dentdale, in Cumbria, lies below Whernside; don't miss **Dent▶▶** with its cobbled streets, the epitome of the rural Pennines.

BARNARD CASTLE
Just beyond the park's northeastern boundary, in County Durham is the town of Barnard Castle, whose namesake castle (EH) perches above the Tees. The Bowes Museum here, built in opulent French château style, houses a splendid collection of fine arts.

209

THE DRUID'S TEMPLE
Lying outside the Dales National Park's eastern boundary and tucked away in the woods at the end of a road west of Ilton, the Druid's Temple is one of Yorkshire's great surprises. At first sight it appears perfectly preserved prehistoric monument, but almost too perfect to be true: in fact it is a scaled down replica of Stonehenge (with additions), created in the early 19th century by a local landowner who wanted to give work to unemployed masons. The site is unstaffed and you need a good map to find it.

Limestone pavement above Malham Cove

Southern Scotland

**Map legend:**
- ★ Walk start point
- ☆ Drive start point

0 10 20 30 40 50 km

0 10 20 30 miles

Southern Scotland

Braemar • Balmoral Castle
Linn O'Dee
1154m
Lochnagar
North Esk
Strachan
Stonehaven
Deeside & Lochnagar
Clova
Fettercairn
Inverbervie
Spittal of Glenshee
Laurencekirk
Johnshaven
ANGUS
Edzell Castle
Kirkmichael
South Esk
Brechin
Montrose
Bridge of Cally
Kirriemuir
Aberlemno
Forfar
Blairgowrie
Alyth
Isla
Glamis
Glamis Castle
Friockheim
Inverkeilor
Dunkeld
Birnam
Coupar Angus
Arbroath
Capith
Stanley
Muirhead
Carnoustie
Balbeggie
Dundee
Monifieth
Scone Palace
Perth
Glencarse
Newport-on-Tay
M90
Echo Castle
Newburgh
Leuchars
Bridge of Earn
Auchtermuchty
Cupar
Eden
St Andrews
Craigtoun
Falkland
Ceres
Fife Ness
M90
Falkland Palace
Ladybank
FIFE
Crail
Rumbling Bridge
Kinross
Loch Leven
Pittenweem
Anstruther
Cowdenbeath
Glenrothes
Leven
Elie
Earlsferry
Buckhaven
Dunfermline
Kirkcaldy
Inverkeithing
Burntisland
Firth of Forth
North Berwick
Hopetoun House
South Queensferry
Gullane
Dunbar
M9
EDINBURGH
Haddington
East Linton
Broxburn
Dalmeny
Cockburnspath
St Abb's Head
M8
Livingston
Musselburgh
EAST LOTHIAN
Gifford
Grantshouse
St Abbs
Loanhead
Dalkeith
Eyemouth
Penicuik
Bonnyrigg
Newtongrange
Chirnside
Berwick-upon-Tweed
MIDLOTHIAN
Lammermuir Hills
Duns
West Linton
Lauder
Greenlaw
Swinton
Dolphinton
Eddleston
Peebles
Tweed
Gordon
Coldstream
Lowick
Biggar
Traquair House
Galashiels
Kelso
Tweed
Ford
Drumelzier
Abbotsford House
Melrose
Upper Tweeddale
Selkirk
St Boswells
Town Yetholm
Wooler
Tweedsmuir
BORDERS (SCOTTISH)
Jedburgh
Cheviot Hills
816m
The Cheviot
Grey Mare's Tail
Hawick
Denholm
Alwinton
Rothbury
Moffat
Teviothead
Coquet
West Woodburn
Beattock
Eskdalemuir
Hermitage
NORTHUMBERLAND
Otterburn
A74(M)
Esk
Liddel
Kielder Water
Lochmaben
Langholm
Border Forest Park
Northumberland National Park
Kirkwhelpington
Lockerbie
Housesteads Fort
Hadrian's Wall
Chollerford
Caerlaverock Castle
Gretna Green
Birdoswald Fort
Vindolanda
Chesters Fort
Annan
Irthing
Tyne
Hexham
Corbridge
Bowness-on-Solway
Carlisle
Brampton
Haltwhistle
Silloth
Crosby
Wetheral
Derwent Reservoir
Wigton
Thursby
Castleside
Aspatria
Eden
Alston
Stanhope
CUMBRIA
M6
Lazonby
Melmerby
893m
Cross Fell
Wearhead
Maryport
Bothel
931m
Skiddaw
Caldbeck
Langwathby
DURHAM
Derwent
Greystoke
Penrith
Cow Green Reservoir
High Force
Cockermouth
Bassenthwaite

Strachan
North Esk
Fettercairn
Inverbervie
Laurencekirk
Johnshaven
Aberlemno
Montrose
Friockheim
Inverkeilor
Arbroath
Carnoustie
Monifieth
Newport-on-Tay
Firth of Tay
Leuchars
St Andrews
Craigtoun
Fife Ness
Crail
Anstruther
Elie
Earlsferry
North Berwick
Firth of Forth
Dunbar
East Linton
Cockburnspath
St Abb's Head
St Abbs
Eyemouth
Chirnside
Berwick-upon-Tweed

The miniature Highland scenery of the Trossachs: Loch Arklet

RECOMMENDED

CITIES Edinburgh, Glasgow.

INLAND TOWNS AND VILLAGES

Scottish Borders: Peebles.

Stirling: Stirling.

COASTAL TOWNS/VILLAGES

Angus: Arbroath, Montrose.

Fife: Anstruther, Crail, Culross, St. Andrews.

GREAT HOUSES

Angus: Glamis

Argyll and Bute: Hill House

Dumfries and Galloway: Culzean, Drumlanrig.

Perth and Kinross: Scone.

Scottish Borders: Abbotsford, Bowhill, Mellerstain, Traquair.

West Lothian: Hopetoun.

CASTLES

Argyll and Bute: Bothwell, Rothesay (Bute).

City of Edinburgh: Edinburgh.

Dumfries and Galloway: Caerlaverock.

Fife: Kellie, St. Andrews.

Stirling: Doune, Stirling.

West Lothian: Linlithgow. Craignethan.

RUINED ABBEYS AND CATHEDRALS

Dumfries and Galloway: Sweetheart.

Fife: St. Andrews.

Scottish Borders: Dryburgh, Jedburgh, Melrose.

Angus: Arbroath.

PALACES AND GARDENS

Stirling: Stirling.

Fife: Falkland.

West Lothian Linlithgow. Gardens

Dumfries and Galloway: Castle Kennedy, Threave.

City of Edinburgh: Edinburgh Royal Botanic Garden.

THE SCOTTISH NATION Scotland is now part of the UK, but has a long history as an independent state. After having fought hard to maintain its sovereignty, Scotland surrendered its independence in an act of Parliamentary Union with England and Wales in 1707. Scotland's parliament was abolished and since then it has been ruled from London by a British parliament in Westminster. However, it was allowed to keep its church, legal and educational systems distinctive and separate. In 1997, the Scots voted to have their own parliament once again. The first elections for the Scottish Parliament were held in 1999 and a new Parliament building near the Palace of Holyroodhouse on Royal Mile in Edinburgh opened in 2004; however, Scotland still retains Members of Parliament representing its views in Westminster.

THE LIE OF THE LAND Southern Scotland is composed of the Central Lowlands and the Southern Uplands, a wide band of hills that stretches from coast to coast. In the west this latter, wild area is known as **Dumfries and Galloway** while the eastern part is known as the **(Scottish) Borders**, though in fact both parts have acted since time immemorial as a war-torn border country, a self-governing shield between England and Scotland. The Lowlands occupy a rift valley, comprising the westward flowing River Clyde and the long eastern intrusion of the Firth of Forth. This is the heart of Scotland, studded with ancient Christian sanctuaries, sturdy medieval burghs, royal palaces, baronial seats, thickly populated manufacturing towns and its great rival cities of Glasgow and Edinburgh. The Central Lowlands, encompassing **Argyll and Bute**; **West, mid-** and **East Lothian**; **Stirling**; **Fife** and part of the **Perth and Kinross** and **Angus** regions, are by no means uniformly low-lying. The handsome capital city of **Edinburgh** is perched among volcanic hills, Glasgow—Scotland's most populous city—is overlooked by the Campsie Fells, Dundee is fringed by the Sidlaw Hills and the Kingdom of Fife is given a backbone by the Ochil Hills. The northern frontier of the Lowlands is the Highland Boundary

Fault. This is strikingly prominent feature cuts Scotland in two, with land rising abruptly on its northern side. The Fault divides the island of Arran in half, continues north-east through Helensburgh to Loch Lomond and skirts through old market towns such as Crieff and Dunkeld to reach Stonehaven on the east coast.

THE HERITAGE Most of the great prehistoric monuments of Scotland are found in the north, but there are good collections of Pictish and early Christian carved stones to be seen in Angus and St. Andrews. Viking invasions in the ninth century destroyed much of the evidence of Celtic Christianity except for the distinctive round towers at Brechin in Angus and Abernethy in Perth and Kinross. Dunfermline Abbey and the famous Norman church in Leuchars, near St. Andrews in Fife, are good examples of the Romanesque influence, which came to Scotland in the late 11th century. This was followed by the Gothic period, well represented by the ruined Border abbeys as well as the surviving cathedrals of Dunblane and Glasgow.

The 15th century is the most distinctively Scottish period: the simpler collegiate church developed then, with battlemented towers and stone-slabbed roofs and spires. This period also saw the birth of the tower house with its thick, vertical stone walls, a concept gradually enriched by combining towers into L, T and Z plans; the roofs budded a playful array of corner turrets, crow-stepped gable ends and balconies. The neat burghs, or market towns, are dominated by a broad high street, typically with a mercat cross and the Tolbooth, which served as both jail and town hall. The 16th-century royal palaces at Linlithgow, Falkirk and Stirling reveal the influence of the Renaissance, but it was not before the more peaceful politics of the late 17th century that Scotland produced a truly classical style. Sir William Bruce ushered in this period, but it was dominated by two generations of the Adam family (William and sons—Robert, James and John), who gave the term Adamesque to their Palladian vision of 18th-century Britain. Mellerstain, Culzean and Charlotte Square in the New Town of Edinburgh are among the family's great works.

In the early 19th century the Romantic movement encouraged a return to a native Scottish spirit, leading to the Gothic-Baronial style of the high Victorian era, which still dominates the land.

By contrast the unsurpassed modernist architect Charles Rennie Mackintosh created an idiosyncratic version of art nouveau in such buildings as Hill House and the Glasgow School of Art, among many others.

O Caledonia! stern and wild,
Meet nurse for a poetic child!
Land of brown heath and shaggy wood,
Land of the mountain and the flood,
Land of my sires! what mortal hand
Can e'er untie the filial band
That knits me to thy rugged strand?
—Sir Walter Scott, *The Lay of the Last Minstrel* (1805)

213

SCOTS GLOSSARY
Some of the Gaelic and local terms you might come across.
Ben Mountain
Broch Circular stone defensive tower
Burn Stream
Ceilidh Impromptu gathering with singing and story-telling
Croft Small farm, often tenanted
Firth Narrow sea inlet
Glen Valley
Law Isolated hill
Linn Waterfall
Loch Lake
Lochan Small lake
Machair Coarse grass beside the sea, often used for grazing
Mull Promontory

Walks

Callander Crags, Stirling *210D3*

Car park on west side of Callander. A marked path from Tulipan Crescent, by the tennis courts, leads into woods. A steep climb is rewarded by splendid views of the Trossachs from the top of the Crags, which form the edge of an abrupt escarpment. (1.5 hours)

Culzean Country Park, *210B2*
South Ayrshire

Car park by Culzean Castle. The park is laced with trails; a detailed map is available on site. Aim to visit the castle, Happy Valley (with its exotic trees), the walled garden and Swan Pond. Maidens village to the south is an alternative starting point, where you can walk along the shore to the estate gates. (1–2 hours)

Grey Mare's Tail, *211B4*
Dumfries and Galloway

Car park by A708 between Selkirk and Moffat. A fine waterfall, visible from the road, but worth taking either of the marked trails for close-up views. The longer trail climbs to the top of the fall and heads for lonely Loch Skeen. (1–2.5 hours)

St. Abb's Head: the view of the cliffs at White Heugh, where guillemots and kittiwakes may be seen

New Lanark, *210C3*
South Lanarkshire

Car park in New Lanark. This 'model' village (see page 220) is quite remarkable, and is the starting point for walks along the Clyde Gorge, with its dramatic waterfalls. Walk south, parallel with the river, through the village, then fork right onto a track and right again onto a path above the river. Cross the river at a sluice bridge and turn right for further views to ruined Corra Castle. Return the same way. (2 hours)

St. Abb's Head, *211C5*
(Scottish) Borders

Car park by nature reserve visitor centre just west of St. Abb's village. A short path leads towards the village, then turns north parallel with the coast for bracing cliff views to the lighthouse at St. Abb's Head, where there are nesting sites for 50,000 birds, including puffins. Either return along the cliffs or take the easier lighthouse access road, with spectacular views of the coast. (1 hour)

► **Angus** 211E5

(Angus andDundee Tourist Board tel: 01382 527527;
www.angusanddundee.co.uk)

The county of Angus extends west from the North Sea across prosperous farmland (renowned for its black cattle) to the Grampians. The best scenery is to be found in the 'Braes of Angus'—beautiful glens such as Glen Isla, Glen Prosen, Glen Clova and Glen Esk—and on the rocky coast between **Montrose►** and **Arbroath►**. Montrose is a delightful summer resort whose Flemish-style architecture reflects centuries of trading with the Low Countries. **Montrose Basin**, the adjacent brackish tidal inlet, is the haunt of thousands of birds, including oystercatchers, curlews and pink-footed geese; there is a wildlife sanctuary on the A934. The fishing and market town of Arbroath, too, has something of a resort air in the summer. Its most famous monument is the 12th-century, red-stone abbey (HS)—a picturesque ruin which is surrounded by tombstones.

Inland and north of Arbroath by 22km (14 miles) is **Brechin**, a red-stone market town on the banks of the River South Esk. Standing proud beside the small cathedral is Scotland's finest **round tower►**. Only three such tall towers are known outside Ireland; they date from the 10th century and were used as the refuge and watchtower of the independent monasteries of the Celtic Church. At **Aberlemno**, 8km (5 miles) southwest along the back road to Forfar, are some fine carved Pictish stones.

Due north of Brechin is **Edzell► ►**. The ruins of its castle (HS) are handsome enough, but it is the Pleasance, the walled garden laid out by the scholar Sir David Lindsay in 1604, that makes the place exceptional.

In the fertile Vale of Strathmore, a little southwest of Forfar, is **Glamis Castle► ►** (as in Shakespeare's *Macbeth*), its brooding bulk standing quiet and solemn in the spacious acres of its deer park. Near the castle, a row of stone-roofed cottages houses the **Angus Folk Museum►** (NTS) of reconstructed interiors and domestic bygones.

►► **Arran** 210C1/C2

(Tourist information: Arran (Brodick) tel: 01770 302140;
www.ayrshire-arran.com; Bute (Rothesay) tel: 0870 720 0619;
www.visitscottishheartlands.com)

The largest of the Clyde Islands, Arran is a traditional holiday island, easily and quickly reached from Glasgow by train and ferry. Sheltered by the Kintyre Peninsula, it enjoys unusually warm weather and has dramatic mountains, deep valleys and sandy and rocky bays. As you approach the island on the ferry from Ardrossan, **Brodick Castle►** (NTS), an ancient stronghold of the Stuarts, dominates the shoreline. Its gardens include one of the finest rhododendron collections in Scotland. Arran is studded with prehistoric stones and is a paradise for hill-walkers, birdwatchers and geologists, who come by the busload because virtually every rock type is represented on the island.

North lies the flatter, fertile **Isle of Bute**. The capital town of Rothesay is reached by ferry from Wemyss Bay. Ruined Rothesay Castle (HS), like Arran's, was once the property of the Stuart kings. Cromwell destroyed it in the 17th century. Following a minor road to the south of the island and then a footpath across a field, you can walk among the ruins of St. Blane's Chapel with views of the Firth of Clyde.

ANGUS TRIVIA

● The Angus market towns proudly boast more fish-and-chip shops per head of population than anywhere else in the world.

● Arbroath has its own, separate culinary status as the home of 'Arbroath Smokies', split smoked haddock on the skin.

● In 1885 Arbroath entered a team in the Scottish Cup that recorded the highest score in British soccer history. They beat Bon Accord 36–0. The score might have been even greater: much time was spent retrieving the ball when a goal was scored, as the goalposts then had no nets and seven further goals were disallowed for offside. The Arbroath goalkeeper was said to have smoked a pipe throughout the match.

● The Declaration of Arbroath was an open letter presented by the abbot of Arbroath in 1320, signed by all the dignitaries of the land and addressed to the Pope. It summarized the case for an independent Scotland.

215

Brodick Castle and Garden, Isle of Arran

ROBERT BURNS

Often described as Scotland's ploughman poet, Robert Burns (1759–96) was well educated for his time. Though his amorous exploits have gained notoriety, his contribution to literature was through poetry that shrewdly observes the foibles of his fellow men. He also wrote numerous sentimental, lyrical and narrative pieces and was an avid 'improver' of Scottish traditional songs. A major theme running through his work was a belief in the universal brotherhood of man.

MORE BURNS SITES

Near the birthplace and Burns Cottage and Museum in Alloway are the Brig o'Doon and 17th-century Alloway Auld Kirk; both feature in Burns's poem *Tam o'Shanter* and Burns was baptized in the Kirk itself. The imposing Burns Monument was erected in 1823 and bears figures (added five years later) of Tam o'Shanter and his drinking companion, Souter Johnny.

► **Ayr** *210B2*

(Tourist information tel: 01292 290300; www.ayrshire-arran.com)

Admirers of Scotland's national poet, Robert Burns, may want to visit his birthplace at **Alloway**►► on the southern outskirts of the coastal resort of Ayr. Burns, who was one of the few European poets to rival Shakespeare for wit, spent his first seven years at the cottage which now forms the **Burns Cottage and Museum**. Close by, the **Tam o'Shanter Experience** is an audiovisual show recounting his famous poem. To the south is the **Burns Monument** of 1823.

High on a clifftop 19km (12 miles) down the coast road from Ayr, **Culzean Castle**►►►(NTS), built 1772–90 and the ancient seat of the Kennedys, hides behind its battlemented exterior a supremely elegant classical interior by Scottish architect Robert Adam, one of his finest Scottish creations. The celebrated oval staircase rises through three tiers of columns to an exceptional second-floor salon. Culzean Country Park, with its walled summer garden, woodland walks, lake and camellia greenhouses, is the most popular of the National Trust for Scotland's properties. Laid out on the dunes a little south of Culzean is the famous **Turnberry Golf Course**.

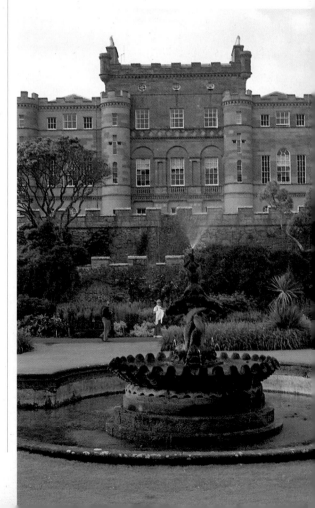

Culzean Castle, Robert Adam's elegant creation

THE (SCOTTISH) BORDERS

Drive

The (Scottish) Borders towns, abbeys and houses to visit

A 160km (100-mile) tour of the best of the (Scottish) Borders towns, abbeys and uplands. See also pages 218–219.

Start from **Peebles** and take the A72 east, following the Tweed, to **Traquair House**▶▶ outside Innerleithen. Continue along the A72 to reach Galashiels. Here, look out for the turning to Walter Scott's house, **Abbotsford**▶▶. From Abbotsford join the A72, but turn off into **Melrose** for the ruined **abbey**▶ (HS). Head back onto the A72 then the A68 for St. Boswells and **Dryburgh Abbey**▶▶ (HS). Detour north on the B6356 to Scott's View. Take the B6404 for a look at **Smailholm Tower**▶ (HS) on your way north to **Mellerstain House**▶▶. From here cross to **Hume Castle** and join the B6364 to Kelso to see its ruined abbey and, to the west of town, **Floors Castle**▶▶.

Follow the A698 south along the Teviot Valley to **Jedburgh**▶▶ with its ruined **abbey**▶▶ (HS), Castle Jail and Museum and Mary Queen of Scots

Visitor Centre. You can detour south of the town to Ferniehirst Castle and the Capon Tree. From Jedburgh take the A68 north to St. Boswells and turn west onto the A699 to **Bowhill House**, west of Selkirk.

Follow Yarrow Water upstream, along the A708, turning north at Mountbenger onto the B709 for the lonely crossing of Deuchar Law to Traquair House. From here a small road on the south bank of the Tweed passes **Kailzie Gardens**, near Cardrona, on the return to Peebles.

Dryburgh Abbey, founded in 1150

Young Walter Scott, in Smailholm Tower

218

THE EILDON HILLS AND WALTER SCOTT
Legend has it that these pink hills that rise prominently out of the valley near Melrose were cleft in three one night by the 13th-century wizard Michael Scott (Michele Scot in Dante's *Inferno*), to settle a dispute with the devil (the wizard's spellbook is said to be buried in Melrose Abbey). Geologists insist they are the relics of old volcanoes. Either way, they make excellent walking territory for those staying in Melrose and were popular with Sir Walter Scott. Visit Scott's View, beside the B6356 north of St. Boswells, for the view of them he so enjoyed.

▶▶ The (Scottish) Borders 211B4
(Scottish Borders Tourist Board tel: 0870 608 0404; www.visitscottishborders.com)

As famous for its salmon as for its tweed, the (Scottish) Borders is a land scarred by centuries of turbulence. Fought over since the days of the Romans, it has many sites that bear silent testimony to this past—tower houses built to ward off border raiders, skeletons of abbeys vengefully destroyed by England's Henry VIII. It is also Sir Walter Scott country, the countryside that inspired Scotland's most celebrated novelist. There is nowhere else quite like it in Scotland—a pleasant coast, no big mountains but lonely, rounded hills, good for bracing moorland walks. Even in the holiday season, there are no tourist jams.

The town of **Jedburgh▶▶** is best known for its **abbey▶▶**(HS) and anyone planning to visit the four great Borders abbeys—Jedburgh, Dryburgh, Melrose and Kelso—should visit the Abbey visitor centre here, which admirably explains their role. Jedburgh Abbey holds the record for border raids—destroyed and rebuilt eight times in its 400-year working life. Its finest features are the two late Norman doorways and the excellent tracery window in the north transept. Also in the town are **Mary Queen of Scots Visitor Centre**, which tells the story of the queen who stayed here in 1556 and the **Castle Jail and Museum**.

Selkirk is a tweed-manufacturing town and a good base. **Bowhill House▶** is 6km (4 miles) west, set in the high ground between two tributaries of the Tweed. Its many works of art include the last Leonardo da Vinci in private hands in Britain. The house is surrounded by grounds.

Just outside Innerleithen, is **Traquair House▶▶**, Scotland's oldest inhabited house, dating from about 1,000 years ago, although most of the structure is 17th century. Its forbidding outline is softened by the pale harling of its walls, but it remains dark and chilly inside. In the gardens the excellent maze is popular with children. The house includes an 18th-century brewery, which produces the excellent Traquair House beers. **Peebles**, a pleasant town set on the River Tweed, is popular for outdoor pursuits, such as walking, golf, fishing and cycling. The 145km (90-mile) long Tweed Cycleway starts at nearby Biggar.

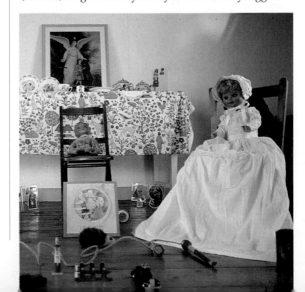

Children's playthings on display in Traquair House

Between Galashiels and Melrose is **Abbotsford▶▶**, the imposing turreted mansion that the great novelist Sir Walter Scott had built on the banks of the Tweed. It is still inhabited by his descendants and houses his extraordinary collection of assorted Scottish curiosities.

Melrose is an appealing town. Close by the compact main square stands **Melrose Abbey▶▶**(HS), its remains being the finest example of the golden age of Scottish ecclesiastical architecture. Its soft pink stone is warm, forgiving and kind and a magical atmosphere pervades the site. Robert the Bruce's heart is said to be buried here. From the town there are delightful walks up to the Eildon Hills (see panel, page 218) and along the River Tweed.

Dryburgh Abbey▶▶(HS), set peacefully in an exquisite bend of the graceful River Tweed near St. Boswells, is the most moving of the four Borders abbeys. Large sections stand astonishingly well preserved, especially the cloisters. If you walk nowhere else, walk here; it's the best way to enjoy the peace and quiet of Scotland's most serene ruin. Leave your car and cross the Tweed by the footbridge.

A little way northeast is **Smailholm Tower▶**(HS), a classic pele tower (see panel). **Mellerstain House▶▶** is found 9km (5 miles) northwest of Kelso. This breathtaking Georgian house, built by William and Robert Adam in

the mid-18th century (see panel page 51), is the perfect example of the Adams' skill in combining stateliness with domestic ease and comfort. Inside, the large, wide, light rooms, in their pale Adam hues, are as perfect as the day they were finished. A museum contains a wonderful portrait of Bonnie Prince Charlie disguised as Flora MacDonald's Irish maid, Betty Burke (see page 246).

Kelso is a proud town, but the **abbey ruins** (*Admission free*) are the least captivating of the Borders' abbeys, the square tower resembling a fortress. To the west of Kelso stands **Floors Castle▶▶**, its William Adam and William Playfair exterior one of the stateliest of all the Border palaces. On a sunny day its pinnacled façade gleams above its terraced riverside grounds. Only the hall retains its original Adam interior, but in the state rooms are many treasures. The 19th-century Gothick bird room is a popular curiosity.

The coast at **St. Abb's Head▶** (see Walks, page 214) is a prime site for naturalists and birdwatchers.

PELE TOWERS

The word 'pele' or 'peel' is derived from the Latin *palus* or palisade and was the name given to the tower houses built around the Scotland-England border against the raiding enemy. Smailholm Tower, near St. Boswells, is a well-preserved example from the 16th century. Then it housed a continuous day and night watch; now it stands square and stern and stark on a moorland crag, overhanging a sullen pool. The 15th-century tower house at Cranshaws in the Lammermuir Hills features in Scott's *The Bride of Lammermuir*.

Founded in the 12th century, Jedburgh Abbey was used as a place of worship until 1875

TWEED MAKING

For countless centuries Borderers have made tweed, a practical, hard-wearing woollen cloth that was formerly known as 'Galashiels Grey'. In the 1820s Sir Walter Scott brought the material to the attention of fashionable London society by making a sensational appearance in black-and-white checked trousers and later tweed enjoyed the patronage of Queen Victoria and Prince Albert. The styles and hues have become more sophisticated and today many spinners, weavers, designers and tapestry makers work in the Borders. In Galashiels, **Locharron of Scotland** is the producer of the world's largest range of wool worsted tartans. The **Locharron Cashmere and Wool Centre**, Waverley Mill, operates guided factory tours with the opportunity to buy.

THE COVENANTERS

The Covenanters were a leading faction of Scottish society in the 17th century that supported a Presbyterian system of church government. The National Covenant was signed in 1638 and the bishops, appointed by the Crown, were abolished the same year. Under the leadership of Archibald Campbell, 8th Earl of Argyll, the Covenanters successfully opposed an army sent north by Charles I. This campaign, known as the First Bishops War, led directly into the greater engagement of the Civil War. Sir Walter Scott's novel *Old Mortality* tells the story of the Lowland Covenanters and the extremes to which their religious zeal led them.

The Falls of Clyde run through a gorge just below New Lanark

MARY, QUEEN OF SCOTS' LOVER

James Hepburn, Earl of Bothwell, is one of history's more exciting characters. He was the lover of Mary, Queen of Scots, the possible father of James VI and certainly the murderer of Darnley, the queen's second husband, whose body was found strangled outside the bombed-out house of Kirk O'Field. He then divorced his wife and rushed the queen out to a secret marriage at Dunbar Castle in 1567. Hounded by their enemies, the lovers were, however, forced to part and Bothwell was eventually imprisoned in the Danish Castle of Dragsholm, where he died insane.

▶ The Clyde Valley   210C3

(Greater Glasgow and Clyde Valley Tourist Board tel: 0141 204 4400; www.seeglasgow.com)

Deep in the wooded Clyde Valley near Lanark (see Walks, page 214) is the 18th-century model cotton mill village of **New Lanark**▶▶▶ (a World Heritage Site). It is linked with such key figures of the Industrial Revolution as the inventor Richard Arkwright and Robert Owen (1771–1858), the social reformer, who attempted through enlightened methods to create a cooperative industrial community here; Owen believed that such ideas would one day replace private ownership. His Nursery building, the Institute for the Formation of Character, the school and apartments housing the workers have all been restored. On an inclusive ticket you can take in a short introductory history 'ride' in the award-winning visitor centre before looking in at Robert Owen's House, the Millworkers' House, Robert Owen's School for Children and the period-style village shop.

West of Lanark, **Craignethan Castle**▶▶ (HS) is a fine example of a 16th-century stronghold. The most exciting feature is the caponier, a vaulted gallery built onto the floor of the moat providing protection from artillery fire (though it nearly suffocated the defenders in smoke); this one is thought to be the earliest in Britain.

Bothwell▶▶, southeast of Glasgow, boasts a 14th-century church and a monument which commemorates the defeat of the Covenanters (see panel) in 1679. The town is chiefly renowned for its 13th-century castle (HS), set high above the Clyde. This strategic castle was much damaged in the Wars of Independence of 1296–1330 against England.

▶ Dumfries and Galloway 210B3

*(Dumfries and Galloway Tourist Board tel: 01387 253862;
www.visitdumfriesandgalloway.co.uk)*

The western hills are wilder and more expansive than
those of the better-known (Scottish) Borders district to the
east. The character of the region is also more solemn,
though it is enlivened by some interesting archeological
sites, some haunting ruins and some splendid castles.
While much of the countryside inland is humdrum, the
southern coast is a pleasant place to wander around, with
an occasional surprising view of the English Lake District
(best from the top of Criffel, south of Dumfries). The area
is never crowded; some of the wildest parts of the
Southern Uplands are in Galloway Forest Park (parts of
which are tediously blanketed in evergreen plantations)
and some of the Lowlands' most beautiful countryside is
in the hills and valleys of the Rivers Nith, Annan and Esk,
to the north and east of the stone town of Dumfries.

Standing beside the Solway Firth 14km (9 miles) south of
Dumfries is **Caerlaverock Castle▶▶**(HS). Its unusual
triangular plan, its full moat and the green serenity of its
site make this, 'the lark's nest' castle, one of the most memorable in the country. It has been much fought over and the
outer walls were beseiged by King Edward I in 1300 less
than a decade after the foundations had been laid. The interior bears a very fine Renaissance façade added by the
enlightened Lord Nithsdale, head of the Maxwell clan, in
the 17th century. Not far away at Ruthwell is the particularly fine carved Anglo-Saxon **Ruthwell Cross▶**. More than
5m (16ft) high and dated to the seventh century, it is one of
the most important monuments of the Dark Ages

Threave Castle▶▶(HS) and **Threave Garden▶▶**(NTS), a
grim castle and a delightful garden, lie near Castle Douglas,
16km (10 miles) northeast of Kirkcudbright. Threave Castle
was built by Archibald the Grim, who boasted how the gallows' knob that sticks out over the entrance 'never wanted a
tassel'. Threave Castle was a 14th-century stronghold of the
notorious Black Douglases, so called because of their merci-
less pillaging, and was besieged unsuccessfully by the royal
forces of James II (of Scotland) in 1455. South of the ruined
castle is the Threave Wildfowl Refuge, where wintering
birds include wild geese and teal.

CURLING
For at least 350 years this
team game, played on ice,
has been enjoyed all over
Scotland. The curling
stones are made from
granite and have handles
sunken into the top. The
object is to slide the
stones along the ice into
a tee, the team with the
most stones at the middle
of the tee being the win-
ner. The best stones are
reputed to be from Ailsa
Craig, a 335m (1,099ft)
volcanic plug of rock
16km (10 miles) off
Girvan that persistently
pops up into view as
you drive around the
Ayrshire coast.

221

*On its island in the River
Dee, Threave Castle
speaks of a strife-ridden
period in Scottish history*

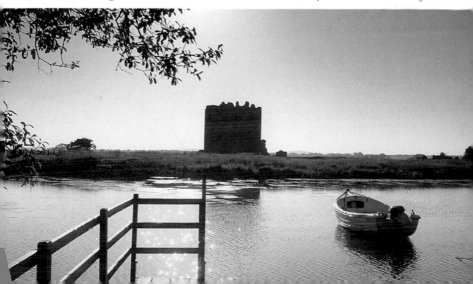

Drumlanrig Castle, ringed by forests and rolling hills

The nearby (but separately administered) Threave Garden is where the National Trust for Scotland trains its budding young horticulturalists. Every type of terrain and condition they are likely to encounter is authentically re-created here, from rose to heather garden, from rock to wood; there are herbaceous borders, a walled garden and fabulous glasshouses in which exotic flowers and fruits grow. In spring there is a display of 200 different types of daffodil.

The town of **Kirkcudbright**▶ is set sweetly on the River Dee around **MacLellan's Castle**▶(HS). With its typical pastel-painted housefronts, it has long been beloved of Scottish artists; Edward Atkinson Hornel was a member of the artists' colony founded here in the early years of the 20th century. There are several art galleries in the town today. It is a tranquil place to spend a day wandering around. Visit the ancient tollbooth, with its curious and beautiful spire, it contains an art gallery (*Admission free*) with paintings from the Kirkudbright Artists' Colony (1880 to the present), or the Stewartry Museum (*Admission free*) with its many local antiquities and curios; a display explains the strange and ancient Scottish pastime of curling (see panel, page 221). In Gatehouse of Fleet, 13km (8 miles) northwest, is the **Mill on the Fleet**▶, a visitor centre based on a restored 18th-century cotton mill that portrays the town's industrial past.

Whithorn, 29km (18 miles) south of Newton Stewart, is one of the oldest Christian areas in Britain; here, in 397, St. Ninian built the first Christian church in Scotland, although the present ruin dates from the 13th century. The Whithorn Story (HS) has finds related to the saint.

The southwesternmost corner of this region is the strange spit of land known as the Rhinns of Galloway (from which there are views of the Mourne Mountains across the water in Northern Ireland). Here is the **Logan Botanic Garden**▶, where plants from the temperate regions of the southern hemisphere thrive in a walled garden. **Castle Kennedy Gardens**▶, near Stranraer, were laid out on a grand scale by the 18th-century Earl of Stair, with ruins, lakes and wooded walks. It is at its most majestic when the rhododendrons and azaleas are in bloom in early summer.

In the northern part of Dumfries and Galloway, set beside the River Nith near Thornhill, is **Drumlanrig**▶ ▶(HS). No building looks more solid or more imposingly rooted in Scotland than this pink 17th-century palace. Within its massive walls are the region's finest collections of Old Masters, including a Rembrandt and exquisite French furniture of the 18th century. Rural craftspeople offer work for sale.

▶ ▶ ▶ **Edinburgh** *211C4*
(Edinburgh and Scotland Information Centre tel: 0845 225 5121; www.edinburgh.org)

The capital of Scotland is an outstanding city. It is rich in open spaces, museums, beautiful buildings and elegant streets, all lit by the clear Lothian light. The dark courts, cobbled streets and steep steps of the medieval Old Town contrast with the gracious squares, circuses and crescents of the Georgian New Town. It is at its most exhilarating during the International Festival from mid-August to early September and Fringe from early to late August.

The Royal Mile▶ ▶ ▶ is the original and chief street of the city. At its western end lies the **castle▶ ▶ ▶** (HS), on the site of an ancient fortress and home to the Scottish Crown Jewels; at the other end are the Abbey and **Palace of Holyroodhouse▶ ▶** , the official Scottish residence of the Queen (open to the public when the Royal Family is not here). The Royal Mile is the heart of the Old Town; many of the city's most historic landmarks are on it and there are numerous museums and houses to visit (see panel).

St. Giles' Cathedral, the High Kirk of Edinburgh, was originally built in the traditional shape of a cross, though later additions have given it an unusual square design. **Canongate Kirk** is a dignified example of a Presbyterian church, with typical white-painted walls and wooden box pews. The **Royal Museum▶ ▶ ▶** (*Admission free*), Chambers Street, is a worldwide collection with decorative art and archeology galleries, natural history and technology galleries. Next door, the **Museum of Scotland** (*Admission free*) concentrates on all things Scottish. In Holyrood Road, **Our Dynamic Earth▶ ▶** uses state-of-the-art technology in a voyage of discovery around our planet. Close by is the startlingly innovative Scottish Parliament building, completed 2004, while the **Grassmarket** is a pleasant part of the Old Town, with its antiques shops and bistros.

The Mound is a causeway between the Old and New Towns. There are views across to breezy **Calton Hill▶ ▶ ▶** where the **National Monument▶** stands, styled on the Parthenon in Greece to commemorate the Scots who fell in

Princes Street and Edinburgh Castle, dramatically perched on a volcanic crag, as seen from Calton Hill

223

THE ROYAL MILE
The **Camera Obscura and World of Illusions,** near the castle in the Outlook Tower, gives a 'living image' of the city projected via lenses (best on a bright day). Opposite, The **Scotch Whisky Heritage Centre** tells all there is to know about whisky. **Gladstone's Land** (NTS), on the Lawnmarket, is a re-creation of a typical Old Town, six-floor tenement house. The **Writers' Museum** (*Admission free*) contains memorabilia of Scottish writers, including Robert Burns, Sir Walter Scott and Robert Louis Stevenson. On the High Street is the absorbing **Museum of Childhood** (*Admission free*). **The People's Story** (*Admission free*), on Canongate, tells the story of ordinary folk from the 18th century on. Opposite, in a striking 16th-century mansion, is **The Museum of Edinburgh** (*Admission free*).

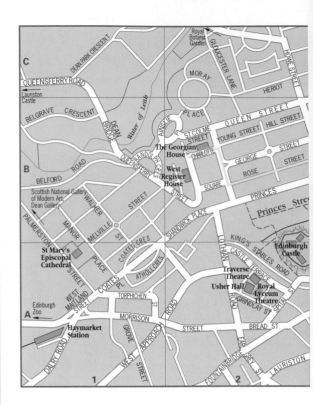

224

THE FORMER ROYAL YACHT *BRITANNIA*

The Queen's famous royal yacht, built in Clydebank near Glasgow and launched in 1953, is now a museum berthed at Ocean Terminal, Leith, on the edge of Edinburgh. There is a self-guided audio tour of the five decks. It is reached by bus numbers 1, 11, 22 and 34 from the city. Leith has pleasant waterfront restaurants.

THE NATIONAL GALLERY OF SCOTLAND

The five national galleries (the nearby National Gallery and Royal Scottish Academy, the National Portrait Gallery, the National Gallery of Modern Art and Dean Gallery) are all free, and connected by free bus. The National Gallery includes Poussin's sequence of *The Seven Sacraments*, a Rembrandt self-portrait at the age of 51, Velasquez's *Old Woman Cooking Eggs*, El Greco's *Saviour of the World* and many Scottish works. *The Reverend Robert Walker Skating on Duddingston Loch* by Sir Henry Raeburn (1756–1823) is one of Scotland's best-loved paintings.

the Napoleonic Wars. Though never completed, it is evidence of the 18th-century boast that Edinburgh had become the Athens of the North. Beside the Mound is the **National Gallery of Scotland▶▶▶** (*Admission free*), a classical building housing the national art collection (see panel).

Princes Street▶ is the principal shopping street. Running along one side are Princes Street Gardens; the **Scott Monument** is the most striking, if endearingly excessive, landmark, covered with statuettes of characters from Sir Walter Scott's novels and poems; you can climb to the top.

In Queen Street, in the New Town, a distinctive red-brick Venetian palace houses the **Scottish National Portrait Gallery▶** (*Admission free*). There is not one second-rate picture in the portrait gallery and no shortage of famous subjects. In 1791 Robert Adam was commissioned to design one superb square to enhance the quality of the New Town. Grand, spacious and elegant, his **Charlotte Square▶** is the quintessence of the New Town. No. 7, **The Georgian House** (NTS), has been restored, giving a glimpse of an interior of about 1800.

The **Royal Botanic Garden Edinburgh▶** (*Admission free, except to the greenhouses*), beyond the New Town, has superb tropical greenhouses. For walks, climb **Arthur's Seat▶▶**, a volcanic hill or follow the **Water of Leith**, west of the New Town. Out this way, the **National Gallery of Modern Art and Dean Gallery▶** has a worldwide collection, including works by Picasso and Matisse.

EDINBURGH

Walk

From the Castle to Charlotte Square

Start at the **Castle**▶▶▶(HS), then enter the **Royal Mile**▶▶▶ at Lawn Market to visit the **Scotch Whisky Heritage Centre**▶, **Camera Obscura and World of Illusions**▶ and **Gladstone's Land**▶(NTS). Continue along High Street past Parliament House, the Tron Kirk, **St. Giles' Cathedral** and the City Chambers. Go on past the **Museum of Childhood**▶ and **John Knox House** along Canongate, to **The People's Story**▶, **The Museum of Edinburgh** and the **Canongate Kirk**▶, to the **Palace of Holyroodhouse**▶▶.

Return up Holyrood Road and along the Cowgate to pass the University, the **Royal Museum**▶▶▶, **Museum of Scotland, Greyfriars Kirk**▶ (and statue of the loyal little dog, Greyfriars Bobby) and then **The Grassmarket**. Turn up Victoria Street, left down Bank Street to **The Writers' Museum**▶ and then down The Mound to the **National Gallery of Scotland**▶▶▶ and the **Royal Scottish Academy Building** (catch the views towards the National Monument on Calton Hill). Turn right onto **Princes Street**▶ to the **Scott Monument**, across and onto St. Andrew Square and Queen Street for the **Scottish National Portrait Gallery**▶.

Follow George Street to Frederick Street, turn left, then right on Rose Street and continue to Robert Adam's **Charlotte Square**▶ to visit **The Georgian House**(NTS).

►► The Firth of Forth

*(Edinburgh and Scotland Information Centre tel: 0845 225 5121;
www.edinburgh.org. Kingdom of Fife Tourist Board tel: 01592
750066; www.standrews.com/fife)*

The Firth of Forth is a wide tidal inlet that bites deep into
the east coast of the country. From a first glance at a map
it appears to have almost severed Scotland into two. It has
functioned more as a trading canal than as a frontier
moat. The long tidal shores are dotted with merchant
towns whose markets and privileges are established in
ancient royal charters. The old local adage says that a
farm by the Forth is better than an earldom in the north—
expressing the realities of this land that formed the
heartland of the medieval kingdom of Scotland.

Six kilometres (4 miles) west of the Forth rail and road
bridges is **Hopetoun House►**, the beautiful stately home of
the Marquis of Linlithgow. Begun in 1699 by Sir William
Bruce and completed by William Adam and his sons, it
houses a sumptuous collection of paintings, tapestries and
furniture. An equal distance east of the bridges, near South
Queensferry, is **Dalmeny►**, a large 19th-century house set in a
fine park. It's home to one of Britain's outstanding Rothschild
Mentmore collections of 17th-century French furniture,
tapestries and Sèvres porcelain. Dalmeny can be reached on
foot along the estuary from Cramond, a lovely walk.
Cramond► is a pretty village of whitewashed cottages and
old mills at the mouth of the River Almond, on the outskirts of
Edinburgh. A little ferry takes you across to the Dalmeny
estates and there are delightful walks up the riverbank.

Farther west, still south of the Firth, **Linlithgow
Palace►►**(HS) stands above the town of Linlithgow. At
the time of Mary, Queen of Scots' birth here in 1542 it was a
magnificent structure, but a fire in 1746 left it a ruin. Its
enormous roofless red body survives and there is a fine
octagonal fountain in the courtyard, a vast Great Hall and a
swath of grass around the outer walls on which to picnic.

Across the Firth, on the western edge of Fife, the small
coastal town of **Culross►►►** (pronounced 'Coo-ross') is

END OF AN ERA
With the opening of the
Forth road bridge, the
villages that stand on
either side of the Firth—
known as North and South
Queensferry—lost the
ferry service that had
existed for some 900
years. Among the earliest
visitors here was Queen
Margaret, wife of Malcolm
Canmore, who used this
route in the 11th century
between her palace
and her abbey near
Dunfermline—hence the
name 'queen's ferry'.

THE FORTH BRIDGES
The Forth train bridge,
built between 1882 and
1889 and illuminated
since its centennial, still
wins the admiration of
young engineers. For most
of its life it was the
longest bridge in the
world. A little west is the
fabulous modern suspen-
sion road bridge (1964),
much lighter and a superb
feat of modern engineer-
ing. The Visitor Centre
(*Admission free*), within
the Queensferry
Lodge Hotel at South
Queensferry explains
the structures.

set in an unpromising landscape of former coal mines with a distant view of the Grangemouth refinery. Persevere, however, for Culross is one of the jewels of the National Trust for Scotland. This perfectly preserved example of an early 17th-century trading burgh made its way in the world by digging coal from under the Forth, smelting iron to be hammered out into girdles and boiling up seawater to extract salt. The cobbled streets are lined with traditional corbeled houses, roofed with the distinctive terracotta pantiles of Fife. You can inspect three period interiors: start at The Town House (NTS) with an exhibition and video show on local history and examine the jail chamber in the basement. Next door is the restored palace (NTS) of Sir George Bruce, the local entrepreneurial landowner, with its painted ceilings and tiled kitchen. Bishop Leighton's Study (NTS), also carefully restored, is the traditional name for the tall corbeled town house that overlooks the Mercat Cross. From there a short walk up steep Kirk Street leads to the slight ruins of a Cistercian monastery standing immediately beside the old abbey chapel, which has functioned, with later additions, as the parish church since the Reformation.

Dunfermline Abbey▶▶ (HS) stands above the wooded glen of Pittencrieff Park in Dunfermline. The abbey was founded as a Benedictine house in the 11th century. Its tower and the eastern end were rebuilt in the 19th century to serve as a parish church, but the sturdy 12th-century nave with its solid pale stone columns, strong round arches and the zigzag chevrons so characteristic of the Romanesque is more interesting. The visitor centre has a good range of display material.

A more recent attraction at North Queensferry is **Deep Sea World**▶▶, an elaborate and innovative aquarium, with the world's largest viewing tunnel, as long as a football field. In summer, boat trips can be taken from South Queensferry, by the Forth bridges, to Inchcolm Island, to see the well-preserved abbey (HS) and a colony of seals.

See page 230 for more information on the fishing villages of the East Neuk of Fife.

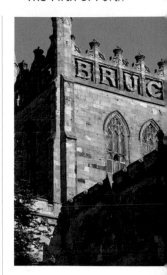

Dunfermline Abbey, burial place of King Robert the Bruce

227

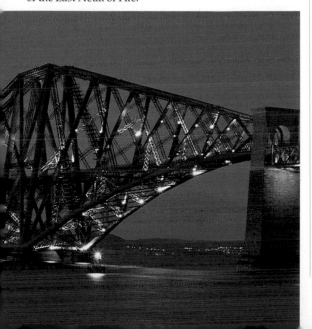

The Forth train bridge, which needs continuous repainting on a four-year cycle

ROYAL TENNIS
The 16th-century Falkland Palace (NTS), inland from Kirkcaldy, was a popular hunting seat for the Scottish kings until James VI died in 1625. The original Royal Tennis Court was built in 1539, though the present court dates from 1625, reputedly it is the world's oldest, and is still in use today. Sir Walter Scott used the palace as the setting for part of his novel *The Fair Maid of Perth*, which was made into an opera by Bizet.

GLASGOW SCIENCE CENTRE

On the south bank of the Clyde in the Govan area and dominated by the rotating Glasgow Tower (Scotland's tallest free-standing tower, which you can go up) this is packed with hands-on encounters with science and is one of Scotland's top family attractions. Also on site are a planetarium and IMAX cinema, while across a footbridge over the river is the Tall Ship *Glenlee* of 1896, one of only five Clyde-built sailing ships afloat in the world. There is a lively schedule of demonstrations and children's events.

SOCCER SHRINE

At Hampden Park, the world's oldest international football stadium, the Scottish Football Museum surveys the game back to the 1860s. Stadium tours visit the changing rooms and Royal Box.

The great shipbuilding yards on the Clyde were born in the 19th-century steam era when Clyde-built vessels acquired a high reputation worldwide

▶▶▶ Glasgow   *210C3*

(Tourist information tel: 0141 204 4400; www.seeglasgow.com)

Glasgow's skyline of chimneys, factories and high-rises is a reminder of Glasgow's 19th-century industrial core, but the middle of Glasgow is today a place of captivating charm. The city's merchant dynasties bequeathed it a legacy of art and architecture—and most of the museums and galleries are free. The grid plan of the streets makes it easy to explore.

The city has three distinct areas: the medieval town, the Merchant City and the West End. The **cathedral▶**, a dark-hued, heavy Gothic glory begun in the 13th century, is one of the two surviving buildings of the medieval town, on the eastern side of the city. St. Mungo (or Kentigern) founded a missionary chapel here in the sixth century, around which the trading burgh of Glasgow later grew. Opposite the cathedral, the unique **St. Mungo Museum of Religious Life and Art▶** (*Admission free*) explores the religions of the world, while in the other direction spread over a hill overlooking the city the **Necropolis▶** is an ostentatious burial ground where Glasgow's richest magnates were buried. In Castle Street, is **Provand's Lordship** (*Admission free*), built in 1471 for a canon of the cathedral and now displaying period artefacts and furnishings; it is the city's oldest house.

The Merchant City district has its origins in the heyday of the 'tobacco lords'. Glasgow was well placed for trade with the New World and the 18th century saw a period of glory as an international trading city. By the 19th century Glasgow was one of the world's greatest shipbuilding hub and, in an expression of bursting civic pride, money was poured into the Merchant City district to create some of the best Victorian streets in Britain, with some of the most innovative architecture of the day. The great rectangular **George Square▶** is the heart of Glasgow today (location of the Tourist Information Centre), flanked on one side by the splendidly overblown façade of the **City Chambers▶▶** (*Free guided tours* of the marbled interior, 10.30am, 2.30pm), built 1883–88. To the north is Queen Street station; Central station, with its even more impressive 19th-century interior, is just a few blocks west. **Trades Hall of Glasgow** (*Admission free*) with its Adam façade dates from 1791; **Hutchesons' Hall** (NTS) and **Stirling Library** are early 19th-century. Glasgow Green is one of many city parks and here is the **People's Palace▶▶** (*Admission free*), an excellent museum devoted to the social history of Glasgow and the huge Winter Gardens conservatory. Nearby is the old Templetons carpet factory (1889), an amazing replica of the Doge's Palace in Venice (*not open to the public*).

In the leafy area of the West End, with its fine early 19th-century town houses around Glasgow University, is the **Art Gallery and Museum Kelvingrove▶▶** (*Admission free*), a Victorian red sandstone mansion in Kelvingrove Park (*Closed for refurbishment until 2006; until late 2005, highlights of the art collection are displayed in the McLellan Galleries near the Glasgow School of Art*). In Kelvin Hall, opposite, is an exciting **Museum of Transport▶▶** (*Admission free*), with reconstructed Underground stations and shops, old trams, cars and motorcycles. The **Hunterian Art Gallery▶▶** (*Admission free*) is renowned for its collection of works of James McNeill Whistler (1834–1903). Also strongly represented is 19th- and 20th-century Scottish art, including works of the Scottish colourists, the 'Glasgow Boys', a group

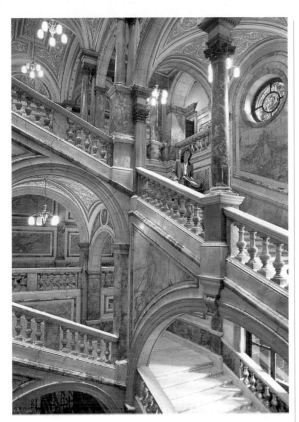

The interior of the City Chambers

CHARLES RENNIE MACKINTOSH (1868–1928)

Mackintosh was prominent in the Arts and Crafts Movement and was the first Scottish architect since the 18th century to achieve international fame. While his stained glass and metalwork used the art nouveau motifs of intertwining tendrils, his buildings have a taut quality of geometric simplicity; his furniture design is typified by the tall, starkly simple ladder-chair. The Glasgow School of Art (1896–1909) is his masterpiece, designed when he was only 28; other notable buildings include Scotland Street School—now a museum of education (*Admission free*), the Willow Tea Rooms on Sauchiehall Street and the Lighthouse (the former *Glasgow Herald* Building) in Mitchell Lane—now featuring architecture and design including a Mackintosh Interpretation Centre. In Bellahouston Park, House for an Art Lover was built in 1996 using Mackintosh's plans of 1901. At Helensburgh, west of Glasgow, Hill House (NTS) is an outstanding example of his domestic style.

229

of painters who advocated realism in art instead of Victorian romanticism. The Mackintosh House (*Admission free*) is an elegant re-creation of the nearby house (now demolished) occupied and furnished by Glasgow architect Charles Rennie Mackintosh (see panel). Within the **Botanic Gardens** is a beautiful 19th-century glasshouse, **Kibble Palace►►** (*dismantled for refurbishment; reopens 2006*), where tree ferns grow amid white statuary.

The **Glasgow School of Art►►►** (*Guided tours daily at frequent intervals*), in Renfrew Street, is the finest completed example of Mackintosh's vision. Still a working art school, it houses a collection of his paintings and designs. **The Tenement House►►** (NTS) on nearby Buccleuch Street is the ordinary city apartment of Miss Agnes Toward, preserved as she left it in 1965, having changed virtually nothing in more than half a century. The simple dignity of her gas-lit four-roomed home and belongings tell more about the realities of Scottish life than a dozen palaces.

A short drive out (or take a bus or train from Glasgow Central station; courtesy bus from Pollok Country Park entrance, 200m/220yd from Pollokshaws West rail station) is a light, glass-walled building, constructed in 1983 in the grounds of **Pollok House** (NTS). It houses the extraordinary art collection of shipping magnate Sir William Burrell. Though vast, the **Burrell Collection►►►** (*Admission free*) is worth a visit, comprising Egyptian alabaster, Chinese jade, Persian rugs, tapestries, stained glass and carved doorways.

Façade of the Glasgow School of Art

St. Andrews, Scotland's first university town, seen from St. Rule's Tower

GOLF IN ST. ANDREWS
To many St. Andrews is synonymous with golf, a sport that has been played there since the 15th century. In 1754 local dignitaries set up the Society of St. Andrews Golfers, which had the title Royal and Ancient ('R & A') conferred upon it in 1834. New courses have been added around the Old Course, where the 18th hole is named after the great Tom Morris. There are more than 500 courses in Scotland and 'round' and day tickets are available at most (including St. Andrews, except for the Old Course); discounted golf passes cover some areas. Contact Visit Scotland (see page 274) for a free copy of *The Official Guide to Golf in Scotland.*

▶▶▶ St. Andrews
211D4

(Tourist information tel: 01334 472021; www.visit-standrews.co.uk)

Scotland's oldest university, its first golf course and the ruins of its principal pre-Reformation cathedral mingle with the everyday business of an old Fife market town and summer resort. It was already a holy place for the southern Picts when a shrine to St. Andrew, patron saint of Scotland, was established on the eastern clifftops in the eighth century. Within a century St. Andrews had become the administrative hub of Christianity in Scotland. The top of 12th-century St. Rule's church tower gives a bird's-eye view over the enormous ruined nave of the adjoining 14th-century **cathedral▶▶**(HS) and of the town's little port with its long pier, known as a mole. West along the coast are the ruins of the bishop's **castle▶**(HS) with its bottle dungeon, from which no one ever escaped and 16th-century mine and counter mine (a defensive tunnel). Below the Martyrs' Memorial, the handsome **Royal and Ancient Club House** (home of the ruling body for golf the world over) overlooks the oldest course in the world and the **British Golf Museum**. Nearby a Sea Life Centre stands by the long West Sands. On the three converging streets that comprise the 'auld grey toun' are lesser but impressive buildings such as the university's 15th- and 16th-century colleges and the West Port gate, all among town houses and secret 'wynds', or alleyways.

The East Neuk A road south leads to **Anstruther▶**, one of several pretty old fishing villages dotted along the southern coast of Fife's East Neuk. Here is the Scottish Fisheries Museum. There are boat trips in summer to the Isle of May. Fishermen's cottages in **Crail▶▶** are now home to artists and holiday-makers. To see a fishing fleet in action go to the port at **Pittenweem▶**. Flemish gables reflect former trading links with the Low Countries. Inland is **Kellie Castle▶▶** (NTS), 16th-century round tower houses typical of the Lowlands; another is **Scotstarvit Tower▶**(NTS), near Ceres. Also in the vicinity is the **Hill of Tarvit Mansion-house** (NTS), rebuilt by Sir Robert Lorimer in 1906 to house the art collection of a jute magnate; there are paintings by Sir Henry Raeburn and Allan Ramsay, fine furniture, Chinese porcelain and an Edwardian laundry.

▶▶ Stirling 210D3

(Tourist information tel: 0870 720 0620;
www.stirling-tourism.co.uk)

Stirling Castle▶▶(HS) stands in a strategically commanding position on a volcanic crag, the symbolic key to Scotland, at the geographical and historical heart of the country. Nearby, the **Old Town Jail**, St. John Street, recaptures the feel of prison life, with the actor-guide playing the role of both guard and prisoner.

On the other side of town, the **Bannockburn Heritage Centre and Battlefield** (NTS) tells the story of the most famous battle in Scottish history (see panel). Midway between them on the banks of the Forth are the restored Gothic ruins of **Cambuskenneth Abbey**. Walk up to the old town to see the **Church of Holy Rude** where in 1543 Mary, Queen of Scots was crowned at the age of nine months. **Cowane's Hospital** (*Admission free*), the shell of **Mar's Wark**—built in 1570 as the town house of the 1st Earl of Mar, Regent of Scotland—as well as **Argyll's Lodging** (HS), are all notable buildings in this vicinity (all *open*). Within the castle walls are 18th-century artillery batteries, gardens, a royal chapel and the Renaissance palace of the Stuart kings. Also here is the **Argyll and Sutherland Highlanders Regimental Museum**.

The **Wallace National Monument▶▶**, on the northeastern edge of the town, commemorates Scotland's first freedom fighter, William Wallace; Wallace rose from obscurity to lead the national resistance to the advancing English king, Edward I, winning a victory at the Battle of Stirling in 1297.

Dunblane▶ is a small residential town beside the meandering River Allan. Although its name is associated with the 1996 massacre, when a gunman opened fire on children at school, Dunblane does have one of Scotland's finer Gothic cathedrals. The tower is 12th-century, but the splendid interior, one long soaring nave, is mid-13th century. The town is also a good base for touring the Ochil Hills to the east. At the foot of the Ochils near Dollar, 16km (10 miles) east of Stirling, **Castle Campbell▶** (HS), built at the end of the 15th century, stands perched on a huge crag. A short trail follows its base through Dollar Glen, part of it hewn out of rock, over catwalks and past cascades. West of Dunblane, **Doune** is worth a visit for a fine 14th-century royal **castle▶** (HS).

ROBERT THE BRUCE
The Battle of Bannockburn was one of the most decisive in Scottish history. For several years Robert the Bruce (1274–1329) had been successfully waging a guerilla war against the English—and those of the Scottish nobility whom he had alienated. In 1314 he was forced into a pitched battle over the vital control of Stirling Castle; with a mere 5,000 men but great cunning, he destroyed an English force of some 20,000. Stirling surrendered and Edward II fled to Dunbar; Scotland later won independence for 400 years and Bruce was acknowledged as king of Scotland.

231

Castle Campbell towers
above the Burn of Sorrow
and the Burn of Care

232

TROSSACHS WALKS

The area's most energetic hikes are the main peaks such as Ben Ledi, Ben Lomond and Ben Venue, but numerous lesser summits have fine views, among them Ben A'an (climb up from the former Trossachs Hotel, now a timeshare development, north of Loch Achray on the A821) and Conic Hill, near the southeast corner of Loch Lomond. For lower-level walks try the forest around David Marshal Lodge near Aberfoyle, where there is an old tramway to explore, or the wooded glen north of Rob Roy's Grave at Balquhidder. (See also Walks on page 214.)

ROB ROY MACGREGOR

Robert MacGregor, known for his red hair as Rob Roy (Red Robert), was a free-booting cattle thief whose exploits frequently involved robbing the rich for the benefit of the poor. He was forced to become an outlaw in about 1712, but having successfully outwitted all attempts to bring him under control, he gradually returned to living openly among his own people. In 1725 he was given a formal pardon. The full story of this Scottish folk hero is told at the Rob Roy and Trossachs Visitor Centre in Callander.

▶▶ The Trossachs   210D3

(Loch Lomond and The Trossachs National Park Authority (Balloch) tel: 01389 722600; www.lochlomond-trossachs.org)

The Trossachs is an area of rugged hills, tumbling streams and picturesque lochs. It may lack the drama of the true Highlands, but its accessibility from central Scotland has made it popular. Strictly speaking, the Trossachs is a narrow strip of country between **Loch Katrine** and **Loch Achray**, but in effect it is considered to stretch west from the busy town of **Callander** to the shores of Loch Lomond, with the somewhat commercialized **Aberfoyle** as its heart. Undeniably beautiful, it is also one of the most visited areas in Scotland and is particularly popular in high summer.

The area became fashionable with the 18th-century Romantics in their cult of the picturesque—it was wild, but not too wild and it was also easy to reach. Sir Walter Scott also helped to popularize the area, using the Trossachs as the setting for his poem *Lady of the Lake* and his novel *Rob Roy*. For this was the territory of Rob Roy's Clan Gregor, a near-criminal band touched by a spirit of romantic lawlessness (see panel). The Trossachs was also the preferred sketching ground of the Glasgow Boys (see page 228), and with Loch Lomond became Scotland's first National Park in 2002.

The 37km (23-mile), **Loch Lomond▶**, Scotland's largest inland loch (in terms of surface area), stretches from the suburbs of Glasgow to the fringes of the Highlands. It is surrounded by a dramatic variety of wooded farmland, empty hills, and rocky shores, but traffic along the road up its western shore is sometimes so busy it can be hard to enjoy its beauty.

There are several pleasant summer **boat trips** (but get there early to avoid waiting): along the length of Loch Katrine on the SS *Sir Walter Scott*; on Loch Lomond from Balloch, Ardlui and Tarbet, on the western shore and from Balmaha or the Inversnaid Hotel pier on the quieter eastern shore; a more modest excursion goes out to the ruins of **Inchmahome Priory** (HS) on an island in the Lake of Menteith. Activities such as 'pony trekking' (riding), cycling, fishing and golfing are available. Walkers can choose between numerous forest trails or hill walks. The area's scenic drives can be combined with short walks from the road, to beauty spots such as the Falls of Leny, off the A84 northwest of Callander and the Trossachs viewpoint at the top of the A821 north of Aberfoyle.

Still waters: Loch Ard

The Highland clans in their 15th-century heyday formed a tribal system strong enough to threaten the authority of the Stuart monarchs. The aftermath of the last Jacobite rebellion of 1745 brought about the final dismantling of their distinctive way of life. However, the dress and tartan of the Highlands of former times then became fashionable—and the scene was set for the once outlawed cloth of a tribal minority to become the most potent symbol for the whole of Scotland.

Life beyond the Highland Line In Gaelic the word 'clann' means family. By the 13th century, clans had evolved into self-governing tribal units, at whose head was a chief or 'father' to whom lesser chieftains and ordinary clansmen gave allegiance. The clan, at least in earlier times, counted its wealth in cattle. Consequently, cattle-raiding was common, as were territorial disputes. However, not all of the clan's preoccupations were warlike. The more powerful chiefs kept extensive retinues, an important member being the clan bard, who was official record keeper as well as composer. By the 18th century, better communications meant that the clans came more into contact with southern or Saxon—hence 'sasunnach'—ways. Some chiefs even sent their children to school in the Lowlands and developed a taste for fine wines or fashionable clothes. Thus the system was already in decline before the shock of Culloden (see page 246).

The dress of the clans The idea of a 'clan tartan' was essentially a marketing device of 19th-century textile manufacturers. Tartan was banned after Culloden, though the Highland regiments of the British army were still permitted to wear it. Later, the fashion industry used the military as a source of inspiration and tartan became very fashionable. Then the visit of King George IV to Scotland in 1822 created an excuse for the new landowners and clan chiefs of Scotland to act the part and dress up in tartan costumes. The cloth has remained popular ever since, creating its own mythology and conventions.

HOW TO RECOGNIZE A FELLOW CLANSMAN
Contemporary evidence from the Battle of Culloden indicates a wide variety of tartans worn even by members of the same clan. The government forces were identifiable by the red or yellow tied badges on their bonnets, while the Jacobites had their famous 'white cockades', inspired by the wild white rose said to have been plucked by Bonnie Prince Charlie as a symbol for the campaign. In fact, the British army was the first to define uniform tartans in the 18th century.

233

THE BLACK WATCH
One of General Wade's ways of policing the Highlands (see page 244) was to recruit local Highlanders. Six independent companies first enlisted in 1725 and from these was formed the 43rd, later the 42nd or Black Watch Regiment. By creating fighting units of this type, the martial spirit of the Highlands was harnessed for Britain's imperial wars of the 19th century.

236

RECOMMENDED COASTAL TOWNS
Argyll and Bute: Inveraray, Oban.
Highland: Portree (Skye), Dornoch, Ullapool.
Orkney: Stromness.

COASTAL FEATURES
Highland: Cape Wrath, Handa Island, Stacks of Duncansby.
Orkney: Old Man of Hoy.

CASTLES
Aberdeenshire: Crathes.
Argyll and Bute: Duart (Mull), Kilchurn.
Highland: Dunvegan (Skye), Eilean Donan.

PALATIAL INTERIORS
Aberdeenshire: Haddo.
Argyll and Bute: Inveraray.
Highland: Cawdor.
Perth and Kinross: Blair.

MOUNTAIN WALKING
Cairngorms, Cuillins (Skye), Fort William area, Glen Coe, Torridon.

PREHISTORIC MONUMENTS
Orkney and Shetland: Maes Howe, Ring of Brogar, Skara Brae, Jarlshof, Mousa Broch.
Western Isles: Callanish Circle (Lewis).

ISLAND ESCAPES
Argyll and Bute: Jura.
Highland: Raasay, Rum.
Western Isles: Barra.

CHRISTIAN ARCHITECTURE
Aberdeenshire: St. Machars Aberdeen,
Argyll and Bute: Iona.
Moray: Elgin Cathedral.
Orkney: St. Magnus Kirkwall.

GARDENS
Aberdeenshire: Crathes.
Argyll and Bute: Crarae.
Highland: Inverewe.

Bagpipes and tartan show that Highland culture is still alive today

NORTHERN SCOTLAND The **Highlands and Islands**, with their awesome mountain and coastal scenery, have contributed much of what is now considered typical of Scotland. Malt whisky, bagpipes, tartans, clans, kilts and Highland flings were all distinctive aspects of Highland culture that today are considered essentially Scottish. This would have amazed any 17th-century Scot, for one of the key facts of Scottish history was the marked division between the northern Highlands and the main body of Scotland. The Highlands and the Lowlands were as different as night and day and they held each other in mutual scorn.

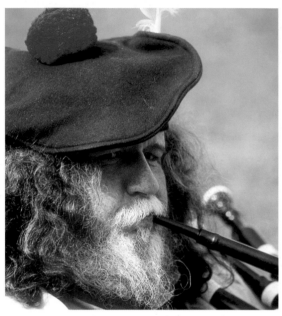

THE GREAT DIVIDE Though they might have traded cattle for grain at market towns, Highlanders and Lowlanders otherwise kept their distance. The Highlanders were Gaelic-speaking with a highly developed oral culture of bards, oaths and undying loyalty to kinship groups; the Lowlanders were English-speaking, literate and fond of lawsuits. The Highlanders were semi-nomads who counted their wealth in cattle and avoided towns, whereas the Lowlanders were firmly rooted in the farms and well-established towns that were evenly scattered over the coastal plains. The Highland Boundary Fault, running from southwest straight across to northeast Scotland, was not merely a geological divide: it was a linguistic, social, military, legal and economic boundary.

A WAR-TORN TERRITORY Though the Highlands brought limited rewards back to the central government in Edinburgh, they provided a vital resource in times of danger. The mountain valleys could be relied upon to produce hardened troops for any military adventure that offered loot. The region also served as a bulwark against foreign conquest, most graphically in the 14th century when the

English occupied the Lowland towns for a generation but could make no effective headway into the Highlands. Even after the Act of Union between England and Scotland in 1707, the Highlands continued to supply manpower for Britain's imperial adventures and to this day there is a tradition of military service.

Jacobite rebellions broke out in 1715 and 1719 as part of a long history of dissidence, but this time the south responded differently. General Wade was commissioned to design and build a string of strategic forts and fortified barracks for the military occupation of the Highlands, all linked by roads and elegant bridges. Several examples survive in the old county of Inverness-shire, in what is now known as the **Highland** region. The Jacobite rising led by Bonnie Prince Charlie in 1745 (see page 246) had catastrophic effects, for the Hanoverian victory at Culloden Moor near **Inverness** was followed by the deliberate destruction of the military basis of Highland society. The legal powers of the clan chiefs were destroyed, the kilt and weapons were forbidden and a series of ruthless judicial commissions brought the gallows to every glen. This was followed, a generation later, by an economic crisis resulting in the Clearances—wholesale eviction of the tenant farmers to make space for sheep pastures (often run by English-speaking farmers from the Lowlands), particularly in **Sutherland** and the **Black Isle**, the **West Highlands** and the **Western Isles**. Today, the shells of single-floor cottages are the desolate reminders of more populous times.

THE HERITAGE The primitive stone castles of the Highland chiefs decayed into romantic ruin while the turf and stone round huts of the tenant crofters were reduced to lumps in the pasture. They were replaced by neat stone farmhouses, crisp neoclassical manses for the influential clergy and the light plain halls of their Presbyterian churches. Ironically, at the same time as the Highland crofters were being packed off in emigrant boats, the fashion for things Highland got into full swing, intensified by Queen Victoria's patronage of **Deeside**. In the late 19th century a series of enormous and exclusive sporting estates were created for the summer recreation of Britain's wealthy, notably in **Angus, Perth and Kinross, Moray, Aberdeenshire, Sutherland** and **Wester Ross**. A series of excessive Gothic Baronial lodges, hotels and palaces still are the dominant architectural note of the Highlands, softened by modern bungalows and the older, stone-built dormer-windowed houses still seen all over the Highlands and Islands. The influx of English speakers helped make the Gaelic tongue obsolete and, though its use is still widespread in the crofting population of the **Western Isles**, Gaelic is now rarely heard on the mainland.

237

Quoth God to the Highlander,
'What will you do now?'
'I will down to the Lowland, Lord,
And there steal a cow.'
—Anonymous

"FHAD'S A DH'FHÀSAS FLÙR AIR MACHAIR MAIRIDH CLIÙ NA H-AINNIR CHAOIMH, THE PRESERVER OF PRINCE CHARLES EDWARD STUART WILL BE MENTIONED IN HISTORY AND IF COURAGE AND FIDELITY BE VIRTUES, MENTIONED WITH HONOUR"
JOHNSON

Walks

Beinn Lora, Argyll and Bute   234B2

Forestry Commission car park just south of Benderloch village (north of Oban). Beinn Lora is a 308m (1,010ft) hill with magnificent views of Loch Linnhe. Follow a path through the forest; follow signs and eventually skirt an area of boggy pools; the summit then comes into view. Return the same way. (2.5 hours)

Findlater Castle, Aberdeenshire   235D5

From Cullen waterfront follow the shore-level road east; this dwindles to a coastal path. On a clear day the Caithness and Sutherland coastline can be seen across the Firth. Walk onto the 15th-century ruins of Findlater Castle, perched high on the cliff. Then return the same way. (2.5–4 hours)

Duncansby Head, Highland   235E4

Car park at Duncansby Head lighthouse. From the northeastern-most tip of the British mainland a fine coastal path heads south to the Stacks of Duncansby, a trio of natural pillars cut off from the mainland by erosion from the sea. Return the same way. (1.5 hours)

Glen Nevis, Highland   234B3

Car park at end of road in Glen Nevis, southeast of Fort William. There is a waterfall by the car park. The path leads into a splendid gorge before entering more open terrain, passing further waterfalls and reaching ruins at Steall. Return the same way. (2 hours)

Kenmore, Perth and Kinross   235B4

Start in Kenmore village square (east end of Loch Tay). Take the road northwest, cross the River Tay, then immediately take a riverside path on the right; a little later, turn right on a road, then left on a rising forest track, which soon levels out; 45 minutes' walking leads to a well-marked vantage point for views over the loch and over Taymouth Castle; return to the last track junction you reach and then turn right downhill to Kenmore. (2.5 hours)

The stacks at Duncansby Head

▶▶ Aberdeen

235C5

(Tourist information tel: 01224 288828;
www.aberdeen-grampian.com)

The 'Granite City' is the third largest in Scotland, but although the oil boom years of the 1970s gave rise to handsome new buildings on the waterfront and huge oil-rig vessels in the port, the town has managed to retain its Georgian roots and its 19th-century dignity. The grand sweep of Union Street reflects the city's rich history. Elegant floral displays soften the imposing Victorian buildings and the silver granite squares and terraces.

St. Machar's Cathedral▶ was founded in 1131; the main part was built in the mid-15th century. It dominates the part of the city known as **Old Aberdeen**, a calm haven of cobbled streets and houses that date from 1500. In this area too is **King's College**, founded 1500–05 and part of the university, as well as the Cruickshank Botanic Garden and Seaton Park. Farther out, the **Brig o'Balgownie** across the River Don is the oldest medieval bridge in Scotland.

Central Aberdeen is more formal, with rows of granite town houses and spacious streets. Its numerous university buildings, markets and museums are dotted on and around Broad Street and Union Street. The **Tolbooth**, on the corner of Broad Street, is the town jail, built in 1627 and open to the public. On Ship Row, in the 16th-century Provost Ross's House, is **Aberdeen Maritime Museum▶▶** (*Admission free*) brings the city's relationship with the North Sea to the fore, with absorbing exhibits on fishing, shipbuilding and the oil industry. **Provost Skene's House** (*Admission free*) has changing exhibits and period furnishings, while **Satrosphere** features hands-on science and technology. The **city library**, **St. Mark's Church** and **His Majesty's Theatre** (*currently closed for refurbishment*) are known as 'Education, Salvation and Damnation'. **Aberdeen Art Gallery▶** (*Admission free*) has works by George Romney, Sir Joshua Reynolds, James McBey, Augustus John and Scottish impressionist William McTaggart among others. The **Duthie Park Winter Gardens** (*Admission free*) are the largest glassed gardens in Europe.

Haddo House▶ (NTS) is a 30-minute drive north, near Pitmedden, a handsome house designed by William Adam in 1731 and relatively unchanged. In Viewfield Road, the **Gordon Highlanders Museum** pays tribute to what Churchill called 'the finest regiment in the world'.

In the tropical hot houses
of Duthie Park

NORTH SEA FLIER
Cruden Bay, north of Aberdeen, witnessed the takeoff of the first flight across the North Sea back in 1914, when solo pilot Tryggve Gran flew 480km (298 miles) to Stavanger in Norway. But with the advent of World War I, his achievement went almost unnoticed. There is a monument to Gran close to the sinister ruin of Slains Castle, which Bram Stoker saw on a visit in 1895, inspiring him to write *Dracula*.

THE BUCHAN COAST
Aberdeen is the gateway to some of the country's most pristine coastline. North to Cruden Bay and on to the busy fishing ports of Peterhead (the biggest whitefish port in Western Europe) and Fraserburgh stretch glorious miles of untouched sandy beaches. Along the north-facing coast of this far corner of Scotland little fishing villages such as Pennan and Gardenstown, west of Rosehearty, hide under spectacular cliffs.

HIGHLAND GAMES

Athletes compete at these traditional Highland gatherings, held all over Scotland in summer. Venues include Inverness, Stirling and Callander, with the most famous being the **Royal Highland Gathering** in Braemar (September), usually attended by the Royal Family. Events include throwing the hammer, hill races, putting the stone and tossing the caber (a long wooden pole). Braemar's caber weighs in at 60kg (132lb), claims to be the longest at 6.02m (19.75ft) and has been thrown successfully (absolutely straight and from end to end) fewer than five times. There are also bagpipe and dancing competitions. The games originated in martial contests held by King Malcolm Canmore back in the 11th century, to find the toughest men to fight the Normans. The tradition was revived in the 19th century.

The River Dee near Braemar

MALT WHISKY

Single malts, as distinct from blended whiskies, have their origins in more than a hundred distilleries, whose whitewashed buildings and barley-drying kilns are a component of the Highlands landscape. Many offer guided tours and in Speyside is the signposted Malt Whisky Trail (see panel, page 257), a road touring route. Malt whisky varies greatly in taste; in Islay, for example, the peat burned for drying out the barley gives a highly distinctive taste. For an overview of the whisky industry, visit the Scotch Whisky Heritage Centre in Edinburgh's Royal Mile.

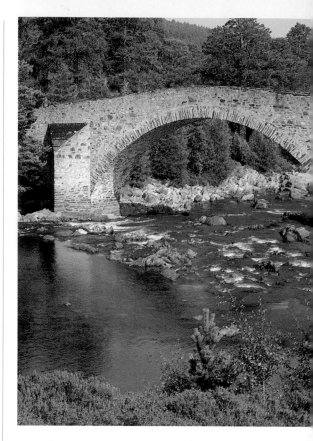

▶▶▶ Deeside
235C4

(Aberdeen and Grampian Tourist Board tel: 01224 288800; www.aberdeen-grampian.com)

The River Dee drains the eastern slopes of the Cairngorms and flows almost 130km (80 miles) east to Aberdeen and the North Sea, passing on its way through a classic Scottish landscape of blue hills and heather moors, woods of larch, juniper and birch, rocky riverbeds and rippling waters.

The village of **Braemar**, 330m (1,083ft) up and circled by layers of hills, is at the heart of the most beautiful stretch of the Dee and a popular summer holiday area. Braemar is famous for its round-towered, L-plan castle, which was built as a hunting lodge by the 2nd Earl of Mar in 1628 and buffeted by the Jacobites in 1689, as well as for the Braemar Gathering held on the first Saturday in September. The Royal Family usually pays a visit to these Highland Games (see panel), which may account for the crowds of around 50,000 people. Robert Louis Stevenson wrote *Treasure Island* while staying in Braemar in 1881. To the west of the village, at the head of the valley just beyond Inverey, is the **Linn o'Dee▶**, where the river waters cascade down into a series of rocky pools. The minor road from Braemar to this beauty spot, often reproduced in Victorian engravings and contemporary postcards, is an attractive drive. From the road, you can set off for some beautiful walks in the Mar Forest and the foothills of Ben Macdhui (1,311m/4,301ft).

Balmoral Castle, some 14km (9 miles) east of Braemar, was bought by Queen Victoria and her husband Prince Albert in 1852. The old castle was too small and today's mansion, typically Scottish baronial in style, was commissioned by Prince Albert. The Royal Family still spends holidays here; the grounds and exhibitions are open to the public from April to July. The peak of Lochnagar (1,154m/3,786ft), which towers over Balmoral, was featured in Prince Charles's first book, *The Old Man of Lochnagar*, an illustrated children's story written to amuse his younger brothers. Across the main road is the granite Crathie Church, attended by members of the Royal Family when staying in Balmoral. Queen Victoria's preferred dram was Lochnagar malt whisky; the Royal Lochnagar Distillery today has a shop and offers visitors a tour of the distillery.

Continuing east along the banks of the boulder-strewn Dee, the A93 passes through the granite village of **Ballater**, built at the end of the 18th century to accommodate visitors taking the spa waters of nearby Pannanich Wells. With its hotels and guest houses, it makes a good base for walking around on the hills of Craigendarroch, Craig Coillich and Glen Muick.

The main road stays close to the river, pausing at **Aboyne**, a town neatly planned around a large level green where the Highland Games take place the first Saturday in August. The valley then opens out to **Banchory**, where the Water of Feugh joins the Dee from the Forest of Birse. Watch the salmon leaping up the rapids from the Bridge of Feugh. Like most of these Deeside resorts, Banchory has a golf course.

North from Banchory about 24km (15 miles), near Kemnay, **Castle Fraser▶** (NTS) is a massive Z-plan castle. It is an excellent example of the Scottish baronial style, notable for its turrets. East along the Dee from Banchory, **Crathes Castle▶▶** (NTS) is a celebrated L-shaped tower house dating to 1553, one of the finest Jacobean houses in the country. Inside, the Room of the Nine Nobles, the Room of the Muses and the Room of the Green Lady are renowned for their remarkable, highly decorative ceilings. The ghost of the Green Lady, carrying a baby and, of course, dressed in green, is thought to haunt certain rooms. The grounds too are special, a vibrant labyrinth enclosed within the dark green walls of a 300-year-old yew hedge. Don't look at the map; just be lured on by the skilfully contrived arches, avenues and enticing prospects.

About 10km (6 miles) down the glen, in the middle of a surviving section of the Caledonian Forest called the Old Wood of Drum, stands **Drum Castle▶** (NTS). A cold, solid 13th-century keep, thick-walled and 20m (66ft) high, adjoins a crow-stepped gabled Jacobean mansion. It houses a fine collection of portraits, silver and furniture, and has pleasant grounds with a café and an adventure playground for children.

RAISING THE OLD PRETENDER'S STANDARD
Only the Highland chiefs were able to raise the men needed to fight the cause of Britain's exiled Stuart king. When George of Hanover became king of Britain in 1714, it was in Braemar, on the spot where the Invercauld Arms Hotel now stands, that the 6th Earl of Mar raised the standard in 1715 to launch the Jacobite Rising, proclaiming the Old Pretender, James VIII of Scotland (and III of England) as king.

241

THE LOCH NESS MONSTER

The alleged appearances of this supposedly dinosaur-like beast lend a hypnotic lure to the loch. The Loch Ness Exhibition within the Loch Ness 2000 Exhibition Centre at Drumnadrochit has photographs of 'Nessie', together with scientific explanations and demonstrations of the latest techniques being used to solve the mystery.

DOLPHIN CRUISES

Dolphin Ecosse run boat trips from Cromarty into the Moray Firth to see bottlenose dolphins (all year, weather allowing) and harbour porpoises and, in summer, minke whales (for reservations, call 01381 600323; www.dolphinecosse.co.uk).

Loch Ness lies in the Great Glen Fault, which runs across the Highlands

►**Inverness** *234C3*

(Tourist information tel: 0845 225 5121 (national contact centre); www.visithighlands.com)

Now, as ever, the Capital of the Highlands, Inverness has a strategic position at the head of the Great Glen. Its often violent history has left it with few historic buildings. The **Inverness Museum and Art Gallery** (*Admission free*) has good, original collections.

Less than 10km (6 miles) out of town, the vast depressing Drummossie moor, renamed **Culloden**, witnessed the last battle fought on British soil, on 18 April 1746. This was the last gasp of Prince Charles Edward Stuart's attempt to gain the throne from George II (see page 246). There is a good **Visitor Centre** (NTS; *Admission to battlefield free*) that tells the story of that rainy day in which a thousand of Bonnie Prince Charlie's Highlanders met their deaths. A mile south lie the prehistoric **Clava Cairns** and standing stones. **Cawdor Castle►**, a little to the east, was built by the thanes of Cawdor in the 14th century. The original keep remains and inside are Jacobean rooms. At the entrance to the Inverness and Beauly Firth sits **Fort George►** (HS), built between 1748–69 to keep the Jacobites at bay.

The largest loch in Scotland in terms of volume of water, **Loch Ness** relies more on the 'Nessie' legend (see panel) than its beauty. Views are good from **Urquhart Castle** (HS).

Visit **Beauly►** for its 13th-century priory remains and for Campbells, a tweed, tartan and woollen shop. **Strathpeffer** is a Victorian spa town; walk from here to the Rogie Falls. The **Black Isle►** is a broad, fertile peninsula with wading birds. In Cromarty look at the old port, the lighthouse and **Cromarty Courthouse Museum►** where you can tour the cells and courtroom. In **Rosemarkie** see the Pictish stone in the churchyard and Groam House Museum (*Admission free*). In nearby **Fortrose** visit the Gothic cathedral ruins.

LOCH NESS AND THE BLACK ISLE

1045m
Ben Wyvis
Alness
Invergordon
Cromarty
Cromarty Courthouse
Blue Head
Glass
Evanton
Cromarty Firth
Balblair
484m
Cloch Mhor
Skiack
Jemimaville
Glenurquhart
Moray Firth
Rogie Falls
Culbokie
Whiteness Head
Dingwall
Alcaig
Black Isle
Rosemarkie
Fortrose
Fort George
Strathpeffer
Loch Ussie
A835
Maryburgh
Contin
A9
Avoch
Chanonry Point
Ardersier
Nairn
Orrin
Conon
Urray
Chanonry Point
A96
Cawdor
Muir of Ord
Tore
Munlochy
Moray Firth
Clephanton
Cawdor Castle
North Kessock
Castle Stuart
Croy
Beauly Firth
Balloch
Contraywood
Beauly
Priory
Kilmorack
Kirkhill
Smithton
Culloden Battlefield
101m
Inverness
Clava Cairns
316m
Cnoc na Moine
548m
609m
Carn Nan Tri-Tighearnan
Dochgarroch
Essich
Daviot
Kiltarlity
Loch Bruicheach
Abriachan
Loch Ashie
A9
Loch Moy
Findhorn
165m
Meall na h-Eilrigh
Dores
Moy
615m
638m
Milton
Drumnadrochit
Loch Ness
Loch Duntelchaig
10 km
Ehrich
Urquhart Castle
miles

243

Drive

Loch Ness and the Black Isle

A 200km (125-mile) tour through varied mountain and coastal landscape.

Leave Inverness on the A9 towards the southeast, turn onto the B9006 to see **Culloden Battlefield and Visitor Centre** (NTS) and nearby **Clava Cairns** prehistoric stones. Continue to **Cawdor Castle▶**, scene of Duncan's murder in Shakespeare's *Macbeth*.

Turn back and take the narrow B9006 to **Fort George▶** (HS) with its museum of period barrack rooms and weaponry. Follow the east coast of the **Moray Firth** into Inverness and out again on the A82 along the northern shore of **Loch Ness** to ruined **Urquhart Castle**(HS) and the Loch Ness Exhibition in **Drumnadrochit**.

From here return north over the hills to the remains of **Beauly Priory**. At Muir of Ord take the A832 northwest to reach **Strathpeffer**. Head east to **Dingwall** and follow the Black Isle shore to reach the old seaport of **Cromarty**. Head south along the A832 to the charming little resorts of **Rosemarkie** and nearby **Fortrose**. Continue southwest to rejoin the A9, crossing over the Moray Firth on the Kessock suspension bridge (1982), which leads back into Inverness.

A sgian dubh (Gaelic dagger) in Inverness Museum and Art Gallery

WADE'S ROADS
In an attempt to disarm the Jacobite supporters of the exiled Stuarts, concentrated in the Highlands, General Wade stationed his government troops, the Redcoats, in forts which he built at Fort William, Fort Augustus and Fort George. He linked these forts with military roads and connected them to the Lowlands. From Fort Augustus one of Wade's roads runs over the Corrieyairack Pass; it was used by Bonnie Prince Charlie's army on its 1745 march to Edinburgh.

244

Ben Nevis and Carn Mor Dearg

The Caledonian Canal

▶ ▶ ▶ **Lochaber**   234C3

(Highlands of Scotland Tourist Board tel: 0845 255 5121 (national contact centre); www.visithighlands.com)

This region, known as the West Highlands, is an area of archetypal highland landscape—bleak moorlands, soft valley meadows and the long reach of still lochs. It is the land of the Camerons and the Macdonnels, clans that provided the core support for the '45 Rebellion (see page 246) and that, a year later, dumped the Jacobite treasure into Loch Arkaig rather than see it in the hands of the Hanoverians.

At the southern end of Loch Ness (see page 242) the little town of **Fort Augustus** sits around the Caledonian Canal, a splendid waterway, with several staircase locks, designed by Thomas Telford. By linking the lochs of the Great Glen the canal joins Fort William on Loch Linnhe with Inverness on the Moray Firth. Fort Augustus has long since lost the fort built by General Wade (see panel).

The resort and aluminum-smelting town of **Fort William** stands in the shadow of **Ben Nevis▶**, Britain's highest mountain at 1,347m (4,419ft). It is not the best in the Highlands for walking, but if you do wish to climb it, allow five hours to get to the top and three hours to pick your way back down (it looks deceptively small because it lacks a definitive peak). It is of course essential to be properly equipped and take all safety precautions. Low-level walks with superb views of the mountains include Glen Nevis (see Walks, page 238), the towpath of the Caledonian Canal (notably Neptune's Staircase, a flight of locks north of Fort William) and Glen Leven (east of Kinlochleven), which threads its way up to the vast Blackwater Reservoir. Fort William is a modern, commercialized place, but makes a convenient base. Its story began in 1655 when General Monk built an earthwork fort here. This was later replaced by General Wade's stone construction in the reign of William III, which was pulled down in the 19th century. The **West Highland Museum** on Cameron Square provides a good introduction to the region and its natural history.

South from Fort William the main road passes through **Glen Coe▶▶**, the scene, in the early hours of 13 February 1692, of Scotland's most infamous slaughter. Acting under government orders, members of the Campbell militia who

Fishing boats at Mallaig: the catch is auctioned on the waterside

**THE WEST
HIGHLAND LINE**
The railway that runs from Glasgow to Mallaig justly claims to be Britain's most scenic route. The construction of the line between Fort William and Mallaig in particular involved some major feats of engineering, with gradients of up to 1 in 48, several rock cuttings and dramatic bridges, viaducts and tunnels. Some services are steam-hauled such as the Jacobite Steam Train that runs from Fort William to Mallaig (for more information tel: 01463 239026 or 0870 124 5511; www.steamtrain.info.

were billeted on members of the MacDonald clan, turned on their hosts—breaking the strict code of hospitality that existed between clans—and indiscriminately slaughtered them. An act, so the government thought, that would dissuade anyone from having doubts about the legitimacy of Queen Mary on the throne instead of her father James VII (James II to the English). The Glencoe Visitor Centre (NTS) is near the foot of the glen.

West of Fort William, at the head of Loch Shiel, the **Glenfinnan Monument▶** (NTS) marks the spot where the Young Pretender, Prince Charles Edward (see page 246), raised his standard on 19 August 1745 and launched the campaign to see his father recognized as rightful king.

The songwriter's 'Road to the Isles' from Fort William leads to **Arisaig** and **Mallaig▶ ▶** past the coral sandy beaches that featured in the movie *Local Hero*. Inland are the dark waters of Loch Morar, the deepest freshwater stretch of water in Britain, with its own lesser-known monster, Morag. On the wooded islands in the loch, the Jesuits maintained a secret seminary to keep the Roman Catholic faith alive. The busy fishing port of Mallaig is the departure point for ferries to the Small Isles of Eigg, Muck, Rhum, Canna and Armadale on Skye (see pages 254–255). All the islands are easy day-trips; only the Skye boat takes cars.

To the south is the untamed **Ardnamurchan Peninsula**, whose far point is the westernmost part of the British mainland. Isolated on a tide-washed island in Loch Moidart stands the empty keep of **Castle Tioram▶**, last used by the MacDonald chief of Clan Ranald, who burned it after the 1715 uprising failed, rather than let the Campbells take possession. A short walk from the hotel in the village of Kilchoan, **Castle Mingary▶** stands in one of the most impressive locations on the peninsula's southern shore, looking across the Sound of Mull to Tobermory.

The small Highland village of **Lochaline▶**, where ferries depart for Mull, sits on the picturesque Morvern Peninsula overlooking the tidal inlet of Loch Aline. The strong square keep of 14th-century Ardtornish Castle was one of the chief bases of the Lord of the Isles (see panel, page 254).

The monument to the '45 at Glenfinnan

**THE WEST
HIGHLAND WAY**
This 152km (95-mile) long distance footpath starts from Milngavie, just north of Glasgow, and heads north of the eastern side of Loch Lomond, before passing Rannoch Moor, Glen Coe, Glen Nevis and Ben Nevis to reach Fort William. As you get farther north, the scenery is more and more magnificent. It is never really steep, but be prepared for plenty of up-and-down sections.

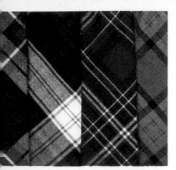

Seen by contemporary opponents as a political and military threat to 18th-century Britain's stability, the Jacobites and their hopeless quest to restore a Catholic monarch to the British throne was soon turned into a romantic lost cause. At its head was the most romantic figure of all: Italian-born Prince Charles Edward Louis Philip Casimir Stuart, know variously as the Young Pretender, the Young Chevalier and, most familiarly, Bonnie Prince Charlie. He was in Scotland for only 14 months.

'Charles was the candle who lighted the bonfire, but they [his Highland supporters] were the timber that filled a dark sky with their splendid ardour.'
—Eric Linklater, in *The Prince in the Heather*

OVER THE SEA TO SKYE
'Carry the lad born to be King over the sea to Skye' is perhaps the best-known line from the corpus of Jacobite songs and alludes to the perilous voyage from Benbecula to Skye which Charles took while disguised as Betty Burke, Flora MacDonald's maid. *The Skye Boat Song*, however, is a 19th-century fake: its famous lyrics date from 1884 and most of the melody from 1879.

Charles set off from St. Nazaire on his escapade with the blessing of a French government eager to see Britain destabilized. When the handsome young man landed on the island of Eriskay in the Western Isles, the local MacDonald chief told him to go home. Charles rather romantically replied that he had 'come home' and, undaunted, went on to raise his standard at Glenfinnan in August 1745.

A persuasive personality The fatal charm of the Stuarts managed to persuade about one-sixth of the estimated 30,000 fighting men in the Highlands of Scotland to take up arms in his cause. The campaign met with early successes but was finally halted on Culloden Moor in April 1746. There the Jacobites were blown away by the superior artillery of the British army. Charles went into hiding and the government forces (which comprised a number of Scottish regiments) went on to commit numerous atrocities in its efforts to destroy the Highland way of life. This policy was implemented by a far-off government in Westminster, which perceived the Highlands as a hotbed of potential Jacobites, where clan chiefs were able to call on what were, in effect, private armies.

The romance of a lost cause From these bare facts sprang the legend of an irresistibly handsome young man on a lost cause. With the real threat out of the way, the Jacobites were soon reinterpreted in song and story. Bonnie Prince Charlie became the figurehead of Jacobite mythology and has been seen on shortbread boxes ever since. Flora MacDonald—whose dealings with the Prince covered only a few days and who had to be persuaded to have anything to do with the business at all—was quickly elevated to a romantic heroine. The notion that the Prince was never betrayed by a sympathetic Scottish people is a still current tale. In reality his supporters had to keep him well out of the way. But none of this matters. With Bonnie Prince Charlie, the romance is all.

▶▶ Mull   *234B2*

(Tobermory tourist information tel: 0870 720 0625;
www.visitscottishheartlands.com)

The beautiful 'isle-of-the-cool-high-bends', 38km (24 miles) long and 42km (26 miles) wide, has many aspects—rocky cliffs, sandy beaches, quiet fishing coves, bleak moors, lone castles and lofty mountains—but is dominated by green terraces of grazing land managed by crofts and small farms. Mull is served by ferries from Kilchoan, Lochaline and Oban.

Duart Castle, perched above the Sound of Mull 5km (3 miles) from Craignure, has its origins in the 13th century. It has been restored as the summer home of the chief of Clan Maclean. **Torosay Castle**, just outside Craignure, is a 19th-century baronial building (designed by David Bryce) with grounds laid out by Sir Robert Lorimer. **Mull Rail**, a narrow-gauge railway runs between the castle and Craignure.

Tobermory▶, named after a holy well dedicated to Our Lady, is the island's main town, its arc of brightly painted houses encircling a bay popular with yacht owners.

The Holy Island of **Iona▶▶▶**, the 'Cradle of Christianity', is served by ferry from Fionnphort on the

ANCIENT BURIAL PLACE OF KINGS

St. Oran's Cemetery on Iona is the oldest Christian cemetery in Scotland. Here are buried 48 Scottish kings, including Kenneth MacAlpin, who first united the Scots and Picts in 843 and Duncan, murdered by Macbeth in 1040. Eight Norwegian kings also have graves here, a reflection of the several hundred years of Norse occupation of Scotland from the ninth century on.

A prehistoric standing stone on the Ross of Mull

247

western tip of the Ross of Mull or by boat excursions from Oban via Mull. No cars are allowed on the island, but all sights can be easily reached on foot. In 563 St. Columba and 12 companions landed here from Ireland and established a monastery as a base for numerous missionary journeys among the pagan Picts. It became the motherhouse of the Celtic church in Scotland and England. This era of great spiritual and creative achievement ended, however, with the Norse raid of 803, which killed 68 monks and persuaded those left alive to return to Ireland. Nothing of their monastery remains, but an astonishing collection of early Christian stone carvings recalls this heroic period. Apart from St. Oran's Chapel of 1080, the existing abbey buildings all date from the second foundation in the early 13th century, when a Benedictine monastery and nunnery were established. In the 20th century, the abbey buildings were restored and are now the home of the Iona Community. The island's sense of peace is a source of spiritual refreshment for many visitors.

FINGAL'S CAVE, STAFFA

The cathedral-like cave that inspired Felix Mendelssohn's *Hebrides Overture* is one of several on this tiny uninhabited island north of Iona. Smooth columns of black basalt, the result of volcanic action, rise out of the sea in what is known in Gaelic as 'An Uamh Ehinn' (the musical cave), because of the echoing sounds that the sea makes within it. Boat trips leave from Oban and Iona throughout summer.

THE CRINAN CANAL

In 1793 work started on the construction of this short 14km (9-mile) canal that would link Loch Fyne with the Sound of Jura, saving ships the long, hazardous journey around the Mull of Kintyre. The chief engineer, Scotsman John Rennie, met with financial and engineering problems (Thomas Telford was also called upon for his expertise) and it was never a commercial success. However, it passes via 15 locks through a beautiful landscape of wooded mountains, and its basin at Crinan is now popular with yachtsmen.

248

A 'Cal Mac' ferry arrives in Oban from the islands

▶ Oban and Argyll   234B2

(Argyll, the Isles, Loch Lomond, Stirling and Trossachs Tourist Board tel: 0870 720 0600; www.visitscottishheartlands.com)
Oban is a popular family resort, accessible by bus and train from Glasgow. The port bustles with fishing vessels and ferries for the islands of Lismore, Mull, Coll, Tiree, Colonsay and the Western Isles. Stroll along the seafront, browse in the woollen mills, then head for Dunollie Castle where the Lords of Lorne used to preside. McCaig's Tower, an unfinished 19th-century folly styled on Rome's Colosseum and built to give work to unemployed masons, overlooks the town with fine views across to the Inner Hebrides. Oban is not known for reliable weather, but there are a number of indoor attractions to enjoy when it rains, such as a glass factory, a small war and peace museum and the distillery (*Guided tours*), best known for its 12-year-old malt whisky. Just east of the town is the Oban Rare Breeds Farm Park. The road north passes the 13th-century MacDougall fortress of **Dunstaffnage** (HS) on its way to the Scottish Sea Life Sanctuary on the shore of Loch Creran.

Just north of the village of Taynuilt is the **Bonawe Iron Furnace▶** (HS). Here you can see the restored remains of a charcoal furnace, founded in 1753, used for iron smelting. The village of Lochawe sits at the head of Loch Awe, the longest loch in Scotland, famous for its fishing. In summer the boat *Flower of Scotland* threads through the romantic burial islands of the MacNaughtons on Innis Fraoch and the MacArthurs on Innishail. The gaunt ruins of Kilchurn Castle, the original fortress home of the Campbells of Breadalbane, stands at the head of Kinloch Awe.

Inveraray▶▶, at the head of Loch Fyne, is a supremely elegant 18th-century town noted for its bridges, fishing port, gibbet pier, judges' lodgings and central double church. Its chief attraction is the **Jail▶**, with its tableaux of jailers and wretched inmates. **Inveraray Castle▶▶**, home of the Campbell Dukes of Argyll, is a heavy stone castellated mansion, but it has delightful 18th-century interiors and is stuffed with Highland weapons, portraits and memorabilia. Walk through the grounds to the stone folly tower on the summit of Duniquaich for a panoramic view over the area.

Crinan▶ is a tiny place at the western end of the Crinan Canal (see panel), its handful of houses and a hotel overlooking the yachting activity in the old basin. The village of Kilmartin▶▶ is surrounded by prehistoric sites, including the Nether Largie Linear Cemetery—an alignment of Bronze Age burial mounds, including one you can climb into by ladder—and the Temple Wood stone circles; in the churchyard is a collection of medieval carved stones and in the church itself a Celtic cross. Kilmartin House contains the Museum of Ancient Culture. **Dunadd Fort** may have been the capital of the early Scots kingdom of Dalriada. On its rocky top are carved a footprint and a boar.

Across the Sound of Jura lies **Jura▶**, the rugged island, home of red deer, where George Orwell wrote *1984*. Next door is the peaty isle of **Islay▶▶** (ferries from Kennacraig on the Kintyre Peninsula), where six distilleries operate. Islay's sights include the ninth-century Kidalton Cross and the Museum of Islay Life at Port Charlotte.

A carved stone at Kilmartin

249

The dazzling interior décor of Inveraray Castle

Drive

Oban and Argyll (see yellow route on map, page 234)

This tour takes in the beautiful Loch Etive, the dramatic Pass of Brander and the shores of Loch Fyne, with its fine Inveraray Castle. Return through an area studded with prehistoric remains on a road past sea lochs with views of the Inner Hebridean islands (about 160km/100 miles). There is an optional detour of about 60km (37 miles) down the Knapdale Peninsula.

Leave **Oban▶** going north on the A85 to pass Connel Bridge. Continue to Taynuilt for **Bonawe Iron Furnace▶** (HS) and then on the A85 through a narrow treeless defile, the Pass of Brander, to **Lochawe**. Take the A819 south to **Inveraray▶▶** with its splendid **castle▶▶** and then turn south on the A83, skirting the shores of Loch Fyne and passing Auchindrain Township Open Air Museum and Crarae Gardens (NTS). Reach the market town of **Lochgilphead** and turn north up the A816. A detour may be taken on the B841 to **Crinan▶** at the end of the Crinan Canal and then south to Castle Sween and **Kilmory Knap** for its medieval carved stones.

Continue north on the A816 to **Dunadd Fort** and **Kilmartin▶▶**, for some absorbing prehistoric sites. Pass **Carnasserie Castle** to the west end of Loch Awe and, twisting in and out of view of the Firth of Lorne, return to Oban.

WILDLIFE

Both island groups are renowned for their seabird colonies, which are among the most important in the world. On Shetland, visit the Island of Noss, accessible by small ferry in summer (weather permitting). Here and at Hermaness on the north of Unst you get wonderful views of puffins, gannets, guillemots, razorbills and many more species.
As you explore the island, watch out for great skuas, arctic skuas and whimbrels, which nest on the moorland. On Orkney, visit Yesnaby Cliffs on Mainland, both for their seabirds and for the rare and miniature Scottish primrose.

250

The relentless pounding of waves at Yesnaby, Orkney, has created a precarious pillar of rock, now detached from the rest of the island

►►► Orkney and Shetland 235A5/E5

(Orkney Tourist Board tel: 01856 872856; www.visitorkney.com; Shetland Islands Tourism tel: 01595 693434; www.visitshetland.com)

These two groups of islands have such a different cultural atmosphere from the rest of Scotland that many visitors feel they have arrived in another country. For 600 years they were under Norse rule and even when this domination ended, in the 15th century, it was another 200 years before the Scottish throne became strong enough to exert authority over these remote islands. Both groups of islands are bleak and treeless, but have splendid cliff and sea loch scenery and rare birdlife. Despite having arguably the finest collection of prehistoric sites in Britain, they receive comparatively few visitors.

ORKNEY ISLANDS►►► In Kirkwall on Mainland the pre-Reformation **St. Magnus Cathedral►►** stands in proud dominance over the town. It was begun in the 12th century and the massive round pillars and arches of the arcades date from this time. In one of the pillars two skeletons were discovered early this century, one of which may be St. Magnus himself. In the cathedral precincts are the ruins of the Bishop's Palace (HS) and Earl's Palace (HS) and **Orkney Museum** (*Admission free*), a 16th-century town house turned into a museum of Orkney. Around the precincts wind streets of crowstepped gabled houses, brightly painted.

Skara Brae►►► (HS), also on Mainland, is an entire neolithic settlement that lay perfectly preserved in sand dunes for 4,000 years until a storm first uncovered a corner of it in 1850. Inside the houses are beds, hearths, dressers, closets, even fish tanks. The inhabitants left pots, clothes and tools, which are displayed in the museum. The **Ring of Brodgar►►** is a wide circle of stones. When first constructed it was surely one of the most magnificent stone circles ever built by neolithic man. The scale is quite breathtaking and although only some of the stones remain, the original majesty is well preserved. Many of the stones reach a height of 4.5m (15ft). Nearby, **Maes Howe►►** (HS) is the finest chambered cairn, or burial chamber, in Europe, both for size and preservation. It was built around 2700 BC and so had been standing for at least a century before the first circle was marked out at Stonehenge in Wiltshire. It remained intact for nearly 4,000 years until the Vikings plundered it; their rude Norse inscriptions can still be seen on the walls.

A more modern curiosity is the **Italian Chapel▶** at Lamb Holm, created from Nissen huts and scrap materials in 1943 by Italian prisoners of war who were building the Churchill Barriers in the bay of Scapa Flow. **The Pier Arts Centre▶** (*Admission free*) is a delightful little gallery in the ferry port of Stromness. It has the best collection of modern British art in the north of Scotland. The masterpieces of Ben Nicholson and Barbara Hepworth admirably complement the island's ancient remains.

The famous **Old Man of Hoy▶ ▶** is an enormous stack of rock rearing a tremendous 135m (443ft) out of the sea off the island of Hoy. Like most of Orkney's cliff scenery, it is best seen from a boat (or the ferry from Scrabster, or you can walk the 4km (2.5-mile) path from Rackwick).

SHETLAND ISLANDS▶ ▶ These are the most northerly part of Great Britain (Shetland is about 95km/59 miles north of Orkney) and the beauty of midsummer nights when there is little or no darkness has to be seen to be believed. The main industries are crofting, fishing and knitting. The fine wool of the Shetland sheep is knitted in distinctive, traditional hues and patterns, often known as Fair Isle.

Some people travel to Shetland just to see **Mousa Broch▶ ▶ ▶**, on a little island to the southeast of Mainland, reached by ferry from Sandwick. The Iron Age fortress tower still stands more than 13m (43ft) high, all its distinctive features wonderfully preserved. Interestingly, when Shetland was covered with brochs (see panel), Mousa was acknowledged to be the smallest and least noble of them all. **Clickhimin▶**, near Lerwick, is a well-preserved broch.

On the southernmost tip of Mainland is **Jarlshof▶ ▶ ▶** (HS), one of the most remarkable prehistoric sites in Europe. Impressive remains, standing several metres high, can be seen of the Bronze Age courtyard settlements, the Iron Age 'wheelhouses' (see panel) that succeeded them and the longhouses of the Viking settlers who came next. There is also a 16th-century laird's house, once home of the Earl of Orkney Patrick Stewart and linked with Walter Scott's novel *The Pirate*. The same earl, renowned for his cruelty, built **Scalloway Castle**. The **Shetland Museum** (*Admission free*) in Lerwick tells the islands' story.

251

This Iron Age wheelhouse is part of Jarlshof's remarkable legacy of 3,000 years of settlement

Sinuous Loch Tay, one of Scotland's great salmon-fishing spots

▶▶ **Perth and Kinross**   *235B4*

(Perthshire Tourist Board tel: 01738 627958; www.perthshire.co.uk)

In the middle of Scotland, and rich in historical associations, Perth and Kinross (formerly Perthshire) is a county of contrasts. As you travel north the farmland of the south is transformed into the rounded heather-covered slopes of the Grampian Mountains. Cut through with great lochs, it is bound into one region by the waters of the Tay.

The town of **Perth▶** enjoys a pleasant position beside the River Tay. Despite its bridges, its Georgian terraces and the Millais paintings in the **Perth Museum and Art Gallery** (*Admission free*) and the distinctive watercolours of John Duncan Fergusson in the **Fergusson Gallery** (*Admission free*), it does not quite live up to the expectations set by its long history. On the north edge of town, the **Caithness Glass Visitor Centre** (*Admission free*) gives the chance to see glass-making in progress (it has a factory shop), while above the town, Kinnoull Hill is graced with two 18th-century follies, imitations of Rhenish castles. **Branklyn Garden▶** (NTS) is a small but delightful collection of rhododendrons, shrubs and alpines. Balhousie Castle houses the Black Watch Regimental Museum (*Admission free*).

Located upriver from Perth is **Scone Palace▶▶▶**, one of Scotland's great treasure houses. Scone (pronounced 'Skoon') was the seat of Pictish government and the site of the famous Stone of Scone (see panel). Until the time of James I all the Scottish kings were crowned here. The present palace was built over the foundations of the ancient abbey by William Atkinson, a pupil of James Wyatt, at the onset of the fashion for Gothick in the first decade of the 19th century. Its state rooms display the treasures from England and France assembled by the Earls of Mansfield, but it is chiefly loved for its lived-in, family atmosphere.

Pitlochry▶ is a Highland resort town, in a beautiful setting of loch, river, mountain and wood. It was created in the Victorian era when the railway station and the Hydro, the large (and originally strictly teetotal) hotel, offered healthy walking breaks away from the smog and sin of the big cities. It boasts a Festival Theatre with a broad summer schedule. Local beauty spots include the Queen's View up Loch Tummel and Loch Rannoch, beneath volcano-shaped Schiehallion (1,064m/3,491ft)—there is a visitor centre. Just outside town is the site of the Battle of Killiecrankie (an early Jacobite victory) with its visitor centre (NTS; *Admission free*).

To the north of Perth the attractive 'Little Houses' of **Dunkeld▶** date from its rebuilding following a siege during the Jacobite rebellion of 1689, in which the vastly outnumbered Lowland Cameronians held out against the Highlanders; the nave of the ruined 14th-century cathedral was later restored to serve as the parish church.

To the northwest is **Blair Castle▶▶▶**, its white walls and turrets surrounded by the rugged beauty of the Atholl Hills. The province of Atholl has been ruled from this tower house since the 13th century. The castle is famous as the seat of the only duke to be permitted a private army, the 100-strong Atholl Highlanders. They parade on the last Sunday of May; the tunics, worn with a white bow tie, enliven many a Highland Ball throughout the year. The castle has rooms open to the public, packed with treasures, including rare surviving examples of 17th-century Scottish furniture. In the model 18th-century village outside the castle gates there is a local folk museum. A 5km (3-mile) track leads to the gorge, bridges and waterfall of Bruar.

Each loch in Scotland has its own marked character, but **Loch Tay▶▶**, overlooked to its north by the 1,214m (3,983ft) summit of Ben Lawers, has a serenity which is totally out of keeping with the bloody clan feuds that went on around its shores. At its western end the village of **Killin** is noted for the **Falls of Dochart▶**. Between the village and Loch Tay are the ruins of Finlarig, the murderous stronghold of Black Duncan of the Cowl, who was the acquisitive chief of the local Campbells. His wealthy descendants built the elegant bridge and model village of **Kenmore▶** at the east end of the loch. The market town of **Aberfeldy**, 11km (7 miles) east, with its monumental Wade's Bridge (see panel, page 244), is a popular base for summer visitors. You can walk to such nearby attractions as **Castle Menzies▶**, a classic 16th-century Z-plan tower house; the old **Kirk of Weem** with its pair of Celtic crosses; and the **Birks of Aberfeldy▶**, a sylvan glen made famous by Burns's poem.

253

Above: Perth city's coat of arms, on a lamppost
Below: a room inside Scone Palace

THE LEGACY OF FORBES

In 1836 Professor James Forbes, a 23-year-old geologist, made what is believed to have been the first rock climb in the Cuillins. He later produced the first accurate map of the range, naming some summits himself, thus bringing the area to the public notice. Soon the sport of climbing for its own sake was born. Sheriff Alexander Nicolson became a leading exponent, and with the setting up in 1889 of the Scottish Mountaineering Club the sport spread to Ben Nevis and Glen Coe.

LORDS OF THE ISLES

The lordship of the Isles was an independent state that controlled the islands and much of the west coast of Scotland in the medieval period. The founder was Somerled, the progenitor of clan MacDonald, who used the conflict between his Norse overlords and the Scots kings to establish a near-autonomous state in the 12th century. When Norse overlordship ended, the MacDonald chiefs agreed to accept the rule of Donald of Islay, as Lord of the Isles. James IV managed to annex the title in 1493 (one still borne by the heir apparent to the British throne).

The path to Moonen bay and cliffs

▶▶▶ Skye   234C2

(Portree tourist information tel: 0845 225 5121 (national contact centre); www.visithighlands.com or www.skye.co.uk)

The most startlingly magnificent of the Hebridean islands, Skye is also the closest to the mainland. Since 1995, Skye has been joined by a bridge from Kyle of Lochalsh to Kyleakin. It is an island of extremely irregular shape, a sort of smudged handprint some 80km (50 miles) from end to end and varying from 6km (4 miles) to 40km (25 miles) in width. It consists of a central nexus—on which are **Portree**, the bustling capital (and hub of the island's bus network) and the Cuillin Hills; a number of long peninsular fingers stretch out from there, intersected by sea lochs. The landscape changes with disorienting ease from alpine peaks, to rolling farmland, bleak moorland, wooded valleys, coves of white coral sand and cliffs dotted with secret caves.

Close to the ferry terminal at Armadale, **Armadale Castle Gardens and Museum of the Isles▶** feature displays telling the story of the clan Donald and its progenitor, Somerled, the first Lord of the Isles (see panel). The castle is a restored 19th-century castellated mansion.

The central chain of mountain peaks, the **Cuillins▶▶**, their jagged silhouette seldom seen without at least a wisp of cloud, provides some of the most splendid scenery and demanding climbing in Britain. Rising to 1,009m (3,310ft), they enclose Loch Coruisk, a great pool of water locked in an amphitheatre of crags of the blackest gabbro; it is a scene of overpowering desolation and grandeur. You can reach it by boat trip from Elgol, or in a full day's walk from Elgol or Sligachan (it is not a walk, however, for the faint-hearted). An easier option is to walk the 6km (4 miles) along the coast from Elgol to Loch na Creitheach on the threshold of the Cuillins.

In Portree, **The Aros Experience▶** tells the island's story from the point of view of the ordinary people rather than the landowners. At Skeabost, a little way northwest of Portree, are the ruins of the tiny **Columban Chapel▶**, one of a number of the earliest Celtic churches known to have been built here.

Farther west, **Dunvegan Castle▶▶** has been home to the MacLeods of Skye since the 12th century. Striking a magnificent attitude on this remote shore of the island, it contains treasures sacred to the clan such as the fairy flag, which when waved has the power to save the clan.

Legend says it will only work three times and it has already been used twice, with miraculous results. In the churchyard at **Kilmuir** lie the remains of Flora MacDonald, Hebridean heroine of the '45 Rebellion (see panel, page 246), beneath an imposing Celtic cross. Nearby, the **Skye Museum of Island Life** uses four thatched cottages to recreate aspects of the simple yet heroic self-sufficiency of the island's crofters.

The **Trotternish peninsula**▶▶▶ constitutes northeast Skye, a surreal terrain of geological oddities: sandstone and limestone layers have collapsed beneath volcanic basalt to form a moonscape. Beneath the peninsula's summit, the Storr, stands a precarious needle of rock, **The Old Man of Storr**. The **Mealtt Falls** thunder into the sea near **Kilt Rock**, so named because of the pleated appearance of the rock strata. **The Quiraing** is one of the strangest and most fascinating hills in Scotland. Seldom seen without its raven guardians swirling around, it is a confused mass of cliffs, scree slopes and towering pinnacles, including features named the Prison, the Needle and the Table. On a wind-blown promontory at the northern end of Trotternish stand the ruins of **Duntulm Castle**▶, a historically impressive fortress built by the MacDonalds of Sleat when they were battling with the MacLeods of Dunvegan for the control of this region (see panel, page 254).

From Sconser a little ferry journeys across to the tranquil island of **Raasay**▶▶. A track follows the island's long spine of hills to end at the silhouetted ruins of medieval Brochel Castle.

Across the Cuillin Sound south of Skye lie the **Small Isles**, Rum, Eigg, Muck and Canna, served by ferries from Mallaig or Arisaig on the mainland. Each has a limited number of hotels. **Rum**▶▶ is the largest of the group and has a volcanic mountain cluster, the highest peak being Askival (810m/2,657ft). The haunt of red deer, wild goats, golden eagles and sea eagles, the island is a national nature reserve and has nature trails and a hotel owned by Scottish Natural Heritage.

Skye style: old croft house, traditionally maintained with white-washed walls, a central doorway and a roof of heather thatch

MIGHT IS RIGHT?
The 1882 Battle of the Braes was a half-heroic, half-comical affair. A group of bailiffs who were attempting to evict crofters from the coastal strip just south of Portree were beaten off by a fierce band of Hebridean house-wives armed with stone-weighted stockings. The English government, used to sending gunboats all over the world to force their way, promptly sent one up to Skye but backed down in the face of universal hostility. Instead they sent a Commission whose report paved the way for the enlightened Crofting Acts.

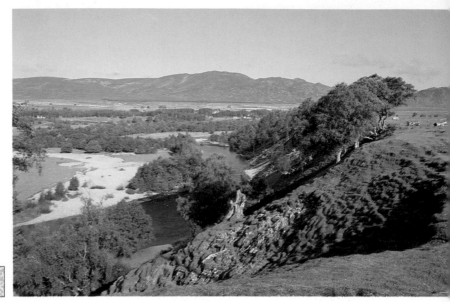

The valley of the River Spey near Newtonmore

GORDONSTOUN SCHOOL
The school, near Elgin, is famous nowadays as the establishment where the Queen's three sons were educated, but its buildings have had a local notoriety since the 17th century, when they served as the residence of Sir Robert Gordon. Known as the Warlock Laird, he laid out the school's famous round square so that his diabolic familiars could never corner him. His accomplice, the local minister, was not so lucky and was found one morning horribly shred by giant claws outside the kirk.

▶ **Spey Valley**   *235C4*
(Highlands of Scotland Tourist Board tel: 0845 225 5121 (national contact centre); www.visithighland.com; Aberdeen and Grampian Tourist Board tel: 01224 288828; www.aberdeen-grampian.com)
One of the broad classifications of single-malt whiskies is the Speyside malts which take their name from the River Spey. It rises in the Monadliath (literally 'the grey moors') and runs northeast, spreading through the wildlife-rich Insh Marshes with the Cairngorms as a backdrop. Beyond Grantown-on-Spey it reaches the whisky-distilling area stretching all the way to the Moray coast. The typical Strathspey view features a pleasing mix of woods and farmlands backed by moorland slopes and, inevitably, a plume of white steam jetting up from yet another distillery tucked into the landscape. Visit Glenfiddich (*Admission free; guided tours*) at Dufftown for a wide-ranging and entertaining interpretation of malt whisky, though there are plenty of other famous names, some on the marked **Scotland's Malt Whisky Trail** (see panel, page 257).

The resort town of **Aviemore** is a creation of the 1960s but it is a popular base for hill walking in the **Cairngorm Mountains**▶▶ in summer and skiing in winter. Cairn Gorm itself rises to 1,245m (4,085ft); take the ski lift (it operates year-round) for a wonderful view. Other activities might include a visit to the osprey reserve at Loch Garten, a ride on the **Strathspey Steam Railway** (tel: 01479 810725; www.strathspeyrailway.co.uk) from Aviemore to Boat of Garten (good walks at either end), or a visit to the Landmark Highland Heritage Visitor Centre. South along the A9 towards Kingussie is the Highland Wildlife Park.

Kingussie▶, pronounced 'Kinusie', is a pleasing town of one main street, with many beautiful walks nearby. If you visit only one highland history museum in Scotland, visit the **Highland Folk Museum**▶▶ here. It is divided into indoor and outdoor exhibitions and includes a 'black house' from the Outer Hebridean island of Lewis, a corn mill and a salmon smokehouse. At Newtonmore, the **Highland Folk Museum**▶▶ demonstrates the life and work of crofters in the early 1900s and has a turfhouse township evoking the 18th century. On a natural escarpment the other side of the Spey and the A9 stands the gaunt roofless ruin of the **Ruthven Barracks**, a sister to the one in Glenelg (see page 258). They were built to police the main Highland trade routes after the 1715 rebellion was suppressed, but a generation later, in 1746, they were blown up by Jacobites.

Elgin▶ is the administrative hub of Moray and the largest town in the popular Laigh of Moray. (Laigh means a sheltered low-lying area and, in this case, refers to its position in the 'rain shadow' of the Grampians.) Elgin's cathedral (HS), 'the lantern of the North', founded in 1224, was burned in 1390 by the villainous Wolf of Badenoch. Though subsequently rebuilt, it is now a picturesque ruin. Beside it, the **Biblical Gardens** claim to incorporate every plant mentioned in the Bible, with paths laid out in the form of the Cross. Elgin Museum features a display on Britain's oldest dinosaurs, found nearby. East of the town is the attractive community of **Fochabers**, with plenty of antiques shops to attract browsers, as well as the absorbing Fochabers Museum of Local History. On the coast, the otherwise rather workaday town of **Buckie** is enhanced by an interpretation of the development of the northeast fishery, the Buckie Drifter Maritime Heritage Centre. Summer boat trips from here provide the opportunity to watch bottlenosed dolphins. At Macduff, the **Macduff Marine Aquarium**▶ displays the sealife of the Moray Firth.

Pluscarden Abbey▶ (*Admission free*) lies in a fertile valley to the southwest of Elgin. Its atmosphere is potent, with Benedictine monks going to and fro amid the Gothic ruins. Founded by Alexander II in the early 13th century, the abbey was damaged by the warfare of the region and fell into further decay after the Reformation. It was partly restored by the Marquis of Bute in the 19th century and in 1943 was bestowed by his son on a Benedictine community from Prinknash in Gloucestershire. The monks moved in five years later and are now rebuilding it.

SCOTLAND'S MALT WHISKY TRAIL
Speyside is home to more than half of Scotland's malt distilleries, many of which are fascinating 19th-century time-warps. On the 110km (68-mile) Malt Whisky Trail (www.maltwhiskytrail.com) are Benramach (at Forres), Cardow (Knockando), Dallas Dhu (Forres), Glenfiddich (Dufftown), Glen Grant (Rothes), Glenlivet (Glenlivet) and Strathisla (Keith). Of these, Glenfiddich, Glen Grant and Glenlivet are free; otherwise admission covers a guided tour, and a voucher redeemable in the shop. Children under 8 are not admitted to some production areas. At Speyside Cooperage (Craigellachie), Britain's only working cooperage open to the public, oak casks are repaired for reuse in whisky manufacture.

257

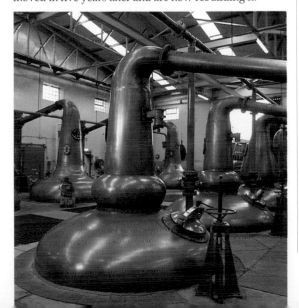

The copper stills at Glenfiddich Distillery; there are seven distilleries on Scotland's Malt Whisky Trail

THE SPEYSIDE WAY
The 75km (47-mile) long-distance path starts at Spey Bay where the River Spey flows into the North Sea and offers fairly easy walking as far as Ballindalloch before tackling the more challenging section through the hills to Tomintoul. The countryside is varied and the path passes near several whisky distilleries.

Dominating the skyline
around the village of
Golspie is a statue of the
1st Duke of Sutherland.
He was the infamous
Leviathan of Wealth who
between 1810 and 1820
evicted 15,000 of his
tenants from their self-
sufficient crofts in order to
turn their small plots into
profitable sheep pasture.

*Eilean Donan Castle, a
Mackenzie fortress, was
rebuilt early in the 20th
century by Colonel
Macrae after he suppos-
edly saw its original
appearance in a dream*

258

DORNOCH'S CLAIMS TO
FAME
Besides having the third
oldest golf links in the
world, considered as far
back as 1630 to be
superior to those of
St. Andrews, Dornoch also
claims the best sunshine
record in northern
Scotland and the dubious
distinction of being the
last place in Scotland to
burn a witch. The Witch's
Stone by the 17th hole of
the golf links commemo-
rates the country's last
judicial execution for
witchcraft, in 1722.

► ► ► **Sutherland, Caithness,
and Wester Ross**   *234C2*
*(Highlands of Scotland Tourist Board tel: 0845 225 5121
(national contact centre); www.visithighland.com)*
The northernmost reach of mainland Scotland is often
referred to as the last great wilderness of Europe. The
eastern coast, a fertile strip backed by brown moorland,
could not be in greater contrast to the green mountains
that overlook the sea lochs of the west coast of Ross.

In a remote and picturesque situation on the Sound of
Sleat, **Glenelg**► was once on the main cattle-droving route
to Skye. Here are found the two best-preserved brochs (see
panel, page 251) in mainland Scotland, a handsome,
ruined Hanoverian barrack block and Sandaig Bay, site of
Gavin Maxwell's otter refuge of 'Camusfearna' so vividly
described in *Ring of Bright Water*. In summer you can take
a ferry across the surging Kylerhea tidal stream to Skye.

North, across Loch Duich, the stunning **Eilean Donan
Castle**► ► stands on an islet at the meeting of three lochs.
On the northern shores of this peninsula are the stone-
built houses and palm trees of the delightful coastal village
of **Plockton**►. West of Lochcarron, the adventurous
should take an exhilaratingly twisty road (certainly not
one for more timid drivers) over **Bealach na Ba (The Pass
of the Cattle)**► ►. The glacier-scarred rocks on the summit of this pass offer a very fine view over Skye, especially
at sunset. The road then leads down to the remote coastal
village of **Applecross**. A carved Celtic cross beside the kirk
marks the site of the once influential seventh-century
monastery of St. Maelrubha.

Torridon► ► lies at the end of one of Wester Ross's
wildest glens. The road along the southern shores of
Upper Loch Torridon offers magnificent views of Beinn
Alligin (985m/3,232ft). A National Trust for Scotland
Countryside Centre in Torridon has a deer museum and
an audio-visual presentation on local wildlife. Farther
north, in one of the most beautiful corners of the west
coast, lies the spectacular, world-famous **Inverewe
Garden**► ► ►(NTS), a collection of some 2,500 species of
tender and hardy shrubs and trees which flourish in the
warmth of the Gulf Stream.

The port of **Ullapool**, placed amidst breathtaking scenery,
doubles as a resort. The A835 east heads down Loch
Broom to the Falls of Measeach in the dizzying

*Himalayan lilies and
other exotic species
flourish in Inverewe
Garden, formerly a
peaty wasteland*

GENERATING POWER
Standing on the clifftops
16km (10 miles) west of
Thurso, the giant golf-ball
shape of Dounreay
nuclear power station can
be seen for miles around;
there is a visitor centre
(*Admission free*).
Elsewhere the waters of
Scotland's mountains and
reservoirs are harnessed
to produce electricity: the
great pipes of the hydro-
electric plant at
Kinlochleven can be seen
on the hillsides south of
Fort William and those of
the Tay-Tummel system
around Glen Affric. The
pumped storage plant at
Ben Cruachan in Argyll
has a visitor centre.

259

Corrieshalloch Gorge▶▶. To the north the same road
passes **Knockan Cliff▶**, in the Inverpolly National Nature
Reserve and glimpses Stac Pollaidh and Suilven, two of
the most striking mountain shapes in Scotland.

In the far north, you can take a ferry and minibus from
Durness to **Cape Wrath▶▶** to see some stupendous
coastal scenery. Britain's highest mainland cliffs are
nearby Clo Mor, east of Cape Wrath. Just outside Durness
itself is the Smoo Cave, which is in fact three vast caves in
the limestone cliffs, with a waterfall. A boat trip can be
taken right into the second and third caves.

Few people who come this far north fail to visit
Britain's most northeasterly point, **John O'Groats**, named
after the Dutchman Jan de Groot (Dunnet Head, nearby,
is actually the northernmost point). It's basically an
untidy collection of tourist shacks, disappointing to many
visitors. Persevere instead to nearby Duncansby Head
(see Walks, page 238): the three dramatic offshore stacks
rise to more than 60m (200ft).

South of Wick, near the village of Lybster, are two
impressive ancient relics, the **Hill o' Many Stones** and the
Grey Cairns of Camster▶▶. The former is a curious and
attractive arrangement of 22 rows of stones in a fan shape,
the latter two excellently preserved neolithic burial
chambers. If you don't mind the idea of crawling into
someone's grave, you can enter one of the handsomest
in the country, 60m (200ft) long and 18m (60ft) wide with
separate chambers inside.

North of Dornoch the fairy-tale towers of **Dunrobin
Castle▶▶** stand on a coastal escarpment, the former seat
of the earls and dukes of Sutherland, the largest landowners in Britain. Despite its fanciful 19th-century exterior, it
is an ancient fortress with a medieval keep as its core. The
collection of paintings inside includes a Reynolds and two
Canalettos. **Dornoch▶▶** is a secluded and ancient royal
burgh, a pretty little sandstone town with several kilometres of safe sandy beaches. The small cathedral of the
Bishops of Caithness dates from the 12th century. The
town is also renowned for its golf links.

WILDLIFE
The flow or marsh country
of Caithness and
Sutherland is a vast
stretch of plantations. It is
home during the summer
months to greenshanks,
dunlins, golden plovers
and other wading birds.
Dunnet Bay, near Wick, is
an excellent birdwatching
spot in winter. Look for
great northern divers,
long-tailed ducks and scot-
ers. The flora of the Arctic
species mingles with
mountain species, almost
at sea level. Handa
Island, off Scourie, is
another wonderful site
for breeding seabirds.
A private ferry runs
April to mid-September
from Tarbert
(tel: 01971 502347).

Scarista Bay, Harris, typifies the majestic remoteness of the Western Isles

A voice so thrilling ne'er
was heard,
In spring time from the
cuckoo-bird,
Breaking the silence of
the seas
Amongst the farthest
Hebrides.
—William Wordsworth,
The Solitary Reaper

THE LEWIS CHESSMEN
The chance discovery in
the 19th century of the
12th-century chessmen on
Lewis caused a storm of
controversy. Their artistry
was of a standard many
found hard to attribute to
the 12th century. Carved
from walrus ivory, they are
now divided between the
British Museum in London
and the National Museum
of Antiquities in
Edinburgh. Replicas can
be bought on Lewis.

▶▶▶ **Western Isles**   *234D1*
*(Western Isles Tourist Board tel: 01851 703088;
www.visithebrides.com)*
Sail west across the Minch and you reach the Western
Isles, or Outer Hebrides. For the most part the eastern side
of the archipelago is barren, rocky and steep. Its west
coast is all silver-white beaches, long and empty and
backed by the 'machair', fertile peaty grassland enriched
by white shell-sand—an almost unique habitat that supports a rich wildlife. Between the two lie watery, peaty
and totally treeless moors.

The Western Isles change their religion with their
latitude: strict Presbyterianism in Lewis, Harris, Berneray
and North Uist; Roman Catholicism in South Uist, Eriskay
and Barra; with Benbecula in between a mixture of the
two. The difference is readily apparent: strict observation
of the Sabbath in the northern islands means people go out
only to attend church services (shops and bars are closed),
whereas Sundays in the south are livelier and more
relaxed. Even the houses on the southern islands have a
brighter look, often with vibrant roofs and painted walls.

It is a perfect place to get away from it all. The people wel-
come visitors, but you will not find organized facilities. The
few 'sights' are mostly archeological; what visitors will
remember is the empty beaches, the lochs, the hills, the
wildlife, the pure quality of the light and the way of life.

LEWIS AND HARRIS Lewis and Harris are in fact one island,
linked to the mainland and Skye by ferries from Ullapool to
Stornoway and Uig to Tarbert. The world-famous Harris
tweed is still produced here. The stone circle of
Callanish▶▶▶ is one of the most haunting and eloquent
places in Britain (there is an exhibition in the nearby visitor
centre). An open-air temple of the Bronze Age that seems to
have related particularly to the moon, it is tucked onto a
broad peninsula on the west coast of Lewis that protrudes
into the sheltered waters of Loch Roag. The inner circle of 13
stones surrounds a central 5m (16ft), 5-tonne menhir. In the
central cairn, remains of a human cremation were discovered when the 1.5m (5ft) banks of peat were removed in
1860. At Arnol, the squat **Black House**▶ (HS) is now a

museum (see panel, page 261); at nearby Shawbost is
another museum evoking crofting life the **Shawbost Folk
Museum** (*Admission free*). To the west, **Dun Carloway▶** is
one of the best brochs (Iron Age towers) in the Hebrides,
dating from the first century BC and with walls rising to 6m
(20ft); its interpretation centre is open in summer. **Rodel
Church▶▶**, a bold cruciform dating from 1500, stands on
the southern tip of Harris. The cold bleak interior preserves
a number of carvings.

NORTH AND SOUTH UIST On the road south from
Lochmaddy is the finest chambered cairn in the Hebrides.
Barpa Langass▶ sits on the side of the hill, Ben Langass; a
little tunnel leads into the communal burial chamber built
by Bronze Age Beaker people. The northwest coast of North
Uist has several beautiful coves and beaches; the one near
Hosta is, on a clear day, the best place to see **St. Kilda**, the
most remote of the Hebrides. **Balranald RSPB Reserve▶**
offers a trail across the flower- and bird-rich machair.

North Uist, Benbecula, South Uist, Eriskay and Berneray
are linked by a causeway, and are connected to the mainland by ferry from Mallaig to Lochboisdale and to Skye
from Uig to Lochmaddy. At Milton a cairn stands on the site
of the birthplace of Jacobite heroine Flora MacDonald . Over
the causeway tiny **Eriskay** is celebrated in the Gaelic
'Eriskay Love Lilt'. It was here that Bonnie Prince Charlie
first set foot in Scotland on his way from France.

Barra▶ ▶ is a microcosm of all the Western Isles with its
rocky coastline on the east, sandy bays and machair on
the west. Small-scale farming is still the main occupation
and Gaelic is still spoken. Ferries connect Castlebay with
South Uist and the mainland.

*Harris wool, here being
sold locally; the tweed is
sold worldwide*

*The standing stones
at Callanish on the Isle
of Lewis*

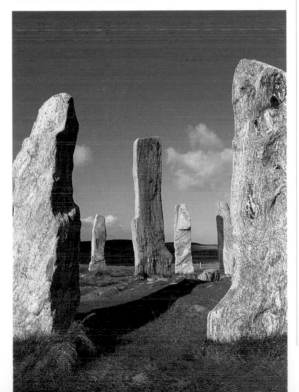

CROFT HOUSES OLD AND NEW

The Arnol Black House on
the west coast of Lewis is
a traditional crofter's
house that gives a fasci-
nating insight into a way
of life that was common
until the 1970s. Inside
the thick stone walls a
peat fire smoulders in the
middle of the floor, the
smoke filtering out
through the oat-straw
thatch held down by
stone-weighted strands of
rope. Many of these old
croft houses can still be
seen, some left in ruin,
some given new roofs.
The modern houses that
replace them are similarly
low buildings, usually with
dormer windows.

Mountains, lochs and glens make a magnificent landscape but a harsh environment in which to live and work. Traditionally the Highlands supported a sophisticated, martial society with its own code of conduct and social responsibilities. This was wilfully destroyed in the mid-18th century and within a generation the infamous Clearances began, when the people were driven from the land.

PROPHET OF DOOM
The 17th-century poet Brahan Seer, born on Lewis in the Outer Hebrides, described how the glens would be emptied of their people by sheep, how the sheep would in turn be displaced by deer before the coming of the black rain that would clear all life from the land. The 'black rain' has been widely identified with fallout from a nuclear war or a disaster at the Dounreay nuclear reactor. Too many of his prophecies have been fulfilled for his dark vision of the future of the Highlands not to cast a chill of apprehension.

Mass evictions and emigrations have left the landscape dotted with ruined crofters' houses

The rule of the Highland chieftain Up until the defeat of the Jacobite clans at Culloden Moor in 1746, the Highlands were divided into small communities by the dramatic landscape of mountains and sea lochs. It was primarily a cattle-breeding society that traded for grain grown in the Lowlands. The Highland cattle, small herds of sheep, goats and chickens were highly mobile and every community required a strongly motivated fighting force to protect its wealth from 'lifting'. This was the economic basis of the closely knit and intensely martial Highland clans. There was a long tradition of paternalistic care, but it was a feudal society for the simple reason that a hundred strong men in times of crisis were of much greater use than a money rent.

The changing tide After their victory at the Battle of Culloden, the Hanoverian government, frightened by the partial success of the Highland army that rallied to Bonnie Prince Charlie, determined to control this militant society. They banned firearms, the martial kilt and the strong legal powers of the clan chiefs—and they were undeniably thorough. Within a few years the Highlands were at peace and money rents began to replace feudal tenures. For a few decades everything seemed rosy—the potato provided a new cheap staple crop for the poor, grain prices stayed down and livestock prices soared. Capitalists built iron foundries, fishing ports, piers, linen and woollen mills, partly financed by enormous profits made by gathering kelp. The population quickly doubled, but the plots of farming land became ever smaller.

The Clearances The end of the Napoleonic wars brought a violent depression with the total collapse of fish, cattle and kelp prices and the near-extinction of rural industries. Only sheep brought in a handsome profit. Sheep farming, however, was incompatible with thousands of tenants packed into the glens and coastal strips and many people began to be evicted from their land to make room for sheep paddocks. They were moved south to the slums of the industrial cities or packed off to Canada, Australia, New Zealand and the US. Gladstone's Crofting Act of 1886 gave the surviving tenants a guaranteed claim on their smallholdings and allowed strong communities to survive in the Hebrides, but many big estates were turned over to deer hunting and grouse shooting. With forestry, fish farming and tourism, these still play a major part in the Highlands' economy.

Travel Facts

Arriving and departing

By air: London has five airports. The largest is **Heathrow** (one of the largest in the world). Airbuses run to London Victoria, Heathrow Express trains to London Paddington (taking 15–25 minutes) and Underground trains (the cheapest option) take 45–60 minutes to central London (not all night). The next largest airport, **Gatwick**, has a direct rail link to Victoria Station. **Luton** (north of London) has a shuttle bus link to the railway station, and **Stansted** has trains to London Liverpool Street (taking 45 minutes). **London City Airport** is served by a shuttle bus from Liverpool Street (25 minutes) and Canary Wharf, as well as overground trains. **Birmingham, East Midlands, Edinburgh, Glasgow, Leeds** and **Manchester** also serve international flights.

By boat: Numerous ports offer cross-Channel services to the rest of Europe. Dover in east Kent (114km/71 miles from London) is the main port connecting with Belgium and France; if you get stuck here for the night, there are plenty of bed-and-breakfasts.

FOR TRAVEL DETAILS

Flight arrivals: see Ceefax (accessed through most TVs via BBC channels), page 440 **Flight departures**: contact individual airlines **Rail Europe Travel Centre** tel: 0870 584 8848 **Eurostar** tel: 0870 518 6186; www.eurostar.com **Eurotunnel** tel: 0870 535 3535; www.eurotunnel.co.uk

By rail: Trains via the Eurotunnel run from the European mainland. Eurostar (passenger) services from Brussels and Paris to London Waterloo International take less than 3 hours. Car-carrying services from Calais to Folkestone take 35 minutes.

Camping

Campsites are abundant in Britain, ranging from small fields with just a single cold tap by way of facilities to large-scale sites with shower blocks

and shops. Useful sources of information include the Visit Britain annual publication *Camping and Caravan Parks in Britain* (on sale at major bookshops or by post from Visit Briatain Mailorder Fulfilment, Westex Ltd., 7 St. Andrews Way, Devons Road, Bromley-by-Bow, London E3 3PA, tel: 0870 606 7204), and *The Big Sites Book* published for members of the Camping and Caravanning Club (Greenfields House, Westwood Way, Coventry CV4 8JH, tel: 024-7669 4995; website: www.campingandcaravanningclub .co.uk). Tourist Information Centres can help with lists of local sites.

Children

Many hotels, particularly larger ones, provide babysitting services, and baby-listening devices are often available. Enquire when booking about child discounts, and if there are any special facilities; British hotels are not generally good about providing entertainment for the youngest visitors—toy boxes, children's books, emergency medical supplies and interesting children's meals are in short supply. Some establishments operate a 'no children' rule.

Child discounts are offered for many admission fees. On the rail network, up to two children under five years of age may travel free with each fare-paying passenger, while children of five and over and under 16 travel at half the full price. Anyone travelling by train with children should invest in a Family Railcard: up to four 5 to 15-year-olds travel anywhere in the country for 20 per cent of the adult fare, and up to two accompanying adults have a discount of one-third on most fares.

Pubs Children under 14 are not allowed in the bar area. Some pubs allow accompanied children on to the premises (in the restaurant, for instance) and in the garden. You have to be 18 or over to buy or consume alcohol in a pub.

Theme parks and safari parks include Alton Towers (Alton, Staffordshire), Camelot Theme Park (Preston, Lancashire), Chessington World of Adventures (Chessington, Surrey),

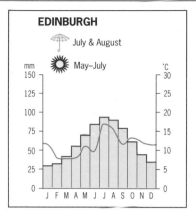

EDINBURGH

July & August

May–July

mm
150
125
100
75
50
25
0
J F M A M J J A S O N D

°C
30
25
20
15
10
5
0

LONDON

July, August,
October & November

May–August

mm
150
125
100
75
50
25
0
J F M A M J J A S O N D

°C
30
25
20
15
10
5
0

Knowsley Safari Park (Prescot, Merseyside), Legoland (Windsor, Berkshire), Lightwater Valley (Ripon, North Yorkshire), Longleat Safari Park (Warminster, Wiltshire), Thorpe Park (Chertsey, Surrey), West Midland Safari and Leisure Park (Bewdley, Worcestershire) and Woburn Safari Park (Woburn, Bedfordshire).

London, the South Coast (Devon, Dorset and Sussex in particular), the North Yorkshire coast and Cornwall are among the most appealing areas for families; older children may also enjoy the Lake District, Exmoor, Pembrokeshire, York, Edinburgh and the Scottish Highlands.

Climate

Britain is a temperate country—the weather is seldom extremely hot or extremely cold and there is no prolonged rainy or dry season—yet where every year seems to break

some meteorological record ('the coldest May this century'; 'the driest November since records began'). In short, the British climate is a fascinatingly fickle beast: the seasons are distinctive but fuse into each other; brilliant mornings often cloud over as they proceed. No wonder the umbrella is such a national institution. Be prepared for sudden changes in temperature: chill winds as well as heatwaves, and bring rainproof footwear and clothing.

The prevailing wind comes from the west, bringing most rain to western Britain; a rain-shadow effect causes eastern areas to have lower rainfall. The south gets less rain than the far north, and the climate tends to get warmer the farther south you go. In mid-June it stays light until 10pm (later in north Scotland); conversely, in winter it gets dark early, and the very far north stays gloomy all day.

265

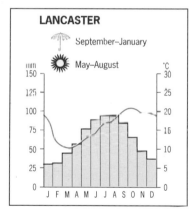

LANCASTER

September–January

May–August

mm
150
125
100
75
50
25
0
J F M A M J J A S O N D

°C
30
25
20
15
10
5
0

NEWQUAY, CORNWALL

October–January

April–August

mm
150
125
100
75
50
25
0
J F M A M J J A S O N D

°C
30
25
20
15
10
5
0

Travel in spring and you could encounter blustery squalls and sleet or sunshine; May and June can be excellent times for a holiday, with the long daylight hours and uncrowded roads and sights (except at Bank Holiday weekends). Oxford and Cambridge colleges are mostly closed in the weeks running up to examination time in late May and early June.

Summer school holidays make late July and all of August extremely busy in many areas, including national parks and coastal areas—Devon, Cornwall, the Lake District, the South Coast, the Scottish Highlands (also cursed by midges over this period) and Snowdonia are among the most crowded regions. Some historic cities fill almost to capacity, York, Chester and Canterbury among them. Other places are manageable, including the Welsh borderlands, Eastern England, East Anglia and the Scottish borders. September can have fine weather; this can be a good time to travel.

Visitor numbers drop appreciably along with the temperature in October and November (the West Country stays reasonably mild), but Christmas is busier, with many hotels offering special Christmas break deals. Many attractions close between October or November and Easter (including most National Trust properties). Scottish winters usually have enough snow for skiing, notably in the Cairngorms.

For 24-hour recorded weather information tel:0906 850 0401 (premium rate) or for a five-day forecast: www.bbc.co.uk/weather.

Crime

Violent crime is still rare in Britain and central cities are mostly quite safe, but minor offences against property have risen over recent years, particularly in some inner city areas. Even in remote countryside, it is wise to be on guard against car theft, and to ensure all valuables are locked out of sight. Be extra vigilant of your belongings at airports and major railway stations: do not let them out of your sight. Because of the threat of terrorist bombs, unattended parcels are likely to be removed.

Customs

People travelling within the European Union (EU) are no longer entitled to import duty-free goods. However, visitors from outside the EU can bring in duty-free goods up to the current EU allowances (see top panel on page 267).

Note the distinction between **duty-free** and **duty-paid** allowances; duty-free goods (bought at duty-free shops in airports, ferry terminals on ferries and on aeroplanes) have had no duty paid on them.

The countries of the EU are Austria, Belgium, Cyprus, Czech Republic, Denmark, Estonia, Finland, France, Germany, Greece, Hungary, Italy, Latvia, Lithuania, Luxembourg, Malta, the Netherlands, Poland, Portugal, the Republic of Ireland, Slovakia, Slovenia, Spain (not the Canary Islands), Sweden and the United Kingdom (not the Channel Islands).

Cycling

You need to be canny to explore Britain by bicycle, as many roads are too busy to be much fun, yet elsewhere you can explore some delightfully quiet countryside. Good areas include East Anglia, the Cotswolds, mid Wales and the Welsh borderlands, Northumberland and the Scottish Borders, the Isle of Wight and (off road) along the South Downs Way in Sussex. The National Cycle Network is rapidly being developed to reach 16,000km (10,000 miles) by 2005, giving access to quiet

A clock in Chester commemorates Queen Victoria's diamond jubilee

DUTY-FREE ALLOWANCES

Duty-free allowances for goods bought outside the EU)

Cigarettes	200
or cigarillos	100
or cigars	50
or tobacco	250g
Still table wine	2 litres
Spirits, strong liqueurs over 22% volume	1 litre
or fortified or sparkling wine	2 litres
Perfume	60cc/ml
Toilet water	250cc/ml
All other goods including gifts and souvenirs	£145 worth for visitors from outside the EU

roads and specially constructed cycle paths. It will pass within 3km (2 miles) of half the UK population. The Network has been established by the charity Sustrans, 35 King Street, Bristol BS1 4DZ, tel: 0117 929 0888 (website: www.sustrans.org.uk); excellent maps of the routes are on sale. The general organization for cycling matters is the Cyclists' Touring Club (CTC), 69 Meadrow, Godalming, Surrey GU7 3HS, tel: 0870 873 0060 (www.ctc.org.uk).

Disabilities, visitors with
The National Accessible Scheme grades hotel, farmhouse, inn, guesthouse and self-catering accommodation according to suitability for visitors with disabilities with four categories for those with mobility problems and two categories each for those with visual or hearing impairment. You can get help finding suitable accommodation from the Holiday Care Service, Information Unit, Seventh Floor, Sunley House, 4 Bedford Park, Croydon, Surrey CR0 2AP, tel: 0845 124 9971 (website: www.holidaycare.org.uk), or Minicom (for callers with hearing impairment) 0845 124 9976 and from the Royal Association for Disability and Rehabilitation (RADAR), 12 City Forum, 250 City Road, London

EC1V 8AF, tel: 020-7250 3222, or Minicom 020-7250 4119, (website: www.radar.org.uk). RADAR publishes the annual *Holidays in Britain and Ireland*.

Some hotel chains have bedrooms that have been adapted for people with disabilities. Many museums and tourist sites have lavatories for wheelchair-users; a booklet showing lavatories for people with disabilities is available from RADAR.

Wheelchair-users planning train travel should first contact the rail network that they will be using— telephone numbers are in the *Yellow Pages* or through directory enquiries (118 500)—so that arrangements can be made for boarding and seating. RADAR has addresses of local disability associations.

Driving
Driving in Britain can be a delightful way to see the country, or a diabolically frustrating experience. In many remote country areas it is the only

DUTY PAID GUIDE LEVELS

Guide levels for duty-paid goods bought in the EU,
You can bring in any amount of goods*, but beyond these guide limits you have to be able to show the items are for your own personal use (this includes gifts); if you are receiving any payment in return for these goods (including payment of your travel expenses) you will be liable for duty.

Beer	110 litres
Cigarettes	3,200
Cigarillos	400
Cigars	200
Tobacco	3kg
Spirits	10 litres
Intermediate products (sherry, port etc)	20 litres
Wine	90 litres

*From some countries there is a limit on the amount of tobacco products which can be brought into the UK without paying duty. Check current limits before you travel.

feasible way of getting around; for village-to-village pottering (such as the Cotswolds, the Weald and Constable Country), where the local public transport is limited, the car really comes into its own. The huge network of narrow, crooked lanes (many very ancient indeed) is a particular feature. Rural honeypots such as the Lake District and the Cornish coastal towns and villages can get so busy in summer that finding somewhere to park requires ingenuity; consider using local buses (if there are any) or finding a footpath. In big cities, finding your way can be difficult; in central London (where parking is something of an ordeal) you should avoid driving if possible and use public transport or taxis. For driving through central London Monday to Friday 7am to 6.30pm (except public holidays) there is a £5 Congestion Charge.

Breakdown Car-rental companies normally provide cover with one or other of the major motoring organizations in Britain, the AA or the RAC. On motorways, there are emergency telephones on the hard shoulder every 1.6km (1 mile). Arrows indicate the direction of the nearest one.

Car rental Large firms with numerous branches and desks at airports include Avis tel: 0870 010 0287 (www.avis.co.uk), Budget tel: 0870 156 5656 (www.budget.co.uk), and Hertz Tel: 0870 844 8844 (www.hertz.co.uk). These may not be the cheapest; telephone around for the best deal.

Hiking is a national pastime

Licences Australian, Canadian, Irish, New Zealand and US driving licences or permits are acceptable for driving in the UK. Holders of permits written in a foreign language are advised to obtain an official translation from an embassy or recognized motoring organization, or an international driving licence before they leave their home country. Car rental firms all require you to have held your licence or permit for at least a year.

Motorways These link most major cities; service areas for fuel and refreshments are indicated well in advance. On some motorway stretches, however, there is a serious dearth of stopping places, eg, the M25 (London's busy orbital route), the M11 and M20.

Parking restrictions Never park on a double yellow line; parking on single yellow lines is generally permitted on Sundays and at other times as displayed on signposts beside the road. Wheel clamps are increasingly used to combat illegal parking and beware, the fee/fine to release your car is hefty.

Traffic regulations Traffic drives on the left (hence clockwise at roundabouts, which are common features at intersections). Speed-limit and destination signs use miles (one kilometre is roughly ⅝ of a mile). Speed limits for cars are 110kph (70mph) for motorways and dual carriageways, 95kph (60mph) for other roads, and 50kph (30mph) in built-up areas unless otherwise indicated. It is compulsory for all passengers to wear seat-belts. Drivers must be at least 17 years old.

Electricity
The current in Britain is 240 volts, alternate current. Plugs have three square pins.

Embassies and consulates in London
Australia Australia House, Strand, WC2, tel: 0870 005 6701
Canada 1 Grosvenor Square W1, tel: 020-7258 6600
Republic of Ireland 17 Grosvenor Place, SW1, tel: 0870 005 6725

New Zealand New Zealand House, Haymarket, SW1, tel: 0870 005 6962 **USA** 24 Grosvenor Square, W1, tel: 020-7499 9000.

Health

Most visitors receive free treatment under the National Health Service. Visitors from countries which do not have a reciprocal agreement with Britain may be charged. Accident victims must be admitted via Accident and Emergency in hospital. Local doctors (GPs) will see visitors; ask at your hotel or a pharmacy for details. If you take medication, make a note of the medicines you use. A charge is made for dental treatment.

Free 24-hour medical advice from a qualified nurse is available over the phone through the government service NHS Direct, tel: 0845 4647.

Pharmacies and larger supermarkets have a fair range of medicines you can buy without a doctor's prescription. Opening time rotas of pharmacies are often maintained: details of locations of the duty pharmacy are posted in the windows.

Hitch-hiking

Hitch-hiking is not illegal in Britain, although the occasional report of violent crime associated with hitching deters many people. It is illegal to stand on the hard shoulder of motorways; however, you may wait near roundabouts by motorway slip roads.

Holidays

Summer school holidays are generally from late July to early September; you may find many places closed from Christmas Day to New Year.
1 Jan New Year's Day
2 Jan New Year (Scotland only)
Late March to early April Good Friday, followed three days later by Easter Monday
First Monday in May Early May Bank Holiday
Last Monday in May Spring Bank Holiday (Whitsun)
First Monday in August Summer Bank Holiday (Scotland only)
Last Monday in August Summer Bank Holiday (England and Wales only)
25 December Christmas Day
26 December Boxing Day

Insurance

Travel insurance should cover accident or illness, loss of valuables, injury or death while driving, and holiday cancellation or curtailment. Travellers may be covered for personal items through their house contents insurance. Be sure to leave the original policy details at home and take only a photocopy on your travels. Shop around for the best buy: prices and what is covered vary enormously.

Language

Although there is nowhere in Britain where English is not understood, in certain parts it is very much the second language. Welsh is the main tongue in parts of Mid-West and North Wales, but less so in South Wales and the Welsh borders. Throughout Wales signposts and so on are in both languages. Gaelic is spoken in a few parts of Scotland, notably the Hebrides. Britain's cultural diversity is often simplified into the notion of a land of two cultures, separated by a north/south divide. But to simplify accents this way would not be possible. In whatever area of the country you visit, you will come across marked regional accents; from 'Scouse' in Liverpool to 'Brummie' in Birmingham, from 'Geordie' in Newcastle to 'Cockney' in London.

Lavatories

Public lavatories are well signposted in towns, and nearly all filling stations have them. Lavatories in pubs and restaurants are reserved for customers.

Lost property

Items are often handed into police stations; they pass on information about lost items to other branches. To make life easier, make sure your address in Britain is shown clearly on all your valuables.

For items lost while on public transport, contact the bus station, train station or airport involved.

The London Transport Lost Property Office is at 200 Baker Street, NW1 5RZ, tel: 020-7486 2496; open Monday to Friday 9am to 2pm.

Maps

The Automobile Association (AA) publishes a comprehensive road atlas of Great Britain; this includes dozens of town and city plans.

Britain has been mapped accurately by the Ordnance Survey (OS). If you intend to spend some time exploring a region, invest in the pink-covered OS Landranger maps, 1:50,000 scale (2cm to the km): contours show relief, and footpaths are marked. For hiking, the orange-covered OS Explorer maps, 1:25,000 scale (4cm to the km), showing field boundaries, are best; for some of the most popular walking areas (including many national parks) the yellow-covered OS Outdoor Leisure maps at 1:25,000 scale, are available instead. Most bookshops have local OS maps; the full range is sold at Stanfords Map and Travel Bookshop, 12–14 Long Acre, London WC2 9LP, tel: 020-7836 1321 (website: www.stanfords.co.uk).

Media

Newspapers Britain is sometimes said to have the best and the worst newspapers in the world. There are the 'quality' broadsheets (*The Times*, *Independent*, *Guardian*, *Financial Times* and *Daily Telegraph*) and the 'popular' tabloids (the *Daily Mail*, *Daily Express*, *Sun*, *Mirror*, *Star* and *Sport*). For London, the *Evening Standard* (Mon–Sat) has national and local news and a useful entertainment section. There are several regional dailies.

Television There are five terrestial channels: BBC1 and BBC2 are funded by licence fees, and ITV, Channel 4 and Five by advertising. Many hotels have cable and satellite TV.

Radio There are five national BBC radio stations, Radio 1 (pop music), Radio 2 (light music), Radio 3 (classical music), Radio 4 (news, drama and general interest) and Radio 5 Live (sport and news). Classic FM, broadcasting lighter classical music, is the most popular independent radio station. Frequencies can be found in newspapers and the weekly TV listings magazines.

Money matters

Credit cards are widely accepted at nearly all filling stations, most restaurants and many shops. Travellers' cheques and Eurocheques are a safe way of carrying money. Using your bank or credit card to draw cash from ATMs can get better exchange rates, but be sure to check the fees first— both your bank and the bank where you're making the withdrawal may charge you. The pound (£) is divided into 100 pence (p). Denominations are 1p, 2p, 5p, 10p, 20p, 50p and £1 and £2 coins, then £5, £10, £20 and £50 notes. Banks in Scotland issue their own banknotes; they are legal currency throughout the UK.

VAT refunds Nationals of countries outside the EU may claim refunds for Value Added Tax (VAT) on goods bought within the EU; ask for a form when you make your purchase.

Tipping Generally, tip 10–15 per cent in a restaurant if service has not already been added (ask if it is not clear), or not at all if you think the meal and/or service was not up to scratch; total payment boxes on credit card slips are often left empty, leaving you to add a tip (whatever you decide, remember to fill it in!). Taxidrivers expect 10 per cent; minicab drivers (whom you order by telephone and are told a price before you travel) generally do not expect anything. Porters in luxury hotels expect £1. Hairdressers and barbers can be tipped 10 per cent.

Opening hours Standard office hours are Monday to Friday, 9am to 5pm; shops generally stay open until 5.30 or 6pm, and operate 9am to 5.30pm on Saturdays. Many open on Sundays. In central London and certain other cities many shops open until 9pm on Wednesday or Thursday.

Restaurants generally open for lunch noon–2pm, and for dinner 6pm–10pm, but times vary. Cafés usually operate 9am–5pm.

Hours and dates when tourist attractions are open obviously vary; many places close from the beginning of November to Easter, and are also closed on Sunday morning, plus maybe all day on Monday or another weekday. Typical hours are 10am–5pm, with last admission an hour before closing. Check with the tourist office (phone numbers given for each entry in this guide) for opening times of an attraction if you are making a special trip there.

Banks are open Monday to Friday from 9am; most close at 4.30pm; a few open on Saturday mornings.

Pubs in England and Wales are open from 11am–11pm Mon–Sat, noon–10.30pm Sun and Good Friday and noon–3pm, 7pm–10.30pm Christmas Day. Some pubs close between 2.30pm and 6pm. In Scotland, they are open from 11am–11pm Mon–Sat, noon–2.30pm and 6.30pm–11pm Sun (though some may stay open in the afternoon).

A 'bobby' on the beat

Organized tours

Tour buses frequently circuit the sights of Oxford, Stratford-upon-Avon, Windsor, Bath, Cambridge, Edinburgh and other historic towns. In London, double-decker open-top sightseeing buses run by the Big Bus Company (tel: 020-7233 9533; www.bigbus.co.uk) take a number of routes in the city, with commentary; for the price of a one-day ticket you can get on and off where you like and switch from one route to another; or you can save money by taking ordinary buses and using a Travelcard. Special interest walking tours are given daily by The Original London Walks (tel: 020-7624 3978; www.walks.com). Themes among the 100-plus walks each week include pubs, ghosts, the Beatles and royalty. Walks last about two hours, usually starting from an underground station; reservation is not necessary. From Westminster Millennium Pier and other central London piers several operators offer Thames river cruises, west to Hampton Court, Richmond and Kew, and east to Greenwich and the Thames Barrier (guide available from piers or central London Underground stations).

Places of worship

The established churches in Britain are Protestant but there are numerous Roman Catholic churches. In London, all major religions are represented. Denominational headquarters include Westminster Abbey (Church of England), Deans Yard, SW1, tel: 020-7222 5152, Westminster Cathedral (Roman Catholic), Francis Street, SW1, tel: 020-7798 9055, United Synagogue (Jewish), Upper Woburn Place, WC1, tel: Head Office, High Road, N12, tel: 020-8343 8989, London Central Mosque (Muslim), 146 Park Road, NW8, tel: 020-7724 3363.

Police

Telephone 999 or 112 (also ambulance and fire) for emergencies only; police stations are listed in the *Yellow Pages* under 'Police'.

Traffic wardens (black and yellow uniforms) deal with parking matters.

Post offices

Main post offices open from 9am to 5.30pm, Monday to Friday and 9am to 12.30pm on Saturday. Many newsagents and corner shops sell stamps in booklets. Inland letters bearing first-class stamps generally take a day less than those with second-class stamps. Postcards and letters are charged at the same rate. Enquire at any post office for details of rates for mainland Europe and the rest of the world. For more information tel: 0845 774 0740 or www.royalmail.com.

271

Letterboxes vary in size and shape but are always red

272

Public transport

Air travel There are 27 regional airports in England, Scotland and Wales. British Airways tel: 0870 850 9850 (www.britishairways.com and BMI British Midland tel: 0870 607 0565 (www.flybmi.com) have comprehensive networks of domestic flights, with discounts available, and domestic flights are also offered by Ryan Air tel: 0541 569569 (www.ryanair.com). There are bargain-price 'no-frills' services run by EasyJet tel: 0870 600 0000 (internet booking available; website: easyjet.com).

Buses Generally speaking, services in rural areas are infrequent. An exception is the Isle of Wight, where bus services are excellent.

Many areas have county-wide timetables and/or bus maps. To obtain one, ask at a tourist information office in the area you wish to travel.

Coach Long-distance buses and coaches serve the towns the railways cannot reach; fares are lower than rail, but the journey may not be as comfortable. The major national network is run by National Express (reservations tel:0870 580 8080 or book online, website: www.nationalexpress.com); cards are available giving discount travel for students, families, lone parents, young persons (16–25), over 50s, and the Tourist Trail Pass gives unlimited travel for a given period. The main London terminus is Victoria Coach Station, Buckingham Palace Road (near Victoria railway station), SW1, tel: 020-7730 3466; for some trips, tickets are purchased on board.

Rail The national network is in the hands of 27 private operators, each covering a different area. You can buy through tickets from any point in the country, even if it means using the services of more than one operator. Staff selling you tickets must sell you the cheapest ticket for that route, but the complexity of ticketing means they sometimes make mistakes. Rail is a comfortable, though not particularly cheap way of seeing the country, although delays do occur. Beware of weekend engineering works: maps showing affected services for each weekend ahead may be posted at stations: special bus services fill in for the closed sections of line but they add to the journey time.

Railway tickets are subject to numerous special deals; day return or saver tickets (return within a given period) are much cheaper than two single tickets for the same journey, but are subject to time restrictions (typically not to be used at peak times Monday to Friday); Saver tickets are more expensive on Fridays and on public holidays. Apex tickets give discounts for booking seven days or more in advance on long distance journeys. (BritRail Passes are only available to non-UK residents but will save money for those intending to make more than one long train journey; website: www.britrail.net.) A Young Persons Railcard (for under-26s and students), Senior Railcard (for over-60s) Disabled Persons Railcard and, in southeast England, a Network Card give a one-third discount. Bicycles are carried free on most services (check before travel).

Apart from the London–Scotland and London–Cornwall lines at peak periods, it is seldom necessary to reserve. For national rail enquiries tel: 0845 748 4950; minicom service for the deaf or hard of hearing tel: 0845 605 0600: website: www.nationalrail.co.uk.

Season tickets and memberships

Those intending to visit a number of stately homes and castles should consider taking out a membership for the National Trust (NT) and National Trust for Scotland (NTS) (see panel, page 102; note that membership of the NT entitles you to entry to NTS properties, and vice versa) and/or English Heritage (EH), Cadw (for Wales), Historic Scotland (HS) (see panel, page 124). Membership is available for all of these at any staffed property. Many other houses are under the Historic Houses Association, (2 Chester Street, London SW1X 7BB; tel: 020-7259 5688; website: www.hha.org.uk).

Senior citizens

Anyone aged 60 or over is entitled to a Senior Railcard and can get discounts for admissions.

Student and youth travel

Youth hostels These offer bargain accommodation. The Youth Hostels Association (YHA) has an excellent network of hostels ranging from primitive converted primary schools to manor houses and medieval castles. These can be better places for meeting people than guesthouses and hotels, especially the smaller and more personal youth hostels; some have stunning locations, such as in the Lake District, Snowdonia and the Scottish Highlands. There is no maximum age restriction.

Beds are usually in dormitories, although some hostels have family rooms; food is served at most hostels at set times, although it is always possible to cater for yourself. Few establishments allow hostellers to stay in during the day; at peak times and weekends it is advisable to reserve. You must join the YHA (unless you hold a youth hostel card from another country) to stay; membership can be taken out at hostels.

The central London information outlet is the YHA shop and YHA travel, both at 14 Southampton Street, WC2E 7HY, tel: 020-7379 0597; the head office is at Trevelyan House, Dimple Road, Matlock, Derbyshire DE4 3YH, tel: 0870 770 8868 (website: www.yha.org.uk). The Scottish YHA is based at 7 Glebe Crescent, Stirling FK8 2JA, tel: 0870 155 3255 (website: www.syha.org.uk).

International student cards These are useful to help gain reduced admission fees to tourist sights and entertainments. A Young Persons Railcard gives under-26s and students a third off the price of rail tickets.

Telephones

In emergencies tel: 999 02 112 (police, fire and ambulance); calls are free. Operator for national calls tel: 100; for international calls tel: 155 (both free). Directory enquiries for national calls tel: 118 500 (£1.10 per minute plus 10p connection charge from pay phones) or 118 141 (from 50p per minute plus 10p connection charge, from pay phones only); for international calls tel: 118 505 (£2 per minute plus 10p connection fee from pay phones). Calls on numbers prefixed 0800 are free.

To make a call from a public telephone, put the money in before you dial (if you put in large denomination coins, beware: you will not get change), and collect any unspent coins when you hang up. Phone cards are useful as some booths no longer take coins; they can be bought from post offices and newsagents in denominations of £5, £10 and £20. Mobile phones are hugely popular, and are sold at electrical shops and supermarkets. Prices vary enormously; very cheap models tend to incur high call charges, but if you are visiting Britain for a week or so this option may be practical. You can either 'pay as you go' and top up your phone account when required, or pay a monthly rental fee.

The dial tone is a continuous purr, the ringing tone is a repeated brr-brr, and a repeated single tone indicates the line is engaged; a continuous tone means the number is unobtainable or you may get an automated message.

To telephone abroad, dial 00 followed by the country's code, then by the local number minus the initial 0.

Australia 61
Canada 1
New Zealand 64
Republic of Ireland 353
US 1

Time

When it is 12 noon in Britain between the last Sunday in October and the last Saturday in March it is

273

CONVERSION CHARTS

FROM	TO	MULTIPLY BY
Inches	Centimetres	2.54
Centimetres	Inches	0.3937
Feet	Metres	0.3048
Metres	Feet	3.2810
Yards	Metres	0.9144
Metres	Yards	1.0940
Miles	Kilometres	1.6090
Kilometres	Miles	0.6214
Acres	Hectares	0.4047
Hectares	Acres	2.4710
Gallons	Litres	4.5460
Litres	Gallons	0.2200
Ounces	Grams	28.35
Grams	Ounces	0.0353
Pounds	Grams	453.6
Grams	Pounds	0.0022
Pounds	Kilograms	0.4536
Kilograms	Pounds	2.205
Tons	Tonnes	1.0160
Tonnes	Tons	0.9842

MEN'S SUITS

UK	36	38	40	42	44	46	48
Rest of Europe	46	48	50	52	54	56	58
US	36	38	40	42	44	46	48

DRESS SIZES

UK	8	10	12	14	16	18
France	36	38	40	42	44	46
Italy	38	40	42	44	46	48
Rest of Europe	34	36	38	40	42	44
US	6	8	10	12	14	16

MEN'S SHIRTS

UK	14	14.5	15	15.5	16	16.5	17
Rest of Europe	36	37	38	39/40	41	42	43
US	14	14.5	15	15.5	16	16.5	17

MEN'S SHOES

UK	7	7.5	8.5	9.5	10.5	11
Rest of Europe	41	42	43	44	45	46
US	8	8.5	9.5	10.5	11.5	12

WOMEN'S SHOES

UK	4.5	5	5.5	6	6.5	7
Rest of Europe	38	38	39	39	40	41
US	6	6.5	7	7.5	8	8.5

8–10pm in Australia, 4–8.30am in Canada, 12 noon in the Republic of Ireland, midnight in New Zealand and 2–7am in the US. The rest of the year, clocks go forward one hour to British Summer Time.

Tourist offices
There are more than 800 Tourist Information Centres in Britain, run by tourist boards for England, Wales and Scotland: most are well-signposted (look for the *i* sign). Many offer hotel booking services. Additionally, national parks have visitor centres with good local information.

The authority for tourism in Britain is Visit Britain at Thames Tower, Blacks Road, London W6 9EL. Their website is www.visitbritain.com, linking on to attractions, events and hotels; for information about England it is www.visitengland.com.

It has a US office at 7th Floor, 551 Fifth Avenue, Suite 701, New York, NY 10176-0799, tel: 1-800/462-2748. Website: www.visitbritain.com/usa.

Visit Scotland is at 23 Ravelston Terrace, Edinburgh EH4 3TP, tel: 0131 332 2433. Website: www.visitscotland.com.

The Wales Tourist Board, is at Brunel House, 2 Fitzalan Road, Cardiff CF4 0UY, tel: 0870 121 1251. Website: www.visitwales.com.

For details of any Tourist Information Centre in Britain, tel: 0900 219 2192 (50p per minute).

Walking and hiking
England and Wales are served by public rights of way, which cross private land but are open to walkers; Scotland has an informal rule tolerating access to open land except in the shooting seasons (see page 266). Public footpaths (marked with yellow arrows) are for walkers only; bridleways (marked in blue) are open to horseriders and cyclists too. National Trails are indicated with acorn motifs. Guided walks are offered by numerous bodies (contact Tourist Information Centres for details). If walking on your own, you need a good map (see Maps) and equipment: do not underestimate the mountains (see page 168).

Hotels and Restaurants

HOTELS

Tourist information offices hold lists of local hotels, and many provide a reservation service.

Bed-and-breakfast ('B&B') is ubiquitous and great value: typically it consists of a room in a private house (some have separate bathrooms) and use of a living room ('lounge'). Regional tourist boards publish lists of farmhouses, inns and guesthouses offering B&B (including Visit Britain's annual publication *Where to Stay: Bed and Breakfast*). Country house hotels give you the chance to stay in period country homes; many are privately run by families. Many pubs have a few rooms for overnight visitors. Generally, supply outstrips demand: provided you are prepared to drive to the next town, you will always find a bed, although be warned that the most popular resort towns and the Scottish Highlands get very busy in season. The following recommended hotels and inns are divided into three price categories, based on bed and breakfast for one person sharing a double- or twin-bedded room:

(£) = inexpensive: generally under £35.
(££) = moderate: generally £35–£60.
(£££) = expensive: generally over £60.

The AA Hotel Booking Service is a free, fast and easy way to find a place for a short break, holiday or business trip; simply visit the AA's website www.theAA.com/hotels to search around 8,000 hotels and bed-and-breakfasts in Britain and Ireland.

LONDON

Bayswater, Kensington, and Hyde Park
Delmere Hotel (£££)
130 Sussex Gardens W2 1UB
tel: 020-7706 3344;
www.bw-delmerehotel.co.uk
Friendly staff, well-equipped rooms, jazz-themed bar and a comfortable lounge.
Millennium Gloucester Hotel (£££)
4–18 Harrington Gardens, SW7 4LH
tel: 020-7373 6030;
www.millenniumhotels.com/gloucester
Cosmopolitan, stylish hotel; marble bathrooms, air conditioning.
Parkwood (££)
4 Stanhope Place, W2 2HB
tel: 020-7402 2241; www.parkwoodhotel.com
Pretty hotel overlooking Hyde Park.
Thistle Hyde Park (£££)
90–92 Lancaster Gate W2 3NR
tel: 020-7262 2711;
www.thistlehotels.com/hydepark
Elegant well-cared-for 'town house' style hotel.

Bloomsbury and West End
Bloomsbury Park (££)
126 Southampton Row, WC1B 5AD
tel: 0870 333 9104;
www.thistlehotels.com/bloomsburypark
Comfortable hotel catering for all markets.

Thistle Trafalgar Square (£££)
Whitcomb Street WC2H 7HG
tel: 020-7930 4477 or 0800 181716 (freephone); www.thistlehotels.com/trafalgarsquare
Popular hotel next to the National Gallery and convenient for many West End theatres.

Chelsea, Knightsbridge, and Victoria
Basil Street (£££)
8 Basil Street SW3 1AH tel: 020-7581 3311;
www.thebasil.com
Formal, old-fashioned yet stylish.
Quality Hotel Westminster (£££)
82–83 Eccleston Square SW1V 1PS
tel: 020-7834 8042;
www.hotels-westminster.com
A well-maintained, comfortable hotel.
The Rubens at the Palace (£££)
39–41 Buckingham Palace Road SW1W 0PS
tel: 020-7834 6600; www.rubenshotel.com
Luxury in an enviable location overlooking the Royal Mews behind Buckingham Palace.

Regent's Park
Hotel Ibis London Euston (££)
3 Cardington Street NW1 2LW
tel: 020-7388 7777; www.ibishotel.com
Popular and convenient for Euston Station, this good-value hotel also has a secure car park.
Thistle Euston (££)
Cardington Street NW1 2LP
tel: 0870 333 9107 or 0800 181716 (freephone); www.thistlehotels.com/euston
Modern hotel close to Euston Station.

Beyond the central area
Thistle City Barbican (£££)
Central Street EC1V 8DS tel: 0870 333 9101 or 0800 181716 (freephone); www.thistlehotels.com/citybarbican
Large, modern, near the Barbican arts complex and the City.
Justin James Hotel (£)
43 Worple Road SW19 4JZ
tel: 020-8947 4271; www.justinjameshotel.com
Pretty, creeper-clad Victorian house just minutes from Wimbledon station.
Thistle Tower (£££)
St. Katharine's Way E1W 1LD
tel: 0870 333 9106 or 0800 181716 (freephone); www.thistlehotels.com/tower
Modern hotel; fine views of Tower Bridge.

THE WEST COUNTRY

Bristol
Berkeley Square Hotel (££–£££)
15 Berkeley Square, Clifton BS8 1HB
tel: 0117 925 4000;
www.bestwestern.co.uk/berkeleysquare
Smart Georgian hotel with tastefully decorated rooms. Near the university and art gallery.
Rodney Hotel (££)
4 Rodney Place, Clifton BS8 4HY
tel: 0117 973 5422; www.cliftonhotels.com
Attractive terraced hotel with brightly decorated rooms. Convenient for the city and M5.

Hotels

Cornwall

Carbis Bay Hotel (££–£££)
Carbis Bay, St. Ives TR26 2NP
tel: 01736 795311; *www.carbisbayhotel.co.uk*
Family-run hotel in fine seaside location.

The Island (£££)
Tresco, Isles of Scilly TR24 0PU
tel: 01720 422883;
www.tresco.co.uk/holidays/island_hotel.asp
Modern hotel; island a refreshing getaway.

Pedn-Olva (££–£££)
West Porthminster Beach, St. Ives TR26 2EA
tel: 01736 796222
Friendly hotel affording glorious views across the bay.

Port Gaverne (££)
Port Gaverne, nr Port Isaac PL29 3SQ
tel: 01208 880244; freephone 0500 657867;
www.portgavernehotel.co.uk
Pleasant inn by a cove on an unspoiled coast.

Skidden House Hotel (££)
Skidden Hill, St. Ives TR26 2DU
tel: 01736 796899; *www.skiddenhouse.com*
The oldest hotel in St. Ives. Comfortable bedrooms, modern facilities.

Devon

Halmpstone Manor (££–£££)
Bishop's Tawton, nr Barnstaple EX32 0EA
tel: 01271 830321;
www.halmpstonemanor.co.uk
Lovely manor house surrounded by farmland.

Holne Chase (£££)
Two Bridges Road, nr Ashburton TQ13 7NS
tel: 01364 631471; *www.holne.chase.co.uk*
Peacefully located by the River Dart; well appointed rooms.

Oxenham Arms (£££)
South Zeal, nr Okehampton EX20 2JT
tel: 01837 840244;
www.theoxenhamarms.co.uk
Pleasant 15th-century inn in village street.

Royal Castle (££–£££)
11 The Quay, Dartmouth TQ6 9PS
tel: 01803 833033; *www.royalcastle.co.uk*
17th-century coaching inn on the waterside.

St. Olaves Court Restaurant and Hotel (££–£££)
Mary Arches Street, Exeter EX4 3AZ
tel: 01392 217736; *www.stolaves.co.uk*
Georgian-style house near cathedral.

Dorset

Plumber Manor (£££)
Hazelbury Bryan Road, Sturminster Newton DT10 2AF tel: 01258 472507;
www.plumbermanor.com
Jacobean manor with 16 bedrooms.

The Priory (£££)
Church Green, Wareham BH20 4ND
tel: 01929 551666;
www.theprioryhotel.co.uk
An 800-year-old priory with riverside gardens.

Somerset

Ashwick House (£££)
Dulverton TA22 9QD tel: 01398 323868
Grand turn of the 20th century country house in large grounds on the edge of Exmoor.

The Oaks (£££)
Porlock, nr Minehead TA24 8ES
tel: 01643 862265; *www.oakshotel.co.uk*
Enchanting Edwardian country house overlooking Porlock Bay.

Bath Paradise House Hotel (££)
86–88 Holloway, Bath BA2 4PX
tel: 01225 317723; *www.paradise-house.co.uk*
Quietly located in an elevated position, minutes from the middle of town.

The Royal Crescent (£££)
16 Royal Crescent, Bath BA1 2LS
tel: 01225 823333; *www.royalcrescent.co.uk*
On Bath's famous street; the interior matches the setting.

Wiltshire

Bradford Old Windmill (£)
4 Masons Lane, Bradford on Avon BA15 1QN
tel: 01225 866842;
www.bradfordoldwindmill.co.uk
Converted windmill with amusing décor.

Milford Hall (££–£££)
206 Castle Street, Salisbury SP1 3TE
tel: 01722 417411; *www.milfordhallhotel.com*
A personally managed Georgian mansion house close to the middle of town.

SOUTHERN ENGLAND

East Sussex

Adelaide (££)
51 Regency Square, Brighton BN1 2FF
tel: 01273 205286
Small hotel in elegant square facing the seafront.

The Courtlands (£–££)
15–27 The Drive, Hove BN3 3JE
tel: 01273 731055; *www.courtlandshotel.com*
Quietly situated, easy walk to town and seafront; swimming pool.

Jeake's House (££)
Mermaid Street, Rye TN31 7ET
tel: 01797 222828; *www.jeakeshouse.com*
Gabled, part tile-hung 17th-century house in cobbled street.

Isle of Wight

The George Hotel (£££)
Quay Street, Yarmouth PO41 0PE
tel: 01983 760331; *www.thegeorge.co.uk*
Historic townhouse between the pier and the castle. Decorated with style; restaurant is highly rated and brasserie is good for less formal meals.

Seaview Hotel (££–£££)
High Street, Seaview PO34 5EX
tel: 01983 612711; *www.seaviewhotel.co.uk*
First-class, ideal for families; nautical trappings.

Kent

Ebury (££)
65-67 New Dover Road, Canterbury CT1 3DX
tel: 01227 768433; *www.ebury-hotel.co.uk*
Fine period detailing; a very comfortable lounge and the restaurant is recommended.

The Falstaff Hotel (££)
8-12 St. Dunstan's Street, Canterbury CT2 8AF
tel: 0870 609 6102
Old coaching inn near Westgate Tower.

Hotels and Restaurants

Hotel Du Vin & Bistro (££–£££)
Crescent Road, Tunbridge Wells TN1 2LY
tel: 01892 526455; www.hotelduvin.com
Pleasantly old-fashioned hotel offering
spacious, simply decorated bedrooms.

The Limetree (££)
*8–10 The Limes, Lenham Square, Lenham, nr
Cranbrook ME17 2PQ tel: 01622 859509;
www.limetreerestaurant.co.uk*
Fine 14th-century timber-framed house with a
relaxed, peaceful air.

Wallett's Court Country House Hotel and Spa
(££–£££)
*West Cliffe, St. Margaret's-at-Cliffe, nr Dover
CT15 6EW tel: 01304 852424 or 0800 035
1628 (freephone); www.wallettscourt.com*
Old-fashioned rooms in manor house, newer
rooms in barn annexe.

HEART OF ENGLAND

Cotswolds
Bibury Court (£££)
*Bibury, nr Cirencester, Gloucestershire GL7 5NT
tel: 01285 740337; www.biburycourt.com*
Old-world Jacobean mansion by River Coln,
offering a relaxed retreat.

Buckland Manor (£££)
*Buckland, nr Broadway, Worcester WR12 7LY
tel: 01386 852626; www.bucklandmanor.com*
Top-class hotel in a medieval manor.

Cotswold House (£££)
*The Square, Chipping Campden,
Gloucestershire GL55 6AN tel: 01386
840330; www.cotswoldhouse.com*
Formal elegance with murals and antiques.

Herefordshire
Feathers (£££)
*High Street, Ledbury HR8 1DS
tel: 01531 635760; www.feathersledbury.co.uk*
Striking, black-and-white timber-framed
coaching inn with traditional interior décor.

Oxfordshire
Beetle and Wedge (£££)
*Ferry Lane, Moulsford-on-Thames OX10 9JF
tel: 01491 651381; www.beetleandwedge.co.uk*
Ideal for exploring the Thames Valley.

Linton Lodge (£££)
*13 Linton Road, Oxford OX2 6UJ
tel: 01865 553461; www.lintonlodge.com*
Large hotel comprising several houses close to
colleges and river.

The Randolph (£££)
*Beaumont Street, Oxford OX1 2LN
tel: 0870 400 8200*
Large, comfortable hotel in the heart of the city.

Stonor Arms (£££)
*Stonor, Henley-on-Thames RG9 6HE
tel: 01491 638866*
An 18th-century inn in peaceful village near deer
park and walks. Two restaurants.

White Hart (££–£££)
*High Street, Dorchester on Thames OX10 7HN
tel: 01865 340074; www.oxford-restaurants-
hotels.co.uk*
Charming, friendly inn located in historic village.

Shropshire
Cliffe (£–££)
Dinham, Ludlow SY8 2JE tel: 01584 872063
Friendly hotel with castle views.

Overton Grange Country House (££–£££)
*Old Hereford Road, Ludlow SY8 4AD
tel: 01584 873500;
www.overtongrangehotel.com*
An Edwardian mansion set in attractive gardens
and surrounded by the Welsh Marches.

Warwickshire
Billesley Manor (£££)
*Billesley, Alcester, Stratford-upon-Avon B49 6NF
tel: 01789 279955; www.billesleymanor.co.uk*
Peacefully sited 16th-century manor house.

The Falcon (££)
*Chapel Street, Stratford-upon-Avon CV37 6HA
tel: 01789 279953*
Traditional inn in the heart of town. Pretty
gardens, pleasant restaurant.

White Swan (££)
*Rother Street, Stratford-upon-Avon CV37 6NH
tel: 01789 297022;
www.thewhiteswanstratford.co.uk*
Half-timbered building with modern facilities.

EASTERN ENGLAND

Cambridgeshire
Arundel House (££)
*53 Chesterton Road, Cambridge CB4 3AN
tel: 01223 367701;
www.arundelhousehotels.co.uk*
Victorian terrace by Jesus Green.

Best Western Gonville (£££)
*Gonville Place, Cambridge CB1 1LY
tel: 01223 366611; www.gonvillehotel.co.uk*
Traditional hotel by Parker's Piece park.

Cambridge Garden House Moat House (££)
*Granta Place, Mill Lane, Cambridge CB2 1RT tel:
01223 259988; www.moathousehotels.com*
Modern riverside hotel, close to colleges.

The George of Stamford (££–£££)
*71 St Martins, Stamford PE9 2LB
tel: 01780 750750;
www.georgehotelofstamford.com*
Splendid coaching inn; elegant public rooms and
a good restaurant.

Lincolnshire
D'Isney Place (££)
*Eastgate, Lincoln LN2 4AA tel: 01522 538881;
www.disneyplacehotel.co.uk*
Red-brick house (1735) offering bed-and-
breakfast, near cathedral.

Norfolk
Beaumaris (££)
*15 South Street, Sheringham NR26 8LL
tel: 01263 822370;
www.thebeaumarishotel.co.uk*
Five minutes from seafront and town.

Morston Hall (£££ inc. dinner)
*Morston, Holt NR25 7AA
tel: 01263 741041; www.morstonhall.com*
By marshes, a 17th-century brick-and-flint house;
four bedrooms; great restaurant.

The Maids Head Hotel (££)
Tombland, Norwich NR3 1LB
tel: 0870 609 6110;
www.corushotels.co.uk/maidshead
Dating from 1272, England's oldest hotel in continuous use; the best bet in the city.
Quality Hotel Norwich (££)
2 Barnard Road, Bowthorpe, Norwich NR5 9JB
tel: 01603 741161;
www.choicehotelseurope.com
Modern hotel on outskirts of the city.

Suffolk
Great House (££–£££)
Market Place, Lavenham CO10 9QZ
tel: 01787 247431; www.greathouse.co.uk
Georgian exterior belies an ancient timber-framed structure. Only four bedrooms.
Swan (£££)
Market Place, Southwold IP18 6EG
tel: 01502 722186
Traditional hotel; good standards of comfort.

WALES

Brecon Beacons
Gliffaes Country House Hotel (££–£££)
nr Crickhowell NP8 1RH tel: 01874 730371 or 0800 146719 (freephone);
www.gliffaeshotel.com
Traditional family-run hotel, overlooking River Usk and set in parkland; good fishing nearby.
Llangoed Hall (£££)
Llyswen LD3 0YP tel: 01874 754525;
www.llangoedhall.com
Stylish Edwardian country house with personal touches; classic cooking.

Monmouthshire
Crown at Whitebrook (£££ inc. dinner)
Whitebrook, nr Monmouth NP25 4TX tel: 01600 860254;
www.crownwhitebrook.co.uk
Small with pretty rooms, comfortable lounge; in densely wooded valley.
Parva Farmhouse Hotel and Restaurant (££)
Tintern Parva, nr Chepstow NP6 6SQ
tel: 01291 689411; www.hoteltintern.co.uk
Comfortable without being cute.
Three Salmons (££–£££)
Porthycarne Street, Usk NP15 1RY
tel: 01291 672133;
www.3-salmons-usk.co.uk
Charming mid-town coaching inn that has a stylish appeal.

Pembrokeshire
Penally Abbey Country House (£££)
Penally, nr Tenby SA70 7PY
tel: 01834 843033; www.penally-abbey.com
Georgian house, close to coast, four-poster beds; French-influenced cooking.

Powys
Lake Country House (£££)
Llangammarch Wells LD4 4BS tel: 01591 620202; www.lakecountryhouse.co.uk
A graceful retreat near Llandrindod Wells.

Snowdonia
Bodysgallen Hall (£££)
near Llandudno, LL30 1RS tel 01492 584466
Historic country house hotel and spa in its own parkland; gardens include a 17th-century parterre and follies.
Maes y Neuadd Country House (£££ inc. dinner)
Talsarnau, nr Harlech, Caernarfonshire LL47 6YA tel: 01766 780200;
www.neuadd.com
Ancient building with splendid views.
The Old Rectory Country House (£££)
Llanwrst Road, Llansanffraid Glan Conwy, Conwy LL28 5LF tel: 01492 580611;
www.oldrectorycountryhouse.co.uk
Fine views of mountains and Conwy Castle; gourmet dinners.
The Hotel Portmeirion (£££)
Portmeirion, Gwynedd LL48 6ET
tel: 01766 770000; www.portmeirion-village.com
Hotel fronts estuary and has lavish interior.
Princes Arms Country Hotel (£ ££)
Trefriw, Conwy, LL27 0JP
tel: 01492 640592; www.princes-arms.co.uk
Family-run hotel with splendid views across the Conwy Valley. A wonderful place to stay.
The St. Tudno Hotel and Restaurant (££–£££)
Promenade, Llandudno, Conwy LL30 2LP
tel: 01492 874411; www.st-tudno.co.uk
Oustanding hospitality on the seafront.

Swansea
Fairyhill (£££)
Reynoldston, Gower, Swansea SA3 1BS
tel: 01792 390139; www.fairyhill.net
Mansion with own trout stream; local dishes feature on an ambitious menu.

NORTHWEST ENGLAND

Cheshire
The Chester Grosvenor and Grosvenor Spa (£££)
Eastgate, Chester CH1 1LT tel: 01244 324024; www.chestergrosvenor.com
Five-star luxury hotel at the heart of the city.

The Lake District, Cumbria
The Mill (££)
Mungrisdale, nr Penrith CA11 0XR
tel: 017687 79659
Comfortable, informal former mill cottage.
The Old Vicarage (££)
Church Road, Witherslack, nr Grange-over-Sands LA11 6RS tel: 015395 52381;
www.theold-vicarage.co.uk
Fine cooking, very comfortable; beneath Whitbarrow Scar.
Patterdale (£–££)
Patterdale, Ullswater CA11 0NN
tel: 0845 458 4333 or 017684 82231;
www.patterdale.co.uk
Fine views of the valley and fells.
Sharrow Bay Country House Hotel (£££)
Lake Ullswater, Howtown, nr Penrith CA10 2LZ
tel: 017684 86301; www.sharrow-bay.com
One of Lakeland's most celebrated hotels, Sharrow Bay is highly rated for comfort and its cuisine.

279

Skiddaw (£££)
Main Street, Keswick CA12 5BN
tel: 017687 72071; www.skiddawhotel.co.uk
Pleasant hotel and restaurant in the heart of town.
The Trout (££–£££)
Crown Street, Cockermouth CA13 0EJ
tel: 01900 823591; www.trouthotel.co.uk
This long established, welcoming hotel is by
the banks of the River Derwent. It also has an
attractive restaurant.
Wasdale Head Inn (££)
Wasdale Head, nr Gosforth CA20 1EX
tel: 019467 26229; www.wasdale.com
Long-established haunt of walkers and climbers;
in spectacular isolated position.
White Moss House (£££ inc. dinner)
Rydal Water, Grasmere LA22 9SE
tel: 015394 35295; www.whitemoss.com
Elegant house (formerly owned by Wordsworth
family); English cuisine.

The Peak District, Derbyshire
Cavendish (£££)
Baslow, Derbyshire DE45 1SP
tel: 01246 582311; www.cavendish-hotel.net
High-class comfort in a civilized retreat in the
Chatsworth estate.
Riber Hall (£££)
nr Matlock, Derbyshire DE4 5JU
tel: 01629 582795; www.riber-hall.co.uk
Charming Elizabethan manor house perched
above Derwent Gorge; period character but
modern facilities.

NORTHEAST ENGLAND

County Durham
The Postchaise Hotel (££)
36 Market Place, Bishop Auckland DL14 7NX
tel: 01388 661296
Old hostelry; lively atmosphere and good value.
Home-cooked meals.
Durham Marriott Hotel, Royal County (£££)
Old Elvet, Durham DH1 3JN
tel: 0191-386 6821
Ample, comfortable hotel, on the river bank.
Swallow Three Tuns (££–£££)
New Elvet, Durham DH1 3AQ
tel: 0191-386 4326; www.swallowhotels.com
Old-established, comfortable central hotel.

North York Moors, North Yorkshire
Lastingham Grange (£££)
Lastingham YO62 6TH tel: 01751 417345;
www.lastinghamgrange.com
Old-fashioned, welcoming, in tranquil village.
Mallyan Spout (£££)
The Common, Goathland, nr Whitby YO22 5AN
tel: 01947 896486; www.mallyanspout.co.uk
Located in a village in fine walking country.

Northumberland
White Swan (£££)
Bondgate Within, nr Alnwick NE66 1TD
tel: 01665 602109;
www.classiclodges.co.uk/swanhome
Elegant 300-year-old hotel in town.

York
Abbots Mews (£–££)
6 Marygate Lane, Bootham YO30 7DE
tel: 01904 634866
Just outside city walls, quiet former coachman's
cottage.
Cottage (£–££)
3–5 Clifton Green, Clifton YO30 6OH tel:
01904 643711
Attractive, friendly, and close to central city.
Mount Royale (££–£££)
117–119 The Mount YO24 1GU
tel: 01904 628856;
www.mountroyale.co.uk
Two early 19th-century houses with antiques,
plants, and a welcoming atmosphere.

Yorkshire Dales, North Yorkshire
Amerdale House (£££ inc. dinner)
Arncliffe, nr Skipton BD23 5QE
tel: 01756 770250
Manor house in beautiful setting; run with flair.
Ashfield House (££)
Summers Fold, Grassington, nr Skipton BD23 5AE
tel: 01756 752584;
www.ashfieldgrassington.co.uk
Small hotel off the Square: rustic décor.

SOUTHERN SCOTLAND

Borders (Scottish)
Burts (££)
Market Square, Melrose TD6 9PL
tel: 01896 822285; www.burtshotel.co.uk
This family-run country town hotel is within
easy driving distance of 16 golf courses.
Welcoming atmosphere.
Cringletie House (££–£££)
Edinburgh Road, Peebles EH45 8PL
tel: 01721 725750; www.cringletie.com
Romantic-looking country house, family-run.

Dumfries and Galloway
Balcary Bay (££–£££)
Shore Road, Auchencairn, nr Kirkcudbright
DG7 1QZ tel: 01556 640217;
www.balcary-bay-hotel.co.uk
Small, lone hotel, pleasantly located on
Balcary Bay.
Knockinaam Lodge (£££)
Portpatrick, Rhinns of Galloway DG9 9AD
tel: 01776 810471;
www.knockinaamlodge.com
Views to Mountains of Mourne in Ireland.

East Lothian
Greywalls (£££)
Gullane, Muirfield EH31 2EG
tel: 01620 842144; www.greywalls.co.uk
Designed by Lutyens, overlooks golf links.

Edinburgh
Caledonian Hilton Edinburgh (£££)
Princes Street EH1 2AB tel: 0131-222 8888;
www.hilton.com/caledonian
Hundred-year-old former railway hotel;
grand foyer, attractive rooms, friendly service,
with castle views.

The Howard (£££)
34 Great King Street EH3 6QH
tel: 0131-557 9303; www.thehoward.com
Five-star comfort in a Georgian terrace in the city's New Town.
Rothesay (£–££)
8 Rothesay Place EH3 7SL
tel: 0131-622 6800; www.festival-inns.co.uk
Reasonably priced, family-run hotel.
Roxburghe (£££)
38 Charlotte Square EH2 4HG
tel: 0131-240 5500; www.roxburghe-hotel.co.uk
Fine example of Adam architecture minutes from Princes Street; range of bedrooms.

Fife

Old Course Hotel, Golf Resort and Spa (£££)
Old Station Road, St. Andrews KY16 9SP
tel: 01334 474371; www.oldcoursehotel.co.uk
By the famous golf course and the sea; elegant, well-equipped and comfortable.
Scores (££ £££)
76 The Scores, St. Andrews KY16 9BB
tel: 01334 472451; www.scoreshotel.co.uk
In two 1880s terraces; seafront view. Convenient for Old Course.

Glasgow

Best Western Ewington (£–££)
Balmoral Terrace, 132 Queens Drive G42 8QW
tel: 0141-423 1152; www.countryhotels.net
Well-equipped, friendly, overlooks Queens Park.
Malmaison (£££)
278 West George Street G2 4LL
tel: 0141-572 1000; www.malmaison.com
The bedrooms at Malmaison are both striking and stylish, with state-of-the-art equipment including ISDN lines and CD players.
One Devonshire Gardens (£££)
1 Devonshire Gardens G12 0UX
tel: 0141 339 2001;
www.onedevonshiregardens.com
Elegant hotel occupying three town houses.

Stirling

Roman Camp Country House (££–£££)
Main Street, Callander FK17 8BG
tel: 01877 330003;
www.roman-camp-hotel.co.uk
Manor house on River Teith.
Terraces (££)
4 Melville Terrace, Stirling FK8 2ND
tel: 01786 472268; www.terraceshotel.com
Welcoming hotel convenient for the central area.

NORTHERN SCOTLAND

Aberdeenshire

Banchory Lodge (£££)
Banchory AB31 5HS
tel: 01330 822625; www.banchorylodge.co.uk
Rambling Georgian house in secluded gardens; antiques, and hearty Scottish fare.
Kildrummy Castle (£££)
Kildrummy, Alford AB33 8RA
tel: 019755 71288
Victorian mansion by castle ruin.

Argyll and Bute

Airds (£££ including dinner)
Port Appin PA38 4DF
tel: 01631 730236; www.airds-hotel.com
Small hotel with views of Loch Linnhe.
Isle of Eriska (£££)
Eriska, Ledaig PA37 1SD
tel: 01631 720371; www.eriska-hotel.co.uk
Idyllic island setting (bridge to mainland); putting green, croquet lawn. Pretty rooms.

Highland

Ardsheal House (££)
Kentallen of Appin, Glencoe PA38 4BX
tel: 01631 740227; www.ardsheal.co.uk
Good base for Loch Linnhe and Glen Coe.
Arisaig Hotel (££)
Arisaig PH39 4NH
tel: 01687 450210; www.arisaighotel.co.uk
Austere exterior, attractive interior. Imaginative menu.
Ceilidh Place (f.f.)
14 West Argyll Street, Ullapool IV26 2TY
tel: 01854 612103
Bookshop, gallery, coffee and wine bar as well as hotel; friendly owners; simple bedrooms.
Columba House (££)
Manse Road, Kingussie PH21 1JF
tel: 01540 661402;
www.columbahousehotel.co.uk
Comfortable 19th-century manse in elevated grounds; good home cooking.
Dunain Park (££–£££)
nr Inverness IV3 8JN tel: 01463 230512;
www.dunainparkhotel.co.uk
Friendly house with good country cooking.
Kilcamb Lodge (££ £££)
Strontian, Acharacle PH36 4HY
tel: 01967 402257; www.kilcamblodge.co.uk
Friendly hotel with fine views of Loch Sunart.
Kinloch Lodge (£££)
Isle Ornsay, Sleat, Isle of Skye IV43 8QY
tel: 01471 833214; www.kinloch-lodge.co.uk
Friendly Gaelic hotel; small and peaceful.
Royal Hotel (££)
Bank Street, Portree, Isle of Skye IV51 9BU
tel: 01478 612525; www.royal-hotel-skye.com
Hotel with health and leisure facilities.

Perth and Kinross

Guinach House (££)
By the Birks, Urlar Road, Aberfeldy PH15 2ET
tel: 01887 820251; www.guinachhouse.co.uk
Edwardian house, off A826, open fire, books; fine cooking, own produce.
Killiekrankie House (££)
Killiekrankie PH16 5LG tel: 01796 473220;
www.killiekrankiehotel.co.uk
Delightful hotel in extensive grounds. Bedrooms are light, and public rooms include a sun lounge and a bar.

Shetland

Busta House (££–£££)
Brae ZE2 9QN tel: 01806 522506;
www.bustahouse.com
Charming 16th-century former laird's home in its own grounds.

RESTAURANTS

Meals at the following restaurants are divided into three price categories:
(£) = inexpensive: probably under £15 per head.
(££) = moderate: probably £15–£30 per head.
(£££) = expensive: probably over £30 per head.

LONDON

For further suggestions, see page 59.

Alastair Little (££–£££)
49 Frith Street W1V 5TE
tel: 020-7734 5183
Unassuming Soho restaurant, minimalist décor, but high-quality modern British dishes.
Crivelli's Garden (£££)
The National Gallery, Trafalgar Square WC2N 5DN tel: 020-7747 2869;
www.thenationalgallery.com
Accomplished innovative cooking on the mezzanine level of the Sainsbury wing.
Le Gavroche (£££)
43 Upper Brook Street W1K 7QR
tel: 020-7408 0881 and 020-7499 1826;
www.le-gavroche.co.uk
Superlative restaurant; a friendly atmosphere.
The Ivy (££)
1 West Street WC2H 9NQ tel: 020-7836 4751
A fashionable brasserie where regulars return again and again; classic dishes. Book ahead.
J. Sheekey (££–£££)
28–32 St. Martin's Court WC2N 4AL
tel: 020-7240 2565
One of London's best-known seafood restaurants, serving traditional English fish dishes.
Lindsay House (££–£££)
21 Romilly Street W1D 5AF
tel: 020-7439 0450; www.lindsayhouse.co.uk
Irish chef Richard Corrigan's Celtic roots are very evident in a gutsy, almost robust style.
Mirabelle (££)
56 Curzon Street W1Y 8DL
tel: 020-7499 4636; www.whitestarline.org.uk
First-rate classic French cooking is especially good-value at lunch. It is essential to book.
St. John (££)
26 St. John Street EC1M 4AY
tel: 020-7251 0848/7251 4998;
www.stjohnrestaurant.co.uk
Fergus Henderson reworks traditional English recipes and explores Mediterranean dishes.

THE WEST COUNTRY

Bristol
riverstation (£–££)
The Grove BS1 4RB tel: 0117 914 4434;
www.riverstation.co.uk
A relaxed bistro as well as an upbeat restaurant. The food has a Mediterranean slant.

Cornwall
The Kitchen (££)
The Coombes, Polperro PL13 2RQ tel: 01503 272780; www.thekitchenatpolperro.co.uk
Cottage featuring fresh fish caught locally.

Old Custom House Inn, Pescadon Restaurant (£££)
South Quay, Padstow PL28 8BL tel: 01841 532359; www.westcountryhotelrooms.co.uk
This attractive restaurant by the waterside has an imaginative fixed-price menu.

Devon
22 Mill Street (££–£££)
22 Mill Street, Chagford TQ13 8AW
tel: 01647 432244
The restaurant is comfortable, though small, and the cooking is assured.
The New Angel (£££)
2 South Embankment, Dartmouth TQ6 9BH
tel: 01803 839425; www.thenewangel.co.uk
French regional and British cuisine, with personal touches. A national institution.
Chough's Nest Hotel (££)
North Walk, Lynton EX35 6HJ tel: 01598 753315; www.choughsnesthotel.co.uk
Interesting dinners in a bright, airy dining room.
Holne Chase Hotel (££–£££)
Two Bridges Road, Ashburton, Newton Abbot TQ13 7NS tel: 01364 631471;
www.holne-chase.co.uk
Former hunting lodge; renowned for lamb and seafood.
The Old Rectory (£££)
Martinhoe, Barnstaple EX31 4QT
tel: 01598 763368;
www.oldrectoryhotel.co.uk
Stylish décor and delicious home-cooked meals.
Rising Sun Hotel (£–£££)
Harbourside, Lynmouth EX35 6EG tel: 01598 753223; www.risingsunlynmouth.co.uk
Former smugglers' inn, now a restaurant and bar; accommodation available.

Dorset
Bistro on the Beach (££)
Solent Promenade, Southbourne Coast Road, Bournemouth BH6 4BE tel: 01202 431473;
www.bistroonthebeach.co.uk
Fresh seafood that draws the crowds. Reserve some weeks in advance.

Somerset
The Moody Goose (£–££)
7A Kingsmead Square, Bath BA1 2AB
tel: 01225 466688; www.moody-goose.com
A stylish restaurant with modern British and French food.

SOUTHERN ENGLAND

Berkshire
Waterside Inn (£££)
Ferry Road, Bray, nr Windsor SL6 2AT
tel: 01628 620691; www.waterside-inn.co.uk
Splendid restaurant serving French cuisine; accommodation available.

East Sussex
Terre à Terre (££)
71 East Street, Brighton BN1 1HQ
tel: 01273 729051; www.terreaterre.co.uk
Innovative vegetarian meals.

Kent

Rankins (£–££)
*The Street, Sissinghurst TN17 2JH tel: 01580
713964; www.rankinsrestaurant.com*
Bistro-style European/Mediterranean cuisine,
using local produce.

Restaurant 23 (££)
*23 Stone Street, Cranbrook TN17 3HF
tel: 01580 714666*
Country pine chic; European/Mediterranean-
based menu that ranges from snacks to
three-course meals.

Thackeray's House (££–£££)
*85 London Road, Tunbridge Wells TN1 1EA
tel: 01892 511921;
www.thackerays-restaurant.co.uk*
Historic house linked with William Makepeace
Thackeray; accomplished, uncomplicated
cooking.

The Whitstable Oyster Fishery Co (££)
*17–20 Sea Street, Whitstable CT5 1AN
tel: 01227 276856* .
The best seafood restaurant in the area. Look
out for native Whitstable oysters. Book a table,
especially at weekends.

New Forest, Hampshire

Simply Poussin (£££)
*The Courtyard, Brookley Road, Brockenhurst
S042 7RB tel: 01590 623063;
www.simplypoussin.co.uk*
Delicious, well-presented ingredients.

HEART OF ENGLAND

Cotswolds

Feathers Hotel (££–£££)
*Market Street, Woodstock, Oxfordshire
OX20 1SX tel: 01993 812291;
www.feathers.co.uk*
A gracious old hotel with daily menu; close to
Blenheim Palace.

Harry Hare's (£–££)
*3 Gosditch Street, Cirencester, Gloucestershire
GL7 2AG tel: 01285 652375*
Popular all-day eaterie, from breakfast (brunch
at weekends) to supper. There's a Mediterranean bias, but fish and chips too.

The Inn for all Seasons (££)
*The Barringtons, Burford, Oxfordshire OX18 4TN
tel: 01451 844324;
www.innforallseasons.com*
Generous portions of home-cooked food, served
in both the bar and stone-walled restaurant.

The Lygon Arms (£££)
*High Street, Broadway, Worcestershire WR12
7DU tel: 01386 852255;
www.thelygonarms.co.uk*
Traditional fare served in the stunning Great
Hall of this distinctive hotel.

Herefordshire and Worcestershire

The Evesham Hotel (££)
*Coopers Lane, off Waterside, Evesham,
Worcestershire WR11 6DA
tel: 01386 765566;
www.eveshamhotel.com*
Friendly, with acclaimed menu and wine list.

The Salutation Inn (£–££)
*Market Pitch, Weobley, nr Hereford,
Herefordshire HR4 8SJ
tel: 01544 318443*
Medieval inn in picturesque village; good-value
Sunday lunch.

Oxfordshire

Le Manoir aux Quat' Saisons (£££)
*Church Road, Great Milton OX44 7PD
tel: 01844 278881; www.manoir.com*
Some of the finest, most inspired cooking in the
land. Splendid bedrooms.

Quod Restaurant & Bar (£–££)
*Old Bank Hotel, 92–94 High Street, Oxford OX1
4BN tel: 01865 202505; www.quod.co.uk*
All-day bar and grill in a converted bank building.

Warwickshire

Billesley Manor Hotel (££–£££)
*Billesley, Alcester, nr Stratford-upon-Avon B49 6NF
tel: 01789 279955; www.billesleymanor.co.uk*
Imposing 16th-century house visited by
Shakespeare. Afternoon tea available.

EASTERN ENGLAND

Cambridgeshire

Cambridge Lodge Hotel (££)
*139 Huntingdon Road, Cambridge CB3 0DQ
tel: 01223 352833;
www.smoothhound.co.uk/hotels/cambridge*
Classic cuisine in comfortable surroundings.

Midsummer House (££–£££)
*Midsummer Common, Cambridge CD4 1HA
tel: 01223 369299;
www.midsummerhouse.co.uk*
A short walk from the central city; excellent
wines and cheeses.

The Old Fire Engine House (££)
*25 St. Mary's Street, Ely CB7 4ER tel: 01353
662582; www.theoldfireenginehouse.co.uk*
Eat in the quarry-tiled rear garden in summer.

Essex

White Hart (£–££)
*Poole Street, Great Yeldham CO9 4HJ tel:
01787 237250; www.whitehartyeldham.co.uk*
Old Tudor pub serving good food and wines.

Lincolnshire

Wig & Mitre (££)
*30–32 Steep Hill, Lincoln LN2 1TL
tel: 01522 535190; www.wigandmitre.com*
Brasserie-style 14th-century inn; on a
picturesque street, close to the cathedral.

Norfolk

Adlard's (££–£££)
*79 Upper St. Giles Street, Norwich NR2 1AB
tel: 01603 633522; www.adlards.co.uk*
Friendly service; fixed-price British/French
menus; good-value lunches.

The Merchant House (£–££)
*8–10 St. Andrews Hill, Norwich NR2 1AD tel:
01603 767321; www.merchants-house.co.uk*
A central, 17th-century merchant's house; mod
ern British with a French influence.

Hotels and Restaurants

Suffolk

The Crown (££)
*90 High Street, Southwold IP18 6DP
tel: 01502 722275; www.adnams.co.uk*
Elegant posting inn with excellent fish;
reservations are recommended.

WALES

Brecon Beacons

The Griffin Inn (££)
Llyswen LD3 0UR tel: 01874 754241
Local produce features strongly in the dishes of
this very popular country inn.

Snowdonia

Castle Cottage (££)
*Pen Llech, Harlech, Gwynedd LL46 2YL tel: 01766
780479; www.castlecottageharlech.co.uk*
Highly acclaimed cooking in 16th-century cottage.
Shakespeare (££–£££)
*Castle Hotel, High Street, Conwy LL32 8DB tel:
01492 582300*
Luscious Victorian setting for Welsh cuisine. The
hotel itself is full of antiques and pictures, and
furnished with great flair.

NORTHWEST ENGLAND

The Lake District

Appleby Manor Country House Hotel (££)
*Roman Road, Appleby-in-Westmorland, Cumbria
CA16 6JB tel: 017683 51571;
www.applebymanor.co.uk*
Imaginative dishes and generous portions.
The Punchbowl (£–££)
*Crossthwaite, Kendal, Cumbria LA8 8HR tel:
015395 68237; www.punchbowl.fsnet.co.uk*
A 17th-century coaching inn. Fine wines and
modern British cooking. Must book.

Cheshire

Broxton Hall Country House Hotel (£££)
*Whitchurch Road, Broxton, Chester CH3 9JS
tel: 01829 782321; www.broxtonhall.co.uk*
A fine collection of dishes; lovely gardens.

The Peak District

Fischer's Baslow Hall (££–£££)
*Baslow Hall, Calver Road, Baslow, Derbyshire
DE45 1RR tel: 01246 583259;
www.fischers-baslowhall.co.uk*
Sophisticated European cuisine.

NORTHEAST ENGLAND

Northumberland

Lord Crewe Arms Hotel (£££)
*Blanchland, Nr Consett DH8 9SP
tel: 01434 675251; www.lordcrewehotel.com*
A 12th-century lodging house for monks.

North York Moors

Milburn Arms Hotel (£–££)
*Rosedale Abbey, Pickering, North Yorkshire
YO18 8RA tel: 01751 417312;
www.milburnarms.co.uk*
Imaginative use of local ingredients.

York

Melton's (£–££)
*7 Scarcroft Road, York YO23 1ND
tel: 01904 634341*
The cooking is Anglo-French and everything is
made on the premises, including the bread.

Yorkshire Dales

Devonshire Arms Country House Hotel (£££)
*Bolton Abbey, Skipton, North Yorkshire
BD23 6AJ tel: 01756 710441;
www.devonshirehotels.co.uk*
Quality dishes featuring local produce.

SOUTHERN SCOTLAND

Borders (Scottish)

Burts Hotel (££–£££)
*Market Square, Melrose TD6 9PL
tel: 01896 822285; www.burtshotel.co.uk*
Fine 18th-century inn with fixed-price menu.

Edinburgh

Iggs (££)
15 Jeffrey Street EH1 1DR tel: 0131-557 8184
Spanish and Mediterranean dishes.
Martin's (££)
*70 Rose Street, North Lane EH2 3DX
tel: 0131-225 3106*
Unpretentious, quality modern British cooking.

Fife

The Peat Inn (£££)
*Cupar, near St. Andrews KY15 5LH
tel: 01334 840206; www.thepeatinn.co.uk*
One of the best-known restaurants in Scotland.
Classical French cuisine.

Glasgow

The Buttery (££–£££)
652 Argyle Street G3 8UF tel: 0141-221 8188
Traditional Scottish and French food in opulent
Victorian surroundings.
Ubiquitous Chip (££–£££)
*12 Ashton Lane G12 8SJ tel: 0141-334 5007;
www.ubiquitouschip.co.uk*
Ex-warehouse off Byres Road; Scottish dishes
(but no chips!).

NORTHERN SCOTLAND

Perth and Kinross

Killiecrankie House Hotel (££)
*Killiecrankie, nr Pitlochry PH16 5LG tel: 01796
473220; www.killiecrankiehotel.co.uk*
Scottish game, meat and fish.

Highland

Hotel Eilean Iarmain (£££)
*Isle Ornsay IV43 8QR tel: 01471 833332;
www.eilean-iarmain.co.uk*
Small inn looking over Sound of Sleat; home
cooking; good wines.
River House (£–££)
*1 Greig Street, Inverness IV3 5PT
tel: 01463 222033*
Riverside-restaurant with fine Scottish ingredients
such as salmon, haggis, Orkney crab and venison.

Index

Index/Acknowledgements

Picture credits

The Automobile Association would like to thank the following for their assistance in the preparation of this book.
ALTON TOWERS 263l; **AMBERLEY WORKING MUSEUM** 97t; **BRIDGEMAN ART LIBRARY** 149c *Fishing Boats off Yarmouth* by John Sell Cotman (1782–1842) Christies, London/Bridgeman Art Libarary, London; **BRITAIN ON VIEW** 152, 160, 161; **TIM LOCKE** 8b; **RITZ HOTEL** 59b; **WOOKEY HOLE** 85

All remaining pictures are held in the Association's own picture library (**AA WORLD TRAVEL LIBRARY**) with contributions from:
M ADELMAN 36, 41, 227, 238, 261t, 261b, 262b; **P AITHIE** 151; **M ALLWOOD-COPPIN** 26/27t, 130t, 130b; **A BAKER** 4, 20b, 64b, 69b, 112, 123b, 179, 198t, 198c, 198b, 208t, 212, 230t, 230b, 231, 232, 252, 256; **P BAKER** 21b, 23b, 26b, 44, 60, 63, 68, 73, 74, 75c, 75b, 77, 101b, 140, 173bl, 186t, 187, 197, 203t, 206t; **J BEAZLEY** 16t, 186c, 190, 194cl, 194cr, 196cr, 199, 200, 214, 216, 217, 218b, 221, 222b, 237, 249t, 259; **A W BESLEY** 70br, 71t; **M BIRKITT** 5b, 28b, 65, 84, 95t, 111, 131, 133, 135; **E A BOWNESS** 18t, 173br, 243; **P BROWN** 12c, 20t, 86, 88b, 90, 91, 99, 104t, 105; **D BURCHILL** 174; **I BURGUM** 110, 123t, 123c, 124b, 150, 155t, 156t, 157b, 162, 164t, 165t, 165b, 167, 168, 169t, 169b, 171b, 269; **M BUSSELLE** 94b; **J CARNIE** 233t, 242, 245t, 245c, 246b, 253c, 258; **T COHEN** 263r; **D CORRANCE** 225, 233c; **D CROUCHER** 159t, 163, 164c, 222c; **P DAVIES** 146, 147; **S DAY** 8t, 117, 176t, 236; **P EDEN** 100b; **R ELLIOTT** 224, 226/227; **P ENTICKNAP** 108; **R FLETCHER** 34b; **D FORSS** 15t, 50, 81b, 89, 92, 95c, 98, 102b, 103, 109t, 109c, 128t, 128b, 142t; **STEPHEN GIBSON PHOTOGRAPHY** 213, 228, 229t, 229b; **J GRAVELL** 166; **V GREAVES** 132; **S GREGORY** 202; **A GRIERLY** 154; **J HENDERSON** 211, 235; **A J HOPKINS** 25, 82/83, 171t, 193; **R JOHNSON** 250, 251; **C JONES** 115, 124t, 177; **A LAWSON** 23t, 61, 69t, 70t, 70bl, 71b, 126/127, 144b; **T MACKIE** 38t; **J McCRAE** 255; **S & O MATHEWS** 31, 80b, 97b, 100t, 107c, 142b, 144t, 145, 148, 155b, 196cl, 218t; **E MEACHER** 5t; **C MOLYNEAUX** 209t; **J MORRISON** 192, 209b; **R MORT** 12t, 12b, 14t, 54b, 272; **R MOSS** 79; **R NEWTON** 21t, 37, 80t, 143, 158, 189, 206c; **D NOBLE** 17, 93, 94t, 104b, 106; **V P OTTER** 116; **K PATERSON** 215, 246t, 249c, 255; **A PERKINS** 15b; **B PERKINS** 156b; **J PERRIN** 153; **N RAY** 3, 19, 67; **G ROWATT** 206b; **P SHARPE** 175, 176, 219, 240, 248; **M SHORT** 118t, 119; **B SMITH** 11t, 45, 56, 59t; **A SOUTER** 10t, 24t, 72, 81t, 118b, 120, 136; **F STEPHENSON** 18c; **R STRANGE** 11b, 13b, 14b, 43, 46, 48, 51, 57t, 57b, 185b; **R SURMAN** 28t, 113; **D TARN** 207; **M TAYLOR** 223; **T D TIMMS** 27b; **M TRELAWNY** 7t, 47, 54t, 58b, 96, 241, 271; **P TRENCHARD** 35b; **R VICTOR** 13t; **W VOYSEY** 9, 16b, 22b, 34t, 35t, 38/39, 49, 53, 53b, 78, 82c, 83b, 87, 88t, 101t, 107b, 175t; **R WEIR** 6, 7b, 239, 244t, 244b, 254, 257, 266; **J WELSH** 184; **L WHITWAM** 10, 30t, 40b, 102, 129, 138t, 138b, 141, 182, 183t, 183c, 184t, 185t, 188t, 188c, 188b, 195, 201, 204, 206t, 208b, 266, 268, 275l; **H WILLIAMS** 24b, 29, 64c, 122t, 262t; **P WILSON** 55, 58t, 149t; **T WOODCOCK** 9t.

Contributors

Original copy editor: Sue Gordon
Revision verifier: Tim Locke
Revision copy editor: www.lodestonepublishing.com